JOURNAL FOR THE STUDY OF THE OLD TESTAMENT
SUPPLEMENT SERIES
314

Sheffield Academic Press

Studies in the Semiotics of Biblical Law

Bernard S. Jackson

Journal for the Study of the Old Testament
Supplement Series 314

From Edinburgh to Ehrhardt

Published by Sheffield Academic Press Ltd
Mansion House
19 Kingfield Road
Sheffield S11 9AS
England

Typeset by Sheffield Academic Press
and
Printed on acid-free paper in Great Britain
by Antony Rowe Ltd
Chippenham, Wiltshire

British Library Cataloguing in Publication Data

A catalogue record for this book is available
from the British Library

ISBN 1-84127-150-0

CONTENTS

ABBREVIATIONS

ANET	James B. Pritchard (ed.), *Ancient Near Eastern Texts Relating to the Old Testament* (Princeton: Princeton University Press, 3rd edn, 1969 [1950])
BA	*Biblical Archaeologist*
BO	*Bibliotheca orientalis*
BZ	*Biblische Zeitschrift*
BZAW	Beihefte zur *ZAW*
CBQ	*Catholic Biblical Quarterly*
HKNT	Handkommentar zum Neuen Testament
HL	Hittite Laws
HTR	*Harvard Theological Review*
IDB	*Interpreter's Dictionary of the Bible* (Nashville: Abingdon Press, 1962)
IEJ	*Israel Exploration Journal*
IOS	*Israel Oriental Studies*
JANESCU	*Journal of the Ancient Near Eastern Society of Columbia University*
JAOS	*Journal of the American Oriental Society*
JBL	*Journal of Biblical Literature*
JCS	*Journal of Cuneiform Studies*
JETS	*Journal of the Evangelical Theological Society*
JJS	*Journal of Jewish Studies*
JNES	*Journal of Near Eastern Studies*
JNSL	*Journal of Northwest Semitic Languages*
JSJ	*Journal for the Study of Judaism in the Persian, Hellenistic and Roman Period*
JSOT	*Journal for the Study of the Old Testament*
JSS	*Journal of Semitic Studies*
JTS	*Journal of Theological Studies*
KAT	Kommentar zum alten Testament
Lauterbach	J.Z. Lauterbach (ed.), *Mekilta de-Rabbi Ishmael* (3 vols.; Philadelpia: Jewish Publication Society of America, 1933-35)
LE	Laws of Eshnunna
LH	Laws of Hammurabi
MAL	Middle Assyrian Laws
OS	*Oudtestamentische Studiën*

PG	J.-P. Migne (ed.), *Patrologia cursus completa...*
	Series graeca (166 vols.; Paris: Petit-Montrouge, 1857–83)
RB	*Revue biblique*
RSV	Revised Standard Version
SBL	Society of Biblical Literature
SVT	*Supplements to Vetus Testamentum*
TDOT	G.J. Botterweck and H. Ringgren (eds.), *Theological*
	Dictionary of the Old Testament
ThWAT	G.J. Botterweck and H. Ringgren (eds.), *Theologisches*
	Wörterbuch zum Alten Testament (Stuttgart: W. Kohlhammer,
	1970–)
VT	*Vetus Testamentum*
WTJ	*Westminster Theological Journal*
ZABR	*Zeitschrift für Altorientalische und Biblische Rechtgeschichte*
ZAW	*Zeitschrift für die alttestamentliche Wissenschaft*
ZTK	*Zeitschrift für Theologie und Kirche*

Translations of biblical passages are from the Revised Standard Version, with relevant amendments noted in text or footnotes.

INTRODUCTION

When I commenced my research into biblical law, in the 1960s, I became increasingly concerned at what I viewed as a lack of theoretical and methodological sophistication prevalent in many studies (including my own). Frequently, one encountered problems where the Bible itself provided insufficient data to come to any strong conclusions. Since the discovery of the Laws of Hammurabi in 1902, and increasingly in the light of the subsequent uncovering of pre-Hammurabi Law Codes, scholars have often resorted to comparative evidence in order both to fill gaps in our knowledge of particular systems of ancient law, and to solve problems of interpretation. Such comparisons have not been restricted to the geographical area of the ancient Near East; Roman and Greek laws were included in a conception which some have described as *Antike Rechtsgeschichte*.

I formed the view that many reconstructions of the history of biblical (and other ancient Near Eastern) legal institutions proceeded from assumptions regarding how law typically develops. These assumptions, I suspected, were based primarily upon nineteenth-century evolutionary views, which were coming increasingly under question.[1] I suspected that the prevailing models were not sufficiently informed by the best available interdisciplinary thinking regarding what were typical patterns of development of human thought, and in particular what within it was most likely to generate regularities of development.[2] In short, a scholarly epoch where theory had not been matched by available data was succeeded by one in which data was used with little concern for underlying theory.

I began to look at studies of linguistic and cognitive development,

---

1. On Maine, see Jackson (1992a), and in the context of the views of Westbrook (1994) see Jackson (1995c: 1750-54).

2. See Jackson (1975a: 8-12); for my developed view, see now Jackson (1995b: Chs. 7–8); (1996a: Ch. 3).

particularly in the school of Piaget.[3] His interest in (a particular form of) structuralism led me to an interest in other varieties of that approach, including that of Lévi-Strauss (Jackson 1979a; 1980b: 5-30; 1982: 147-60; 1982–83: 1-43), who had written about the 'primitive mind' in contexts quite close to the concerns of ancient law. I became increasingly aware that the assumptions that informed contemporary scholarship on biblical law went far beyond those of a particular form of evolutionary anthropology, and encompassed our whole conception of rationality and indeed of the workings of language.[4] My main inspiration became a structuralist-inspired form of semiotics, that promoted in the school of A.J. Greimas,[5] an approach that combined theories of semantics, pragmatics and discourse, and which prompted me to enquire into related questions addressed by linguistics, philosophers and psychologists.[6] All such approaches—insofar as they seek to answer different aspects (synchronic and diachronic) of the question: How do we make sense?'—may be termed 'semiotic', even though the term is more narrowly used to denote theories (such as those of Greimas and Peirce) that offer general theories of signification not restricted to language or the functioning of one particular sense. It may seem odd that anyone should pursue an interest in an apparently formalist and purely synchronic account of sense construction, when the object was to enrich the methodology of comparative ancient law. I was increasingly convinced, however, that any exercise in making sense of ancient legal texts, both individually and in their historical relationships, needed to be based upon some conception of making sense in general.

The result, perhaps, is a more radical scepticism than that anticipated at the outset (Jackson 1995b; 1996a). It is not merely models of how

---

3.   My interest—and even more, my resolve—was fortified by the Edinburgh Gifford Lectures of 1972–73, in which the 'quartet' of Anthony Kenny, John Lucas, C.H. Waddington and Christopher Longuet-Higgins debated the development of mind, paying particular attention to the models offered by Chomsky and Piaget (see Kenny *et al* 1973).

4.   On this intellectual journey, see further Jackson (1997: 127-32).

5.   This general semiotic theory had already been applied directly to law: see Greimas and Landowski (1976), now translated (see bibliography). For my account of its implications for jurisprudence, see Jackson (1985b, 1988b).

6.   Particularly, Bartlett, Bernstein, Bruner, Chomsky, Ong, Strawson and the later Wittgenstein; see further Jackson (1995b: §§3.2, 5.1, 5.4, 6.1, 6.4-5, 7.1-2, 8.2, 10.2-3; 1996a: §§7.5, 9.2, 4).

law typically *develops* that we have to question. The modern, Western scholar necessarily brings to the study of biblical law assumptions as to (a) how language works (based on a conception of 'literal meaning'), and (b) how law functions in society (based on a rule-based conception of adjudication).[7]

Some of the issues that arise from the statement of talion in Exod. 21.22-25 may be used by way of illustration. First, there is a problem of meaning: what did 'an eye for an eye' really mean to the original users? Some ancient sources seemed to indicate that we should take the phrase 'literally': the Roman Twelve Tables prescribed *talio* for maiming another's limb, while explicitly including the possibility of monetary composition;[8] the Laws of Hammurabi include the following.[9]

196.	If a man has put out the eye of a free man, they shall put out his eye.
197.	If he breaks the bone of a (free) man, they shall break his bone.
198-99.	(provide for money payments where the victims are persons of lower status or slaves.)
200.	If the man knocks out the tooth of a (free) man equal (in rank) to him(self), they shall knock out his tooth.

By contrast, the Rabbis were unequivocal: '"An eye for an eye"—that means money' (*Mekhilta ad Exod.* 21.24). The problem was compounded by the fact that very few instances can be found in the Bible of the actual implementation of talionic punishment: the one clear example involved the mutilation of a foreign, captured king, who is made by

---

7. These assumptions are not necessarily always well informed. On definitions of law used in biblical scholarship, see Marshall (1993: 22-24); Jackson (1998b: 218-29). A healthy scepticism is expressed by Wilson (1993: 91): 'The nature of the legal process is still unclear. Little is known about the court system or the mechanisms of law enforcement. The relationship between law and custom has yet to be fully explored. Links between law and other social institutions remain to be studied in detail. In general, the relation of law to its social matrix is still imperfectly understood. To put the matter more bluntly, we still do not know how law worked in ancient Israel.' He is particularly reserved in relation to the premonarchical period (p. 92).

8. XII T. VIII.2: *Si membrum rupsit, ni cum eo pacit, talio esto* (if a person has maimed another's limb, let there be retaliation in kind, unless he makes agreement for composition with him).

9. Translation of Driver and Miles (1952–55: II, 77).

the narrator to view his fate as an instance of *divine* justice (Judg. 1.5-7; see §10.1, *infra*)!

In debating this issue, students of biblical law tended to line up in fairly predictable secular versus religious teams (I was in the former). The secularists saw the monetary 'explanation' as unduly influenced by later religious tradition, and as essentially 'apologetic'. The religious team viewed the secularists as equally motivated by an underlying ideology, that of denying any distinctiveness to the biblical tradition, and reducing it to the common fare of other ancient (and impliedly less ethically sensitive) cultures. In short, the pragmatics of the issue appeared to dominate the semantics; in the absence of clear criteria favouring one side or the other, one decided in accordance with the team with which one wanted to be identified. Nor, of course, was the line-up limited to religious versus secular. The words that Matthew put into the mouth of Jesus in the Sermon on the Mount added further tensions (Mt. 5.38-39):

> You have heard that it was said, 'An eye for an eye and a tooth for a tooth.' But I say to you, Do not resist one who is evil. But if any one strikes you on the right cheek, turn to him the other also.

Here, one ethic was being superseded, or at the very least supplemented, by a new, superior morality. 'An eye for an eye' was thus presented as inferior, even crude or barbaric (at least, again, if viewed 'literally'). The Jewish secularists at least took heart from the fact that biblical law was not alone in espousing such a view.

Such debates, however, beg a fundamental question: what do we mean by 'literal meaning', and is it appropriately deployed in the present context? The concept is closely tied, historically, to the emergence of writing (as, indeed, its very etymology suggests). Even the sentence (to which the concept of literal meaning is most appropriately applied) is itself a unit of writing, not speech. When we talk about literal meaning, we often ask what situations the words 'cover'. That metaphor itself suggests the material word, writing. What if talion, as is widely believed, originated in an *oral* formula? Should we then seek the socially understood use of the formula, rather than the 'literal meaning'? And would not the socially understood use of the formula best be sought in evidence derived from biblical society (including its narratives), rather than comparative evidence? The latter, doubtless, may provide useful hypotheses, but such hypotheses may be more relevant to the 'literary' manifestations of talion in the biblical legal collections than to its origins and social use. Given both the cognitive and pragmatic differences which may be discerned between orally transmitted custom and written formulations of law, separate attention must be given to questions of meaning in each different communicational context.

This was not, however, the direction which scholarly discussion on biblical talion took. The discovery of pre-Hammurabi codes—where the sanctions for bodily injuries were 'fixed fines' rather than physical retaliation—prompted debate on the significance of talion in evolutionary terms. Talion had previously been regarded as 'primitive', an aspect of the vengeance system—redeemable, at best, by the understanding that it served to impose a limit: a single eye, and nothing but an eye, for the loss of an eye. The fact that the pre-Hammurabi codes, both Sumerian (Ur-Nammu)[10] and Akkadian (Eshnunna),[11] indicated specific sums of money for bodily injuries was seized upon by A.S. Diamond as sufficient to reverse the previous understanding of the normal evolution of the law in such cases (Diamond 1957: 151-55; 1971: 98-101, 398-99; Marshall 1993: 133). These 'fixed fines' did not represent 'real compensation' (as understood by later lawyers[12]), but rather arbitrary sums representing rough-and-ready justice. It was only later, he suggested, that this was seen as inadequate, and was replaced by the (often religiously inspired) penal provisions of talion (which later gave way to real systems of compensation).[13]

This debate lacked any real criteria as to what might count as an evolutionary progression. In the absence of such criteria, latter-day diffusionists have rejected entirely the possibility of evolutionary schemes, and sought explanations in terms of direct historical influence, sometimes entirely eschewing controls in terms of comparable, or even

10. §§18–22, commencing: 'If [a man] cuts off the foot of [another man with...], he shall weigh and deliver 10 shekels of silver' (§18, Roth's translation); similar provisions follow in respect of the 'bone' (§19), 'nose' (§20), '??' (text damaged) (§21), and 'tooth' (§22): see Roth (1995: 19).

11. Laws of Eshnunna (LE) §42: 'If a man bit and severed the nose of a man,— 1 mina of silver he shall weigh out. An eye—1 mina; a tooth—1/2 mina; an ear— 1/2 mina. A slap in the face—10 shekels he shall weigh out' (cf. LE 43-46) (see Yaron 1988: 69).

12. Diamond, we may note, was a Master of the Supreme Court.

13. Diamond was a proponent of Liberal Judaism; he did not feel bound by the rabbinic interpretation of biblical texts. Yet with this data he was able to avoid the apparently 'primitivizing' approach of the secularists.

compatible, social conditions.[14] In the present context, a diffusionist solution was certainly attractive. There are many different ways in which the principle of talion might be, and has been, expressed. The choice of an eye, and (especially) a tooth, is hardly inevitable, yet both are found not only in the biblical formulations (or at least two of the three of them) but also in the Laws of Hammurabi. More generally, we find evidence that biblical law represented, in some ways, the climax of a scribal tradition of written law.[15] What view, then, do we take of the relationship between the biblical legal collections and the oral sources that preceded them?

The structure of this book mirrors one of its central claims: that modern understandings of the cognitive and communicational differences between orality and literacy are important,[16] and provide a basis for developmental claims. An attempt has been made to distinguish the semiotic processes at work at various points in the transition from orality to literacy: oral speech acts (Chapter 2), simple written laws (Chapter 3), the combination of such laws into small units of discourse ('paragraphs') (Chapter 4), the functions of different written media of communication (Chapter 5), the attribution of endurance (Chapter 6) and symbolic meaning (as values) to concrete laws (Chapter 7), the development of reiteratory techniques in larger units of discourse (Chapter 8), and the application of narratology to the macro-narrative of the law (Chapter 9).

But two caveats are appropriate at the outset.

First, the principal value of the use of such models is to raise new questions and sharpen debate on old ones; they do not provide mechanical tools that need only be applied to render correct answers. While the study of biblical law may frequently profit from hypotheses derived from external sources—whether implicit comparison with modern

14. Notably, Alan Watson, in a series of books commencing with *Legal Transplants* (1974). This approach has proved highly controversial, but has been followed by Fitzpatrick-McKinley (1999). See further my forthcoming review in *JSS*.

15. Compare, for example, the provisions on goring oxen in LE §§53-55, Laws of Hammurabi (LH) §§250-52 and Exod. 21.28-32, 35-36.

16. In many respects, this book complements the work of Niditch (1997), particularly her insights into the persistence of oral traits in early literacy, and the 'mixed economy' of orality and literacy through much of the pre-exilic period. I have, however, attempted to deploy developmental models to a greater extent than Niditch, in seeking to trace the transformations.

models of law or explicit comparison with the ancient Near Eastern legal collections—it must ultimately be viewed within the semiotics of biblical literature. From this perspective, I seek here to raise a number of new questions and make some fresh suggestions; I do not claim to have exhausted either the analysis of the biblical texts here considered, or the possible forms of semiotic analysis that may usefully be deployed.

Second, the texts of biblical law are not such as admit of the application of these various semiotic issues as a unified system (as is possible, in principle, in modern law, where the range of data is so much more extensive). In particular, none of the sources we have available presents a complete version of the communicational model. The narrative sources, which tell us about the senders and receivers of written law, the types of medium used for this purpose, and the different functions of both writing and reading, do not at the same time provide the texts of the documents they describe. We cannot, therefore, analyse the 'code' used to communicate these particular messages. Conversely, the biblical legal collections present us with ample opportunities to study their communicational codes, but we have no direct access to the history of their pragmatics: the identities of their senders and receivers, the media used to transmit them and the functions for which they were actually used. We do, of course, have narrative accounts of those pragmatics, and these narrative accounts must be treated very seriously, in combination with the content of the laws, in order to understand the message of the final authors (the editors) of the Pentateuch. But as far as historical questions are concerned, the best we can do is to compare the results of internal analysis of the law-codes with the communicational settings whose existence we have identified from other sources.[17] We have to look at each biblical 'law-code' separately, in this respect; they may not all have fulfilled the same communicational function.

In the first chapter, I present the general theories of sense construction, from Greimassian semiotics and the cognitive developmental tradition in psychology, which I have found most useful. Such models do not seek to exclude more traditional forms of analysis. Rather, they provide a set of epistemological positions that have the merit of being explicit and research-based, and thus challenge the inarticulate assumptions regarding language and development that underlie much work on

---

17. That is not to say, however, that we should accept the historical accounts that reveal different communicational contexts as themselves unimpeachable historical evidence; they, too, have their own narrative functions.

biblical law. Some of the problems addressed below are discussed quite directly in terms of the concepts discussed in this chapter: the development of legal drafting in the light of theories of cognitive development (Chapter 4) and the macro-narrative of covenant in the light of Greimassian narratological analysis of the interrelationship of the individual narratives within it (Chapter 9). Other chapters use more specifically focused semiotic approaches (which I argue should be viewed within the context of the more general synchronic and diachronic models set out in Chapter 1). In particular, Chapter 2 draws on speech act analysis; Chapter 3 applies some results of studies of orality and literacy together with Bernstein's sociolinguistic distinction between 'restricted' and 'elaborated' code; Chapter 5 addresses the issue of the media of transmission depicted in the Bible within the context of a basic communicational model. Chapter 6 inquires into the construction of the temporal endurance of law: an issue that has been highlighted in modern legal philosophy but which may also be posed in semiotic terms. Chapter 7 asks how values are expressed in the biblical texts, revisiting the debate on Greenberg's 'postulates', and argues that more weight should be accorded to literary criteria. Chapter 8 considers the forms of repetition encountered in biblical law, and seeks to assess them in both narrative and developmental terms, locating them within the transition from orality to literacy. Finally, in Chapter 10, I return to the example of talion, and indicate the contributions I believe several of these forms of semiotic analysis may make to its manifestations in the biblical texts.

I have not attempted in the present work any full assessment of the biblical 'law codes', though the contribution that a communicational model may make to this problem is outlined in §5.1. This is not because even the identification of the biblical 'law codes' (unlike those of the ancient Near East) is a matter of inference (we have the Book of Deuteronomy in front of us; we do not have the Deuteronomic Code); I am prepared, with most students of biblical law, to make inferences as to the original contours of such documents. The reason resides rather in the complexity of the issues, which can hardly be examined usefully through a limited number of examples. In a forthcoming work, I do seek to address this issue, in relation to the 'Covenant Code' (and in particular the *Mishpatim*).[18]

18. Jackson, B.S., *Wisdom-Laws: A Study of the Mishpatim* (Oxford: Clarendon Press, forthcoming [2002]), being a much expanded and revised text of my

It is hoped that the arguments pursued in this book will encourage greater sensitivity to the analysis of semiotic issues within biblical law. Such analysis may in turn contribute to the development of the semiotic models themselves.

Chapter 1 and the semiotic introductions to other chapters are largely drawn from my *Making Sense in Law* (1995) and *Making Sense in Jurispudence* (1996). I have also drawn, often with substantial revision and development, upon parts of a number of earlier articles, particularly 'Law, Language and Narrative: David Daube on Some Divine Speech-Acts', in C.M. Carmichael (ed.), *Essays in Law and Religion: The Berkeley and Oxford Symposia in Honour of David Daube* (Berkeley: University of California at Berkeley, 1993), 51-66 (Ch. 2); 'Some Semiotic Questions for Biblical Law', in A.M. Fuss (ed.), *The Oxford Conference Volume* (Jewish Law Association Studies, 3; Atlanta: Scholars Press, 1987), 1-25: 'The Original "Oral Law"', in G.W. Brooke (ed.), *Jewish Ways of Reading the Bible* (JSS Supplement X; Oxford: Oxford University Press, forthcoming [2000]) (Ch. 3); 'Practical Wisdom and Literary Artifice in the Covenant Code', in B.S. Jackson and S.M. Passamaneck (eds.), *The Jerusalem 1990 Conference Volume* (Jewish Law Association Studies, 6; Atlanta: Scholars Press, 1992), 65-92 (Ch. 3 and elsewhere); 'Legal Drafting in the Ancient Near East in the Light of Modern Theories of Cognitive Development', in *Mélanges à la mémoire de Marcel-Henri Prévost* (Paris: PUF, 1982), 49-66 (Ch. 4); 'Ideas of Law and Legal Administration: a Semiotic Approach', in R.E. Clements (ed.), *The World of Ancient Israel: Sociological, Anthropological and Political Perspectives* (Cambridge: Cambridge University Press, 1989), 185-202 (Ch. 5); 'Talion and Purity: Some Glosses on Mary Douglas', in J.F.A. Sawyer (ed.), *Reading Leviticus, A Conversation with Mary Douglas* (Sheffield: Sheffield Academic Press, 1996), 107-123, and 'An Aye for an I?: the Semiotics of Lex Talionis in the Bible', in W. Pencak and J. Ralph Lindgren (eds.), *New Approaches to Semiotics and the Human Sciences: Essays in Honor of Roberta Kevelson* (New York: Peter Lang, 1997), 127-149 (Ch. 10). Chapters 6, 8 and 9, where not entirely new, are based on the first series of my Speaker's Lectures in Biblical Studies at the University of Oxford, 1983–84 (hitherto unpublished). Less systematic use has been made also of other articles, as indicated in the footnotes. These earlier articles

Speaker's Lectures in Biblical Studies, University of Oxford, 1985 and 1986.

retain, I hope, some independent value. Here I have tried to develop and integrate them into something somewhat more systematic and essentially new, a set of pilot studies of some of the semiotic dimensions of the transformation of biblical law from orality to literacy.

It is a pleasure, in conclusion, to acknowledge the institutional setting in which it has proved possible (at last) to bring this to fruition. My Chair would not exist without the support of Sir David Alliance. The Centre for Jewish Studies, within the Department of Religions and Theology of the University of Manchester, has since the summer of 1997 provided a most congenial and stimulating environment in which to work. Three papers delivered to the Department's Ehrhardt Seminar provided valuable feedback on material in Chapters 3 and 9. Too many colleagues to mention have been generous in their intellectual and moral support. A particular debt of gratitude is owed to Roger Tomes (Manchester) for comments on a number of earlier papers and to Jack Welch (Brigham Young) for reviewing the present manuscript.

Chapter 1

SOME SEMIOTIC THEORIES

1.1 *Synchronic Models*

The concept of narrative has become popular in the social sciences in recent years (see, e.g., Polkinghorne 1988). Sociologists give accounts of social knowledge in terms of 'frames', 'schemas', 'scripts', 'stereotypes', very commonly describing them in terms of narratives circulating within a particular society (see, e.g., Bourcier 1978: 136-371; Mandler 1984; Tannen 1986; Sherwin 1994: 50-51). Psychologists have considered the role of narrative in the operation of perception,[1] memory[2]

1. A particularly striking example is the phenomenon termed 'confabulation': we make sense of perceptions not as individual, isolated events or moments (like stills taken out of context from a film) but rather in their (often temporal) relationships to each other. We expect them to make sense in sequence, thus as a narrative. If there is a 'gap' in the story, we are apt to fill it. An example is given by Trankell (1972; see Jackson 1995: 363): a lawyer in a taxi saw the car in front of him stop suddenly and one of its doors swing open. He also saw an old man lying in the road. He thought he had seen the old man fall out of the car or be pushed out. In fact the old man was a pedestrian who had been knocked down; he had never been in the car whose door had opened. Such confabulation is explicable in narrative terms: the lawyer here assumed that there was a link between things that he perceived in sequence. There is an operating assumption that such sequences are meaningful, rather than being a mere series of unconnected events.

2. Making sense of 'fading' memories involves recourse to forms of social knowledge in order to fill the gaps. The use of internalized 'schemas' for this purpose has been recognized since the classic study of Bartlett (1932). In routine matters, particularly, we may forget specific features of an event, but replace them with details from the schema. More recent psychologists of memory have made the use of narrative models more explicit. 'Story grammarians' have shown that the clearer the narrative structure of a story, the more accurately it will be recalled. See Mandler and Johnson (1977: 111-51), on the importance of story schemata. The same may be claimed for real events. Fuller (1982: 134), writes: '[T]he number of information "bits", or "chunks", we can keep in mind at one time is limited to five

and elsewhere.[3] Its importance has been stressed in the study of oral cultures.[4] Speech act analysis has also been reformulated in narrative terms.[5] Jerome Bruner (1990) has argued for a 'narrative competence'[6]

or maybe seven. The story as the engram bypasses the limits set on chunk size. One story can contain an enormous load of information "bits" within its framework. Also, since memory storage and retrieval takes time, the story engram allows more information to be processed and retrieved per unit of time.'

3.   See further Jackson (1995b: 185-93, 228-39, 362-75). See esp. pp. 234-39. on the work of Theodore Sarbin (1986). The account of narrative structure offered in that volume by Gergen and Gergen (p. 26) is particularly close to the Greimassian account (below). They write: 'To succeed as a narrative the account must first establish a goal state or valued end point. For example, it must succeed in establishing the value of a protagonist's well-being, the destruction of an evil condition, the victory of a favoured group, the discovery of something precious, or the like. With the creation of a goal condition, the successful narrative must then select and arrange events in such a way that the goal state is rendered more or less probable. A description of events unrelated to the goal state detracts or dissolves the sense of narrative. In effect, all events in a successful narrative are related by virtue of their containment within a given evaluative space. Therein lies the coherence of the narrative. As one moves from one event to another, one also approaches or moves away from the desired goal state. Through this latter means one achieves a sense of directionality.'

4.   See Ong (1982: 113-14), describing narrative as 'a device for the management of knowledge...narrative is particularly important in primary oral cultures because it can bond a great deal of lore in relatively substantial, lengthy forms that are reasonably durable...'

5.   For the Austin/Searle model and its modification by Sbisà and Fabbri, see *infra*, §2.1. It may be reformulated in terms of the Greimassian semiotic described below: there is a need for a 'Contract'—the construction of a Subject endowed with 'competence' to perform the goal in question. The 'essential' conditions relate to the 'accepted conventional procedure having a certain conventional effect, the procedure to include the uttering of certain words by certain persons in certain circumstances' (Austin). In semiotic terms, this is the 'Performance'. Finally, there are 'sincerity' conditions, whose violation does not deprive the speech act of its intended meaning, but nevertheless represents an 'abuse'. In semiotic terms, the perceived sincerity of a speech act is a form of 'Recognition' attributed to it.

6.   At p. 45, he writes: 'Is it unreasonable to suppose that there is some human 'readiness' for narrative that is responsible for conserving and elaborating such a tradition in the first place—whether, in Kantian terms, as 'an art hidden in the human soul', whether as a feature of our language capacity, whether even as a psychological capacity like, say, our readiness to convert the world of visual input into figure and ground? By this I do not intend that we 'store' specific archetypal stories or myths, as C.G. Jung has proposed. That seems like misplaced concreteness.

underlying child linguistic and social development.[7] There is an argument that narrative structures are also at the foundation of linguistic competence as conceived by Chomsky (Jackson 1995b: 198-99, 203-204).

The semiotic approach of Greimas and his followers stresses the role of narrative in the deep structure of signification of *any* form of discourse. The Greimassian school looks for 'basic structures of signification', and finds them in a level of sense construction based upon a semiotic notion of 'narrative' that stresses the communicational processes inherent in it. Its approach is sometimes called 'semio-narrative'.[8]

Rather, I mean a readiness or predisposition to organize experience into a narrative form, into plot structures and the rest'. See Jackson (1995b: 228-32), for further parallels with Greimassian semiotics, including the following account (Bruner 1990: 42-43) of the narrative element that informs his conception of 'folk psychology': 'Folk psychology is about human agents doing things on the basis of their beliefs and desires, striving for goals, meeting obstacles which they best, or which best them, all of this extended over time'.

7.   He invokes both speech act theory and narrative models in his account of the early development of speech behaviour amongst children (Bruner 1990: 86-87): 'The child, in the nature of things, has her own desires, but given her reliance upon the family for affection, these desires often create conflict when they collide with the wishes of parents and siblings. The child's task when conflict arises is to balance her own desires against her commitment to others in the family. And she learns very soon that action is not enough to achieve this end. Telling the right story, putting her actions and goals in a legitimizing light, is just as important. Getting what you want very often means getting the right story. As John Austin told us many years ago in his famous essay 'A Plea for Excuses', a justification rests on a story of mitigating circumstances. But to get the story right, to pit yours successfully against your younger brother's, requires knowing what constitutes the canonically acceptable version. A 'right' story is one that connects your version through mitigation with the canonical version. So...children too come to understand 'everyday' narrative not only as a form of recounting but also as a form of rhetoric. By their third and fourth years, we see them learning how to use their narratives to cajole, to deceive, to flatter, to justify, to get what they can without provoking a confrontation with those they love. And they are en route as well to becoming connoisseurs of story genres that do the same. To put the matter in terms of speech-act theory, knowing the generative structure of narrative enables them to construct locutions to fit the requirements of a wide range of illocutionary intentions'.

8.   For a survey of the history of narratology in semiotics, see Nöth (1990: 367-73). See further Greimas (1989, 1990), and Jackson (1985b: II).

Greimas sought to extend the ideas of semantic structure of Saussure (Jackson 1995b: 18-24) by applying them also to 'discourse': we have to make sense not merely of individual sentences, nor even of the relations of contiguous sentences, but also of texts as a whole. The folklorist Vladimir Propp had analysed 100 Russian folktales, and identified some 31 narrative themes in them, recurring in different forms. Through a re-analysis of this material, Greimas derived a much more abstract, general (and, as he claimed, universal) model in which

(a)   the syntagmatic level of Saussure generated an 'actantial' model, in which discourse makes sense in terms of underlying patterns of intelligible action;

(b)   the associative (or 'paradigmatic') level generates choices (often structured as oppositions) of story elements that are used in the story-sequence (or 'syntagm').[9]

The combination of these two levels, Greimas claimed, represents the 'basic structures of signification' (*structures élémentaires de la signification*) of all discourse—a set of underlying patterns used in all our sense-making activities. We make such sense by understanding the data in terms of meaningful sequences of action. What is a 'meaningful sequence of action' can be specified (the 'syntagmatic axis', described below). Thus the Greimassian theory claims to provide an account of the construction of the sense of behaviour (including speech behaviour), and not merely of the language we use to tell stories. In subsequent work, members of the Parisian school have applied the Greimassian scheme to many different forms of discourse and behaviour. This is possible because the Greimassian concept of 'narrative' is a highly abstract one, lacking many of the connotations associated with one of its particular manifestations, the 'story'.

In seeking the 'basic structures of signification', Greimas took sense construction to involve the interaction of three different levels:

(1)   The 'level of manifestation': the sense data actually presented to us, and the particular sense attributed to it. The data includes both the content of the text (or behaviour) and its manner of expression—whether oral or written. This 'level of

9.   This generates the famous 'semiotic square', on which see Jackson (1995: 148-50). This is relevant to the analysis of the oppositional relationships observed in the examples discussed in §7.2, *infra*, but will not be pursued further in the present context.

manifestation' is sometimes termed the 'surface' (versus 'deep') level of the text.

(2) The 'thematic level' is the stock of social knowledge, itself organized in narrative terms, that is implicit within and helps us to make sense of the data presented at the 'level of manifestation'. It is part of the equipment we deploy in making sense of the world. This knowledge derives from the environment in which we live.

(3) The 'deep level', that of the 'basic structures of signification' themselves. This, too, is part of the equipment we deploy in making sense of the world. However, these basic structures do not derive from the environment in which we live, but are claimed to be universal.

In short, we have to distinguish (a) the particular meaning of any text or utterance (to whatever genre it belongs: law, literature, etc.); (b) the social knowledge we bring to bear in assigning meaning to (a), this social knowledge commonly being stored and transmitted as (substantive) narrative stereotypes, themes, images or typifications of action; (c) the universal[10] narrative structure (or 'narrative competence') that we use to assign meaning to both actual discourse and social knowledge.[11]

---

10. The claim that such structures are 'universal' is said by some Greimassians to mean that the theory has proved useful in the explanation of the construction of meaning in all those phenomena to which it has thus far been applied. Unlike the 'universal grammar' of Chomsky, it is thus derived from empirical observation, rather than from *a priori* argument. Its universality is, therefore, open in principle to qualification. Some go further. Claims for the innate status of story structure as the basic structure of cognition are advanced by Fuller (a psychologist), independently of the Greimassian semiotic tradition. For her, 'the essential components of the story engram are someone(s) or something(s) (a noun) acting or being acted on (a verb)' (1982: 134). However, such a 'grammatical structure' is accompanied by a form of emotional encoding: 'What I am suggesting is a double encoding of the story engram, first on the basis of grammatical structure, and second on the basis of emotional category. Such double encoding would allow for an enormous number of information bits to be stored and expeditiously and appropriately retrieved' (1982: 136).

11. It does not follow from this that we must reduce meaning to nothing more than narrative structure, to the exclusion of rhetorical, stylistic and other features of the level of manifestation: the claim that narrative structure is a necessary condition of sense construction does not entail the view that it is also a sufficient condition. For further discussion, see Jackson (1995b: 157-58; 1996d: 176).

This last may be described as follows. Every human action, for Greimas, begins with the establishment of a *goal*, which thereby institutes someone as the *subject* of that action, with the goal of *performing* it. In realizing the action, the subject will be helped or obstructed by other actions of other social actors. This help or obstruction will affect the 'competence' of the subject to perform the action. The desired action itself will be achieved, or not achieved. But it is a characteristic of human action that the sequence does not finish there. Human beings reflect upon past actions. As a consequence, the syntagmatic axis of Greimas concludes with the concept of *recognition* (or 'sanction'). Human action (whether real or fictional) thus appears meaningful in terms of a basic three-part 'narrative' sequence, for which Greimassians have adopted the following technical vocabulary:

(1)   'Contract': the institution of the subject through the establishment of goals[12] and competences.
(2)   'Performance': (or non-performance) of those goals.
(3)   'Recognition': of that performance (or non-performance).

Any narrative involves a set of interactions, in the course of setting goals, performing them, and assisting or obstructing their accomplishment. At the 'deep level', the theory sees these interactions as involving a set of abstract actors, termed *actants*,[13] which appear in pairs: Sender–Receiver (of goals), Subject–Object, Helper–Opponent. Latterly, the 'helper' and 'opponent' have disappeared as independent *actants* and been replaced by a more abstract notion of the presence or absence of the competences—the *savoir-faire* and *pouvoir-faire*—required to perform the action. At the end of the narrative syntagm there is another communicational element, the sending and receiving of messages of recognition of what has occurred: that the task is recognized as having

12. The goals of action may be of any kind: they may include communicative goals.

13. The actants at the 'deep level' may be expressed at the level of manifestation by one or several *acteurs* (real people in social life; 'characters' in literature): conversely, a single *acteur* may perform different actantial roles at different times. At the level of manifestation, the Sender and Receiver may even be the same person; thus, the model has no problem with self-generated action, or with the 'internal' recognition of the performance of a goal by the Subject. But the fact that we are able to make sense of social action (whether real or fictional) at all is due to the fact that we are able to identify in the data presented to us some manifestation of these basic narrative roles.

been performed, not performed, well performed, badly performed, etc. The scheme may be represented diagrammatically:

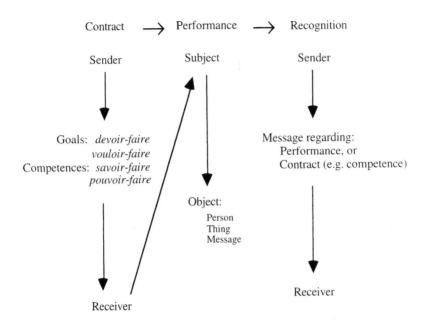

Though this pattern may be described generally as 'goal-oriented action'—in which, no doubt, conscious goals may form a type of paradigm—the model does not require that the goals be conscious. Indeed, the whole emphasis of semiotics is not upon the state of mind of the actors, but on the sense-effects of what they do. Thus, a 'Sender' may even be an impersonal agency, a custom, a social force.

'Below' the 'deep level', there is a level of construction of meaning here termed 'thematic'. Some years ago, George Fletcher argued that some technical intricacies in the history of the common law of larceny were best understood in terms of the relationship of different fact situations to the collective image of acting like a thief.[14] That collective image served as a kind of paradigm: the typical image of thieving in the

14. Fletcher (1976), p. 473 ('unanalyzed perception'), p. 476 ('intuitive sense of stealing', 'shared image of stealing'); *idem* (1978), p. 7 ('shared understanding of what larceny is').

history of Western legal thought was the nocturnal burglar.[15] From this it does not follow that the daytime pickpocket would not be regarded as a thief: some cases are closer to, others more distant from, the paradigm case. The collective image was not merely a description of typical action; it also included a tacit social evaluation. *This* collective image of acting like a thief involved a particular *frisson*, a fear of the intruder, a horror of the crossing of territorial boundaries, with all the attendant danger that, socially, such boundary-crossing is thought to entail. In semiotic terms, such tacit social evaluations represent the transfer of 'modalities' within the 'recognition' element of the underlying narrative grammar: the activity of the thief is recognized as dangerous.

In my version of semiotic theory, I call such paradigms 'narrative typifications of action'. From this example, three important elements emerge. First, it is not a definition in terms of necessary and sufficient conditions; as a model that informs our perception, it does not generate (as the positivist might wish) 'demonstrable' judgments as to what is 'within' or 'outwith' the image.[16] But it is capable of generating judgments of relative similarity. Secondly, such a typification is not a neutral description; it comes, always, laden with a form of evaluation (for even 'indifference' is a form of evaluation). Thirdly, some typifications may be relative to particular social and/or professional groups, sometimes called 'semiotic groups' (Jackson, 1995b: 93-98), distinguished one from another by the (often overlapping but still distinct) systems of signification operating within them.

There is clearly some common ground between this level of sense construction—'thematization' in the language of the Greimassian school (Greimas and Courtés 1982: 343-44)—and a number of other theories in the social sciences.[17] Such social knowledge is internalized by members of the group concerned, and is deployed very often unself-consciously. But the theory of 'narrative typifications of action'—

---

15. Fletcher (1978: 31): 'In the early stages of history there were no clearly marked boundaries among burglary, larceny and robbery. All were collapsed in the single image of the thief coming at night, breaking the close and endangering the security of the manor'. Fletcher includes Exod. 22.1 in his evidence for this image. See further *infra*, §3.2 for further support for the nocturnal element. On this theme in Roman law, see Kernéis (1999).

16. Hence the conception of 'narrative' meaning deployed in §3.2, *infra*.

17. See particularly the sociological and psychological theories referred to at pp. 21-22, *supra*.

unlike other forms of social construction theory—seeks to locate thematization within an overall semiotic framework. For narrative typifications to make sense, they must themselves satisfy the general conditions of sense construction, and are therefore to be analysed in terms of the underlying narrative structure, the 'narrative syntagm', described above.

Greimassian semiotics is applicable not only to the content of a message (its semantics), but also to the act of enunciation (or communication) of that message (its pragmatics). I call this the 'narrativization of pragmatics'. The enunciation of messages is as much an action as anything else that human beings do. It is generally assumed to be a meaningful action. We therefore have to ask whence derives its meaning. A Greimassian would argue that there are necessary conditions for the attribution of such meaning, including the semio-narrative syntagm ('deep level'). But within any particular society or social group, what counts as a successful enunciation, and what type of enunciative meaning is attributed to it (assertion, threat, play, irony, etc.) are matters of internalized social knowledge ('thematic level'), as indeed are the signs (at the 'level of manifestation') of successful performance. I have argued elsewhere that we may observe the importance of the narrativization of pragmatics particularly clearly in the business of the courtroom (Jackson 1988b: 33-36 and Ch. 3, esp. pp. 67-76; 1995b: Chs. 10–12 *passim*). The idea may prove particularly fertile also in biblical, and especially Pentateuchal, studies, which is rich in narratives of divine speech, direct and mediated. The Pentateuch provides not simply an account of the content of law qualified as divine; it provides a series of accounts of the enunciation of such laws, all of which may be analysed in narrative terms.[18] Differences between these accounts, and their

18. Watts (1999) has recently argued that the Pentateuchal legal collections (if not their final redaction: see pp. 30-31) were designed for (instructional) public reading. He bases this on their rhetorical structure, which he sees as informed by a narrative pattern of story-list-sanction, a model he takes (at pp. 37-40) from O'Banion (1992). In this context, the laws are the 'list'. But 'narrative' and 'list' have been viewed as characteristic, respectively, of orality and literacy (see Havelock 1963: 176-80; Ong 1982: 42-43; Goody 1986: 54-55; Jackson 1995b: 80-81), but Watts seeks to elide this distinction, viewing the texts as written (*ab initio*) for the purpose of public reading, and continuing to be informed by the rhetorical structure designed for this purpose even when the institution of public readings disappeared (1999: 61 n. 1): 'The distinction between hearers and readers, which has been so fruitful for studies of orality and literacy, is blurred by the practice of read-

relations to other aspects of the text, deserve serious study.

Criticisms of both the Greimassian tradition in general, and of this particular version of it, have not been lacking. Some say that the notion of narrative typifications is a descendant of a mechanical structuralism, in which choices must be made between already defined structures of knowledge, without the opportunity to create new structures of understanding.[19] It is not, however, claimed within this tradition that narrative typifications of action operate as mechanical structures, automatically triggered by a certain measure of similarity with the data at the level of manifestation, and generating an unavoidable interpretation of that data. We may use here the insightful account of models of pragmatics offered by Sbisà and Fabbri (1981: 301-19; see §3.2, *infra*). As against the rule-bound model of speech act analysis, they oppose a negotiated, interactional model. There may exist stereotypes of the kind of people, appearances and speech that persuade, but these at best create

ing aloud for aural reception. Since Israel's legal texts and law-reading tradition do not differentiate between readers and hearers, I do not distinguish them either, regarding both as part of the text's 'audience'.' He thus seeks to apply the story-list-sanction model not only to texts which purport to be discrete speeches, notably those of Moses in Deuteronomy, but also to stories of the giving of law (Exod. 19–24: at pp. 49-52, 137) which purport to come from the anonymous narrator. Ong and others have indeed stressed that lists require a narrative presentation in order to be remembered and transmitted; clearly, some of the biblical genealogical material may be viewed in this light. But that implies a far closer connection between the contents of the list and the narrative than is apparent in Watts's model—other than the occasional use of motive clauses referring to narrative history (Watts 1999: 65-67) and some thematic connections (e.g. at p. 58, regarding the regulations for the construction of the Tabernacle). At best, Watts's account assists in understanding the meaning of the giving (enunciation) of the law; it makes little contribution to the understanding of the content of the law. He himself writes (at p. 39) that narrative allows one to understand 'the possible reasons for and implications of the list's very existence'. Moreover, even if O'Banion's model is regarded as useful, it falls short of providing a general narrative model, since it applies only where that which is communicated is a list. It does not follow from the fact that lists require a narrative presentation to be comprehensible in oral communication that story-list-sanction should be taken as the only form of narrative structure discernible in the Pentateuch. Elsewhere, the object of the 'performance' (in the sense of Greimas, described above) may not be the communication of a list (of laws, or anything else) but something quite different.

19. See Douzinas, Warrington and McVeigh (1991: Ch.5). For my response to their arguments, see Jackson (1992d: 103-117).

presumptions, and do not generate mechanical conclusions. The acceptance of particular narrative images is a function in part of the meaning attributed to their acts of enunciation. Narrative, in this sense, is mediated through rhetoric. But the meaning of rhetoric is itself a function of the narrative understanding of its own performance.[20]

1.2 *Diachronic Models*

Diachronic models have not been favoured by structuralist-inspired semioticians, for reasons not dissimilar from James Barr's protest at the uncontrolled use within biblical theology of etymological arguments divorced from general linguistic theory (1961: 295)[21] (which parallels my own in relation to the methodology of comparative ancient law). Both see contemporary practice as unduly influenced by the tacit survival of models derived from nineteenth-century German romanticism—where the links between comparative philology, comparative mythology and comparative jurisprudence were strong and explicit.[22] In both contexts, what has been lacking has been *general* theories of development rather than theories restricted (often, as a matter of principle) to particular cultures.

Cognitive developmental psychology does now purport to offer such general theories. In so far as they propose generally applicable patterns for the development of language and thought, they may be viewed as a form of diachronic semiotics, helping us to understand how our capacities for sense construction develop. It is the choice of a cognitive base for the evolutionary progression that represents the distinctive contribution of the cognitive developmentalist. Historical Jurisprudence lacked a strong response to the problem of choosing an appropriate measure of evolutionary advance. The cognitive developmental approach comes far closer to satisfactory solutions to these problems. In

---

20. This, again, distinguishes my approach from that of Watts, discussed *infra* n. 25.

21. His attack on the use of the concrete-abstract distinction (pp. 11-12) is well taken in the context of approaches informed by 'ethno-psychology' (p. 24), but there are better bases for it, as argued later in this section.

22. On Sir Henry Maine's use (or misuse) of comparative philology, see Jackson (1992a: 256-71).

this respect, Kohlberg has gone further than Piaget (Mays 1974: 241): while Piaget, at least in his early work, regarded logic and morality as parallel phenomena, the one regulating thought while the other operated on action and the affective life (1932: 404-405), Kohlberg has demonstrated, particularly in respect of the first four stages, the dependence of moral upon cognitive development (1971: 166, 182, 183, 186, 187-88, 197-98, 203). One strong implication of the work of the cognitive developmentalists is that we are more likely to identify evolutionary progressions within the form of institutions, and their linguistic expression,[23] than in their substance.

In Piaget's view, where cognitive development takes place—for it is not inevitable—it proceeds through an invariant set of stages, each one of which is required for progression to the next. He saw a strong parallel between the development of science and the development of the capacities of the individual child. He sometimes called his theory one of 'genetic epistemology', a theory of how individuals come to acquire and exercise the capacity to know. Advancing firstly through a sequence of 'prelogical' sub-stages, the child reaches at about the age of 7 the stage of 'concrete mental operations', and progresses at adolescence, around 11 or 12 years of age, into the stage of 'formal mental operations'. Piaget's theory relies fundamentally upon notions of systemic equilibrium within 'stages':[24] each of the stages builds upon and reorganizes the cognitive level of the earlier stage. Piaget does not, however, claim that progress to the highest levels of the stage of formal mental operations is inevitable for every child, nor that the child necessarily advances at the same rate in all areas of activity.

Intelligence begins with a 'sensorimotor' stage—a form of practical intelligence, the ability to discriminate between different sense inputs (e.g. food and drink) and coordinate bodily movements accordingly. In the sensori-motor stage, the infant learns to coordinate actions and per-

---

23. For Piaget, linguistic development itself reflects and depends upon the general development of intelligence in the child. See further Jackson (1995b: 241-42).

24. Through their concepts of equilibration and structure, Piaget and Kohlberg are able to show distinctions in kind rather than degree within the constructivist process: the determination of whether x is within a stage or between stages is no longer an arbitrary labelling process, and the structural nature of 'stages' has (as a result of its formal character) considerable explanatory power (see, e.g., Piaget 1932: 77; 1971: 141; Kohlberg 1971: 169, 184, 186, 225-26, 226, 230; Jackson 1980a: 351 n. 20).

ceptions into 'schemas of action', but the schemas represent reactions to immediate stimuli. 'Operational thinking', on the other hand, requires the development of a 'representational schema', with the ability to comprehend and use symbols.[25] Language is but one form of symbolic communication, and depends—like other forms—upon the development of a general capacity to use symbols, to see one thing (or word, smell or other immediate sensation) as representing something else. The reason why representational schemas can develop from sensori-motor schemas, it is argued, is that the latter involve the recognition of resemblances (for example, in obtaining various objects too distant to reach by dragging their supports, or through imitating the actions of other persons), this leading the infant to recognize similarities between self and others (Beard 1969: 8).

From 2 to 4 years old, the child, though capable of handling symbols, cannot yet place objects in classes, and thus form concepts. The child still lacks the relationship between *all* and *some* and uses what Piaget calls 'pre-concepts', which 'remain midway between the generality of the concept and the individuality of the elements composing it' (Boden 1979: 54). This stage is characterized by 'egocentricity': things are meaningful only in so far as they derive from the child's own experience or are perceived to affect the child. This is reflected also in both speech behaviour and moral development: the typical viewpoint on why something is wrong is exemplified by: 'It is wrong to tell a lie because you will be smacked' (Beard 1969: 9). The next sub-stage is called 'intuitive' and extends from the age of about 4 until 7.[26] Children can begin to give reasons for their beliefs and actions, but these are 'intuitive', based on immediate perceptions, rather than upon mental operations such as comparison. We find here the beginnings of a capacity to classify, but only on one dimension at a time (Jackson 1995b: 246).

A particularly significant advance occurs at the stage of 'concrete mental operations' (age 7–11). For Piaget, the conception of a mental

25. Cf. Bruner's account of the development from enactive to ikonic to symbolic representation, stressing the 'motivated' character of even the earliest stage, enactive representation: discussed in Jackson (1995b: 252-61, esp. pp. 254-55).

26. For criticism of the ages assigned to these various stages, see the work discussed in Jackson (1995b; 250-51), particularly that of Margaret Donaldson, claiming that the experimentation did not take account of the social pertinence (or its absence) of the tasks to the children.

operation involves 'reversibility' (1958: 6; quoted at Boden 1979: 71). At the intuitive stage, a child given two buttons and then three more may be able to add them up to obtain five (though the same operation may not yet be possible without the buttons), but will not realize that the three can be subtracted from the five in order to (re)produce the original two (unless the buttons are actually taken away). At the stage of 'concrete mental operations' the child can understand both the initial process and its reversibility, without the presence of the buttons. The concrete mental operations are thus accompanied by an awareness of the techniques being used and not merely a prediction of their success. This stage is also characterized by the capacity to form and handle classes and series of objects, and to generate reversible mental operations on them (Beard 1969: 76-89). The child can now draw the 'smallest' and 'largest' square without needing to make intermediate members of the series; can sort objects by more than one criterion simultaneously; appreciate the interrelationships of a whole with its parts, or a class with its subclasses, or 'symmetrical relations' (e.g. that a distance is unaltered in whichever direction it is measured). But there are still limitations in verbal reasoning: the child at this stage, for example, cannot be asked to assume the truth of a statement without believing it to be true ('Suppose that...') or to use general laws in argument. Similarly, children at this stage find it difficult to provide meaningful definitions.

By the age of 11, the child may be ready to enter the final stage of cognitive development, that called the stage of formal mental operations. Whether such progress is in fact made will depend upon the child's social (interactive) environment. The stage of formal operations is characterized by the capacity to reason abstractly, to think about the possibilities of differences in situations and their likely effects—thus, for Piaget, to apply the classical method of science, hypothetico-deductive thinking.[27] There also develops the capacity to reason about one's own reasoning independently of content. Assumptions may be made for the sake of argument. The child 'begins to look for general properties which enable him to give exhaustive definitions, to state general laws and to see common meanings in proverbs or other verbal material' (Beard 1969: 98-99). Inductive argument develops: 'An adolescent

---

27. Piaget has been criticized for identifying intelligence too directly with scientific ability, and for viewing social development as no more than a precondition of such intellectual development (see Jackson 1995b: 251-52).

quickly sees that several instances of a kind suggest the existence of a law which should hold good in all similar cases, but a child tends to see successive instances as separate, unrelated events' (Beard 1969: 101). The moral reasoning associated with the period of formal operations represents a change from previous periods. Whereas earlier the child believes rules and conventions to be unalterable, an adolescent comes to realize that they have been decided by adults, and that they may differ among different groups of people. The substance of moral judgments becomes less extreme; the child now appreciates that a good man may have some bad characteristics and points out what there is to be said both for and against him (Beard 1969: 98).

Piaget himself applied his three main stages of cognitive development—preconceptual, concrete, formal—to what is termed 'moral development': the child's capacity to make sense of rules and to apply them to human behaviour (its own or that of others), especially behaviour that deviates from those rules. The preconceptual stage was characterized by egocentricity, a basic lack of understanding that there can be external reasons for rules; the concrete stage was characterized by heteronomy; the formal stage by autonomy (Piaget 1932; cf. Jackson 1995b: 285-86). Kohlberg has proposed and tested a more detailed scheme of moral development, largely within the Piagetian tradition. He regards the Piagetian cognitive stages as *necessary* but *not sufficient* for development through the stages of moral development (Kohlberg 1987: 12-13).[28] Within this cognitive framework, Kohlberg argues that we have the capacity to develop a form of specifically moral sense, a sense that is 'intrinsically moral in nature, rather than a logical or social-cognitive structure applied to the moral domain' (1987: 15). Moral development is thus regarded as neither a different name for social development, nor a description of the way in which children describe and justify their social relations. Social development, and the accounts given by children of their social relations, constitute a parallel but distinct sphere: there is convincing data, he argues, that 'the domains of social conventional judgment and moral judgment are

28. Thus, Piagetian concrete operations are regarded as necessary for stage 2 moral judgments in Kohlberg's scheme (below), and 'early formal operations' are necessary for stage 3, while 'consolidated formal operations' are necessary for stage 4. On the relationship between Piaget and Kohlberg, see also Weinreich-Haste (1983: 5-6).

differentiated by young children' (Kohlberg 1987: 14-15).[29]

Kohlberg identifies six stages of moral development, divided into three levels (which broadly correspond to Piaget's three principal stages). The first level is the *preconventional* level, where social rules are external to the self, and the child conforms to them for reward or out of fear of punishment. This is the level of 'most children under age 9, some adolescents, and many adolescent and adult criminal offenders' (Kohlberg 1987: 16). The second is the *conventional* level, where morality consists in 'socially shared systems of moral rules, roles, and norms' that are now internalized: the child identifies with them, especially those emanating from authority. This is the level of 'most adolescents and adults in American society and in most other societies'. The third is the *postconventional* level, where society's rules and the individual's own moral principles become differentiated, moral values being identified with the latter. This is reached only by a minority of adults, and usually only after the age of 20–25. Here, 'acceptance of society's rules is based on formulating and accepting the general moral principles that underly these rules' (Kohlberg 1987: 16).[30] In other words, they are accepted not merely because they represent the morality accepted by society, but rather on the basis of some critical evaluation. Hence, the individual's own general moral principles will, at the postconventional stage, be preferred to the rules of society in cases of conflict.[31]

Do studies in this tradition have the potential to assist us in assessing purported regularities of *social*, rather than individual, development? After all, it is a safe assumption that the authors of biblical literature (if not always their audiences) were adults, perhaps even reasonably intelligent adults! Piaget hailed Brunschvig's *Progrès de la conscience dans*

---

29. A theme pursued further by Turiel (1983; cf. Jackson 1995b: §8.3). However, retention of increasing differentiation as a central feature of development continues to link the modern cognitive developmentalists with nineteenth-century social evolutionary thought. It is this, for example, that leads Piaget (1965: 201) to suggest that primitive peoples differentiate between law, religion and morality only by nuances (though this should perhaps be taken more as an external claim that appeals to Piaget rather than a result of his own psychological investigations).

30. For a more detailed account of the six stages into which Kohlberg divided these three levels, see Jackson (1995b: 289-92).

31. For methodological critique of Kohlberg's work, and its focus upon verbalised moral reasoning rather than moral decision-making, see Jackson (1995b: 294-99).

la philosophie occidentale as 'the widest and the most subtle demonstration of the fact that there exists in European thought a law in the
evolution of moral judgments which is analogous to the law of which
psychology watches the effects throughout the development of the
individual' (1932: 402). Similarly, Kohlberg concluded that the stages
of moral evolution of culture identified by Hobhouse 'parallel our own
stages in many ways' (1971: 178). In his book, *The Foundations of
Primitive Thought*, the anthropologist C.R. Hallpike argues strongly
against objections to applying arguments based on child psychology to
early peoples:

> One of the great mistakes of anthropologists, both in the nineteenth cen-
> tury and today, is to suppose that there is a contradiction between saying
> that the cognitive processes of primitive man are more childlike than
> those of educated men, and that they can also attain more complex and
> profound representations of reality than those of which children are
> capable. The root of this mistake is the failure to distinguish between
> cognitive processes on the one hand, and knowledge and experience on
> the other. In our own society cognitive development such as mastery of
> logical relationships ceases for the average child at about sixteen, though
> the brighter child continues to develop longer, and the development of
> the dull child ceases before sixteen. We can say that, cognitively speak-
> ing, the adult in our society has the mentality of an adolescent. But
> knowledge, skills, and maturity of judgement continue to develop over
> an indefinitely long period, and it is these attainments that distinguish the
> adult from the child and the adolescent in every society. In primitive
> societies, however, because there is less stimulus to cognitive growth
> from the social and natural environment, developmental psychology
> maintains that cognitive growth ceases earlier and that formal thought
> and the more advanced concrete operations in particular are not devel-
> oped. For want of a better terminology, we can refer to cognitive growth
> of the kind studied by Piaget as 'vertical' development, and the growth
> of experience and judgement as 'horizontal' development. While
> 'vertical' development will vary according to the milieu, 'horizontal'
> development, the accumulation of experience and wisdom, will always
> distinguish the thought of the adult from that of the child, in primitive
> societies as well as in our own. And it is surely an extraordinarily narrow
> assessment of human beings to say that wisdom, experience, and emo-
> tional maturity count for nothing by comparison with the ability to con-
> serve quantity or to grasp logical inclusion. One is therefore not imply-
> ing that adults in primitive society are intellectually merely the equiva-
> lent of children in our society, but that in primitive societies cognitive
> skills predominantly of the preoperatory type will be developed to a very

high degree of skill and that these will be complemented by the accumulation of experience and wisdom throughout the lifetime of the individual (1979: 39-40).[32]

Hallpike defines as 'primitive' societies 'that are non-literate, relatively unspecialized, pre-industrial, small-scale, and characterized by
"face-to-face" relations in everyday life' (vi). He seeks to elucidate
those characteristics that seem to be most distinctive and prevalent in
the thought processes of such peoples. Primitive thought 'tends to be
idiosyncratic, elusive, unsystematic (at the explicit level), inarticulate,
and frequently expressed through the imagery of symbolism and metaphor ...' (vii). Central to this view is an argument about the relationship
of language to thought, of writing to language, and of the role in primitive societies of symbolic systems other than language.

Language—by definition, in nonliterate societies, speech—is only
one form of symbolism, and is not a precondition of the development of
thought: 'Nothing could be more false than to suppose that the lack of
ability to put thoughts into words signifies the absence of any form of
thought...' (47). It is largely false to assume that 'the cognitive processes employed in problem solving, learning, and in our interaction
generally with people and things are linguistic in nature' (67). Indeed,
the effective use of language has no simple correlation with other

32. Page references in the rest of the text of this section are to this book.
Support for such an approach is also to be found in the work of Morris Ginsberg,
Talcott Parsons, and a number of legal scholars (see further Jackson 1980a: 349-
50). The claim that the cultural development of peoples in historical times mirrors
the cognitive development of the individual is quite distinct from, and does not
depend upon, any claim that ontogeny recapitulates phylogeny—that is, that the
development of the individual recapitulates the evolution of the species to which he
belongs. Moreover, the proposition that the history of legal drafting may be compared to the development of the individual child (see Chapter 4, *infra*) does not
entail any complete equation of the two. If we conclude, for example, that the
draftsman of the Laws of Hammurabi displays the cognitive level of a child of 9,
we are not thereby saying that the draftsman was either a child of 9, or had the mind
of a child of 9 (i.e. was a retarded adult). We are claiming merely that in the sphere
of legal drafting he had activated his capacity to that particular level. Not only may
he have been capable of abstract mental operations, he may indeed have applied
such abstract mental operations to other spheres. The Laws of Hammurabi do not
represent the sum total of the intellectual achievement of the period; it is, however,
significant that they are still used today to introduce students of Akkadian to the
language, precisely because of their relative simplicity.

aspects of intelligence (73). Hallpike's view of the role of language in social and cultural development leads him also to reject any notion of linguistic determinism.

What we find lacking in primitive thought are mental operations, with the characteristic of reversibility associated with the stage of concrete operations. This affects the thought of primitive societies in relation to number, measurement, analysis, conservation, time and space (Chapters 6–8). Thus (338):

> primitive representations of space are highly dependent on the phenomenal appearance and contextual associations of the physical world which are experienced in everyday life, such that representations tend to be static and heavily loaded with symbolism.

And as regards time (383):

> the fundamental distinction between primitive, pre-operatory conceptions of time and those of concrete and formal operations, which we employ in many areas of our thinking, is that primitive time is based on sequences of qualitatively different events, such as those of the seasons or of daily activities.

The use of language and modes of thought of primitive societies derive from the integrated nature of those societies on the one hand and the absence of written communication on the other (484). Developmental psychology, Hallpike argues, sees literacy as producing fundamental changes in cognitive processes (e.g. 127 n. 9, 234). For example (193):

> It has been found in almost all tests that there is a very clear correlation between literacy, with a tendency to classify by form, and a developmental tendency whereby young and/or non-literate children classify by colour and only later, as a result of acquiring literacy, switch to classification by form.

Indeed, the arguments of Ong on the characteristics of oral and written cultures (Ong 1982; Jackson 1995b: 79-83) may readily be related to such aspects of cognitive development.

So what forms of symbolization are used in primitive societies? They are 'non-linguistic symbolic representations based on imagery and the shared associations of everyday objects derived from co-operative action' (135). These ideas of symbolism are encapsulated in action, ritual, and social institutions rather than at a verbal level (cf. Savigny [1867] quoted *infra*, §7.1). But the emphasis on imagery does not entail any absence of thought. Hallpike is confident that both classification and abstraction are to be found, but they differ from Western forms of classification and abstraction in being applied to images rather than linguistic propositions :

> primitive classification is based on functional, associational relationships derived from concrete properties and everyday associations... Such classification is inherently closely associated with prototypical images, and while some hierarchical classification exists in most primitive societies, it is not well formed or of particular utility. More significant are categories based on realms of experience, which need not be hierarchically organised (234-35).

Abstraction, he argues, occurs at every level of cognitive functioning but is encountered in three different types—of perceptual properties, of relations, and of propositions (174). It is this last application of abstraction that is missing in primitive thought—a function of both the absence of writing and the presence of shared social background:

> the verbal analysis of experience, of social behaviour and custom, will be given a low priority in societies where experience is roughly the same for everyone, where behaviour is largely dominated by custom, and where institutions are part of the social structure that is not the subject of debate... Generalisation is required for instruction out of context, for comparison and analysis, for reconciling felt contradictions between different aspects of life or different representative modes... and for planning and deliberate experiment. As we have seen, the circumstances of primitive life do not generally present problems requiring generalisation (132).[33]

How should we assess all this? The same general criticisms levelled at Piaget (see Jackson 1995b: 25-52) apply equally here. The members of 'primitive' societies may not become 'little scientists', but that does not negate the judgment that they have complex cultures—often more complex in their observational classifications and social (e.g. kinship) relationships than our own. The term 'primitive' remains value-laden (even if we do not ascribe to it some type of substantive moral inferiority), and reflects here a privileging of intellectual skills over other forms of sense perception. Many of those forms of sense perception that Hallpike finds strongly represented in 'primitive' societies—such as the

---

33. Elsewhere (at p. 67), he invokes explicitly Bernstein's concept of 'restricted code', on which see *infra*, §3.1. Cf. Bruner's 'instrumental conceptualism' (1966: 319-24).

deployment of 'prototypical images'—continue to play an important role in our own, both 'beneath' the surface of cognitively more advanced thought and in the speech and thought patterns of particular (socially subordinated) groups within society.[34] Hallpike's work alerts us to the developmental importance of the transition from orality to literacy, and at the same time to the persistence within literacy of earlier patterns of cognition—what Ong has referred to as 'oral residue' (1982: 115). All the more important, within the study of biblical law, that we should seek to distinguish the phenomena that belong to the period of orality from those that are generated by incipient literacy.

The recovery of the transition from orality to literacy may appear remote. There is, however, a possible source of guidance quite readily available to us. We are not restricted to either historical reconstruction or anthropological linguistics.[35] Within modern society, educational difference has produced 'semiotic groups' of genuinely literate people on the one hand—those whose cognitive processes have been structured by literacy to such a degree that they even speak much as they write—and incipiently literate people on the other—those whose cognitive processes remain characterized by 'oral residue' and who thus write much as they speak (Jackson 1995b: 79). It is this distinction, as much as the technical argot of the lawyers, that results in the incomprehensibility of many contemporary legal texts to a major section of the population. Indeed, one definition of 'Plain English', into which the movement of that name seeks to translate legal documentation, is 'writing that is straightforward, that reads as if it were spoken' (Redish 1985; cf. Jackson 1995b: 114-15). There is much common ground both within academic studies[36] and with this applied field of sociolinguistics in identifying features of legal expression that depend upon the internalization (through education, at the appropriate developmental stage) of the cognitive processes associated with literacy.

---

34. See particularly Jackson (1995b: 84-66, 93-94, 104-10, 305-19, 409-12) on educational, class and gender differentiations.

35. On the research of Luria and others, see Jackson (1995b: 81-82; §3.1, *infra*).

36. Studies of the relations of orality and literacy (Ong, Goody), the cognitive developmental tradition (Piaget, Kolhberg), and approaches which, in different ways, seek to integrate them, notably Bruner's studies of child linguistic development and the work of Hallpike.

Chapter 2

SPEECH ACTS AND SPEECH BEHAVIOUR

2.1 *Introduction*

The oral and the written are not merely alternative media (or 'channels') for the transmission of meaning. They reflect different modes of thought. But this difference goes beyond issues of semantic structure (see §3.2, *infra*). The paradigm of speech is face-to-face interaction. There, we need to take account not only of what the participants say, not only of what they are seeking to *do*—a perception that has generated the philosophically influential speech act theory (Jackson 1995b: 47-52)—but also of the other sensory elements involved in that interaction. The notion of speech acts can itself thus be expanded into one of speech behaviour, the latter including such matters as voice production (intonation etc.) and 'body language'. The semiotics of speech behaviour—the sense produced by face-to-face communication—must also take account of the visual impression created by the speaker.

Indeed, of the various senses, Sekuler and Blake regard vision as preeminent:

> of all the senses, vision represents the richest source of information...this pre-eminence of vision is mirrored in the proportion of the human brain that is devoted to vision (1990: 21).

But it is not only a quantitative measure (of information received, of brain area involved) that leads them to this conclusion:

> When pitted against the other senses, vision dominates them. Suppose, for example, you are looking at some object held in your hand. If your fingers and your eyes give you conflicting information about the shape of that object, your experience follows what your eyes have told you... A ventriloquist exploits the dominance of vision to fool you into thinking that the sound originates from his dummy rather than from himself (Sekuler and Blake 1990, citing Rock and Harris 1967: 96-104; Power 1981: 29-33).

Chomsky (1980: Ch. 6) discusses the relationship between language and other semiotic systems. One of his examples is face-recognition. He applies to this process the same Cartesian argumentation that he applies to language acquisition: we cannot account for the rapid development of this skill in terms of response to the nature and quantum of the sensory inputs actually received. Jackendoff, too, seeks to 'show that vision, too, is governed by a mental grammar' (1993: 171-83; see also Jackson 1995b: 22-26; 1994a: 329).

In other respects, too, classical speech act theory has been broadened in recent years. Austin's original conception (1975; cf. Blakemore 1992: Ch. 6; Mey 1993: Ch. 6; Schriffin 1994: Ch. 3) was that certain uses of language did not merely make statements, but performed actions. The classical ('direct') speech act was characterized by a particular grammatical form: the utterance 'I name this ship the *Exodus*' does not describe the naming of the ship or claim that the ship has that name: rather, it performs the act of naming. Before the utterance, the ship did not have that name; after the utterance, the ship does have that name. The utterance has an effect in the world (albeit the world of our social knowledge and consciousness). Promising is another act, with social consequences, that may be performed by an utterance. The grammatical form 'I promise' is 'performative' in this context though it is not the only possible performative expression: in a conversational context, 'It's a promise' or just 'Promise!' might do equally. Legal systems have often insisted on particular (sometimes highly stylized) grammatical forms for this purpose, in order to remove doubt as to whether there was a genuine intention to promise, and to facilitate the recognition of the utterance as a speech act of a legal character. In Roman Law, for example, a promise made by 'stipulation' originally required a question and answer form: '*Spondesne...?*'—'*Spondeo...*' ('Do you promise...?' —'I promise...') (see, e.g., Buckland and Stein 1963: 434-35).

Austin (1975: Ch. 3) set out a series of conditions that must be fulfilled for a speech act to be performed.

(1) There must exist an accepted conventional procedure having a certain conventional effect, the procedure to include the uttering of certain words by certain persons in certain circumstances.

(2) The particular persons and circumstances in a given case must be appropriate for the invocation of the particular procedure invoked.

(3)   The procedure must be executed by all participants correctly.

(4)   The procedure must be executed by all participants completely.[1]

Failure in any of the above conditions would render the speech act void, in the sense that it would not produce the social consequences sought. But there may also be, in some cases, further accompanying conditions regarding the thoughts or feelings of the participants, breach of which will render the speech act not void, but rather an abuse.[2] Isaac's blessing of Jacob, believing him to be Esau, illustrates this conception.[3]

More recently, however, it has been argued that this conception of the operation of speech acts is too rigid. Sbisà and Fabbri have proposed a significant modification to speech act theory (1981: 301-19). They point out that the Austin/Searle model is based upon a logical structure: for the performance of any speech act there exists a set of conditions, every one of which is necessary for the successful performance of that speech act. Thus, if any one is unfulfilled, the speech act necessarily fails; conversely, if all the conditions are fulfilled, the speech act necessarily succeeds. But such a logical account may not describe how speech acts always function. In practice they operate through the use (and indeed negotiation) of such conditions in particular contexts of social interaction. Just as imperfect grammar and inappropriate semantics may, within some groups of users, not only prove intelligible, but also be regarded as acceptable, so too the conditions of speech act theory are capable of modification both through the conventions of particular groups and through actual negotiation—explicit or implicit—in social

---

1.   This statement of speech act conditions is, of course, a statement merely of the *general* form of such conditions; for any particular speech act, a far more concrete set of conditions will be generated, within which the persons, circumstances and procedure will be determined.

2.   Searle (1969: 60, 66-67) classified the different types of condition as 'preparatory' (concerning conditions surrounding the performance of the act, including the authority of the speaker to perform the speech act [cf. Kurzon 1986; 8]), 'essential' (concerning performance of the act itself) and 'sincerity' (concerning the intention with which the act is performed).

3.   Gen. 27, esp. vv. 35-36, where Isaac says: 'Your brother came with guile, and he has taken away your blessing' and Esau complains: '...he has supplanted me these two times. He took away my birthright; and behold, now he has taken away my blessing' (see Daube 1947: 91; further §9.2, *infra*). On speech acts of blessing and cursing in the Bible, see further Levenston (1984: 135-38).

interaction. Thus the speech act should be viewed within the wider narrative context of the relations between the participants (for the narrative model, see §1.1, *supra*).

We may view within this context a relaxation of speech act theory that Austin himself accepted: the first-person form of utterance, 'I promise, I warn, etc.' is not the only possible verbal form for speech acts. Among the alternatives he notes are the use of the passive voice and the second or third person (singular or plural). For example:

> 'You are hereby authorised to pay…'
> 'Passengers are warned to cross the track by the bridge only.'
> 'Notice is hereby given that trespassers will be prosecuted.'

He notes that this last example is a type of speech act usually found on formal or legal occasions, and that the use of 'hereby', especially (but not exclusively) in writing, is a useful indicant that the utterance is performative.[4] What is significant, for Austin, is the capacity of the language to be reformulated in the classical speech act form of a first person present indicative.

Today, we recognize that 'indirect speech acts' may be expressed in a perhaps limitless range of linguistic forms. Lecturing on a hot day in a large lecture theatre, I might direct my gaze at a student sitting near the window and say, 'It's rather stuffy in here!' or 'Isn't it rather stuffy in here?' The response I expect is not, 'Certainly is!' or, 'Yes, but that's because of your lecture,' but rather, 'Shall I open the window?' or an actual movement to open the window. In context, and as interpreted in the light of my non-verbal behaviour, my speech act clearly does not function either as an assertion or as a question about facts,[5] but rather as

---

4. Kurzon (1986: 6-7), goes further. While agreeing that 'hereby' is an optional element in a performative, he notes that it cannot be used in any other context: whether it may *potentially* (by rephrasing) occur in a given sentence is therefore a test of whether we are dealing with an instance of a performative. 'Hereby' is thus 'a marker of a performative, and more specifically a legal performative'.

5. Levenston (1984: 129-30) argues that many of the questions posed by God in the Bible are not true questions in speech act terms, since they lack the preparatory condition that the speaker does not know the answer. He notes that mediaeval Jewish commentators supplied alternative views of the function of such questions: for example, Rashi said that the question to Cain ('Where is Abel your brother?' Gen. 4.9) gave him an opportunity to confess and repent; similarly the question to Eve ('Then the LORD God said to the woman, "What is this that you have done?"':

a suggestion, request, or proposal for action. The effect of the speech act might well be the same as the direct command, 'Open the window!', but the choice of an indirect mode, as Tannen argues (1986: 48-52), also communicates a 'metamessage', a message about the form of relationship the speaker has, or seeks to establish, with the hearer. We may, indeed, be able to convert the indirect speech act back to the classical, first-person form, 'I suggest that you open the window,' 'I request you to open the window,' if not 'I command you to open the window,'[6] but that, as Tannen indicates, would be to change the 'metamessage'. It affects the narrative of the ongoing relationship between the participants.

Austin at first proposed a distinction between 'performatives' and 'constatives'. A 'performative' is where 'the issuing of the utterance is the performing of an action—it is not normally thought of as just saying something' (Austin 1992: 6-7); a 'constative' is where the utterance makes a (descriptive) statement. Yet Austin was aware that the utterance of a descriptive statement was also a type of speech act, even if its social consequences were more limited. When I make an assertion (in Austin's terms, a 'statement'), I do not merely put into circulation, or communicate to my listener, a 'proposition'; by uttering the proposition as an assertion, I perform the action of claiming it to be true. If it proves to be false, that will indeed have consequences, not merely at the propositional level (that people will no longer believe the proposition to be true), but also at the level of utterance (the pragmatic level), in that it will be known that I, who have committed myself to that statement as true, have made what proved to be a false truth-claim, and thus appear

---

Gen. 3.13): thus, these are indirect speech acts, admonitions in the form of questions, though neither Eve nor Cain responds to the true illocutionary force of the utterance. More generally, this raises the question of the extent to which divine speech acts in the Bible are modelled upon human. Levenston notes that genuine questions are excluded if God is regarded as omniscient. On the other hand, he observes (at 137) that, despite theological grounds for distinction, there is a considerable formal resemblance between human curses and divine curses (citing Gen. 9.25). Thus we should pause before accepting the more radical claim of Sternberg (1985: 108, quoted by Watts 1999: 96), that 'the biblical convention of divine performative works against convention, deriving its affective force from the infringement or the transcendence of all the norms that would govern a human equivalent'.

6.   Or even, 'I hereby suggest that you open the window,' 'I hereby request you to open the window,' or 'I hereby command you to open the window' (following Kurzon, *supra* n. 4).

either as a liar or as unreliable. The distinction between 'performatives' and 'constatives' was later replaced by one between the locutionary, illocutionary and perlocutionary aspects of utterances—locutionary acts being the behaviour of speaking, illocutionary force being that which such behaviour amounted to in conventional terms (e.g. making a promise), and perlocutionary effects being the psychological and other effects of speaking, such as persuasion (Jori 1993: 2092).

In this chapter, I provide some examples of issues within biblical law that may advantageously be viewed within the above framework.

2.2 *Speech Acts in Biblical Law*

The Bible provides an array of speech acts.[7] We have several examples in domestic relations. Perhaps the best-known is the oral divorce formula in Hos. 2.4: 'She is not my wife and I am not her husband.' The use of the first person[8] does not suggest, of course, that the particular grammatical convention by which English expresses the performative in Austin's classical form (first person indicative) is transferable to other languages. A systematic comparative investigation of such speech forms in different languages would be valuable. Not only do biblical speech acts appear to require direct address (particularly appropriate for face-to-face transactions involving domestic relations); the use of the deictic formula *hineh* might be compared with the English 'hereby', and might at the same time suggest use in an oral setting.[9]

Direct access to the forms of biblical speech acts is available, of course, only where the text purports to provide us with *oratio directa*. And even there, we cannot always be sure that the narrator's understanding of the speech act is the same as the original. Take the account of the 'naming' of Moses in Exod. 2.10. We read that Moses grew up

7. The only study appears to be Levenston (1984). I am grateful to Dennis Kurzon for having drawn it to my attention, and also for useful comments on this chapter.

8. Levenston (1984: 138-39) cites also Gen. 9.9 (God covenanting with Noah), 17.4 (God covenanting with Abram and at the same time renaming him Abraham), Exod. 34.10 (God covenanting with the people after the golden calf) for the use of the first person in speech acts.

9. After writing this, I was happy to find that I had been anticipated by Levenston (1984: 139), describing the more common translation of *hineh*, 'behold', as somewhat inept. He observes that 'the culture described in the Pentateuch is predominantly an oral culture, where the spoken utterance is supremely important'.

(nursed by his mother, on behalf of Pharaoh's daughter), and that then (probably at adolescence) he was brought to Pharaoh's daughter 'and became to her as a son, and she called his name Moses, saying that it was because she had drawn him forth from the water' (כי מן המים משיתהו). At the narrative level, Moses is given a new name on entry into the Egyptian court. If any incongruity would have been perceived by the audience at the fact that the Egyptian princess apparently justified her choice of name in terms of a Hebrew etymology, this may have been taken as an element of humour, adding variety to the tone of the narrative. At any rate, the recorded speech act is explicitly described as 'naming': ותקרא שמו משה. But two factors lead us to suppose that a different speech act may originally have been intended. *Mosheh*, as has plausibly been argued, is neither a Hebrew nor an Egyptian name, but rather the common Egyptian suffix to personal names, as found for example in *Thutmose* (Cazelles 1986: col. 35). *Thutmose* means 'son of Tut'; the *'mose'* is equivalent to the Hebrew *ben*. Should we conclude, therefore, that we have a record of the boy's 'kitchen' name—'Sonny'? I think not. We have to relate this to the phrase that immediately precedes: ויהי לה לבן (and became to her as a son). Pharaoh's daughter adopted Moses. How was adoption performed? Probably, by a formulaic speech act, examples of which are found in ancient Near Eastern sources, such as 'You are my father and I am your son' (see Paul 1978). Thus the words ותקרא...משה may themselves very well be a record of the speech act of adoption: 'And she called him...son.' Knowledge of the relevant institution was apparently lost to our narrator, who reinterpreted the speech act as that of simple naming,[10] with the result that we now have before us. If correct, there is a sad conclusion. Not only are we ignorant of Moses' Hebrew name; we no longer know his Egyptian name either.

Even when we get apparently verbatim quotations of speech acts in the Bible, we have to ask ourselves whether they are likely to represent speech acts taken from life, or whether the realities have been given a literary gloss. When Jacob adopts Ephraim and Menasseh, in effect to give Joseph a double portion,[11] his speech is reported as (Gen. 48.5):

10. Of course, adoption may itself involve renaming. But adoption is not treated in the laws of the Bible, though there are a number of allusions to it in the narratives. See Falk (1964: 162-64), arguing that the need for it was reduced by both polygyny and levirate marriage.

11. Cf. Falk (1964: 163), citing a parallel from Ugarit. See further §8.3, *infra*.

> And now your two sons, who were born to you in the land of Egypt before I came to you in Egypt, are mine; Ephraim and Manasseh shall be mine, as Reuben and Simeon are (Gen. 48.5).

The two sentences have different functions: it is the narrator's audience, not Joseph, who are being told (through Jacob's speech) that Ephraim and Menasseh were born in Egypt before Jacob's arrival; so too, the comparison with Reuben and Simeon is hardly performative. What is performative is the declaration that Ephraim and Menasseh belong to Jacob. The opening *ve'atah*, moreover, may be taken as a marker of a speech act, comparable to *hineh*.

Another example of the literary refashioning of speech acts occurs in Deut. 20.5-7. When Israel goes to war against its enemies, the commanders are to issue the following proclamation to the people (ודברו השטרים אל העם לאמר):

> What man is there who has built a new house and not dedicated it? Let him go back to his house, lest he die in the battle and another man dedicate it. And what man is there that has planted a vineyard and has not enjoyed its fruit? Let him go back to his house, lest he die in the battle and another man enjoy its fruit. And what man is there that has betrothed a wife and has not taken her? Let him go back to his house, lest he die in the battle and another man take her.

It is difficult to believe that a commander on the eve of a battle issues his exemptions in the form of questions backed up by motive clauses. Surely what we would expect is no more than a statement of the conditions of exemption. Our *oratio directa* may indeed reflect a *Sitz* of oral proclamation in that it uses a separate clause for each individual category.[12] But the terms of the proclamation are clearly attributable to the didactic interests of the narrator. No one would dream of using Shakespeare's battle speeches as direct evidence of speech forms in actual battle situations. Would they?

Not totally unrelated to the speech act of naming is the process of classification. Num. 35.16-18 contains a sequence of homicide provisions, expressed in the following form: 'But if he struck him down with an instrument of iron, so that he died, he is a murderer—*rotseach hu* (רצח הוא)—the murderer shall be put to death' (v. 16). Daube observed that *rotseach hu* is logically superfluous.[13] Why not merely say, as in

---

12. This may cast light also on the development of drafting (see §4.4, *infra*).
13. Cf. the famous argument of Alf Ross (1957) as to the redundancy of legal

the normal casuistic form, 'If he struck him down with an instrument of iron, so that he died, he shall be put to death'? Daube called this the 'diagnosis form' (Daube 1944–45: 39-42; 1981: 100-106).[14] Between the statement of the facts, and the provision of the legal remedy, a diagnosis of the legal condition is inserted. Its origin, he suggested, lies in medical texts. Between the description of the symptoms and the prescription of a treatment, we have a diagnosis of the ailment. Yet here too, one might conclude, the diagnosis is logically redundant. If we know that a raw egg will cure a hangover, the treatment is not the product of discovery that the symptoms are 'a hangover'; it is the result of experience that those symptoms are relieved by that treatment. Generations of patients, and perhaps as many generations of doctors, have successfully relieved medical conditions while being totally wrong in their diagnosis of what that condition was. The diagnosis, we may think, is a matter of medical science, the treatment a matter of medical practice, just as the classification of the offender here as a 'murderer' may be a matter of legal theory, while what matters for legal practice is purely the punishment.

But such an analysis, Daube claimed, neglects the ancient medical idea that to conquer a sickness it is necessary to discover its name or that of the demon that causes it.[15] If correct, this means that the naming of the disease was not merely a matter of scientific speculation, but a speech act that formed a necessary part of the treatment. But when the form is transferred to the legal context, the need for such a speech act largely disappears. The diagnosis form is very much the exception rather than the rule. We find it in circumstances where the facts go beyond the normal image of the offence in question. It is not self-evident that a man who strikes another with an iron instrument, but without the evidence of ambush or prior hatred that the biblical sources normally require for the offence of murder (see §8.2, *infra*), should be so treated. Here, a decision is taken to that effect. To make this offender

concepts; see further Jackson (1985b: 183-91; 1996a: 141-44).

14. On the developmental significance of this, see further §4.2, *infra*.

15. Cf. Olivecrona, Preface to Hägerström (1953: xvii), observing that magic includes 'every kind of belief in the possibility of producing desired effects by other means than those belonging to natural causality. A typical instance of magic is the production of an effect by representing it or proclaiming its occurrence in formal words... A usual feature of magical acts is the formality that attaches to them: the act has to be performed exactly in the right manner, if it is to produce the effect.'

into a murderer, a speech act is necessary.[16]

But where do we find evidence for such a speech act? Though there is a possibility that *rotseach hu* originates in the formal pronouncement of a court (or perhaps an oracular decision), the text of Numbers 35 neither presents it as a direct speech act formula (*oratio directa*), nor does it refer to the performance of a speech act, as in the case of the naming of Moses. But reference to the speech act is, I maintain, present, if we take the total narrative context into account. God instructs Moses to tell the children of Israel that he, God, says that the accused in these circumstances is a murderer. The institutional speech act of naming is here incorporated into the narrative structure, and indeed into the very structure of the legal norm itself. The audience will not doubt that this offender now really is a murderer, given that it is God who has applied that name to him.

I used to think of this clause, *rotseach hu*, as a 'justification' of the norm, albeit in the form of an arbitrary classification. But it is worth noting, in the light of Austin's speech act theory, that naming and justification are quite different. Austin would classify 'naming' as an 'illocutionary act', but he would not so regard 'justify'. If I say, 'I name this ship Queen Mary,' I thereby perform the speech act of naming (provided the preparatory conditions are fulfilled, notably those relating to my authority to do so). But if I say: 'I justify,' I do not thereby perform an act of justifying. Rather, justification may be a perlocutionary effect of what I say by way of justification (Austin 1975: Ch. 9). In the biblical text, however, justification does appear as an illocutionary speech act, given the narrative context. Because this is a report of divine speech, the very act of classification—unsupported by reasoning, but carrying the weight of divine authority—constitutes also its own justification of the legal conclusions.

The opening of the Decalogue may be viewed as an indirect speech act, having the form of a constative but the force of something different: 'I am the LORD your God, who brought you out of the land of Egypt, out of the house of bondage' (Exod. 20.2). Jewish tradition

16. At first sight, such a speech act might be viewed as a constative, being declaratory of a state of affairs. But the issue here is not whether the offender is found to have acted in the way described, but rather what should be their legal status, with appropriate normative consequences. In so far as this classification is new, the speech act is performative, in that it constitutes a new legal classification that did not exist before.

regards this as the first 'commandment'; for Christians, on the other hand, it is the introduction to the next commandment, that against idolatry, rather than an independent commandment (Sarfatti 1990: 410-11, citing Augustine in *PG*, III, pp. 620, 644). We may put the issue in the terms of modern linguistics. Is this sentence the mere making of a truth-claim, or is it a different kind of (indirect) speech act?[17] We might compare an utterance like 'I am your father,' delivered by an irate father to his infant in reaction to some insulting speech or behaviour, or in connection with the laying down of rules of behaviour that the infant questions. Rationally, we might view this as the statement of a 'motive' for obedience, but this would be insufficient. The utterance is designed to evoke a feeling, a sentiment, and not merely a course of behaviour: it is a demand for loyalty and respect.[18] If we view—as we should—this Biblical speech act in its narrative context, much the same conclusion applies: 'I am the LORD your God, who brought you out of the land of Egypt, out of the house of bondage' is not a mere truth-claim (such as might evoke the response, 'Sure, everyone knows that. So what?'), but rather a demand for loyalty, the loyalty inherent in adherence to a covenant under which God has already demonstrated his performance of his role of protector. The demand for belief thus involves not just cognition but also an affective state: the feeling of loyalty.

17. Levenston (1984: 142-44) argues that *anokhi YHWH* should be regarded as the enacting formula, a 'divine oral signature', and therefore that the first commandment is 'You shall have no other gods before me' (Exod. 20.3). But that does not take account of the historical description appended to the name (either here or in the Prologue to the Laws of Hammurabi, which Levenston compares: 143 n.13). In this respect, the Decalogue differs from most of the other examples Levenston cites from Leviticus. As he indicates, in Lev. 19, we find, most commonly, simply 'I am the LORD', and also frequently 'I am the LORD your God', but only once 'I am the LORD your God, who brought you out of the land of Egypt' (19.36), which he himself describes as an expansion. The pattern is similar elsewhere in Leviticus. The reference to the Exodus occurs also in Lev. 11.45, 25.38, 26.13. These expansions may well be allusions to the opening formula of the Decalogue. The only other narrative expansion of the formula in Leviticus is in 20.24: 'I am the LORD your God, who have separated you from the peoples'. The theme of separation is closely linked to the other form of expansion found in Leviticus: 'I am the LORD who sanctify them' (22.16), which derives from the priestly writer's theological concerns.

18. This, of course, is quite compatible with the common historical explanation, in terms of ancient treaty forms, where loyalty and obedience are pledged in exchange for protection.

An example of a 'negotiated' speech act may be found in the story of Susanna and the elders. Susanna is convicted of adultery, on the false evidence of the elders, whose attempt to blackmail her into gratifying them she has resisted. The elders testify that they had observed her *in flagrante delicto* with her lover; they had attempted to detain the young man, but he had been too strong for them and had escaped. In deference to their position, the assembly believes them and condemns Susanna to death, in accordance with Deut. 22.22. Susanna cries out in protest: the omniscient God must know the falsity of the charge.

> The LORD heard her cry. And as she was being led away to be put to death, God aroused the holy spirit of a young lad named Daniel; and he cried with a loud voice, 'I am innocent of the blood of this woman.' All the people turned to him, and said, 'What is this that you have said?' Taking his stand in the midst of them, he said, 'Are you such fools, you sons of Israel? Have you condemned a daughter of Israel without examination and without learning the facts? Return to the place of judgment. For these men have borne false witness against her.' Then all the people returned in haste. And the elders said to him, 'Come, sit among us and inform us, for God has given you that right.' And Daniel said to them, 'Separate them far from each other, and I will examine them' (vv. 44-51).

To each, he posed the question: 'Under which tree was the offence committed?' The first responded, 'Under a mastick tree,' the second, 'Under a holm tree.'[19] In the light of this contradiction in the evidence, the assembly immediately acquitted Susanna, and (more problematically)[20] turned on the two elders and put them to death in accordance

19. In the Greek, the names of the trees figure in a skilful double pun, which has prompted scholarly discussion, from ancient to modern times, as to the original language of the story (see further Jackson 1977: 38).

20. Mediaeval Jewish versions of the story sought to remove the possibility that the inconsistency in the testimony had resulted from error (see Jackson 1977b: 39-40). In the *Summa Decretorum* of the Bolognese Decretist Rufinus, written between 1157 and 1159, the argument is advanced that both elders could have been telling the truth: the couple could have made love under *both* the mastick *and* the holm tree. But to this, he noted, there was a rejoinder: the elders had claimed to have witnessed the act *together*. Thus, only one act of love could have been in issue, and therefore the evidence remained contradictory. Nonetheless, the analysis produced an important negative conclusion: inconsistency as to the time or place of the offence did not *necessarily* indicate false testimony: there were circumstances in which both witnesses might be telling the truth. In the doctrinal argument of Rufinus, this became relevant not only to the position of the elders, but also to the

with the Mosaic law against malicious testimony (Deut. 19.16-19).

We are entitled to ask: how was it possible for Daniel to get the court reconvened in the first place? We can hardly imagine a similar incident today: sympathizers in the public gallery will not infrequently protest the innocence of the accused who has been convicted and sentenced. It is inconceivable that the court would reconvene in the light of any such protest. For the narrative to make sense, we have to distance ourselves from the privileged knowledge of the narrator—that Susanna is actually innocent, and that God has indeed inspired Daniel to intervene on her behalf, in the light of her own invocation. We have to ask how God performed this semiotic trick: how was Daniel endowed with authority such as to secure the reconvening of the court? If we regard this as a speech act of summons, we need to reconstruct the preparatory conditions for its performance: the authority of Daniel to make such a demand. The first thing we are told about the intervention of Daniel is that he 'cried with a loud voice, I am innocent of the blood of this woman'. This implies, on the one hand, that the court was 'popular'—reflecting, perhaps, the Hellenistic environment of the ancient versions—and, secondly, that there was something special in Daniel's tone of voice, in making his intervention. This is confirmed by the terms in which the other elders (apparently reacting to the impression made by Daniel upon his fellow-members of the popular jury) invite him to take an active part in the reconvened proceedings: 'Come, sit down among us and show it us, seeing God hath given thee the honour of an elder.'[21]

weighing of evidence against the accused. For the canonists were beginning to develop a doctrine according to which the two-witness rule could be satisfied in appropriate cases by *testes singulares*, single witnesses each to separate occurrences of the same offence. This was permissible, according to the canonists, only where the offence was inherently likely to be repeated. That condition was fulfilled in the case of adultery (though the early canonists limited this to adultery with the same lover); it was not admissible in the case of murder of a bishop (especially the same bishop!). For the history in canon law and its influence in England and Scotland, see Jackson (1977b: 37-54). There may possibly be a link with CDC 9.16-23, on which see Jackson (1975a: 172-83).

21. This presentation by the narrator of Daniel's speech as an inspired, thus divine speech act, is carried forward into the language that Daniel uses in examining the two elders and in commenting upon their replies. For example, to the response of the first elder, Daniel comments: 'Thou has lied against thine own head; for even now the angel of God hath received the sentence of God to cut thee in two.'

If Daniel had no actual authority to demand that the court reconvene, it appears that the members of the court were prepared to ignore this failure of the normal preparatory conditions. Indeed, they were prepared to institute him as a member of the court, with the right to examine witnesses. The normal preparatory conditions appear to have been 'negotiated'.

2.3 *Speech Acts and Form-Criticism in Biblical Law*

2.3.1 *Apodictic Forms*
The search for the oral origins of Israelite law has been conducted largely through form-critical arguments, in which the pioneering analysis of Albrecht Alt still looms large. He distinguished between the (to him, Israelite) apodictic forms and the (to him, non-indigenous) casuistic, associating the former with the Israelite cult and the latter with an administration of justice that reflected the practices of the Canaanite environment (Alt 1989: 93-103, 125-32). Neither the Israelite/Canaanite distinction nor the cultic *Sitz* of the apodictic law are widely followed today (Crüsemann 1996: 11). But the basic quest for the settings in life of the speech patterns whose traces survive in the literary sources remains a useful starting point for the investigation of the prehistory of Israelite law.[22]

As for the apodictic law, Alt (controversially) saw it as having three

---

22. Alt's argument for the cultic setting of the apodictic law (1989: 123-32), however, was methodologically flawed. He fixed on the reading required by Deut. 31.10-13 (§9.4, *infra*) every seventh year at the Sukkot festival (despite accepting that it was 'the solemn reading of Deuteronomy' that was to take place there: [1989: 127]), and endowed that occasion with the function of covenant renewal, while at the same time conceding (at 129) that no such description is actually given of it in the text. His starting point was the form, completely extrapolated from any of the narrative contexts in which we actually find it. From the form alone, he inferred a use and therefore a *Sitz im Leben*. In order to substantiate that *Sitz im Leben*, he rewrote Deut. 31.10-13 to fit it. A preferable approach would start from quite different assumptions. It would not assume a one-to-one relationship between form and setting and infer the setting from the form; rather, it would infer the significance of the form from those narrative settings where we actually find it (taking account of the complexities that can arise when our accounts of those settings are literary: the relationship between speech acts and their narrative settings [see further §2.2, *supra*]).

versions: participial, prohibition, curse (1989: 109-23).[23] For each one
of them, it is possible to locate the *Sitz im Leben* in the domestic setting.
Thus, we find in Proverbs the use of the participial form in precisely the
same context—domestic relations—as we find it used in the participial
section of the *Mishpatim*. In the latter, two of the four participial provisions are offences against parents:

ומכה אביו ואמו מות יומת :Exod. 21.15

ומקלל אביו ואמו מות יומת :Exod. 21.17

with which we may compare

מקלל אביו ואמו ידעך נרו באישון חשך :Prov. 20.20

גוזל אביו ואמו ואמר אין פשע חבר הוא לאיש [24]:Prov. 28.24

משחית

It is hardly difficult to reconstruct the setting which explains these
parallels in both form and content. Within the constant theme of domestic instruction in Proverbs[25] (one in which the role of mother[26] as well

---

23. The classification of the participial form, in particular, has proved controversial. Alt associated the caesura between subject and predicate with 'the metre of
a five-beat Hebrew verse' (at 109). In favour of such an apodictic classification, see.
e.g., Boecker (1980: 194-201 [reviewing earlier German scholarship]); Schwienhorst-
Schönberger (1990: 213-16). Houtman (1997: 14) regards them, essentially, as
casuistic in form but apodictic in force. In favour of a casuistic classification, see
Wenham (1971a: 97, 102) and Weinfeld (1973: 63). Patrick (1985: 156-57), who,
while seemingly approving Alt's view that all three types of apodictic law 'would
engender a different sort of transaction with an audience than would those carefully
calibrated conditional statements Alt termed 'casuistic', and therefore must belong
to a different oral setting', sees similarities between the participial and casuistic
forms: 'like casuistic law, these laws are impersonal and judicial, whereas apodictic
commandments are personal and moral (nonjuridical)' (at 72). See also Prévost
(1976: 357).

24. The terminology of *pesha* is also used in two narratives of *domestic* disputes: Laban's accusation that Jacob or a member of his family had stolen his
household gods (Gen. 31.36), and the kidnapping of Benjamin (Gen. 50.17). On the
possible relationships of these sources, see further Jackson (2000b: 49).

25. E.g. Prov. 4.4,11 and the frequent address to 'my son': Prov. 1.8, 15; 2.1;
3.1, 11, 21; 4.1 (plural); 4.10, 20; 5.1; 6.1, 21; 7.1; 23.15, 19; 27.11. Cf. Greenberg
(1995: 17) on the family as the natural educational environment, citing particularly
Deut. 6.20: 'When in time to come your children ask you: 'What mean these

as the father is stressed) we frequently encounter references to physical correction.[27] Indeed, the very term *musar* is sometimes used with that connotation (Prov. 13.24; 22.15; 23.13). Some children will react against that correction, either verbally (cursing) or physically.[28] In narrative sources, we encounter the participial form used of a proclamation, as in the protection accorded Cain.[29] This, it seems, may have been the form of the speech act used for domestic regulation, where the instruction was issued to the household as a whole (including those not present at the oral proclamation itself).

The form *lo* or *al* + second-person verb, as in the Decalogue and frequently elsewhere, is often regarded as the 'classical' version of the apodictic form. It is, of course, a natural way of expressing a prohibition. It is also found used for face-to-face prohibitions in the domestic setting. as in Gen. 28.6, where Isaac prohibits Jacob from taking a Canaanite wife in the words:= ויצו עליו לאמר לא תקח אשה מבנות כנען, the text conveniently here providing us with both a description of the force of the speech act (command) and its formula.

Alt's third form was that of curses: *arur*. Here too, we do not have to search far in the biblical narratives for a domestic setting: not only cursing in reaction to domestic discipline (Prov. 20.20 [*supra*]; cf. 30.11, 17), but also the use by both Isaac and Jacob of deathbed blessings and curses in regulating the future of the clan.[30]

decrees, laws and rules...'

26. Prov. 1.8; 6.20: *torat imekhah*, and the role of the mother in Prov. 29.15 (which seems to imply that the mother also has a role in physical correction); 30.11. 17; 31.1-2, 26.

27. E.g. Prov. 13.24 and see the use of the *shevet* in Prov. 10.13; 13.24; 22.15; 23.13-14; 29.15.

28. For parallels to Exod. 21.15 from the ancient Near East as well as the Bible. see Fitzpatrick-McKinley (1999: 120-21).

29. Gen. 4.15: כל הרג קין שבעתים יקם, presumably directed to those mysterious people Cain fears may kill him in his wanderings (v.14). Cf. Gen. 9.6, on which see further §7.1, *infra* (esp. n. 24).

30. See esp. Gen. 27.12 (Isaac), where Jacob fears that if the ruse is discovered he will receive a curse rather than a blessing. In the event, that is, in effect, what Esau receives (Gen. 27.39-40), though described in the language of blessing—what we might term a 'mixed blessing'. Cf. Jacob's blessing of Reuben in Gen. 49.3-4. There may well be a connection here with the wisdom theme of the relationship between good conduct and the motivation that you 'live', as explored very recently by Burkes (1999: 253-76).

2.3.2 *The Casuistic Form*

As for the casuistic form, it is much more difficult to find an oral life setting with which to associate it. It might be thought that the Bible itself provides us with good evidence on this question, in the incident of the daughters of Zelophehad (Num. 27.1-11, 36.1-10) and parallel sources regarding the adjudication of disputes during the wandering of the Israelites in the desert. Originally, I myself argued that the story of the daughters supported the view that the casuistic form originated in the law court (Jackson 1975b: 488-99 n. 43). We have a complaint, followed by an oracular decision, followed by an instruction by God to Moses to proclaim a generally binding rule. However, though the rules applicable for the future are indeed expressed as a paragraph of casuistic laws,[31] the narrative does not use that form to express the pronunciation of the decision-making in the case itself: כן בנות צלפחד דברת נתן תתן להם אחזת נחלה בתוך אחי אביהם (Num. 27.7) and the authority of the casuistic paragraph derives not from the decision *per se* but rather from God's command to Moses to proclaim it.[32] Indeed, the terms in which Moses is to make this proclamation are given in *oratio directa*: 'If a man dies (איש כי ימות), and has no son, then you shall cause his inheritance to pass to his daughter. And if (*ve'im*) he has no daughter… And if (*ve'im*) he has no brothers… And if (*ve'im*) his father has no brothers…' (27.8-11). Without such proclamation, no precedent would have been set for the future.[33] That being so, we have more reason to associate the casuistic form, on the evidence of this narrative, with the setting of a proclamation by the supreme

---

31. Though not precisely in the form of the *Mishpatim:* the first (Num. 27.8) commences with *ish ki,* commonly found in the priestly source, followed by three *ve'im* clauses. Moreover, the apodoses (but not protases) are expressed in the second person.

32. Crüsemann (1996: 84) has plausibly suggested that these narratives are designed to provide authority to propound new, divinely authorized rules, that are *not* claimed to have been given on Sinai.

33. Cf. Jackson (1987: 6-9). An argument to similar effect has been advanced by Knierim (1989: 16-17) against Liedke's account of the casuistic laws. The latter, Knierim argues, fails conceptually to distinguish between a case decision and the use of prescriptive language in formulating a binding (legislative) rule for the future. See also Greenberg (1995: 15): 'The law is embedded in a narrative framework, which tells of God's command that every law be proclaimed to the Israelites…publication is manifestly of the essence of lawgiving.'

authority, than with a case law precedent.[34] Indeed, we may question, here as elsewhere in the early history of law, whether our own categorization of legislation and precedent as two separate 'sources' of law is applicable to the ancient material. What is clear is that the narrator does not rely here on any conventions known to his audience in order to communicate the force of decision as a precedent for the future: he makes that force absolutely explicit, through the narrative framework, 'And you shall say to the people of Israel' (v. 27.8); '...and it shall be to the people of Israel a statute and an ordinance, as the LORD commanded Moses'.

In the second case involving the daughters, where the tribal leaders seek successfully to prevent the land inherited by the daughters from being alienated from the tribe,[35] the same speech form as in Numbers 27 is used in relation to the decision itself: כן מטה בני יוסף דברים (The tribe of the sons of Joseph is right, Num. 36.5), but the rules for the future are here stated in an apodictic form (Num. 36.7-9). In the case of the blasphemer, the decision is stated as a direct command (הוצא את המקלל..., Lev. 24.14) while the rules for the future, again introduced by a direct command from God to Moses to proclaim them, follow in an elaborate literary mix of short casuistic (איש כי, vv. 15, 17, 19) and participial (vv. 16, 18, 21) provisions and other apodictic forms (vv. 16, 20, 22) (see Jackson 1996b: 119-21). The case of the passover defaulters does not state the decision separately, but the rules for the future are again a mix of casuistic forms (איש איש אשר...איש כי) and apodictic (Num. 9.10-13).

As regards the proclamations that Moses is commanded to make in the wake of these various desert disputes, there is thus no one-to-one correlation between form and use (cf. Schwartz 1983: 161-63). Such proclamations may be made in a variety of forms. The narrative contexts in which we find them generally tell us far more about the force of the utterance than does the form itself.

It is worth comparing the narrative of the daughters of Zelophehad with the story of David's division of the booty after the defeat of the Amalekites.[36] For there we encounter a similar pattern: a dispute, its

---

34. On biblical indications of divine legislative speech acts, see Levenston (1984: 139-44).

35. On the relationship between the two cases, and the narrative function of their separation in the text, see Sakenfeld (1988); Ulrich (1998: 529-38).

36. 1 Sam. 30.21-25. For the text and further comment on the place of the narra-

resolution and the enunciation of a rule generally binding for the future. Again, the adjudication and the enunciation of a new rule are attributed to a person of high authority, though not one who (currently) enjoys the title of king. After the defeat of the Amalekites, and the recovery from them of the booty they had taken from David's city of Ziklag (including his two wives) and the capture of their livestock, David is met with the argument, from the 'wicked and base fellows' in his army, that only the 400 warriors who had actually engaged the Amalekites should share the booty, to the exclusion of the other 200 who had started the pursuit with them, but had been too exhausted to complete it, and had been left behind at the brook of Besor (1 Sam. 30.22). David rules for equal shares. We have in 1 Sam. 30.23-25 a passage that, like Deuteronomy 20, calls for careful sifting of the speech forms that might have been used in an historical context, from the narrative presentation of what happened. David certainly starts off with a direct prohibition, responding to the proposal put to him by his men: 'You shall not do so' (לא תעשו כן, v. 23).[37] He continues with the reasons: it was God who assured the victory. Then he gives his positive order, stated apodictically[38] (if not proverbially): כי כחלק הירד במלחמה וכחלק הישב על הבלים יחדו יחלקו (Behold the share of he who goes down into battle and of he who stays behind with the equipment shall be divided equally, v. 24). Then the narrator continues: 'And it was so from that day onwards, and he established it as a statute (לחק ולמשפט) for Israel, until this very day' (see further §6.2, *infra*).

The pattern that we observe here is the same as that in the story of the daughters of Zelophehad in Numbers 27. We have a complaint, followed by a decision, followed by the enunciation of a general and continuing rule. In the case of the daughters of Zelophehad, the latter stage is given more prominence through the reiteration of the terms of the

tive in the development of the notion of enduring legislation, see further §6.2, *infra*.

37. There is more consistency in relation to the statement of the decision, with Num. 27.7, 36.5 and 1 Sam. 30.23 all using formulae involving *ken*. This would appear to suggest that adjudication is viewed in primarily reactive terms: a proposal is put to the adjudicator, which is approved (*ken*) or not.

38. I cannot agree with Whitelam (1979: 96), who, though acknowledging the metrical form of the decision, seeks to associate it with the casuistic form of the *Mishpatim*: the *ki* here is deictic, not a conjunction. He may well be correct, however, in suggesting that this was not a Davidic innovation. He points also (at 97) to the 'similar ruling' in Josh. 8.22, though we are not told there what is to be the basis of division of the booty.

general rule; indeed, the general rule that Moses is commanded by God then to pronounce goes beyond the circumstances that had actually arisen in the case of the daughters themselves, since we are told what is to happen even when there are no daughters. Here, in the case of David, we also have a degree of discrepancy between the decision in the particular case, and the general law that follows. In the preceding narrative, we are nowhere told that the reason for leaving the 200 men behind at the brook of Besor had been to look after the equipment; on the contrary, we are twice told that they were left because they were exhausted,[39] with no hint on either occasion of any further reason. But in the general rule that David pronounces, the equal shares are to be between the warriors and those who stayed behind looking after the equipment.[40]

The comparison with the case of the daughters of Zelophehad is significant for a number of reasons. First, we see how tenuous is the distinction between adjudication and edict. In both passages, a particular incident has occurred that calls for a decision, and that decision is made by the supreme authority on the spot. How meaningful is it to characterize the case of the daughters as a 'case', or litigation, and to adopt some other characterization of the request of the 400 warriors? Certainly, Num. 27.5 uses the phrase, ויקרב משה את משפטן לפני יהוה (Moses brought their case before the LORD). But that does not justify us in taking *mishpat* as restricted, or even especially connected, to a dispute which is to be judicially determined. Here, in the case of David, the ultimate rule is imposed on Israel *lechok ulemishpat* (v. 25). In fact, this passage may provide significant evidence of the meaning of the phrase, *vayasem lo chok umishpat,* which we find not uncommonly of kings starting from Moses in Exodus 15 and continuing through Joshua at Shechem in Joshua 24. In *chok umishpat, mishpat* appears to reflect the fact that the general rule has been prompted by an individual decision (but not necessarily a judicial decision), while *chok* signifies that that individual decision has indeed been elevated to the status of a general rule. For it is clear, from the incidents of both the daughters and the booty, that a decision, even if made by authority, did not *eo ipso* count

39. 1 Sam. 30.10, 21. Whitelam (1979: 95-96) notes the discrepancy and argues that the theme of exhaustion was a late accretion, though 'why this took place appears impossible to decide'.

40. The distribution that God commands Moses to make of the booty of the Midianites is different again. On Num. 31, see §6.2, *infra*.

as a general rule for the future. In both cases, there is a further act to be performed in order to make it so.

Thus, though we have a number of narratives regarding disputes, their resolution and the resultant statement of rules for the future, the casuistic form does *not* appear as the regular formula of either decision/judgment or rule for the future (though it is found sometimes in the latter context). Indeed, the most influential contemporary theory that associates the casuistic form with judicial decision-making in individual cases is *not* based on Alt's kind of form critical argument, seeking the underlying *speech* patterns: rather it is what we might call a primitive *literary* theory, that of the derivation of the casuistic form from (written) 'trial transcripts'. In surviving ancient Near Eastern trial transcripts, we find a statement of the circumstances followed by a statement of the verdict. Liedke has argued that by excising the names of the parties and other purely circumstantial detail, the two statements could be combined so as to generate, respectively, the protasis and apodosis of the casuistic form (1971: 39, 54-56)[41], a view that has been followed by both Otto (1993: 4, 18, 22) and Crüsemann (1996: 60).

Such arguments, we may note, assume the existence of written trial records in ancient Israel, no evidence for which has yet been found.[42] But even if they existed in the form we know from the ancient Near East, there is no necessity in identifying them as the source of the form: the clauses follow a natural narrative sequence.[43] The 'trial transcript'

---

41. For such trial records, see more recently those from Nippur, discussed by Locher (1986: 93-109). As Boecker (1980: 153), puts it: 'For the account of a suit to become a casuistic legal principle, it had to undergo a radical process of abstraction. Names and above all circumstances and details were excised. The only thing finally remaining was the case and its verdict raised by its conditional formulation to the level of universal validity', citing Gerstenberger (1965: 24 n. 2), and quoting Liedke (1971: 55-56) 'the development of the casuistic principle began...as the attempt to preserve and hand on, in written or oral form, a judicial sentence'. Note the indeterminacy here regarding the form of transmission. Goody (1987: 74) sees the process as associated specifically with literacy: '...the stripping away of the individual and the casual, as well as the process of selection this involves, is part of the process of recording a court case or any other set of events. Moreover the very fact of writing them down means that one can make, record, and hence *compare* repeated observations in a precise away'.

42. We do, by contrast, have reflections of orally delivered verdicts: *tsadik ata* (Prov. 24.24; cf. Boecker (1980: 38).

43. For the theoretical foundations of this claim, see §1.1, *supra*, and Jackson

theory does highlight, however, an apparent paradox in dealing with the *Mishpatim*. On the one hand, they are widely regarded as the earliest of the biblical legal collections; in terms of content they are compatible with an early, pre-institutional stage of legal development (see further §3.3, *infra*). On the other hand, they seem to have the closest literary connection with the codes of the ancient Near East. This would appear to suggest that the oral tradition that preceded the scribal formulation of these laws itself had elements in common with the orally transmitted custom of the region.

2.4 *Visual Dimensions of Speech Behaviour*

Sense perception is rarely neutral, objective, value-free. In biblical Hebrew, the verb *shama* (hear) is regularly used to mean 'obey'. In English, we say 'Seeing is believing'! This section illustrates the importance of vision in biblical law.[44]

(1995b: 144-48, 203-205, 218-19, 228-34). On the use of the casuistic form in other legal cultures, see Jackson (1968: 381 and n. 48); Segert (1973: 164-65).

44. See also §§9.2, 9.3, *infra*, on visible signs in the covenant narratives. For law, more generally, see Jackson (1994: 311-34), including reference to a paper by Bernard Hibbitts entitled 'Making Sense of Metaphors: Visuality, Aurality and the Reconfiguration of American Legal Discourse', delivered to the Law and Society Association conference in Phoenix, June 1994, a copy of which Professor Hibbitts kindly made available to me. Hibbitts' theme is that there has been a discernible movement from visuality to aurality as the privileged metaphors describing legal sense construction. Thus: 'While American legal discourse has embraced a range of figurative expressions evoking all sorts of sensory experience, it has long favored visual metaphors. We frequently consider law itself as a looking: we "observe it": we evaluate claims "in the eye of the law"; our high courts "review" the decisions of inferior tribunals. Alternatively, we speak of law as something one would look at: it is a "body", a "structure", a "bulwark of freedom"...' On the other hand, more recently: 'Our everyday language is picking up a growing number of aural or aurally-related terms. The process of auralization accelerated possibly in the 1960s, when American youth began to "tune in" and "turn on". Today, when we make a proposal to someone, we first "sound them out". An appealing idea or proposal "sounds good" even if it is written down. Jargon of all sorts is routinely labelled as a form of speaking... In conversation, acknowledgement...seems increasingly to be communicated by the phrase "I hear you" as opposed to "I see". Ignorance is increasingly portrayed in aural as well as visual terms. Where we were once overwhelmingly inclined to "turn a blind eye" to something, we now seem more likely to "turn a deaf ear". When two individuals or groups refuse to pay attention to one

Take the account of the reactions of the children of Israel, assembled at Mount Sinai in preparation for the revelation of the Law. Preceding the theophany and the speaking of the 'words',[45] the awesomeness of what was about to occur was signified by 'natural' manifestations: thunder, lightning, dense cloud on the mountain 'and a loud trumpet blast' (Exod. 19.16). The people were duly terrified. A little later, their reaction is described thus:

> All the people saw the voices and the lightning and the voice of the trumpet and the mountain burning and trembled (Exod. 20.18).

Some translations seek to solve the difficulty—the verb 'saw' equally governing objects both visual and auditory—by substituting a neutral verb such as 'perceived'.[46] But there is no doubt that the verb used in the Hebrew, *ra'ah*, does mean 'see' in the visual sense. Indeed, that verb is used in other contexts of divine revelation. One of the Hebrew nouns translated in the English Bible as 'prophet' means, literally, 'one who sees' (*ro'eh*—in some older translations rendered as 'seer'). The language of the narrative thus appears to attach particular privilege to the visual form of perception.[47]

I was reminded of Exod. 20.18 when reading about some neuroscientific research on the effects of sensory inputs (through the five senses: sight, hearing, touch, smell, taste) on the brain. These various senses, it appears, are perceived as different (as sight, sound, touch, smell, taste, respectively) by virtue not of properties of the input,[48] but rather as a function of the particular sector of the brain to which the neural impulse is directed. For example, stimulation at a particular point on the back of the brain can elicit sensations of light flashes, while stimulation at a particular point on the side of the brain can cause the recipient to hear

other, they are analogously engaged in a "dialogue of the deaf".'

45. The Hebrew term, *dibrot*, normally rendered commandments, literally means no more than this.

46. Stahl (1995: 53) adopts a surprisingly modernist interpretation here, in describing this as a 'blurring of the senses indicated by the synaesthesia of seeing and hearing'.

47. See further Carasik (1999: 257-65), on the Deuteronomic privileging of hearing, and its reinterpretation of Exod. 20.18 in Deut. 4.12 and 5.1-5.

48. The brain does not receive the entire soundwave or light energy, but only the neural impulses (electrical signals) produced by those sources. Moreover, the particular sensory organ (eye, ear, nose, etc.) does not transform the impulse in such a way as to distinguish the nature of the sense.

tones. Sekuler and Blake suggest the following thought experiment in illustration of this phenomenon:

> Suppose you were able to reroute the nerve from your eye, sending it to the part of your brain that normally receives input from your ear. Suppose that while you were at it, you also rerouted the nerve from your ear, sending it to that part of your brain that normally gets visual information. Now imagine that with this revised nervous system, you are caught in a thunderstorm. You should *hear* a flash of lightning and then *see* a clash of thunder (1990: 12).

It is also possible to make claims about the relative potency of different forms of sensory perception. My own interest in this question was aroused by some work in the psychology of evidence, which suggests that a witness's memory of the *face* of someone previously unseen survives significantly longer than does our memory of the *voice* of someone previously unheard.[49] More generally, visual perception has claims to greater 'originality' than language, in both philogenic and ontogenic terms. The visual stimulus produces an iconic image on the retina, unlike the symbolic (or 'arbitrary') connections characteristic of linguistic representation. The latter form of representation, characteristic of the human species, may be regarded as a later development in evolutionary terms. Some accounts of the development of representation in the individual offer a similar pattern: Jerome Bruner speaks of 'the successive emergence of action, image, and word as the vehicles of representation' (Bruner 1974: 349; 1966: Chs. 1–2).

In the legal context, we regularly speak of 'images of justice'. Indeed, we have specific images of how judges ought to appear and behave in court. One recent occasion in which a judge violated the image of how a judge ought to behave occurred in Arizona,[50] where the case of a man charged with a speeding offence was decided by the toss of a coin. The arresting officer had followed the defendant and had claimed (without benefit of radar) that he was driving at 45 mph in a 35 mph area. The defendant denied it, and contested the speeding ticket in court (apparently without benefit of legal representation). Municipal Judge Ralph Turco said that he wanted to give the defendant 'the benefit of the doubt', obtained a quarter coin, and invited the defendant

---

49. See Gudjonsson (1992: 86-87), and literature there cited. Of course, face recognition may not be typical of visual perception in general.

50. Reported in *Lawyers' Weekly*, Canada, April 1992. See further Jackson (1996: 119-22).

to toss it: 'You call it, you won your case. You don't, you lost.' The defendant lost the toss, whereupon the judge upheld the ticket but cut the fine from $47 to $20. The defendant was not happy, and complained: 'I'm glad not everything comes down that way. It's not the fact that I lost, it's just that that's not how you do it in a courtroom. It should be either yes or no.' The judge accepted that the coin toss was 'not a standard procedure. The Supreme Court might not approve it, but what the heck. That's why you have judges instead of computers.'

Many students to whom I have recounted this incident doubt that there would have been such an outcry if the judge had tossed the coin himself, in the privacy of his chambers—even, perhaps, had knowledge of his action emerged later. It is the visual incongruity of the judge's behaviour, by comparison with what is expected of a judge, that proves particularly offensive. As the defendant put it, '[I]t's just that that's not how you do it in a courtroom.'

That justice is conducted in public—thus, that it is '*seen* to be done'—is, indeed, part of the Western cultural tradition. But this value is not universal. Indeed, there are occasions when the very concealment of the process from sight is used to construct a sense of sanctity and thus special validity. Such is the case of decision by oracle: the face, sometimes even the identity, of the decision-maker remains concealed.[51]

Perhaps the biblical story of the judgment of Solomon (1 Kgs 3.16-28) reflects either a transitional period between 'private' and 'public' justice or a play upon the tensions between them.

> Then two harlots came to the king, and stood before him. The one woman said, 'Oh, my lord, this woman and I dwell in the same house; and I gave birth to a child while she was in the house. Then on the third day after I was delivered, this woman also gave birth; and we were alone; there was no one else with us in the house, only we two were in the house. And this woman's son died in the night, because she lay on it. And she arose at midnight, and took my son from beside me, while your maidservant slept, and laid it in her bosom, and laid her dead son in my

51. This seems to be the best explanation of the difficult passage concerning Moses' veil in Exod. 34.29-35. The people could not tolerate the divine glow on Moses' face after he spoke directly to God, so (at least) when he repeated God's commands to the Israelites, he did so wearing a veil. In narrative terms this repeats the theme of the terror caused by the theophany at the time of the Decalogue (Exod. 20.18-19); the effect is to present Moses' mediation of revelation in oracular form (see also Stahl 1995: 69-71).

bosom. When I rose in the morning to nurse my child, behold, it was dead; but when I looked at it closely in the morning, behold, it was not the child that I had borne'. But the other woman said, 'No, the living child is mine, and the dead child is yours.' The first said, 'No, the dead child is yours, and the living child is mine.' Thus they spoke before the king. Then the king said, 'The one says, "This is my son that is alive, and your son is dead"; and the other says, "No; but your son is dead, and my son is the living one."' And the king said, 'Bring me a sword.' So a sword was brought before the king. And the king said, 'Divide the living child in two, and give half to the one, and half to the other.' Then the woman whose son was alive said to the king, because her heart yearned for her son, 'Oh, my lord, give her the living child, and by no means slay it.' But the other said, 'It shall be neither mine nor yours; divide it.' Then the king answered and said, 'Give the living child to the first woman, and by no means slay it; she is its mother.' And all Israel heard of the judgment which the king had rendered; and they stood in awe of the king, because they perceived that the wisdom of God was in him, to render justice.

Divinely inspired justice in the Bible is, as I have argued, essentially a private matter, the operation of direct inspiration by God to the decision maker, rather than adjudication in public by virtue of a previously-announced rule (Jackson 1989: 187-88; 1990: 244-48; §4.1, *infra*). Yet Solomon here utilized a divinely inspired intuition *in public* (see further §3.4 [end], *infra*).[52] This was neither an oracular decision nor the natural dialogue of the public domain. Allied with this is the opposition of symbols: the sword of war, the justice of peace.[53] Perhaps it is these combined oppositions that have made the scene of Solomon's judgment so powerful an image in art. However that may be, the importance of Solomon's judgment as an *image* of justice resides neither in the correctness (from the narrator's viewpoint) of the outcome, nor in the psychological ingenuity of the test used by Solomon in order to elicit the

52. The point of this story is to validate the wisdom of Solomon. In Greimassian terms (§1.1), it is Solomon who is the subject (it is he who has the problem to solve), and it is his solution of the problem that ultimately receives recognition (the final verse). The fact that it is so recognized then validates the performance by God of his promise (in the immediately preceding section of the narrative) to give Solomon 'a wise and discerning mind, so that none like you has been before you and none like you shall arise after you' (vv. 9-12).

53. The sword in the traditional Greek symbol of justice is normally taken as expressing the power of justice to enforce its decisions, not the means by which it arrives at those decisions!

truth. For it is the visual retelling of the scene—in art—that constitutes it as an image of justice. The biblical account itself concludes: 'And all Israel *heard* of the judgment which the king had rendered...' The recognition of the king's wisdom is recounted as a reaction to their hearing of the narrative, not their direct observation of the scene. Would the story have become as famous had it not been taken up by the artistic tradition? I suspect not. The reason: it is only when we see the painting that Solomon's act of adjudication becomes a public matter, a case where justice is indeed seen to be done—even though it is we, some three thousand years later, who 'see' it!

To conclude, a remark on the range of senses regulated in the first half of the Decalogue (on the structure, see §7.2.3, *infra*). Take, first, the prohibition of idolatry (Exod. 20.3-6):

> You shall have no other gods before me. You shall not make for yourself a graven image, or any likeness of anything that is in heaven above, or that is in the earth beneath, or that is in the water under the earth; you shall not bow down to them or serve them; for I the LORD your God am a jealous God, visiting the iniquity of the fathers upon the children to the third and the fourth generation of those who hate me,[54] but showing steadfast love to thousands of those who love me and keep my commandments.

In context, this is the converse of the loyalty demand.[55] But it goes much further, in specifying the prohibited forms of worship. Idolatry is particularly identified with (a) the making of visual images, and (b) worshipping them. Such worship involves the language of the body ('you shall not bow down to them') and the rituals of sacrifice ('or serve them'),[56] thus involving the senses of both smell[57] and taste (the smell of the burning, the taste of part of the animal consumed by the priests). The text of this commandment concludes with further stress upon the affect of breach: such manifestations of disloyalty will make God feel jealous; he will requite disloyalty (shown by such idolatry) with withdrawal of protection, by contrast with the reciprocity of 'love for love' that informs the relationship of covenantal loyalty deriving from observance of the first commandment (Exod. 20.2).

The next prohibition regulates a particular form of speech, banning

---

54. On transgenerational punishment, see further §6.3 and §8.1 n. 11, *infra*.
55. Exod. 20.2, discussed in §2.2, *supra*.
56. The verb *avad* in biblical Hebrew is often used in this technical sense.
57. For biblical views of perception through smell, see Ritchie (2000: 59-73).

the utterance of the divine name:

> You shall not take the name of the LORD your God in vain; for the LORD
> will not hold him guiltless who takes his name in vain (Exod. 20.7).

Speech is not to be equated either with mere thought or with behaviour.
There is a form of sacred speech peculiar to those loyal to this God, and
that must not be abused, used for alien purposes.

Next comes the Sabbath:

> Remember the sabbath day, to keep it holy. Six days you shall labor, and
> do all your work. But the seventh day is a sabbath to the LORD your
> God; in it you shall not do any work, you, or your son, or your daughter,
> your manservant, or your maidservant, or your cattle, or the sojourner
> who is within your gates... (Exod. 20.8-10).

The Sabbath regulation represents not just a particular ordering of time,
but the attribution of a special religious feeling, that of sanctity, to the
seventh day. The command on sacred speech is thus followed by one on
sacred time.

In describing the behaviour taken to be fundamental to the particular
identity of the people of Israel, the Decalogue thus presents an integrated semiotic—the construction of the sacred through the dimensions
visual images, body language, smell, taste, speech and time.

Chapter 3

'WISDOM-LAWS'

3.1 *Introduction*

It is a basic assumption of contemporary methodology, both historical and legal, that in addressing a text we should look in the first instance for its 'literal meaning'. Indeed, in the legal sphere, literal meaning has ideological as well as methodological significance: it is a vital part of the modern, Western conception of the 'Rule of Law'.

The modern liberal ideology of the Rule of Law makes assumptions about both language and behaviour. It assumes that human behaviour consists in the making of rational, informed choices on the basis of the available information. 'Informed choice' on the part of the autonomous individual is the supreme value of what we call liberalism. It follows that a liberal legal system has a duty to present individuals with the relevant legal information needed to inform their choices of action. That duty is conceived to be fulfilled by the communication of the texts of the law, since it is assumed that those texts normally have a 'literal' meaning, which is equally accessible to the citizen (at least through a lawyer) determining his/her action in advance and to the judge adjudicating on such action *ex post*.

The modern Western model of law thus endorses the following propositions:

(a) People can rely ultimately on their disputes being resolved by court adjudication.

(b) Such court adjudication involves the application of rules expressed in language.

(c) The meaning of those rules is normally available in advance, the assumption being that the 'literal' meaning is that both intended by the legislator and to be applied by the court.

By contrast, a different model of law is discernible in early biblical law, whose features may be described thus:

(a)   People should avoid having their disputes resolved by court adjudication. Dispute settlement is conceived as an essentially private, rather than a public matter: shaming a neighbour in public is reprehensible and self-defeating.

(b)   Both private dispute settlement and, later, court adjudication do not necessarily involve the application of rules expressed in language.

(c)   Where such rules are used, their application is not to be identified with the notion of 'literal meaning', but rather with their narrative, contextual sense.

In this chapter, I contrast the traditional 'literal' conception of meaning with a 'narrative' conception rooted in orality (§3.2) and argue that this narrative conception often goes hand in hand with a pre-institutional form of dispute resolution (§3.3), the two together generating what I call 'wisdom-laws'.[1]

Modern conceptions of meaning seek a very close relationship between *verba* and *voluntas*: we (normally) are expected to mean what we say, and to say what we mean. In principle, there should be no gap between the meaning we intend and the meaning of the words we utter. If there is, we are judged incompetent. Another way of expressing this notion is through the conception of literal meaning. But that very expression gives the game away. 'Literal' meaning is a conception of meaning bound to writing, not just words; it is a form of meaning construction associated with literacy.

But literacy, as scholars like Walter Ong and Jack Goody stress, is not simply an alternative channel of transmission of meaning; it is a way of thought. 'Writing restructures consciousness'.[2] Two aspects of

1.   This is the major theme of *Wisdom-Laws*, my long-delayed commentary on the *Mishpatim*, now nearer to completion, where further examples may be found. On the relationship of these issues to that of the relationship between 'law' and 'wisdom' in the Bible, see Jackson (2000b).

2.   The title of Ch. 4 of Ong (1982); see also Goody (1977); Jackson (1995b: 79-83). Olson (1994) is basically sympathetic to Ong's views, though he claims that 'no clear logical or empirical arguments have established any direct causal linkages between writing with thinking' (at 16). He summarizes his position thus: '...the failure of earlier theories of the implications of literacy comes from their assumption that literacy has its effects through advances *in ways of writing*, that is, the form of the script; in contrast I shall argue that conceptual implications arise from

the transformation of structures of consciousness, between orality and literacy, are particularly relevant here. First, orality favours events rather than concepts or system; the kind of connections we can best process through speech are those of narrative rather than logical sequence. We can tolerate a complex story told orally, but not a complex legal document. Secondly, the distinction between orality and literacy very frequently coincides with what the linguist Basil Bernstein has termed 'restricted code' rather than 'elaborated code' (Bernstein 1971: I, Chs. 5–7, 108-109, 123-37; cf. Jackson 1995b: 93-95; Douglas 1975: 173-80); indeed, for Ong restricted and elaborated linguistic codes 'could be relabelled 'oral-based' and 'text-based' codes respectively' (1982: 106).[3] In restricted code we need *not* say everything that we mean, because we can rely upon the shared social knowledge within a small community to fill in what, at the explicit level, would be gaps; elaborated code, by contrast, makes no such assumptions. Everything we want to say must be elaborated; the people with whom we are communicating are not expected to share our cultural, contextual assumptions; any such assumptions therefore need to be spelled out. This extends also to the pragmatics of communication (of which the illocutionary force of speech acts is one aspect). As Olson argues, many of those signs of an utterance's illocutionary force that are available in direct, interpersonal oral communication are lost in the written form, and therefore have to be supplied ('elaborated') by the writer, failing which the reader must make judgments about them.[4]

the *ways of reading*, for it is the art of reading which allows a text to be taken as a model for verbal form...' (at 18-19).

3.   Douglas (1975: 78) remarks: 'Another mistake is to assume that restricted code has little scope. On the contrary, its basis in metaphor makes it a good narrative form because it is richly allusive, highly condensed, and can dispense with slow and complex syntactic forms. But these are not linguistic criteria.'

4.   Olson (1994: 264-65): 'Principle six: an important implication of literacy derives from the attempt to compensate for what was lost in the act of transcription. As we have seen, while scripts well represent lexical and syntactic properties of speech they do not adequately represent the author's audience-directed intentions—how the author means his text to be taken. But this lapse should not be seen as merely a loss, a poverty of writing as some have implied, but as an indirect contributor to the significance of writing. For if writing cannot capture speaker's stance, gaze, tone of voice, stress and intonation, reading such texts calls for a whole new world of interpretive discourse, of commentary and argument as to how, precisely, an utterance, now transcribed, was to be taken.'

These two facets of the distinction between orality and literacy come together in the following opposition: literal meaning assumes elaborated code[5] and is applicable in principle to any content, so long as we spell it out and expect the reader to pay full attention to everything we have written (and no attention to what we have not written); narrative meaning, by contrast, consists not in a paraphrase, the substitution of one set of words by another, but rather the typical stories (see §1.1, *supra*),[6] or narrative images evoked by the words within a group which shares the social knowledge necessary to evoke those images without fully spelling them out. Such a conception of narrative meaning is not, however, lost the moment speech is reduced to writing: in the early stages of literacy, we encounter what has been termed 'oral residue' (Ong 1982: 115).[7]

The claim that 'writing restructures consciousness', supported by considerable research into preliterate peoples,[8] is explained thus. In writing, as one reads through a text, that which has been read remains available for consultation. It is possible to engage in 'backward scan-

5.   In fact, one major philosophical critique (that of Searle) of the notion of literal meaning claims precisely that full elaboration is never possible. For debate within linguistics and the philosophy of language on 'literal meaning', see Jackson (1995b: 42-45).

6.   Despite the analytical tendency to understand meaning in terms of formal definitions, there is some recognition in modern jurisprudence, influenced by ordinary language philosophy, that in practice the 'core' meaning of a rule is understood in terms of its 'standard' uses or instances (see Hart 1994: v, 127; 1958: 606). Bix (1995: 9), describes Hart as using a 'mixture of a paradigmatic and a criteriological approach to meaning...our first move in defining a general term for the purpose of a rule is to invoke the image, example, or particular situation at which the rule was aimed'. He quotes Hart (1994: 127): we start by considering 'whether the present case resembles the plain case 'sufficiently' in 'relevant' respects'. Hart, however, also points to the limitations of 'the communication or teaching of standards by example', taking as his non-legal example an instruction by a father to a child (1994: 124-25). For the arguments of Hart and Fuller utilizing these notions, and the revealing stories taken by Fuller, in particular, to instantiate his hypothetical rules, see Jackson (1996a: 191-97). Hart seems to have been influenced by Wittgenstein's notion of following (as opposed to interpreting) a rule, which he takes to be an 'unreflective' process (see Jackson 1996a: 186-87).

7.   Narrative images still underlie much of our case law and jurisprudential theorizing about it (see Jackson 1988b: Chs. 3–5).

8.   E.g. Luria's fieldwork in Uzbekistan and Kirghizia (1976: 108-109); see also Ong (1982: 52-53) on Fernandez, Karp and Bird (1980); Hallpike (1979).

ning' (Goody 1977: 128; Ong 1982: 104). This is not possible in traditional oral cultures (though it is now possible with technologies that allow for the permanent recording of speech, as in film, video, tape recordings). In order to remain intelligible, therefore, oral language requires a great deal more repetition and redundancy, clues that allow the listener to grasp the direction of the ongoing argument. On the other hand, 'sparsely linear or analytic thought and speech is an artificial creation, structured by the technology of writing' (Ong 1982: 40). The very act of writing (at least in traditional ways, before the use of modern computer keyboards) is so much more consuming of time and effort than is speech—it has been calculated that oral speech is typically ten times faster than handwriting—that relative economy in the written word becomes a very practical necessity.

Other differences in thought structures are also claimed to follow from the orality/literacy distinction. Oral cultures lack abstract categories;[9] their knowledge is expressed in terms of relationships in the human world of their immediate experience (Ong 1982: 42, 49). Even the notions of fact and time, it is suggested, differ in oral and literate societies: the past is not regarded as an expanse of time in which particular facts occurred on particular dates, but rather as 'the domain of the ancestors, a resonant source for renewing awareness of present existence' (Ong 1982: 42, 49). Luria found that requests for definitions of even the most concrete objects met with resistance. Precision, too, is a feature of the culture of literacy:

> The distancing which writing effects develops a new kind of precision in verbalisation by removing it from the rich but chaotic existential context of much oral utterance...orally managed language and thought is not noted for analytic precision...written words sharpen analysis, for the individual words are called on to do more. To make yourself clear without gesture, without facial expression, without intonation, without a real hearer, you have to foresee circumspectly all possible meanings a statement may have for any possible reader in any possible situation, and you

9. Kress (1989: 46) puts it thus: 'Writing has a structuring logic which differs fundamentally from that of speech. It is a logic of the nominal rather than of the verbal; of objects rather than processes; of abstraction rather than specificness/concreteness; a logic of hierarchy and of integration rather than a logic of sequence and addition'. Cf. Olson (1994: 34-35): 'Those least literate were more likely to treat tasks in a concrete, context-bound way while the more literate took an abstract, principled approach to the series of tasks.' On the nature of and reasons for greater decontextualization with literacy, see further Jackson (1995b: 82 n. 57).

have to make your language work so as to come clear all by itself, with no existential context (Ong 1982: 103-104).

3.2 'Literal Meaning': Narrative versus Semantic Models

As argued above, it is far from clear that the conventional meaning of speech (and indeed of writing in its early stages, before the cognitive structures associated with literate thought develop) is to be conceived according to the model of 'literal meaning'. Instead of asking: 'What situations do the words of this rule cover?' we may inquire: 'What typical situations do the words of this rule evoke?' While the quest for literal meaning may produce a paraphrase (the substitution of one linguistic formulation by another), the alternative model looks to the typical narrative images—of situations within known social contexts— evoked by the words. Here are a number of examples from the *Mishpatim* of Exodus 21–22,[10] usually regarded as the oldest legal collection in the Bible, and thus the one whose written formulations may be most susceptible to analysis in terms of 'oral residue'.

> Exod. 22.2-3 (= MT 22.1-2):
> 2   If a thief is found breaking in, and is struck so that he dies, there shall be no bloodguilt for him;
> 3   but if the sun has risen upon him, there shall be bloodguilt for him.

> 22.1 אם במחתרת ימצא הגנב והכה ומת אין לו דמים
> 2   אם זרחה השמש עליו דמים לו

The overall effect of this paragraph is equivalent to the Twelve Tables provisions (VIII.12-13): *si nox furtum fa<x>it, <ast> im occisit, iure caesus esto, si luci <furtum faxit, ast> se telo defendit...endoque plorato*, which (broadly, and subject to some reconstruction) say that a thief intruding during the night may lawfully be killed, while one intruding by day may not lawfully be killed, unless he defended himself with a weapon. But there is a significant drafting difference between the biblical and Roman versions. The Roman explicitly distinguishes between night (*nox*) and day (*luci*), while the biblical provision has appeared to many as badly drafted in this respect: the first verse, which

---

10. In Jackson (2000c) I present also the rabbinic interpretations of these examples, characterised by a rejection of self-help remedies in favour of judicial (rabbinic) adjudication, associated with interpretations which presuppose literal meaning.

allows self-help, makes *no* explicit mention of the time of the incident; the only explicit reference to the time occurs in the second verse, which denies the legitimacy of self-help during the day. It is in the light of that qualification, apparently, that the permission of self-help in the first verse has to be restricted to the nocturnal incident. This would appear at first sight to be a very strange type of drafting. Apparently, the audience is first given the impression that self-help is *always* available, then this is qualified by denying its availability when the incident occurs during the day. Indeed, some scholars have wondered whether the second verse may be a later addition: originally the householder was entitled to kill the intruding thief at any time of day or night; later this form of self-help was restricted to the daytime intruder.[11]

This argument, we may note, derives from a 'literal' reading of the first verse: 'If a thief is found breaking in, and is struck so that he dies, there shall be no bloodguilt for him.' If we pose the question of meaning in the (semantic) form: 'What situations do the words of this rule cover?' then since the provision makes no mention of day or night, we infer that this is irrelevant, so that the rule 'covers' the intruder both by day and night. If, on the other hand, we pose the question of meaning in the (narrative) form: 'What typical situations do the words of this rule evoke?', then we are entitled to take into account the image of typical thieving presented in the book of Job (24.14, 16):

> The murderer rises in the dark;
> that he may kill the poor and needy
> and in the night he is as a thief.

14 לאור יקום רוצח יקטל עני ואביון ובלילה יהי כגנב

> In the dark they dig through houses;
> by day they shut themselves up;
> they do not know the light.

16 חתר בחשך בתים יומם חתמו למו לא ידעו אור

This indicates that nocturnal activity was the primary image of acting like a thief. Exod. 22.1 (MT) did not have to make that explicit: it was part of the narrative image evoked by the words. Such a rule, when orally transmitted, would be understood as evoking that situation.

The example illustrates also another aspect of the difference between

---

11. Discussed and rejected in Jackson (1972: 204-206).

speech and writing. As noted above (§3.1), writing permits us to engage in 'backward scanning'. If we have these two rules in written form, and we read them 'semantically', we may indeed be puzzled initially: the literal meaning of the first provision seems to overlap with and thus conflict with the second. We are prompted then to read the first provision again, in the light of what comes later: if self-help against the daytime thief is not permitted, we will conclude, the first provision must be restricted to the nocturnal offender, even though it does not say so explicitly.[12] We can do this only because the text of the first provision is still in front of us, available for 'backward scanning'. Suppose, however, that these rules were communicated in speech, not writing. Speech is 'evanescent': it disappears as soon as it is uttered. Any cognitive difficulty of reconciling the two texts thus depends upon having retained the *words* of the first rule in memory. Exact words are more difficult to retain in memory than are images: hence the greater likelihood that in an oral society, the meaning of the first rule would have been identified with its typical image—here, that of the nocturnal intruder—and thus no cognitive conflict between the two rules will have been perceived.

My second example concerns the civil liability of the owner of an ox that has killed another ox:

> When a man's ox hurts another's, so that it dies, then they shall sell the live ox and divide the price of it; and the dead beast also they shall divide (Exod. 21.35).

Finkelstein has stressed the different approach to compensation in modern accident law compared with the principle found not only in this biblical provision but also in LE §53. In the absence of negligence, modern law traditionally (that is, leaving aside the operation of insurance) lets losses lie where they fall, whereas

> the aim of the rule, both in Exodus and the Eshnunna laws, is to achieve an equitable distribution of loss when the circumstances of the case suggest that there was no clear justification for shifting the burden of the loss from one party to the other' (Finkelstein 1981: 36).

Thus far, I am fully in agreement. But how was such 'equitable distribution' to be achieved? As has been widely observed from the time of the earliest rabbinic commentaries, an equal division of the loss will

---

12. Or, for the lawyer, by applying a 'synchronic' rule of interpretation: *specialia generalibus derogant*.

result from the *literal* application of the ancient procedure (dividing the carcass and dividing the price of the live ox) only if the two oxen had been of equal value. If the dead ox had been worth more than the live, then the result of the procedure of division will be that the owner of the dead ox will lose more than the owner of the live, since half the price of the live ox will be less than half the price the dead ox would have commanded had it been sold live.[13] Conversely, if the surviving ox had been the more valuable of the two, its owner will lose half its value, whereas the owner of the dead ox will be compensated by more than half the original value of the latter.[14] In the highly unlikely case of the surviving ox being worth more than double the value of the dead ox when alive, the owner of the dead ox will make a profit.[15] Indeed, there is even a theoretical possibility that the owner of the gorer could make a profit, if the value of the carcass is worth more than the value of the gorer.[16]

To avoid such results, both the Rabbis, and with a minor qualification Finkelstein, add a condition that is not found in the text: this procedure applies only when the two oxen (when both were alive) were of equal value. Where this was not the case, a court would have to calculate what sum of money would in fact produce equal loss division[17] (this, of

13. Example: value of dead ox when alive, 300; value of carcass, 50; value of goring ox when sold, 200. Each party gets equivalent of 125; owner of dead ox has thus lost 175, owner of gorer has lost 75.

14. Example: value of dead ox when alive, 200; value of carcass, 50; value of goring ox when sold, 300. Each party gets equivalent of 175; owner of dead ox has thus lost 25, owner of gorer has lost 125.

15. Example: value of dead ox when alive, 200; value of carcass, 50; value of goring ox when sold, 500. Each party gets equivalent of 275; owner of dead ox has thus gained 75, owner of gorer has lost 225.

16. Example: value of dead ox when alive, 600; value of carcass, 150; value of goring ox when sold, 100. Each party gets equivalent of 125; owner of dead ox has thus lost 475, owner of gorer has gained 25!

17. I.e. the difference between the animal's value before and after the incident. In the circumstances of Exod. 21.35 this meant that the plaintiff retained the carcass of his dead ox, and deducted the whole of its value from that of the ox when alive, in order to ascertain the loss that should be divided. See, e.g., Maimonides (1954: 4 [*Hilkhot nizke mamon* 1.3]): 'Thus, if an ox worth one hundred *denar* gores an ox worth twenty and kills it and the carcass is worth four, the owner of the ox must pay eight, this being half of the residual damage.' In this case, a literal application of Exod. 21.35 would have given each party 50 denar plus half the actual carcass, thus considerably profiting the owner of the dead ox. The Rabbis expressed this as 'half

course, requiring them to decide how much the dead ox had been worth when it was alive—a decision quite unnecessary where the biblical procedure itself was applied). Finkelstein assumed that

> the procedure is to be imposed by an impartial authority in the event that the two parties could not settle the matter amicably between themselves... The court, or the public authority felt that it had the right and the duty to intervene in what in all respects was recognised as a private, that is, civil, matter in order to allocate loss' (Finkelstein 1981: 36).

But the rule produces such objectionable consequences *only* if it is read 'semantically' (literally), i.e. as covering all cases which may be subsumed under the meanings of its words. Since no mention is made of the relative values of the two animals, the literal argument goes, that factor is irrelevant, and the rule applies whatever the relative values of the two animals. If, however, we adopt a narrative rather than a semantic approach to the meaning of the biblical text, then this problem largely disappears.[18] It applied to the typical cases whose images are evoked by the words of the rule, and these typical cases will, indeed, be those where the relative values of the two animals are equal or roughly equivalent.

What, then, would have happened in practice where the values of the two animals were substantially unequal? On this, we have no direct knowledge. If the text does reflect a real social custom, I see no overriding reason to exclude its operation, even in many cases where there was a reasonable degree of inequality in the values of the two oxen. For the possibility of resolving the dispute without the need for a formal adjudication is itself a benefit, and may well have been a necessity. That degree of 'arbitrariness' merely represents the price that has to be paid for such a benefit.[19] There is no need to trouble ourselves with the highly unlikely cases (suggested above) of the owner of the victim or

---

damages from its body': *Mishnah B. Qam.* 1.4, *Mekhilta ad Exod.* 21.29 (Lauterbach, III, 82-83).

18. As I argued in Jackson (1974: 74-77).

19. It is interesting to note that Roman law also had an 'arbitrary' procedure in its strict liability remedy for damage or injury caused by animals, the *actio de pauperie*. Here, the owner was liable to pay the full damage, but could, if he preferred, hand over the offending beast in noxal surrender. Clearly, he would always do this where the value of the animal was less than the value of the damage it had caused. And in such a case (and only in such a case—hence the 'arbitrariness' of the remedy) there would be no need for a formal assessment of the value of the loss.

even the gorer making a profit.[20] In such an instance we may assume that the parties would either agree to an *ad hoc* settlement or refer the matter to some form of third party arbitration.

I turn next to a (partially) 'apodictic' example from the Covenant Code, the homicide provisions of Exod. 21.12-14:

> Whoever strikes a man so that he dies shall be put to death. But if he did not lie in wait for him, but God let him fall into his hand, then I will appoint for you a place to which he may flee. But if a man wilfully attacks another to kill him treacherously, you shall take him from my altar, that he may die.

12 מכה איש ומת מות יומת
13 ואשר לא צדה והאלהים אנה לידו ושמתי לך מקום אשר ינוס שמה
14 וכי יזד איש על רעהו להרגו בערמה מעם מזבחי תקחנו למות

Verse 12 is the first of a series of four 'participial' provisions,[21] which continues in vv. 15-17; vv. 13-14 are generally viewed as a 'casuistic' interpolation.[22] But what was the meaning of v. 12, when it stood alone? A 'literal' (semantic) reading might lead us to conclude that the provision is 'absolute', applying to anyone 'who strikes a man so that he dies': no qualifications having been stated, it may be argued, none apply. Alt put the argument thus:

> It refers to homicide; but it makes no distinction between murder and manslaughter, using expressions, indeed, which seem deliberately chosen to leave no doubt that both are included. It treats every killing as a crime punishable by death—and it does not restrict this by any reference

20. Even modern legal systems have safety devices to protect themselves against utterly absurd applications of literal meaning: in English law, the 'golden rule'.

21. On the domestic orientation within the group, see §2.3.1, *supra.*

22. E.g. Patrick (1985: 73); Otto (1988: 31-32); Schwienhorst-Schönberger (1990 39-40); Crüsemann (1996: 150); *contra,* Sprinkle (1994: 74-75) on the 'dubious assumption that an author must slavishly adhere to a literary "form"'. But the problem goes beyond that: vv. 13 and 14 could not, in any other document, have stood alone. Verse 13 clearly presupposes facts already stated in v. 12, namely that a man has been smitten and died; without that presupposition, v. 13 would be meaningless. In *literary* terms, therefore, it is not presented as a separate offence, but rather as a qualification of a more general norm. Brin (1994: 32-33) recognizes the difficulty but argues that the order of vv. 13-14 has been transposed: if read with v. 14 first, the two verses could have stood independently. The transposition, according to Brin, is due to the redactional activity of combining the two laws (v. 12 with vv. 13-14): '...had v. 14 followed immediately upon v. 12, it would have appeared as a simple repetition'. And see further, §4.2, *infra.*

to the possibility of allaying one's guilt by paying an indemnity or seeking sanctuary. Its content, then, is as unconditional as its form, and this is what distinguishes it so sharply from what follows. We must ask why it allows of no conditions. The outlook of the whole Old Testament leaves us in no doubt of the answer: it is Yahweh who demands a stern retribution for every drop of blood that is spilt.[23]

Against this, Schenker has recently argued that vv. 13-14 should be viewed not as a correction of v. 12, but rather as a process of making it more explicit (1998: 210-11): the institution of (altar) refuge in Israel is ancient, as is shown by the narratives regarding Adonijah and Joab (1 Kgs 1.50-53; 2.28-35). Exod. 21.12 should be understood against the background of the contemporaneous institution of places of refuge, and the distinction between intentional and unintentional killing is implicit in that institution. Such an approach rightly takes account of the institutional context and use of Exod. 21.12. That is part of the social knowledge that we rightly impute into the meaning of the provision when we apply the notions of 'narrative reading' and 'restricted code'.[24] If, then, we ask what was the typical narrative image evoked by the words, the case of homicide which would typically generate a demand for death, the most likely answer is a direct (Jackson 1985a: 663; cf. Otto 1991: 162-63), deliberate assault accompanied by an intention to kill. The further we move away from the case of the typical killer, the less strongly will the normal expectation regarding the penalty hold good.[25] Again, we may reasonably assume such implications as to the typical case and its typical treatment to have been encoded in the original, oral use of the apodictic formulation.[26]

23. Alt (1989: 110); cf. Childs (1974: 469-70); as regards the exclusion of composition: Greenberg (1960: 13-14); *contra*, McKeating (1975: 66-68).

24. Schenker (1998: 211), adopts a semantic approach in arguing that Exod. 21.12-14 distinguishes three cases: unintentional (verse 13), intentional (verse 12), premeditated (verse 14).

25. This is, in principle, different from the approach that views Exod. 21.12 as a 'guiding principle' (e.g. Alt [1989: 109]: 'Whoever placed it in this prominent position must have regarded it as the guiding principle for the treatment of the whole matter' of murder and manslaughter). A principle, as understood in the context of a literate society, is a formulation whose meaning is semantic, but whose application may nevertheless not be rigid. See further §§7.1, 7.3, *infra*.

26. For a further application of the semantic versus narrative distinction, see the discussion of the talionic formula in §10.4, *infra*.

3.3 *Self-Executing Laws*

Such a conception of narrative meaning has implications for our understanding of the manner in which such rules may have been used in order to resolve disputes. The question is no longer whether the immediate dispute is 'covered' by the literal meaning of the words of the rule, but rather whether the immediate dispute is sufficiently similar to the narrative image evoked by the rule to justify the use of that rule in order to resolve the dispute. That in itself suggests a more popular form of dispute resolution than that which we nowadays associate with the activities of courts. Nor should we assume that the moment courts come into play, they function as we would expect according to the modern model of the 'Rule of Law'. They may operate partially or entirely without rules; such rules as they may deploy may not be in written form; and where they are in written form, their sense may not be constructed according to the model of literal meaning.

A significant number of the individual rules of the 'Covenant Code' may be described as 'self-executing laws'—rules so formulated (through the use of evidentiary tests and dispute-resolving mechanisms that are easy to administer, sometimes because of their somewhat arbitrary character) that the need to have recourse to third-party adjudication seems to be avoided altogether. Not surprisingly (if we are disposed to correlate the cognitive and linguistic aspects of orality with institutional development), this is a prominent feature of the examples of laws to be understood in terms of 'narrative meaning', as discussed in §3.2, above. Thus we know from several narratives that redress for homicide was initially in the hands of the kin of the deceased. Even when 'cities of refuge' were established, formal adjudication did not take place until and unless the offender reached that city; the kin were still entitled to pursue the offender and kill him en route (without any third-party adjudication) if they caught up with him (Deut 19.6, 12; Num 35.25). It is in this context that we should understand the test of justifiability for killing the intruding thief: the act is justifiable if it takes place at night, but not during the day. The reasoning underlying the law may very well be that self-help is to be used only where it is justified in terms of the danger to the owner. But conclusive, objective tests of when such a danger (and therefore such a justification) exists are laid down: it is justifiable to kill by night, not by day. Thus, the kin of the deceased thief would know, without an adjudication, whether the killing had been justified or not. The law is clear enough to be applied by the parties directly, without the need for third-party adjudication. Similarly, in the case of the goring ox. There is no need to ask which ox 'started it'. There is a live ox and a dead one. The farmers need not even argue about how much the dead ox had been worth when alive. They simply divide the carcass of the dead ox and take the live one to the market. In the typical case evoked by a narrative reading of the text, that of at least *approximate* equality of the values of the oxen, some inequity, or arbitrariness, may result. But this is the price to be paid for the ability to settle the matter immediately, without recourse to third-party adjudication. [27]

There are also other examples. Take the law of release and re-enslavement of the debt-slave (Exod. 21.2-6). The debt-slave has a fixed period of service. Once six years have been served, there can be no quibbling over whether the debt has been fully paid or not by the slave's labour. We should not necessarily assume that earlier release could be *enforced* on the grounds that the debt has been paid off, though certainly an earlier release was always possible by agreement (and thus not requiring the intervention of third-party adjudication). Most likely—though this is speculation—such debt-slavery would only be contemplated when the debt was substantial, and when it was anticipated in advance that six years of labour—though an arbitrary period—was more or less fair in the circumstances. In exchange for not demanding release *before* six years, the debt-slave knew, from this rule, that the master could not claim to detain him for more than that period.

The procedures for change of status by the male debt-slave themselves also accord with such notions of practical wisdom. Release in the seventh year is automatic, and, according to our text, is marked by no formality whatsoever.[28] It is, by implication, simply a reversion to the

---

27. Example: value of dead ox when alive, 200; value of carcass, 50; value of goring ox when sold, 250. Each party gets equivalent of 150; owner of dead ox has thus lost 50, owner of gorer has lost 100.

28. The formulation of the comparable rule in LH 117 (*anduraršunu iššakkan*) has been viewed as implying some official adjudication or participation. See Lewy (1958: 27 n. 58), though basing himself also on a contemporary document. At Rome, we know that the censor was available to enforce release from *mancipium*. deciding whether the original debt had been worked off by the service of the debt-slave. (Whether his participation was required where the release was non-contentious is less clear.) But we can say with certainty that the author of the text in Exodus wishes to stress the difference in kind between the two changes of status,

man's normal status. On the other hand, if the debt-slave wished to convert his status into that of *permanent* slavery, a ceremony was required (Exod. 21.5-6). What is exceptional, and therefore requires due signification to the community, is the choice to remain in bondage (Piattelli 1984: 1236).

Another example of a self-executing rule that can function in that way precisely because of its use of an 'arbitrary' test is the law of relapse after injury:

> When men quarrel and one strikes the other with a stone or with his fist and the man does not die but keeps his bed, then if the man rises again and walks abroad with his staff, the striker shall be clear; only he shall pay for the loss of his time, and shall have him thoroughly healed (Exod. 21.18-19).[29]

and to emphasize that the conversion of debt-slavery into permanent slavery is far more significant than the termination *ex lege* of debt-slavery.

29.   For an extreme example of a 'semantic' reading of this law (taken to exemplify casuistic law), treating it very much as we would a modern, written statute, see Alt (1989: 89-91): 'Here we have the use of the objective conditional clause carried to its fullest extent: there are no less than six conditional clauses, four for the main case and two for the subsidiary case, and then three main clauses, all in the third person. For the Israelite the co-ordination of sentences was the more natural usage, and he would be put to some difficulty to construct such a lengthy period, with its complicated degrees of subordination. But we can understand at once the intention which led to such a forced use of the language. In the conditional clauses the case envisaged by the law had to be exactly described and distinguished from similar cases, before the negative and positive consequences laid down by the law could be set out. In our chosen example it was not a case of a premeditated attack of one man upon another 'with a high hand' but only of such an attack as might have arisen without any considered intention from the momentary excitement of a quarrel; it is not a question of an attack with a weapon brought specially for this purpose, but with an object lying within sight and reach of the attacker at the psychological moment; not an attack leading to death, but only such as to confine the victim to his bed. All this, however, merely defines the general features of the case in question. Next, therefore, the conditions of the subsidiary case, for which alone the prescriptions of the main clause are valid, must be set out in two further subordinate clauses: on the one hand the patient must not be confined to his bed permanently, but on the other hand he does not have to regain his previous capacity for work, particularly in the fields, but has only to be sufficiently restored to health to take his full part in the life of the community in the street (and in the gate). Only by the provisions of the two subsidiary clauses is the case given the precise limits intended by the lawgiver: cases that lie on one side or the other outside the lines drawn by him would obviously be judged and dealt with differently by the law.

The significance of the man's walking abroad independently is that once he has made that degree of recovery, any subsequent death cannot be attributed to the original assailant. We have here a fairly arbitrary causation rule.[30] Romanists may recall the argument of Daube about the original significance of the 30-day rule in the *Lex Aquilia* (1936: 253-68). Nor is the adoption of arbitrary tests of causation unknown in English law. In the crime of murder, death traditionally had to take place within a year and a day.[31] Contemporary insurance policies still sometimes use the same technique. The purpose is not merely to limit the number of claims; it is also to avoid those claims that may prove the most difficult to assess in terms of causation, because the end result has occurred so long after the acts allegedly causing it.[32] What characterizes

'Once this is done, the necessary details of the penalties to be imposed in this particular case can be summarized in the main clauses. These are also set out with great precision—there is first the negative provision, that the use of capital punishment is expressly excluded, and then the positive provision, that the accused is required to compensate his victim. He must in fact pay a double compensation—first for the time when the injured man could not take part in public life, and secondly for the cost of his restoration to health. This means that each of the nine clauses plays an indispensable part in the structure of the whole law, and that there is not one redundant word in any of them. The apparently pleonastic diction is not so in reality, and the overloaded subordination of conditional clauses to one another is unavoidable. It follows as a necessary result of the complicated nature of the matter that is being dealt with, and especially of the need to make clear distinctions in the application of basic principles. These principles are not stated in the law, but are none the less rigidly applied to the case in question. Many other pieces of casuistic legislation in the Hexateuch are simpler in form, but only because the cases they deal with are less complicated. The fundamental purpose in using the casuistic form remains the same.'

For a different view, see Jackson (2000a).

30. Another (though this is not the only factor) is the restriction of the master's homicide liability in respect of his slave to death occurring within a day (Exod. 21.20-21).

31. This mediaeval rule, affirmed in modern times in *Dyson* [1908] 2 K.B. 454, was repealed only in 1996: Law Reform (Year and a Day Rule) Act 1996. However, the Attorney-General's consent to the prosecution is still required if death occurs more than three years later, or if the defendant has already been convicted of another (i.e. non-fatal) offence in connection with the incident.

32. Daube (1961: 249-69) rightly stressed that we ought not to interpret such rules as 'primitive', exhibiting a state of legal evolution where causation could be conceived only in 'direct' terms. He noted, for example, that within the Bible itself, direct forms of causation are required where death occurs, and the life of the

many of these early tests of causation is their very arbitrariness. The arbitrariness, we may suggest, is evidence of the fact that they are directed to the general public, not to experts.[33]

This same arbitrariness is apparent also in the provision of Exod. 22.2 (MT), that if a thief does not have the ability to pay the prescribed penalties, 'he shall be sold[34] for his theft'. This seemingly straight-forward apodosis, ונמכר בגנבתו, is ambiguous: the noun *genevah* can mean either 'the thing stolen' (the stolen property) or 'theft'. It is clear, however, that the noun is used in the former sense in the very next verse, where the *genevah* is said to be found in the hand of the accused. This provides a very strong case for understanding the slavery provision in the same sense. The prefix *b'* is found elsewhere, in conjunction with the verb *makhar*, to mean 'in exchange for'.[35] It is unlikely, however, that the value of the thief, or of his labour for the period involved, would happen to coincide with the value of the stolen animal (or of the multiple restitution, if we view that as included). In its way, the remedy is very comparable to that of Exod. 21.35. The thief has nothing. The economic value of the animal has disappeared, whether the animal has been slaughtered or sold (for thieves, then as now, are likely to spend the proceeds pretty quickly). The remaining economic value, in this

defendant may be at stake; on the other hand, in cases of damage to property, leading only to payment of damages, causation can be far less direct: witness the law of the pit (Exod. 21.33-34), damage by depasturation (Exod. 22.4), and damage by fire (Exod. 22.5).

33. The Bible does recognize that expert determination of such matters may take a different course from determination by the man in the street. But the expert, for the biblical writers, is God himself. Even in cases of homicide, indirect causation is recognized, but judgments as to its existence are left to God. The classical case is that of the liability of David for the death of Uriah the Hittite (2 Sam. 12.9). David had ordered his military commander to have Uriah placed in the front line, with a view to his falling in the battle with the Ammonites. It takes the prophet Nathan, conveying the judgment of God, to charge David on this basis: 'Why have you despised the word of the LORD, to do what is evil in his sight? You have smitten Uriah the Hittite with the sword, and have taken his wife to be your wife, and have slain him with the sword of the Ammonites.'

34. Falk (1967: 243), pointed out that the verb *makhar* is not restricted to the concept of sale, but may refer more generally to delivery. I have suggested that the apodosis be rendered 'he shall be handed over in exchange for the stolen animal', and compared the Roman institution of *addictio* (Jackson 1972: 140-41).

35. For example, Deut. 21.14 forbids a warrior from selling his captive woman *bakesef*—in exchange for silver.

case, is that of the thief himself.[36] Indeed, there is one more element of arbitrariness, if, in accordance with the rabbinic view, one views this sale as creating a form of debt-slavery[37] which is subject to the six-year rule of Exod. 21.2. The enslaved thief will therefore go free after six years. What is being exchanged is not the value of the thief on the slave-market, but the value of his labour for six years. If that does not reach the value of the animal he has stolen (or the multiple, if we take that view[38]), then that is the price which is to be paid for the ability to resolve the matter without requiring institutional assistance.

3.4 *Early Adjudication*

Even if I am correct in stressing the 'arbitrary' character of these rules, each designed to provide a so-called 'objective'[39] test that can readily

36. Even if we understand *venimkar* as 'sale', the meaning that it certainly does bear in Exod. 21.35, we are *not* told of any division of the purchase price (which is explicitly mentioned in Exod. 21.35), such as might compensate the owner (whether for the capital value of the lost animal alone, or for a multiple thereof, as required by Exod. 21.37, 22.3, MT), leaving the thief himself with any residue should his value be greater than that of the animal. But of course, this is *not* a case of dividing the loss between two equally blameless parties; if the effect of the 'arbitrariness' is to the detriment of the thief, who in this way will pay more than the normal amount of compensation, then that is too bad; the thief has brought the situation upon himself.

37. The view that the thief should be handed over to the victim, rather than sold so that the money raised should be so transferred, gains support from the narrative of Joseph's cup, where the brothers propose that they be enslaved if Benjamin is proved guilty, but where the steward counters that only 'he with whom it is found shall be my slave' (Gen. 44.10).

38. On this, later opinion was divided. Both Philo and Josephus take the sale to be in relation to the 'fine' (the multiple restitution), whereas the Rabbis took it to be restricted to the value of the stolen property, in accordance with a narrow interpretation of *bignevato* (see Jackson 1972: 142-44).

39. At one time, there was a tendency to see such rules as manifestations of a 'primitive' stage of legal development, one where 'objective' tests were preferred to those focusing upon the moral responsibility of the accused. But this is hardly a credible picture, when we take account of the totality of biblical literature, even that ascribed to an early period. Subjective guilt was hardly beyond the cognitive competence of the ancient Hebrews. Rather, the rules we have in the Covenant Code represent a choice that we may describe in contemporary economic language as a wish to avoid the transaction costs of adjudication. By means of these rules, those who had disputes could solve them more or less on the spot, without involving

be applied in practice, without entering into difficult issues of fact, it is still possible to dispute the significance to be attached to this phenomenon. I first became aware of this in the context of the evidentiary rules regarding theft. Daube argued that there was a stage when sale or slaughter of the stolen animal (Exod. 21.37) was the only admissible evidence of theft, followed later by a stage when the evidence could extend to 'hot possession'; he assumed that the purpose of such rules was to make life easier for the courts (1941: 242-61; 1947: 88-96; see also Jackson 1972: 41-48). Even today, we find in some circumstances the use of somewhat arbitrary tests in order to make dispute-resolution that much easier for the courts, even though we know that a more sophisticated approach to the issue would be preferable in an ideal world. But it is precisely because this phenomenon fits with—and no doubt is drawn from—a modern legal model that I suggest that we should pause, and ask whether the evidence really does support our reading back of that model to the ancient sources. Legal anthropology presents non-institutionalized models of dispute resolution, either purely bilateral (involving only the parties) or with assistance from bystanders who volunteer to mediate on a purely ad hoc basis.[40] It

themselves in the time and trouble of dispute-processing.

40. See, e.g., Barkun (1968: Ch. 6); Starr (1992: Ch. 6), remarking (127): 'Gulliver... has convincingly demonstrated, in research among the Arusha and Ndendeuli of Tanzania, that in face-to-face communities disputes may be settled despite the lack of developed legal institutions, such as judges, law courts, or adjudicators. In most societies, if two people from the same community get into a dispute, "hostility or the constant threat of it must give way to discussion, negotiation, an attempt to reach some kind of *rapprochement*, and a settlement of the matter in dispute" (Gulliver 1969.25)'. Starr's own fieldwork was conducted in Mandalinci (Turkey), where she found (127): 'there were no special settings, times, or contexts for handling disputes. Villagers did not form action-sets to negotiate in small groups or larger moots. There were no public assemblies for dispute management, no village council meetings, no persons who consistently played the mediating, and no lineage feuding'. She distinguishes 'dyadic and triadic interactions', the former involving the disputing parties themselves alone, the latter being household heads, patrons, village gendarmes, and even 'outsiders to the village, such as government officials, bureaucrats, gendarme commanders—all of whom appear by chance in the village at a critical point in a dispute and are asked to intervene by a principal or his supporter' (132). She quotes also (at 123) an observation of Bisharat (1989: 32), on dispute resolution on the West Bank in modern times: 'Disputes are affairs of great interest in Palestinian communities. In fact, it is typical that many people, even anonymous bystanders, intercede in streetside quarrels and attempt to mediate

makes a great deal of sense to see the 'arbitrary' objective tests encountered in the Bible as originating in a period before institutionalized dispute resolution was the norm. As the process of institutionalisation increased, of course, such rules could very readily be taken over into the forensic context.

Moreover, Prov. 25.7-9 provides evidence of a strong cultural prejudice against the use of judicial adjudication:

> What your eyes have seen
> do not hastily bring into court
> For what will you do in the end
> when your neighbour puts you to shame?
> Argue your case with your neighbour himself
> and do not disclose another's secret.

Conversely, the several descriptions we find in the Bible of the judicial role all omit, until the time of Ezra in the postexilic period,[41] any mention of their use of written rule-books. What, then, was the function of such judges? Clearly, it was not the 'application' of written rules to facts (see further §5.1, *infra*). Taking these sources together with the internal evidence of the Covenant Code and the cultural antipathy towards formal adjudication, we may suggest that the original function of courts was restricted to cases perceived as too far distant from the typical narrative images evoked by (what I have called) the 'wisdom-

---

between the disputants, who themselves seem to welcome a public hearing. Thus what may begin as a private confrontation often rapidly assumes the dimensions of a community event. Gratitude is showered on the mediator who can produce a resolution on the spot and a boost is given to his status in the community. Conflicts that are not immediately resolved become the topics of discussion and speculation. Those with knowledge of the relevant principles of *shari'a* or *'urf* (customary law) hold forth, it being an occasion for public display of religiosity and general wisdom.' See also the jurisdiction of the *tsu* in Manchu China: van der Sprenkel (1962: 82-85); Roberts (1979: Ch. 7, esp. 131-33). On the problematic nature of norms (as a resource, rather than a source of determination of disputes) amongst the Tswana, see Comaroff and Roberts, in Hamnett (1977: 77-112). On the definitional problem in the anthropology of law, see Pospisil (1971: Ch. 2, ultimately adopting an institutional definition).

41. Ezra 7.25: 'And you, Ezra, according to the wisdom of your God which is in your hand, appoint magistrates and judges who may judge all the people in the province beyond the River, all such as know the laws of your God; and those who do not know them, you shall teach.' For the written form of the laws, see Neh. 8.7-8 and further §5.4, *infra*.

laws', and that in resolving them the judges were expected to deploy their intuitions of justice—intuitions claimed to be divinely inspired.

Two well-known narratives in the Bible appear to bear out the claims that (a) adjudication initially concerned cases where a narrative understanding of the rules failed to produce a clear result, and (b) the biblical judges are presented as enjoying a form of authority more 'charismatic' than 'legal-rational' (Weber).[42] As part of a plot to secure the return to court of the exiled Absalom, during the reign of King David, a 'wise woman' is recruited to present a fictitious case to David to serve as a parable to influence him to pardon and recall Absalom (2 Sam. 14).[43] The claim she presents to the king is as follows:

> Alas, I am a widow; my husband is dead. And your handmaid had two sons, and they quarrelled with one another in the field; there was no one to part them, and one struck the other and killed him. And now the whole family has risen against your handmaid, and they say, 'Give up the man who struck his brother, that we may kill him for the life of his brother whom he slew'; and so they would destroy the heir also. Thus they would quench my coal which is left, and leave to my husband neither name nor remnant upon the face of the earth (vv. 5-7).

The king is thus asked to intervene to prevent the normal operation of blood vengeance for homicide. On what grounds? Partly, because the supplicant is a widow[44] (or perhaps that is the basis of jurisdiction, rather than the cause of action [see also Whitelam 1979: 129-35]). More substantially, because this is hardly a typical narrative of homicide such as might be evoked by the biblical rules:[45] the narrative of homicide

42. The evidence, however, is complicated by the fact that the narratives largely concern *royal* adjudication, and thus invoke also an ancient Near Eastern tradition that the king had a special duty to protect certain otherwise unprotected groups (particularly, the widow, the orphan and the poor), and had a discretion to override normal law in so doing (see Fensham 1962: 129-39).

43. On the nature of her wisdom, see further Jackson (2000b).

44. See further Jackson (1998a: 249-50), comparing the concern for posterity in the case of the daughters of Zelophehad, itself a 'hard case', here resolved by divine consultation.

45. Niditch (1997: 19-20) points, however, to the themes the story has in common with that of Cain and Abel. She eschews questions of literary dependence as the wrong questions: 'rather, the field, the open spaces, are places traditionally where subversion can take place, where social mores can be overturned...' Thus, it is the imagery and social understanding of narrative that is transmitted, rather than the specific words of an earlier source—whether oral or written. On the relationship

does not typically result in the total extinction of the deceased's immediate family! David, nevertheless, proves reluctant to intervene. He agrees only when the woman urges the king to apply a measure of *divine* justice (v. 11): 'Pray let the king invoke the LORD your God, that the avenger of blood slay no more, and my son be not destroyed.'

David is here presented as responding to the 'wisdom' of the woman of Tekoah. That wisdom was itself viewed as a form of divine inspiration.[46] David's son, Solomon, is also depicted as deploying divinely inspired wisdom in the case of the two prostitutes.[47] He resolves the matter by what many have regarded as a psychological ordeal. The conclusion to the narrative shows that the narrator's main purpose was to stress the fact that Solomon was endowed with divine wisdom and that he deployed such wisdom in the course of adjudication:

> And all Israel heard of the judgment which the king had rendered; and they stood in awe of the king, because they perceived that the wisdom of God was in him, to render justice (1 Kgs. 3.28).

The claim is made general in Prov. 16.10:

> Inspired decisions are on the lips of a king;
>   his mouth does not sin in judgment.

The claim here is not merely that the adjudication is *on behalf of* God, but that—failing perversity or corruption—adjudication mediates divine decisions. Oracles, wisdom and prophecy are all possible media for the transmission of the divine will. The king has special claims to be the mediator, but where delegation is required, as here in the exercise of the judicial function, divine inspiration is also claimed to be delegated.[48]

There are indications in the Bible that this kind of charismatic judicial authority was originally intended to be hereditary.[49] That was soon

to the Cain and Abel story, see further Lyke (1997).

46. The identification of such wisdom with *torah,* however, appears to be later than the period here described. Cf. Greenberg (1995: 20-22), who dates it to late monarchic times.

47. 1 Kgs. 3.16-28; for the text and further discussion, see §2.4, *supra.* On the story's disinterest in adjudicating on the death of the deceased child, see further Jackson (1998a: 250-51).

48. See 2 Chron. 19.6, *ve'imakhem bidvar mishpat*; Deut. 1.17, *ki hamishpat lelohim hu,* discussed in §5.1, *infra.* On the claims of 'divine jurisdiction', see further Jackson (1995c: 1818-26).

49. Indeed, abuse of *mishpat* became a focus of opposition to the hereditary

found to invite abuse. Neither the hereditary principle of succession nor bureaucratic practices of delegation could be guaranteed to produce judges and officers who would live up to the standards expected of those in receipt of a divine mandate. According to 1 Sam. 7.15–8.3, this problem became manifest already in the period of the judges:

> Samuel judged Israel all the days of his life. And he went on a circuit year by year to Bethel, Gilgal, and Mizpah; and he judged Israel in all these places. Then he would come back to Ramah, for his home was there, and there also he administered justice to Israel. And he built there an altar to the LORD. When Samuel became old, he made his sons judges over Israel. The name of his first-born son was Jo'el, and the name of his second, Abijah; they were judges in Beer-sheba. Yet his sons did not walk in his ways, but turned aside after gain; they took bribes and perverted justice.

It is likely that the earliest use of written law in the Bible was designed precisely to limit the (hereditary) powers of the monarchy (1 Sam. 10.25; Deut. 17.14-17; §6.2, *infra*; see further Jackson 1998a: 252-54). We may see in this just one manifestation of a more general pattern. Contrary to the theory of Sir Henry Maine, who saw 'equity' as a stage later than the 'early codes', the biblical evidence suggests that laws (in the modern sense) were a reaction against discretionary justice. Comparison may be made with Greek and Roman views of the origins of their own earliest codes as representing democratic opposition to the exercise of royal and aristocratic discretion.

principle. See, e.g., the succession of Abimelekh to Jerubba'al (= Gideon), and his slaughter of his step-brothers, which provokes Jotham's antimonarchical fable of the trees (Judg. 9.1-14).

Chapter 4

THE DEVELOPMENT OF LEGAL DRAFTING

4.1 *Introduction*

Chapter 3 considered the manner in which we should 'read' individual rules when they make the transition from orality to literacy. We should not assume that they quickly lose their 'oral residue': it takes not only the development of institutions of literacy but also changed contexts of use for the reading to become genuinely literate. Yet once the writing of law commences, the barrier against the development of discourse units and structures larger than the individual rule disappears. In what is generally regarded as the earliest of the biblical legal collections, the *Mishpatim* of Exodus 21–22, we already encounter small, structured paragraphs of laws. Yet that collection itself has a compositional history. This chapter considers examples of the contribution that a developmental semiotics, based on studies of linguistic and cognitive development (§1.2), may make to the history of biblical drafting. No claims of mechanical developmental progression are intended. As with the use of other forms of comparison, external sources provide no more than hypotheses for the assessment of the biblical material.

4.2 *Terminology: Concrete to Abstract*

The movement from the concrete to the abstract is a theme common to legal history,[1] developmental psychology[2] and orality/literacy studies

---

1. E.g., in this context, André-Vincent (1974: 96-97); Boyer (1965: 50-51).
2. §1.2, *supra* (stage of formal mental operations). The issue is not entirely unproblematic (see Brown 1958: 18-21; Inhelder and Piaget 1969: 3). It is necessary to distinguish abstraction from generalization (as Barr [1961: 31] has rightly stressed in the biblical context). The problems are particularly acute in respect of generic terms, where there may be tension between the tendencies towards greater abstraction on the one hand and greater differentiation on the other. Moreover, the

(see §3.1 n. 9, *supra*) (including the 'Plain English' movement[3]). Many examples could be noted at the level of drafting. Take that provided by Fritz Schulz from Roman law (1946: 64, 66).[4] A man who borrowed a horse to ride from Rome to Aricia, but rode through Aricia up the hill beyond, was held liable for *furtum*; in the second century BC the jurist Brutus advanced one step beyond the reported case, laying down the rule that one who borrowed an animal was guilty of theft if he took it elsewhere or further than he had stated when borrowing it; Q. Mucius then increased the level of abstraction of the rule, making it apply to any *res* handed over under *depositum* or *commodatum*; ultimately the matter was further generalised, the principle now being expressed as *furtum fit si quis usum alienae rei in suum lucrum convertat*. At the grammatical level, the process is often associated with the movement from use of the verbal form (e.g. 'if a man steals') to a nominal form ('theft'). Daube described this in terms of the normal priority of the verb to the 'action noun' derived from it.[5] Legal systems express themselves in verbal forms — 'if a man steals'—before they adopt nominal forms— 'theft'.[6] The Bible, he notes, uses the verb *shamar* in the context of deposit; it is only in the tannaitic period that we encounter *shemirah* (Daube 1969: 52). In the Bible the verb *matsa* is used of finding lost property; it is not until the tannaitic period that we find

child's use of a generic term may be both imitative and goal-oriented. Thus it may be dangerous to assume that the term has the same referents as for the adult, *a fortiori* that the child possesses the concept on which the class is based.

3.   See Jackson (1995b:118, 120 [on the avoidance of nominalizations], 125). For example, 'The property in the goods delivered pursuant to this agreement shall pass to the buyer on delivery' is recommended to be rewritten as 'You will own the goods as soon as they are delivered to you.')

4.   This example might serve to illustrate the difference between the current argument for (cross-cultural) development from the concrete to the abstract, and the use made of it in 'ethno-psychology', where it is taken to characterize the difference between Greek thought and Hebrew thought. The latter is severely criticized by Barr (1961: 11-12, 15-16, 28-33). It is no objection to the approach here adopted that development may be 'related to particular sectors of the culture', so that one sector may, for specific socio-cultural reasons, not have 'advanced' to the same stage of abstraction as other sectors of the same society at the same time. Barr, however, appears more sceptical in general about the links between language and cognition.

5.   Daube (1969: 11-63); see also Boyer (1965: 47), on the terminology of LH.

6.   In the Bible, *genevah* means 'the stolen property', not 'theft' (see Jackson 1972: 140). Cf. *avedah* in Exod. 22.8; Lev. 5.22.

metsi'ah.[7] The phenomenon is not, of course, confined to law: the Bible tells us only that the children of Israel *yats'u mimitsrayim*; we must wait for the rabbinic period for the phrase *yetsi'at mitsrayim* (Daube 1969: 53-54). Daube notes that the speed of this development will not be uniform in all spheres (1969: 44-45 *et passim*), an observation similarly made of child development.[8] We seem to encounter advance particularly in those areas where the priestly writers have an interest. Whereas conversion by a bailee is described in the Covenant Code by the rather awkward verbal phrase *shalach yad b'* (Exod. 22.7, 10), Lev. 5.21 has the nouns *pikadon*[9] and *teshumet yad*;[10] similarly, the same passage has two different nominalizations, *gezel* and *gezelah*, to denote respectively 'robbery' and 'property taken by robbery' (Lev. 5.21, 23)[11] —a clear contrast with the language of the *Mishpatim* that has an equivalent (*genevah*, Exod. 22.2, 3) only for the latter. Daube was in no doubt as to the frequency of such developments, or their significance:

> To put it at its lowest, there has been some reflection on the activity in question, there is some trend towards abstraction, systematization, classification, perhaps, and the thing is becoming more of an institution... This kind of development is met throughout the entire realm of language, in all areas of human engagement, in philosophy, science, politics, architecture, everywhere. Its neglect vitiates or simplifies much of the intellectual history of civilization... [It produces] a revolutionary new picture of the unfolding of thought (1969: 11-12).

Daube's identification of the 'diagnosis' form is relevant also in this context.[12] Recall this example from the priestly account of the law of homicide: 'But if he struck him down with an instrument of iron, so that he died, he is a murderer; the murderer shall be put to death' (Num.

---

7.   The further abstraction, *metsi'ut* —existence—is mediaeval (Daube 1969: 53).

8.   In Piagetian terms, 'décalage' (see Ginsburg and Opper 1962: 162; Gruber and Vonèche 1977: xxxv).

9.   Used apparently in v. 21 to mean 'in (a relationship of) deposit', although in v.23 it undoubtedly means 'the deposited property'.

10.   If original to the passage (see Jackson 1972: 57).

11.   It may be noted that terms like *genevah, gezelah, avedah,* referring to property transferred out of its original possession in a certain way, do not thereby evidence the presence of a concept of 'theft', 'robbery' or 'loss'. Children may recognize 'cats', without having a concept of cattiness (a manifestation of the distinction between generalization and abstraction).

12.   See §2.2, *supra*, on the illocutionary force of the diagnosis.

35.16). Here, the legal consequences are impliedly derived not directly from the facts, but from the categorization of the facts as falling within an accepted legal class. We have here an expression of the consciousness of the draftsman of the importance of classification—a vital step, one might think, towards the propositional logic that Piaget has identified as a principal characteristic of the stage of formal mental operations. The incidence of this form suggests the existence of a developmental pattern. In the Bible the diagnosis pattern occurs only in priestly sources (e.g. Lev. 11.4, 41; 13.3, 40; 20.13; Num. 35.16-18, 21; cf. Ezek. 18.9); in the Akkadian tradition we find it in LH (7, 9, 10, 11, 13: see further §4.7, *infra*) but not in LE.[13] At the same time we may note Daube's observation that the form is not met in Greek or Roman legislation. That in no way detracts from its cognitive significance in the semitic sources. Conceptual advance is not coterminus with its particular expressions in classical culture. While cognitive analysis suggests the universality of underlying developmental sequences, it does not claim that the particular forms expressive of those universal sequences will equally be universal.

The priestly homicide laws reflect the movement from concrete to abstract also in semantic terms. The Covenant Code has a participial provision, מכה איש ומת מות יומת (Exod. 21.12), followed immediately by two casuistic provisions that distinguish cases where asylum is available from those where it is not. On conventional form-critical grounds it appears indisputable that vv. 13 and 14 are interpolated: not only do they interrupt the sequence of four participial provisions; they are introduced by *asher* and combine first- and second-person verbs—

13.	Yaron (1961: 112 n. 2, suggests that it does occur in LE 24, 26. The reference is to the phrases *din napištim...imat*. But this seems quite different from the priestly and Hammurabian pattern, in which, according to Yaron's own definition, the second element is 'a definition of th(e) act, or name given to its perpetrator'. In LE, on the other hand, we merely have a somewhat tautologous reference to the death penalty: 'It is a capital case; he shall die'; there is no categorization of the act in the protasis, other than in terms of its legal consequences. It is, however, possible that the tripartite grammatical structure itself opened the way towards the conceptual advance.

The possible derivation of the biblical pattern from other sources—whether Egyptian or Babylonian medical codes, or from the Laws of Hammurabi, or indeed from medical sources of the biblical period itself—in no way negates the cognitive significance of the pattern (see further Jackson 1980a: 365).

features found nowhere else in the *Mishpatim*.[14] Cognitive analysis supports this interpolationist theory. In v. 14, the premeditated murderer is described as determining to kill his victim *be'armah*, by treachery. This is the only occasion in the Covenant Code where a mental state is described by an abstract noun—a feature later to become common in the priestly writings. Indeed, we see the contrast demonstrated in this very context. Two other verbal forms in the interpolated Exod. 21.13-14 are later represented by abstract nouns: *lo tsadah* (Exod. 21.13) becomes *bitsediyah* in Num. 35.20, and *yazid* (Exod. 21.14) generates the opposite of *bitsediyah*, *bishgagah* (Num. 35.15). In this respect, Deuteronomy remains closer to the Covenant Code: in expressing the notion of antecedent hatred between the parties, it maintains a verbal form, והוא לא שנא לו מתמל שלשם (Deut. 19.4), while P speaks of 'hatred', *sin'ah* (Num. 35.20).

4.3 *Consistency*

Studies of language acquisition show that the very young child (aged 2-4 years) is inconsistent in his use of words, and only gradually acquires a usage that is internally consistent (Ginsburg and Opper 1969: 81). In studying the issue of consistency, we need to distinguish two different issues: (a) whether the same word can be used with different meanings (especially if the latter are in some respect mutually inconsistent); (b) whether the same concept can be expressed by different words. An entirely logical semantic system might seek to avoid both forms of inconsistency (though with a loss of those aspects of signification[15] which flow precisely from the connotations of such overlapping meanings). In legal discourse, (a) is generally regarded as a greater problem than (b). Yet even modern legal discourse does not succeed entirely in eliminating the use of the same word with different meanings, even though law—like other technical discourses—has been found to achieve a greater degree of what is termed 'monosemicity'.[16] Some students of biblical law have, in practice, assumed that even criterion (b) is applicable to biblical law: in the context of the *Mishpatim*, we

14. Other than the second-person verb in Exod. 21.23. On the interpolation of vv. 13-14, see further §3.2 n. 22, *supra*.

15. On the distinction between communication and signification, see Jackson (1995b: 68-70).

16. See Jackson (1985b: 41-43), on a pilot study of French legal terminology.

have various expressions that appear to indicate a death penalty: *mot yumat* (Exod. 21.12, 15-17), *nakom yinakem* (Exod. 21.20), *venatatah nefesh tachat nefesh* (Exod. 21.23), *yumat* (Exod. 21.29). Some have argued that such differences in terminology must imply differences in meaning, though there is no clear answer as to what such differences might be.[17] There are, in my view, good arguments for regarding some of these variations as originating in different documents (where they may or may not have had different meanings). That does not, however, eliminate the problem, if such it be: the differences were still tolerated by the compiler of the *Mishpatim,* and within a relatively short text. Each case has to be determined on its merits: if there are good supporting arguments for the correlation of different meanings with different expressions, we should follow them. But the mere existence of different expressions should not lead to the conclusion that differences in meaning *must* be intended.

The converse problem, whether the same word can be used with different meanings, takes us back again to the very structure of semantics and the question whether we should view the meanings of words in definitional or narrative terms.[18] We may use the example of the verb *ratsach.* Even today, there are still those who debate issues such as capital punishment in terms of whether *lo tirtsach* in the Decalogue (Exod. 20.13; Deut. 5.17) means 'You shall not kill' or 'You shall not murder'. At a purely semantic level, there is no doubt that *ratsach* extends to 'kill': the offender who *is* to be protected in the cities of

---

17. The issues are discussed in my forthcoming *Wisdom-Laws.* Suffice, for the moment, to note the arguments that *nakom yinakem* (Exod. 21.20) refers to (a) a fine (Driver 1911: p. 218); (b) an institutional death penalty—as opposed to action by the *go'el hadam* (e.g. Greenberg 1962: 738; cf. LXX: δικὴ ἐκδικηθήσεται); and (c) vicarious punishment (Westbrook 1988b: 89-100). Interestingly, the Samaritan version already responds to the perceived problem of inconsistency by harmonization, rendering the text 'will be put to death', reflecting *mot yumat* (cf. Cazelles 1946: 54).

18. This is closely related to the semantic (literal) versus narrative distinction for which I argued in §3.2, above. Most of the examples there related to the meanings of sentences rather than words, and there has been a strong tendency, in philosophy (Wittgenstein, Hart), to avoid defining words rather than explaining their use in the context of sentences. However, the example of the image of the thief discussed in §3.2 suggests that narrative images do not attach only to sentences—indeed, the sentence (as opposed to the 'utterance') is a unit of writing rather than speech. On the avoidance of definitions in oral culture, see also §3.1 (end), *supra.*

refuge is classified as a *rotseach* (Num. 35.12); indeed, the verb is used even of the (justified) action of the blood-avenger who catches the manslayer outside the city of refuge (Num. 35.27) (cf. Cohn 1973a: 945; Rofé 1986: 232-34; Haas 1989: 78). But what does this prove? Is the Decalogue really saying to the *go'el hadam:* you are entitled to pursuit, but (morally) you ought not to do it? A better approach is narrative: not to seek what is the full range of situations that, semantically, *lo tirtsach* might 'cover', and then seek to apply them consistently to the texts, but rather to ask what typical situations the term might evoke. The typical narrative evoked in this context is surely 'murder', in the sense of pre-meditated homicide. The further one departs from that typical case, the more the issue becomes not one of narrative sense but literary interpretation.[19] Thus *ratsach* may primarily, or typically, mean 'murder', but it can also, in context, refer to accidental killing or even legally mandated execution. Surely there is nothing surprising in this. Precision, we have noted, is a feature of the culture of literacy (§3.1 [end], *supra*). The biblical text itself affirms that the original communication of the Decalogue was oral.

Whether, within the biblical corpus, there is any tendency towards increasing semantic consistency, parallel to that of speech development in the individual, is undetermined. The issue of increasing consistency in *forms* is easier to address, though a clear conclusion is difficult to derive from the biblical material. In the ancient Near East we do appear to encounter a progression from the use of a variety of drafting forms towards convergence upon formal consistency. This is particularly notable in the relationship between the Laws of Eshnunna, which displays a variety of forms (casuistic, apodictic, relative) and the Laws of Hammurabi, which predominantly adopt the casuistic form, even converting to the casuistic form some of the price and rent lists that in LE stand, in formal terms, even further apart.

On this occasion there is a potential conflict between cognitive analysis and conventional form-criticism. Yaron regards the use of several different forms in LE—regulatory sections, conditional sentences, split protases,[20] apodictic commands and relative formulations—as evidence

19. On Wittgenstein's distinction between the unreflective following of a rule and the reflective process of interpreting it, see §3.1 n. 6, *supra*.

20. The classification itself involves assumptions. Yaron himself rightly warns (1969: 64; 1988: 103) that the split protasis should not be relied upon as a form separate from the conditional sentence (*šumma awilum...*) for the purposes of deter-

that the document was compiled from a variety of different sources: '[T]here is no reason to assume that any one legislator would wish to express his rules in greatly divergent ways' (1969: 59-60; 1988: 97). Yet when Yaron comes to assess formal differences within the price and hire regulations,[21] he prefers to conclude that 'when all has been said, that variety does not exceed what may have been done by one person (or by one group of persons) not particularly careful in drafting or not attaching great importance to uniformity' (1969: 59-60; 1988: 98). Yaron may well turn out to be correct in all these substantive judgments; hitherto, however, no objective criterion has been offered for their demonstration. We should certainly not take modern draftsmanship as our model, to the neglect of the developmental pattern that, if my overall hypothesis is correct, we may expect to have been involved.

The point, if established by further cross-cultural studies, would have important repercussions for the study of biblical law. The *Mishpatim* themselves (Exod. 21.1–22.16 [MT]) are formally diverse; *a fortiori* the 'Covenant Code', within which they are located (Exod. 20.23–23.19). A developmental argument may be offered, if not in favour of the integrity of the wider Covenant Code, then at least in rebuttal of any presumption that formal diversity necessarily indicates (at an early developmental stage of legal drafting) compilation from discrete sources. We may note that Piaget recorded his 12- and 13-year-old Swiss 'legislators', in explaining the rules of their game of marbles, as using indiscriminately the forms 'whoever...', 'When you...whoever', 'When there are...you can', 'If you...',[22] 'the first who...', and 'you can't say...if you' (1932: 38-39). It would not be unreasonable to conclude that these children had covered casuistic, apodictic and relative forms. Nor is it easy to argue for increasing formal consistency within biblical law. As argued in §2.3.2 above, the proclamations that Moses is commanded to make in the wake of the various desert disputes

---

mining origins, since it 'may well be nothing more than an attempt to improve on the ordinary *šumma awilum* formulation'. The source of the judgment that the split protasis may represent an 'improvement' on, rather than merely a chronological development of, the standard casuistic form is not revealed by Yaron. On the cognitive significance of the split protasis, see further §4.5, *infra*.

21. E.g. 'the hire of X is Y', contrasted with 'Y is the hire of X'.

22. From R, the youngest. Cf. Gilmer's (1975) rejection of the view that the 'if you...', form, prominent in Deuteronomy, is a combination of earlier casuistic and apodictic forms.

(normally assigned to the priestly source), come in a variety of forms.

4.4 *Increasing Combination of Variables*

The child in the stage of concrete mental operations deals with each problem in isolation (Piaget 1980: 61) and cannot focus simultaneously on more than one aspect of a situation.[23] Thus he must learn to think with a single variable before he operates with multiple variables. Compare the drafting of the following provisions regarding theft. The Hittite Laws (HL) have separate provisions for theft of bulls and theft of horses, even though those provisions are in all other respects identical:

HL 57: If anyone steals a bull... Formerly they gave 30 cattle. But now he shall give 15 cattle...

HL 58: If anyone steals a stallion... They used to give 30 horses. But now he shall give 15 horses ...

HL 59: If anyone steals a ram, they used to give 30 sheep. Now he shall give [15] sheep...[24]

In terms of grammatical structure, the draftsman was not able to deal with more than a single variable—the historical development of the penalty—in a single clause.[25] So he had to repeat himself in order to cope with the variation of subject-matter. Contrast this with the approach of the Laws of Hammurabi:

LH 8: If a man has stolen an ox or a sheep or an ass or a swine or a boat, if (it is the property) of a god (or) if (it is the property) of a palace he shall pay 30-fold; if (it is the property) of a villein, he shall replace (it) 10-fold...[26]

The explanation for this difference does not reside in the different styles of Hittite and Akkadian draftsmen. For the earlier stage in

---

23. Ginsburg and Opper (1969: 115), with an example from the child's moral judgment: he cannot consider both degree of damage and intention, and bases his judgment solely on the former.

24. Translation of Hoffner in Roth (1995: 226).

25. I have omitted the 'definition clauses', which, in identical terms (in HL 57 and 58; there is none in 59), stipulate that the animal concerned must be two years old to qualify (for these purposes) as a 'bull' or a 'stallion'. We need not go into the question of whether these clauses, which abruptly interrupt the protases, are original or not.

26. Translation of Driver and Miles (1952–55: II, 17).

Akkadian drafting, represented by the Laws of Eshnunna, provides a text on a related theme that is far closer to the Hittite than to the Hammurabian model:

> LE 12:   A man, who will be seized in the field of a subject, in the *crop*, in broad daylight, 10 shekels silver shall weigh out. (He) who will be seized at night in the *crop*—he shall die, shall not live.
>
> LE 13:   A man, who will be seized in the house of a subject, in the house, in broad daylight, 10 shekels silver shall weigh out. (He) who will be seized at night in the house—he shall die, shall not live.[27]

Here the draftsman has not been able to combine into a single clause the day/night distinction with the alternative place of the trespass. He has repeated the clause, even though he has needed to change only a single word.

The Covenant Code provides a similar example, but with a significant variation:

> Exod. 21.26:   When a man strikes the eye of his slave, male or female, and destroys it, he shall let the slave go free for the eye's sake.
>
> Exod. 21.27:   If he knocks out the tooth of his slave, male or female, he shall let the slave go free for the tooth's sake.

Each clause contains two norms, incorporating the variant *eved/amah*. A further clause is required to cope with the variant *ayin/shen* (and the verbs related to them). There is, however, one difference between Exodus and Eshnunna. In Exodus, we have the uses of a paragraphing device (first protasis introduced by *vekhi*, second by *ve'im* [further §4.5, *infra*]) to link the two provisions, thereby allowing the draftsman to omit repetition of the subject, *ish*. LE has such a paragraphing device (represented by *šumma awilum* followed by simple *šumma*), but it is not used in this case; in LE both clauses are introduced by the same independent formula, here the 'relative' form, *awilum ša*.

The proposition that we have here a developmental pattern, which distinguishes LE from LH and the *Mishpatim* from later biblical codes,[28] would not be falsified[29] by the discovery that the 'earlier'

---

27. Translation of Yaron (1988: 51) (slight variations from the 1969 edition).

28. It is no part of the present argument to suggest that there is complete stylistic uniformity with regard to any of the features here discussed within any particular document. Thus multiple variants within a single clause are found elsewhere in the *Mishpatim* (e.g. Exod. 21.37). The methods by which overall cognitive comparisons

pattern, reiteration of a clause in order to cover a further subject matter under the same principle as the norm of the first clause, occurs also in 'later' sources. What is important is the movement from an earlier stage of lower capacity to deal with multiple variants in a single clause to a later stage of greater capacity to deal with multiple variants in a single clause, notwithstanding the retention of the earlier pattern for particular purposes at a later stage. There may always be other considerations leading to the retention of the earlier style of drafting. Such is the case in Deuteronomy's regulations in favour of those about to go into battle (Deut. 20.5-7). As argued in §2.2, it is here the *Sitz* of oral proclamation that prompts the use of a separate clause for each individual exemption (new house, new vineyard, new wife!). Repetition is more suited to the oral medium than compression of all possible contingencies into a single clause (which today we associate with the 'small print' technique). The fact that such repetition occurs at the beginning of written law is a sign of 'oral residue'. In the absence of some particular reason for its retention, it does not survive very long.

4.5 *Increasing Combination of Clauses*

The development of the capacity to integrate previously isolated units into a system can be measured, at the linguistic level, by the degree of grammatical complexity represented by sentences with more than a single verb, often linked by conjunctions (Limber 1973; Crystal and Davey 1969: 203-204). On this criterion, we can again discern development as between LE and LH. Ignoring the basic two-clause structure that constitutes the casuistic form, we can count the number of additional clauses, normally but not exclusively subdivisions of the protasis. More important, perhaps, than gross totals[30] is the fact that LH is able, on occasion, to go much further than LE in the cumulation of additional clauses. LE never goes beyond 5; LH 9 (which is only the first part of an integrated paragraph) has 14. Comparable development may be

might be made between documents are briefly discussed and exemplified in Jackson (1982a: 62-64) (an issue not revisited here).

29. Falsification is discussed further at Jackson (1980a: 368).

30. I compared the whole of LE, minus paras. 1-4, 7-8 and 10-11 (price and rent lists), with the first 34 paragraphs of LH, the two corpora being exactly comparable in terms of word count. I identified 85 additional conjunctive clauses in the former, 95 in the latter.

observed as between the Covenant Code and Deuteronomy.[31]

The forms of grammatical integration are also of interest. Both LE and the Covenant Code have paragraphing devices, in the Covenant Code represented by *ki* or *vekhi* followed by *im* or *ve'im*, in LE by *šumma awilum* followed by plain *šumma*. Such paragraphing allows the draftsman to avoid repetition of some of the facts for each particular norm. In the *Mishpatim* these paragraphs already extend to some four or five provisions, and there are signs in the slave laws (Exod. 21.2-11) of a formalized sequence of conjunctions, wherein, after an initial *ki*, there follow clauses introduced by *im*, until the last clause of the paragraph, which is introduced by *ve'im*. The Akkadian sources appear not to have made use of such alternative conjunctions.

A further advance in the logico-linguistic integration of rules is presented by what Yaron has called the 'split protasis'. It appears to have begun as a simple stylistic variation, where the occurrence of *šumma* within the protasis is deferred, perhaps in order to stress one element as particularly significant (1969: 65; 1988: 101-102). For example:

> LE 9:   Should a man give 1 shekel for harvesting to ?/for ? a hired
> man—if he (*šumma*) (the worker) was not ready for him,
> and did not at all harvest for him the harvesting—he shall
> weigh out 10 shekels silver.

But there is one occasion in LE, Yaron points out, where this form is used to encompass alternative hypotheses.[32]

> LE 17/18:   Should a son of a hired man bring bride money to the house
> of the father-in-law
> (i)   if one of the two went to the fate, to its owner
> indeed the silver shall return;
> (ii) if he took her and she entered his house, verily
> ?/either ?...the young wife went to the fate,

---

31. Cf. Levinson (1997: 18): 'Deuteronomy is a learned text, a literary composition that is the product of skilled scribes.' I think this is reflected also in the kind of legal problems addressed in Deuteronomy, as compared to those in the *Mishpatim*. The latter regulate typical, standard situations; Deuteronomy is interested in (scholastic?) variations on those situations, what might be termed 'second-order' problems (e.g the context in which the primogeniture issue is presented: see *infra*, §8.3). In my forthcoming *Wisdom-Laws,* I argue that Exod. 21.22-23 is atypical of the *Mishpatim,* on this criterion.

32. The numeration is that of Yaron; the layout is mine. However, the two '*šumma*' clauses each begin on a new line on the original.

> whatever he ?/she ? has brought, he will not
> cause to go forth; its excess indeed he will take.

Yaron recognizes the advance and elegance of this formulation, and mourns its passing: '[T]he form did not meet the desire for the uniformity and standardization of sections, all of which should start in the same way. I have not found the form outside the LE' (1969: 63; 1988: 101-102). Taken literally, Yaron is correct. If deferral of the *šumma* within the protasis is taken as definitive of the split protasis, then it occurs only in LE, and its suppression in LH may be taken as another aspect of growing standardization of forms.

But that is not the end of the story. Even where *šumma* is indeed deferred, the opening clause is still conditional in sense. More important, in my view, is the fact that this initial conditional proposition (whether the conjunction *šumma* is used or not) is not followed immediately by a consequence, but rather is interrupted by a (further) conditional subclause. On this criterion, the form is found also elsewhere:

LH 8:   If a man (*šumma awilum*) has stolen an ox or a sheep or an ass
        or a swine or a boat
        (i)   if (*šumma*) (it is the property) of a god (or) if
                (*šumma*) (it is the property of) a palace, he shall
                pay 30-fold;
        (ii)   if (*šumma*) (it is the property) of a villein, he
                shall replace (it) 10-fold.[33]

Here we have a general protasis, introduced by *šumma awilum,* but one which does not proceed to an apodosis; rather, it introduces two formally complete norms (each with a protasis introduced by *šumma*, followed by an apodosis), the function of the initial *šumma awilum* ('split') protasis being to supply information relevant to *both* the subsequent norms. Yaron accepts that this form is 'somewhat similar' to his split protasis.[34]

LH takes a further step in the development of this form. It applies the subdivision to the apodosis, contemplating different fact situations

---

33. The paragraph then concludes with a grammatically independent concluding norm: 'If the thief has not the means of payment, he shall be put to death.' With the structure as noted in the text, cf., e.g., LH 3/4 and 30/31, both of which are less elegant in that the split in the protasis occurs in what logically is not the ideal place.

34. He cites LH 163/164 (1988: 102 n. 47). However, LH 163/164 is by no means unique in LH. See also Yaron's comparison with LE 27/28 (1988: 102 n. 47).

consequential upon the legal procedures required by an initial norm. Examples include LH 2, where the alternative results of the water ordeal are stated as alternative norms following on the requirement to invoke the ordeal (which forms the apodosis of the first clause of the paragraph), and LH 13, where the draftsman deals with the contingency that a party cannot produce his witnesses within the period stipulated in the primary apodosis.

The 'split protasis' structure (on my definition) is extended to an introductory protasis followed by *three* (grammatically) complete casuistic norms, in

> LH 32: If either a runner or a fisher, who is taken captive on a mission of the king (and) a merchant has ransomed him and so has enabled him to regain his city
>
> (i)   if[35] (*šumma*) (he) has the means for ransoming (himself) in his house, he shall ransom himself;
>
> (ii) if (*šumma*) there are not the means of ransoming him in his house, he shall be ransomed out of (the resources of) the temple of his city;
>
> (iii) if (*šumma*) there are not the means of ransoming him in the temple of his city, the palace shall ransom him.

We may term this form a 'ladder'.[36] There is a 'narrative' sequentiality within (i)–(iii); they are not simply logical alternatives within the initial protasis. (ii) comes into play only in the absence of (i); (iii) only in the absence of (ii). Moreover, the merchant will clearly have to approach, successively, the captive (or his family), failing which the temple, failing which the palace in order to recover the ransom: neither of the latter are likely to pay up without evidence that those ahead of them have defaulted. In formal terms, we find an interesting parallel to this structure in Leviticus 5: as a penalty for various sins an offender is required, *inter alia*, to bring a lamb or a goat as a sin offering (v. 6); but if he cannot afford a lamb, he may bring two turtledoves or two pigeons (v. 7), and if he cannot afford two turtledoves or two pigeons he may bring a tenth of an ephah of fine flour (v. 11).

---

35. Wrongly omitted in the translation of Driver and Miles (1952–55: II, 23): see col. xia line 20.

36. The proclamation in the case of the daughters of Zelophehad (Num. 27.8-11) has a similar 'ladder' structure in the relationship between the clauses, though it does not follow a split protasis.

One can readily understand the functioning of the 'split protasis' (on either definition) where the initial protasis is followed by more than a single casuistic norm: what occurs in the initial protasis is common to the succeeding norms, and does not have to be repeated. Where, on the other hand, the initial protasis is followed by only a single casuistic norm, the form is more difficult to understand. The one example appears to be LE 9 (discussed above), which lacks an initial *šumma*, and is explained by Yaron on different, primarily aesthetic/stylistic grounds.

The form of an initial protasis followed by more than a single casuistic norm is common in modern statutory drafting, and is clearly designed for the written medium, where the reader can look back to see the relevant elements mentioned earlier.[37] Indeed, even in writing, it can readily lead to cognitive strain. We may compare the problem of 'embedding' as discussed in linguistics: the greater the separation between subject and verb, the more likely the sentence will be difficult to understand.[38] The reason appears to be that the underlying narrative sequence is thus obscured.[39] The Plain English movement counsels against the use of embedding.[40]

In this context we may review the two apparent examples of the form that are found in the *Mishpatim:*

> Exod. 21.18-19: When (*vekhi*) men quarrel and one strikes the other with a stone or with his fist and the man does not die but keeps his bed, then
>> (i) (*im*) if the man rises again and walks abroad with his staff, the striker shall be clear; only he shall pay for the loss of his time, and shall have him thoroughly healed.

There has been debate as to whether we have here a single norm dealing only with the issue of compensation for the victim of a non-fatal assault, or whether it also regulates fatalities. As it stands, the paragraph

---

37. Cf. Francis (1975: 162), noting the apparent early occurrence of 'different decision procedures between writing, when the first part of the sentence remains evident, and speech in which it may more easily be lost' in the context of evidence that written sentences in young children tended to begin with subordinate units more frequently than speech patterns.

38. Illustrations in Jackson (1995b: 32-35).

39. Jackson (1995b: 205), in the context of Chomsky's theories.

40. Illustrations in Jackson (1995b: 126-28).

is awkward and unusual. It is hardly redeemed by the aesthetic/stylistic argument Yaron applies to LE 9; moreover, it differs from the latter in that we have an initial *vekhi* (and thus nothing equivalent to the deferred *šumma*). Moreover, nowhere else in the *Mishpatim* do we encounter either a split protasis followed by only one subsidiary norm or the use of *im* (Exod. 21.19) to introduce a co-ordinate clause within a protasis.[41] That *im* perhaps raises the expectation of a second casuistic norm, comparable to LE 17/18 or LH 8. We do have one example of such a form in the *Mishpatim*.[42]

<blockquote>

Exod. 22.6-7:   If (*ki*) a man delivers to his neighbor money or goods
                  to keep, and it is stolen out of the man's house, then,

    (i)   (*im*) if the thief is found, he shall pay
            double.

    (ii)   (*im*) If the thief is not found, the owner
            of the house shall come near to God, to
            show whether or not he has put his hand
            to his neighbor's goods.

</blockquote>

Exod. 21.18-19, as we presently find it, begins as if it has such a structure in mind, but provides only one complete norm after the initial 'split' protasis. To parallel Exod. 22.6-7, we would require something like the following:

<blockquote>

Exod. 21.18-19:   When (*vekhi*) men quarrel and one strikes the other
                    with a stone or with his fist and the man does not die
                    but keeps his bed, then

    (i)   (*im*) if the man rises again and walks abroad
            with his staff, the striker shall be clear; only
            he shall pay for the loss of his time, and
            shall have him thoroughly healed.

    (ii)   if the man does not rise again, then …

</blockquote>

I have suggested elsewhere (Jackson 2000a) that a better solution to this particular problem is a transposition of clauses:

<blockquote>

Exod. 21.18:   When (*vekhi*) men quarrel and one strikes the other
                 with a stone or with his fist and the man does not die
                 but keeps his bed, he shall only pay for the loss of his
                 time, and shall have him thoroughly healed.

</blockquote>

---

41. That function is normally performed by *vav consecutivum*, occasionally *ow*.

42. There is an argument that it is not original to that context. It interrupts a sequence of entirely agricultural offences.

Exod. 21.19:   If (*im*) the man rises again and walks abroad with his
staff, he that struck him shall be clear.

This is typical of the 'paragraphing' technique of the *Mishpatim*: we
have what grammatically are two entirely independent norms, each regulating a separate situation, each with a protasis and apodosis, but with
some aspect of the situation carried over from the protasis of the first to
the protasis of the second. This common element is achieved without a
common introduction; it is implied by context/common theme and,
seemingly, by the conventions attaching to the conjunctions *ki* and *im* in
this form of biblical Hebrew. Yet the cognitive problem is identical to
that presented by the 'split protasis': in the case of the second norm,
there is an effective interruption of the 'story': a clause not applicable
in v. 19 is 'embedded' between the opening of v. 18 (which is common
to the two situations) and v. 19 itself. At the very least, the understanding of such paragraphs is aided by writing, providing the possibility of
'backward scanning'. We may suspect that formulations such as these
were written down *ab initio*.

4.6 *Rule Elaboration and Systematization*

At the beginning of the stage of formal mental operations, the child is
said to develop 'a kind of legalistic fascination with rules. He enjoys
settling differences of opinion concerning the rules, inventing new rules
and elaborating on them. He even tries to anticipate all of the possible
contingencies that may arise'.[43] Piaget described an occasion on which
eight (Swiss) schoolboys, aged 10–11,

> in order to throw snow-balls at each other, began by wasting a good
> quarter-of-an-hour in electing a president, fixing the rules of voting, then
> in dividing themselves into two camps, in deciding upon the distances of
> the shots, and finally in foreseeing what would be the sanctions to be
> applied in cases of infringement of these laws (1932: 41).[44]

Legal historians are not unfamiliar with this phenomenon; Beseler

---

43. Ginsburg and Opper (1969: 102); cf. Piaget (1932: 40): 'they seem to take a
particular pleasure in anticipating all possible cases and in codifying them'.

44. In the version at Ginsburg and Opper (1969: 102), by the time all the details
were fixed, it was time to return home, and no game of snowballs was played at
all—yet the 'players' seemed content with their afternoon!

coined the term 'completomania' for it.[45] Yaron has noted that LE exhibits a far lesser concern for comprehensiveness than does LH (1969: 55-56; 1988: 86-87). Thus we very frequently find that self-evident matters left to implication in earlier sources are explicitly mentioned in later versions,[46]—a clear movement from 'restricted' to 'elaborated' code (§3.1). We also find later drafting that includes elements that, while not perhaps self-evident, were clearly not considered necessary at the earlier stage. LH 9–10 amplifies sevenfold (in terms of the number of words used) the procedures involved where a man in possession of 'hot' property claims that he bought it, by comparison with the formulation at LE 40. And LH 237 attempts to specify what constitutes the lost load in the case of the boatman responsible for the sinking of his boat (LE 5). In several of these cases, Szlechter (1970: 92-107) has seen evidence of positive interpretation by LH of LE—a claim which in no way invalidates my suggestion that we have here examples of cognitive development.

The collocation of clauses with but a single variant (§4.4) may be viewed also in this context: despite the need for virtual repetition of clauses, the author is concerned that all the variants should be explicitly included. Thus in LE 56/57 the law of the biting dog follows in both sequence and terms[47] that of the goring ox in LE 54/55. The draftsman is not yet sure that the same rules would be applied to the dog if the provision were not stated.[48] In LH, on the other hand, only the goring ox is included (LH 250-52).[49] In the light of the other evidence as to the

---

45. See Daube (1973: 127); on the phenomenon, see further Jackson (1975a: 161-66, 169-71).

46. Examples discussed in Jackson (1975a: 162-64) are LE 36/LH 125 and Lipit Ishtar 10/LH 59.

47. One might add also the case of the falling wall LE 58. But here there is a further substantive variant: by a decree of the king the offence has become capital.

48. Perhaps an indication of a movement towards 'literal' meaning, associated with the transition from orality to literacy. On the other hand, Yaron (1988: 87) now observes: 'The style of a considerable number of sections in the LE seems to reflect mnemotechnic needs, the desire to facilitate memorizing. They flow smoothly, can be chanted, and committed to memory without much difficulty.'

49. This is unlikely to be explicable on the grounds that the inclusion of LH 250 makes the ox provisions special. Exod. 21.28 lends support to the view that LH 250 represented a common approach to the liabilities of the owner, implied equally in LE. Similarly, any change in the dog law as between LE and LH would have been likely to prompt the inclusion of a dog law in LH.

respective attitudes of LE and LH to completeness, this may well indicate that the goring ox in Hammurabi is now being used as a symbol for a wider class.[50] In both LE and LH we find the ultimate example of the draftsman's concern for completeness—in the use of a 'catch-all phrase' (*u lu mimma šumšu*) at the end of a list of objects any of which may form the subject matter of the clause.[51]

Here too form-critical and cognitive approaches may prove complementary. Yaron, having sought to distinguish precedent-based from 'statutory' provisions in LE according to the presence or absence of an opening *šumma awilum* (1969: 69; 1988, 111),[52] then notes that 'sections based on precedent are, on the whole, of a rather narrowly defined formulation (and)…only rarely cumulate parallel, equivalent facts', whereas 'the combination of equivalents indicates the "statutory" origin of a provision, or at least reformulation by the compiler' (1969: 70; 1988: 112-13). This last qualification is, of course, very important. Though court proceedings gave rise to written documentation, the latter was concerned with recording the parties, the dispute and the decision, not the norm on which the decision was based (cf. §2.3.2 [end]). Thus norm-formulation, even where based on precedent, was indeed the concern of the compiler; at the very least, it was he who was faced for the first time with the task of committing it to formal, written language. But even if we accept that he would tend to keep norms of a case law origin narrower in formulation than those deriving from decrees, the latter *Sitz im Leben* would not be sufficient to explain some of the features we actually find. Whatever his bureaucratic tendencies, cognitive analysis suggests that he needed practice or training to achieve the kind of comprehensiveness we find even in LE, *a fortiori* in LH.

4.7 *Reasons for Rules*

The incapacity of young children to give reasons or justifications for

50. I do, of course, assume, here and throughout, that LE—or something rather like them—were known to the draftsmen of LH (see Driver and Miles [1952–55: I. 6-11]). The literary connections as regards the goring ox laws are particularly strong.

51. E.g. LH 7 (erroneously cited as LE 7 in Jackson [1975a: 164]): 'If a man buys silver or gold or slave or slave-girl or ox or sheep or anything else whatsoever…' Cf. LH 122, 124, 237, LE 40, 50 (*mala ibaššu*).

52. Yaron does not claim a complete correlation, for while 'all sections not using *šumma awilum* reflect one form or another of statute law, most of the sections using *šumma awilum*, but not all of them, reflect litigation and precedents'.

their assertions is taken to reflect an incapacity to recognize the possibility that others may take a different view to their own—an aspect of the well-noted characteristic of 'egocentricity'.[53] Jacques Michel has compared this with the development of law at Rome: the pontiffs did not justify their decisions, which were handed down like oracles and accepted only by reason of the authority *(auctoritas)* of their authors; it was only towards the end of the Republic that reasoning appears in legal argument, under the influence of Greek philosophy.[54] We may compare the development and incidence of motive clauses in the legal collections. Motive clauses are far more frequent in Deuteronomy and the Priestly Code than in the *Mishpatim*, where there is but one clear example.[55] The far greater frequency of motive clauses in D and P than in the ancient Near Eastern collections is, no doubt, attributable to different types of editorial concern, as Gemser has suggested. But Gemser is wrong in claiming that motive clauses are not found at all in the ancient Near Eastern collections (1953: 52). While there are none in Eshnunna, LH 11 concludes its treatment of the alleged finding of lost property in the possession of another with the judgment that the owner who fails to produce witnesses corroborating his identification of the property 'is a felon since he has uttered a slander'—*sar tuššamma idki.*[56]

This, in fact, may represent a more advanced cognitive stage than the mere appending of clauses that provide motives—whether historical, ethical, or religious—for obedience, and which are taken to be characteristic of the religious nature of the biblical collections (Paul 1970: 39, 100). In LH 11 *tuššamma idki* is offered as a reason for classifying the owner as *sar*, this classification being an example of what Daube has termed the 'diagnosis form', which itself represents a significant cognitive advance towards greater abstraction (§2.2, 4.2, *supra*). We may compare Num. 35.16: 'But if he struck him down with an instrument of

---

53. E.g. Ginsburg and Opper (1969: 89). The data is drawn mostly from 4–7-year-olds, thus before the child enters the stage of concrete mental operations. On 'egocentricity', see further §1.2, at pp. 33, 35 *supra*.

54. Unpublished lecture delivered at the University of Edinburgh in 1975.

55. Exod. 21.21 (*ki kaspo hu*, often regarded as interpolated). Gemser (1953: 51), includes Exod. 21.8, and counts 9 in the larger Covenant Code. On the classification of motive clauses, see further Gemser (1953: 53-55).

56. *Per* Driver and Miles (1952–55: II, 16); Roth reads *iddi*, and translates: 'he is a liar, he has indeed spread malicious charges'.

iron, so that he died, he is a murderer; the murderer shall be put to death.' Here, the legal consequences are impliedly derived not directly from the facts, but from the categorization of the facts as falling within an accepted legal class. Classification is here assuming an importance of its own—a vital step, one might think, towards the propositional logic that Piaget has identified as a principal characteristic of the stage of formal mental operations. The incidence of this form suggests the existence of a developmental pattern. In the Bible the diagnosis pattern occurs only in priestly sources (§4.2 p. 96, *supra*); in the Akkadian tradition we find it in LH (7, 9, 10, 11, 13) but not in LE.

Chapter 5

THE WRITTEN MEDIA OF LAW

5.1 *Introduction*

Archaeology has not served well the study of the legal institutions of biblical society. We lack 'court' records—using that term in both its legal and politico-administrative senses. What we possess is a rich literature, into which it is *possible*—to put the matter at its highest—that some original sources from the real legal and administrative milieux may have been incorporated.[1] Certainly, we cannot assume without careful argument that the biblical codes come from any such milieu. And if they do, they have assuredly not survived in their original forms. But this situation should not be regarded as entirely negative. Irrespective of the origins of their materials, the biblical authors have provided us with a wealth of material that informs us of their views about the documentary sources of law.

The study of biblical law has been influenced to some extent by debates regarding the character of the ancient Near Eastern 'codes'. There, we encounter two distinct genres of 'legislative' documents: the *mišarum*-acts and the 'codes'. The former reflect immediate measures of debt-relief, for the most part being retrospective rather than prospective and thus intended to have only temporary force; the latter, on the other hand, state rules whose effect is presented as enduring. Finkelstein has commented upon the pattern of enactment of these two forms of law: the *mišarum* act is found normally at the beginning of a reign, while the 'code' occurs some years later.[2] The ideal character of

---

1. The biblical record may serve us better as an historical source in respect of administrative matters and the (related) legal functions of the king (see Mettinger 1971; Whitelam 1979; Frick 1985).

2. Finkelstein (1961: 91-104, esp. 101); the late dating of the Code of Hammurabi is evidenced by the list of conquests mentioned in the prologue.

the codes may be inferred, *inter alia*, from the fact that they contain provisions that, if made effective, would render the *mišarum* acts unnecessary. Moreover, we have a large corpus of records of decided cases from the courts of Old Babylonia, and they fail to bear out any expectation that the codes were applied in the courts like modern statutes. Sometimes the rulings of the courts conform to the code, but frequently they do not; and the court records contain no quotations or even citations of the rules contained in the codes.[3] The conclusion (though not undisputed)[4] seems to be that our modern model of law, based upon the 'application' of statutes in court, is not applicable to the ancient Near East. The following alternatives have been canvassed:

(a) The 'codes' were to be consulted by judges, as a source of persuasive though not binding authority (Westbrook's 'judicial reference' model).[5]

(b) Their purpose was academic or didactic, whether for some kind of advanced 'civics' education[6] or in some cases as purely scribal exercises[7].

(c) They were designed for professional education, specifically for the training of judges.[8]

3. Cf. Figulla (1951: 95-101); on the lack of citation, see recently, Levinson. (1991: 141-48); Watts (1999: 135).

4. See Westbrook (1985: 247-64); Leemans (1991: 415-16). Westbrook has since modified his view (see 1989: 201-22; 1994: 24-25; Jackson 1995c: 1748-49 n.14; Fitzpatrick-McKinley 1999: 96-100). Even on this 'legislative' view, questions still arise as to the 'reach' of the codes. When, in 1985, Westbrook favoured a more 'normative' view of the function of the law codes, he still viewed the intended audience as the 'royal judges' (1985: 254).

5. Westbrook (1989: 202): it 'refers the court to the real authoritative sources...whether they be statute, precedent or custom... Its text has no independent value. Courts need not cite it or pay attention to its wording, since they are essentially looking beyond it to the source that it reflects' (cf. Greengus 1994: 79). For criticism, see Jackson (1995c: 1747-48, esp. n. 10) on Westbrook's argument from the omen texts (see also Westbrook 1990: 547-48; 1998: 215 and n. 3).

6. Kraus (1960: 283-96); Otto (1994: 161): 'school literature without any practical concern'. For the argument from a Sargon inscription and a parallel in 2 Chron. 17.7-9, see §5.3.2, *infra*.

7. Notably, the Sumerian sources in Roth (1995: 40-45).

8. Otto (1994: 160-63); *contra* Greengus (1994: 84), who cites (n. 60) with approval the view of Harris (1975: 116-17): 'The Old Babylonian judge was, therefore, not necessarily a learned man—he might even be illiterate—but was one who

(d)   Their purpose was monumental, ideological, a 'royal apologia' (Finkelstein 1961: 103; Fitzpatrick-Mckinley 1999: 143-44; *contra* Otto 1994: 161-62).[9]

In fact, it may be dangerous to adopt a single model in respect of the ancient Near Eastern texts.[10] The debate does not, however, fundamentally alter the importance of Finkelstein's distinction between two literary genres,[11] the one primarily for 'ad hoc' legislation, the other for seemingly enduring rules.

Although our data for comparison with the ancient Near East is relatively sparse, it is possible to discern a similar pattern in the Bible. The story of the *deror* of King Zedekiah in Jeremiah 34 is important in this respect.[12] It tells us of a legislative act of the king, freeing debt-slaves,

---

knew what the community considered just and whose attitudes were respected by it and by the litigants. Thus qualifications for the office of judge would be a position of respect in the community, and wealth, to remove the suspicion of personal interest.'

9.   The apologia function is particularly plausible when the laws are displayed publicly on a stela.

10.   See the discussion of the various arguments by van Houten (1991: 26-30), who concludes (29-30): '...the legal collections so far unearthed in Mesopotamia fall into three distinct literary genres. When the laws are sandwiched between a prologue and epilogue which proclaims the deeds and divine mandate of the king, then the law collection is part of a royal apologia. When the laws are preserved without the prologue and epilogue, when there is evidence that they are being recopied with changes and additions being made, and when they are uncovered in a location at which legal disputes are settled, then the laws are functioning as a set of precedents which are referred to in the process of adjudication. Finally, when the laws are uncovered in scribal schools, and show no signs of revision, then the laws have become canonical, or classical literature—part of the venerated tradition which is passed on unchanged.'

11.   This is not, however, to exclude the possibility of a literary relationship between them, as Finkelstein accepts (see further Weinfeld 1995: Ch. 4; Jackson 1998a: 229-32).

12.   Chavel (1997: 74-75): 'Zedekiah makes no reference to the pentateuchal codes. He simply declares *deror*, similar more to the ancient near Eastern *andurarum* acts than to the law in Leviticus 25.' But the background here may well have been military more than economic: the need to recruit personnel for the army, to defend Jerusalem against the Babylonians (see further §6.2, *infra*). The reference in vv. 13-14 to the Deuteronomic version of the law of release of debt-slaves is regarded by several scholars as secondary (see Lemche 1976: 51-52; Houtman 1997: 100). Chavel (1997) argues that the text reflects editorial activity, in or after

comparable to the ancient Near Eastern *mišarum* or *andurarum;* more-over, the narrative itself states that the necessity for this *deror* (legitimated by a covenant) derived from the fact that the previous 'covenant' provision (described in terms of the law of *ex lege* liberation of the debt-slave, found in both Exod. 21.2 and Deut. 15.12) had not been observed. We do not possess a corpus of records of the Judaean or Israelite courts to compare with the provisions of the 'codes', and it would be unwise to treat the narratives of royal judicial activity as typical in this respect. However, the form in which the biblical 'codes' have been transmitted is such as to distance them even further than the ancient Near Eastern codes from the model of modern legislation. The biblical codes are found within a complex literary and narrative frame-work. To a large extent their character is best understood in terms of the literary and narrative relationships they bear with the surrounding material (cf. Levinson 1991:147; §§7.1, 7.3, 8.3, 10.2, *infra*).

If we reject the legislative model, we have to look for something to put in its place. To do so, I propose the adoption of a methodology derived from communication studies and semiotics. If we take account of what the Bible itself tells us about the communication of laws in ancient Israel, we may make progress in understanding the true nature of the biblical 'law codes'.

The classical model of communication involves the following elements:

(a)   the people between whom messages are exchanged—the sender and receiver;
(b)   the choice of medium or channel of communication (writing, inscription on stone, and now electronic data);
(c)   the 'code' in which the message is expressed (a particular natural language, a particular register of that language, or a non-linguistic code, such as the colour code of traffic lights).

Viewed in this light, modern legislation has the following characteristics. The 'sender' is the 'legislator', the 'receiver' the judge. The medium is the written word (finite, enduring, clearly identifiable). But a particular 'code' is used to decipher the meaning of those words. Modern legislation has a peculiar form of force: every single word in it is regarded as being of 'binding' character; the judge must take into

the time of Nehemiah, seeking to abolish Hebrew debt-slavery altogether.

account all of the canonical words (applying strongly this aspect of the notion of 'literal meaning': §3.2, *supra*), and cannot substitute as his primary source of authority words from any other source. He cannot extrapolate from the words some 'main point'. It is this that generates the technical rules of statutory interpretation, and it is in this sense that the words of a statute constitute a message in a particular (communicational) 'code'.

Once the character of modern legislation is made explicit in this way, we can ask whether it is applicable to the Bible. I maintain that it is not so applicable, at least until we reach the period of Ezra. The modern legislative model breaks down for the following reasons. When communication takes place between the legislator (whether the king or the divinity) and the judges, there is no suggestion that the medium of a written text is used;[13] conversely, when we do have the communication of a written text of laws, the judges are not the receivers. Moreover, there is no evidence that the texts of biblical law enjoy that form of force here described in relation to modern statutes, certainly before the time of Ezra.

The evidence for these claims can be summarized quite briefly. The norms of Deuteronomy and the account of Jehoshaphat's reform in 2 Chronicles present a very significant parallel on one central point, despite other differences in detail. Both of them record that the instructions given to the judges are of an entirely general character—to do justice and avoid partiality/corruption (cf. Deut. 1.7; 16.19-20).

The charge given to the judges in the fortified cities of Judah by king Jehoshaphat is simply this:[14]

---

13. So argued earlier in Jackson (1989:187-88, 192-94; 1990: 244-49; 1995c: 1818-23). Cf. Fitzpatrick-McKinley (1999: Ch. 5 esp. 86-88, 100-105); Watts (1999: 135).

14. Whitelam (1979: 185-88) concludes in favour of its historicity, still the dominant view (cf. Williamson 1982: 288-89; Dillard 1987: 147-48; *aliter*, Levinson 1997: 126 n. 73). For a review of the literature, see Knoppers (1994: 59-60). Against its historicity, Knoppers makes a strong case, based on the literary structure of the story of Jehoshaphat as presented by the Chronicler, the language of the Chronicler and his particular theology. See also my argument on Ezra 7.10 at the end of §6.3, *infra*. This does not, however, exclude (though it reduces the strength of) the case for his use of an earlier tradition. I am less convinced by Knoppers's arguments regarding the relations between the various sources on judicial organization and the history of ideas of the role of divine justice (see further Jackson 1995c: 1806-26). In particular, Knoppers, though rightly stressing the

Jehoshaphat dwelt at Jerusalem; and he went out again among the people, from Beer-sheba to the hill country of Ephraim, and brought them back to the LORD the God of their fathers. He appointed judges in the land in all the fortified cities of Judah,[15] city by city, and said to the judges, 'Consider what you do, for you judge not for man but for the LORD; he is with you in giving judgment. Now then, let the fear of the LORD be upon you; take heed what you do, for there is no perversion of justice with the LORD our God, or partiality, or taking bribes' (2 Chron. 19.4-7).

The claim here is not merely that the adjudication is *on behalf of* God, but that—failing perversity or corruption—adjudication mediates divine decisions: ועמכם בדבר משפט.[16] We may compare the terms in which God promises that he will put words into Moses' mouth:...'and I will be with your mouth and teach you what you shall speak' (ואנכי אהיה עם פיך והוריתיך אשר תדבר, Exod. 4.12).[17]

Very similar is the Deuteronomic conception of the judicial role:

You shall appoint judges and officers in all your towns which the LORD your God gives you, according to your tribes; and they shall judge the people with righteous judgment. You shall not pervert justice; you shall not show partiality; and you shall not take a bribe, for a bribe blinds the eyes of the wise and subverts the cause of the righteous. Justice, and only justice, you shall follow, that you may live and inherit the land which the LORD your God gives you (Deut 16.18-20).

The Deuteronomic version of 'Jethro's' reform again stresses the application of a general conception of justice and the avoidance of

different literary and substantive functions of the actions ascribed to Jehoshaphat in 2 Chron. 17 and 19 (62-63, 67), does not address the question why there should be no reference to a written source of law in the *judicial* reform. If the account reflects (only) the aspirations of the post-exilic polity, this is rather surprising. Nor is it clear, on Knoppers's account, why Jehoshaphat should have been chosen for such treatment.

15. On the jurisdiction of the judges in the fortified cities, see Whitelam (1979: 195-96).

16. Dillard (1987: 149) comes close to this in arguing for a conception of judicial activity as 'the agents of Yahweh who was present at their decisions'. The very name Jehoshaphat makes a stronger claim: 'God judges'. Weinfeld (1977: 66-67) notes (but disputes) the significance attached to this by Wellhausen in arguing that the Chronicler here projects back a reform that dates to the Josianic period.

17. Knoppers (1994: 78-79), however, views 2 Chron. 19.6 as reflecting the Chronicler's particular theology of reciprocity in human–divine relations and compares 2 Chron. 15.2.

corruption. Again, there is no mention of recourse to a written text, but Jehoshaphat's invocation of divine guidance (ועמכם בדבר משפט) may also be implied in Deut. 1.16-17:

> And I charged your judges at that time, 'Hear the cases between your brethren, and judge righteously between a man and his brother or the alien that is with him. You shall not be partial in judgment; you shall hear the small and the great alike; you shall not be afraid of the face of man, for the judgment is God's [כי המשפט לאלהים הוא[18]]; and the case that is too hard for you, you shall bring to me, and I will hear it.'

The narrative of Jehoshaphat does indicate a two-tier judicial system. Members of the educated elite are appointed to be judges in Jerusalem, 'to give judgment for the LORD and to decide disputed cases' (2 Chron. 19.8).[19] But even here, no mention of a written source of law is found, and the charge to the judges, once again, is predominantly general:

> Thus you shall do in the fear of the LORD, in faithfulness, and with your whole heart: whenever a case comes to you from your brethren who live in their cities, concerning bloodshed, law or commandment, statutes or ordinances, then you shall instruct them,[20] that they may not incur guilt before the LORD and wrath may not come upon you and your brethren. Thus you shall do, and you will not incur guilt. And behold, Amariah the chief priest is over you in all matters of the LORD; and Zebadiah the son of Ishmael, the governor of the house of Judah, in all the king's matters; and the Levites will serve you as officers. Deal courageously, and may the LORD be with the upright! (2 Chron. 19.9-11).

There is, indeed, a tension in this passage, which appears to speak of sources of law ('statutes or regulations'), while at the same time insisting upon the authority of specified officials. In fact, the phrase *lechukim ulemishpatim* can hardly refer to 'sources of law' in the modern sense; the whole context, commencing with *dam ledam*, indicates that the meaning to be assigned to these words is in terms in the type of subject

18. Weinfeld (1977: 67 n. 10) compares this rather with כי לא לאדם תשפטו כי ליהוה in 2 Chron. 19.6.

19. RSV: the NEB has here 'to administer the law of the LORD and to arbitrate in law suits', offering a far more specific interpretation of the judicial function than the Hebrew (למשפט יהוה ולריב) justifies. On the textual difficulty here, see Whitelam (1979: 199-200).

20. Prefer here NEB 'you shall warn them' (והזהרתם אתם). Knoppers (1994: 76-77) compares Exod. 18.20, noting that these are the only two texts where *zahar* is found with a double accusative.

matter, rather than the source of rules for adjudication. It is in just this sense that *mishpat* is used in the introduction to the 'Covenant Code' (Exod. 21.1). It is very likely, moreover, that the reference to 'bloodshed, law or commandment, statutes or ordinances' reflects an attempt by the Chronicler to harmonize this model with later conceptions.

On the other hand, both Deuteronomy and 2 Chronicles also provide explicit information about the use of a written text of law. In Deuteronomy, this is a book (*sefer*) that is to be prepared for the use of the king himself, and through the study of which the king shall learn to be god-fearing and not rise above his station—a combination of positive and negative generalities comparable, in this respect, to the charge to the judges (Deut. 17.19-20). In 2 Chronicles the king orders his officers to take copies of the book around the country, and to teach it to the people. In both sources, written law has a didactic function (see further §5.3.2, *infra*); it is not the basis of adjudication.[21]

As for the force of the words of biblical law—the 'code' in which they are expressed—we may infer from the evidence of the internal revision of a number of laws within the biblical period (notably the laws of slavery) that their words were not sacrosanct (even though they could be used as the basis of a ritual reading). It is only when we reach Ezra that the notions of 'text' and 'interpretation' are separated.

5.2 *The Use of Inscriptions*

If biblical law fails to conform to the communicational model of modern legislation, we have to look for alternatives. A good starting point is to consider the functions of different media that the Bible records as having been used to communicate rules of law, and to consider for what purposes they were used. Two such media are found: inscriptions and the '*sefer*'. In both cases, we find them used for a variety of functions. Nevertheless, these two media are distinguishable one from the other in terms of two general characteristics. The inscription provides the opportunity for greater permanence of a record than does the *sefer*, and the inscription also has a spatial dimension that the *sefer* lacks: the inscription is normally placed at some particular site, while the *sefer* is, of its character, moveable. However, both of these differences are

---

21. Knoppers (1994: 62-63, 67) rightly insists on not conflating the two separate notices about the teaching activity (2 Chron. 17) and the judicial reform (2 Chron. 19).

reduced once we contemplate the deposit of a *sefer* in an archive.[22]

Sometimes, stone monuments were erected in an *uninscribed* form, relying upon folk memory to identify the event whose place they marked or the significance of their erection. For example, in Gen. 31.43-54 a pillar is erected to witness the covenant *(berit,* v. 44) between Jacob and Laban, and its significance is marked by giving the site a name that recalls that function; the monument also serves a function, according to the text as transmitted, analogous to that of a boundary stone:

> And Jacob said to his kinsmen, 'Gather stones' *(avanim),* and they took stones, and made a heap *(gal)...* Laban said, 'This heap is a witness *(ed)* between you and me today,' Therefore he named it Galeed... Then Laban said to Jacob, 'See this heap and the pillar *(matsevah)* which I have set between you and me. This heap is a witness, and the pillar is a witness, that I will not pass over this heap to you, and you will not pass over this heap and this pillar to me, for harm. The God of Abraham and the God of Nahor, the God of their father, judge between us.'[23]

There is no suggestion in the narrative that the stone was inscribed. The covenant solemnities accompanying its erection—the mutual declarations, the sacrifice and the joint feast—were sufficient to fix its significance.

This feature of the covenantal model, the use of uninscribed stones to mark the place and serve as a monument to the event, occurs also in the Sinaitic narrative, in close proximity to—but distinct from—the writing down of the *sefer haberit* :

> And Moses wrote all the words of the LORD. And he rose early in the morning, and built an altar at the foot of the mountain, and twelve pillars *(matsevah),* according to the twelve tribes of Israel (Exod. 24.4).

Any possibility of interpreting this passage as indicating that the divine message was written *on* the pillars is excluded by Exod. 24.7, which tells us that Moses 'took' *(vayikach)* the *sefer haberit*, which he then read to the people, thus implying that the message was written on something moveable—here, indeed, described as a *sefer*.[24] Moreover,

22. Or, indeed, of an inscription, if of a suitable size: the deposit of the *luchot* in the ark, whatever its other functions, may be viewed in this sense.

23. The inconsistent terminology of both *gal* and *matsevah* may reflect editorial activity in the wake of the ban on the *matsevah*: Deut. 16.22; Childs (1974: 498) notes that this accounts also for the replacement of *matsevah* by *avanim* in LXX and the Samaritan version.

24. On this passage, see further §5.3.3, *infra*. There is no reason to infer that the

matsevah is one of the terms used for the stone monument in the account of the Covenant between Jacob and Laban, where there is no suggestion that the terms were reduced to writing. We find a similar combination in Joshua's covenant ceremony at Shechem:[25]

> So Joshua made a covenant with the people that day, and made statutes and ordinances for them at Shechem. And Joshua wrote these words in the book of the law of God; and he took a great stone, and set it up there under the oak in the sanctuary of the LORD. And Joshua said to all the people, 'Behold, this stone shall be a witness against us; for it has heard all the words of the LORD which he spoke to us; therefore it shall be a witness against you, lest you deal falsely with your God' (Josh. 24.25-27).

It is not unreasonable to suggest that, historically, the use of the uninscribed stone as a monument preceded the use of the inscribed form.[26] As for the latter, the most obvious function of inscribed stone is to mark the boundary of a territory (private or public), and to seek to deter potential violators of that boundary through the use of curses, as in the *kudurru* inscriptions of the ancient Near East (see King 1912; Steinmetzer 1922). It was but one step beyond this to add the record of an historical event that provided the source of title to that property. The victory stela has this dual function. On the one hand, it celebrates the prowess of the victor, or of the god who sponsored him. On the other hand, it marks the place of victory, thus of conquest and acquisition. But both the boundary function and the memorial function could be served by *uninscribed* stones. We have seen an example of the former in the story of Jacob and Laban. Joshua's monument at Gilgal exhibits the latter function too:

pillars are the supports of the altar, as is implied, e.g., by Childs (1974: 505).

25. On this and other covenant ceremonies, see the narrative analysis in Chapter 9, *infra*.

26. Cf. Weinfeld (1972: 165-66), on the relations between Exod. 24.3-8, Josh. 4, 8 and 24, and Deut. 27.1-8. He argues that the author of Deuteronomy, which expressly prohibits the erection of pillars (Deut. 16.22, *matsevah*, cx. Exod. 24.4; Gen. 31.51), 'converted the ritual ceremony into an educational one... [he] transformed the stones [in Deut. 27] into a law document...[and thus] divested the ceremony of its original character... In the Sinai and Shechem ceremonies the stones and the document play two distinct roles: the stones stand as mute testimony to the event, whereas the *sefer* contained the stipulations of the covenant.'

> When all the nation had finished passing over the Jordan, the LORD said
> to Joshua, 'Take twelve men from the people, from each tribe a man, and
> command them, "Take twelve stones from here out of the midst of the
> Jordan, from the very place where the priests' feet stood, and carry them
> over with you, and lay them down in the place where you lodge tonight."'
> Then Joshua called the twelve men from the people of Israel, whom he
> had appointed, a man from each tribe; and Joshua said to them, 'Pass on
> before the ark of the LORD your God into the midst of the Jordan, and
> take up each of you a stone upon his shoulder, according to the number
> of the tribes of the people of Israel, that this may be a sign among you,
> when your children ask in time to come, "What do those stones mean to
> you?" Then you shall tell them that the waters of the Jordan were cut off
> before the ark of the covenant of the LORD; when it passed over the
> Jordan, the waters of the Jordan were cut off. So these stones shall be to
> the people of Israel a memorial for ever' (Josh. 4.1-7).[27]

But folk memory was not always relied upon in order to fix the
meaning of a monument. Both the boundary stone and the victory stela
(genres that overlap on some occasions) came to be inscribed. The
famous Moabite stone, erected by Mesha around 840 BCE to record his
victory over King Omri of Israel,[28] provides archaeological confirmation of a genre that we find mentioned also in the Bible. Immediately
after the victory over the Amalekites, God instructs Moses to record in
writing (but here in a *sefer,* for the benefit of Joshua) that 'I will blot
out the memory of Amalek' (Exod. 17.14). This was designed to signify
the permanence of the victory, just as Mesha proclaimed that 'Israel
hath perished for ever.'

These functions of the inscription seem to precede the recording of
law on stone. However, it is easy to understand the development. There
is a tradition of the victorious lawgiver, extending from Hammurabi[29]

27. The chapter continues with what may well originally have been independent
accounts of the same incident. But in all of them the *avanim* are uninscribed, even
though their function is that of commemoration of the event.

28. *ANET* (3rd edn, 1969: 320-21). Niditch (1997: 55) notes in this context that
no comparable stone stelae have been found in ancient Hebrew script, in the sense
of publicly displayed monuments with writing upon them to indicate what is being
monumentalized.

29. E.g. the Prologue to the Code of Hammurabi: 'I am Hammurabi, the shep-
herd...the capable king, the restorer of the city Eridu...the onslaught of the four
regions of the world...the mighty one...the warrior, who shows mercy to the city of
Larsa...dragon among kings...the enemy-ensnaring throw-net...the fierce wild bull
who gores the enemy... The promulgator of justice...wise one, the organizer, he

through Justinian[30] to Napoleon,[31] which appears quite explicitly in the official documentation. Culturally and psychologically, the connection is easy to understand: the military victor who has shed blood (albeit in what he may claim to be a good cause) nevertheless has a need to redress the balance by promoting peace, and the ideological form of the promotion of peace is the establishment of law and order. I suggest that this, as much as any purely literary connection, explains the form of the Decalogue, which commences with an allusion to a victory: 'I am the LORD your God, who brought you out of the land of Egypt' (Exod. 20.2) and then continues with prescriptions.

I do not use the term 'ideological' loosely. The inscription of laws on stone cannot serve a primarily pragmatic function.[32] This is not a form for easy reference,[33] certainly when we conceive of substantial monu-

who has mastered all wisdom, leader of kings, who subdues the settlements along the Euphrates River by the oracular command of the god Dagan... When the god Marduk commanded me to provide just ways for the people of the land (in order to attain) appropriate behavior, I established truth and justice as the declaration of the land, I enhanced the well-being of the people' (Roth 1995: 76-81; cf. the Epilogue at p. 133).

30. The Prooemium to the Institutes of Justinian commences with the words *Imperatoriam maiestatem non solum armis decoratam, sed etiam legibus oportet esse armatam, ut utrumque tempus et bellorum et pacis recte possit gubernari et princeps Romanus victor existat non solum in hostilibus proeliis, sed etiam per legitimos tramites calumniantium iniquitates expellens, et fiat tam iuris religiosissimus quam victis hostibus triumphator.* ('Imperial majesty should be not only embellished with arms but also fortified by laws so that the times of both war and peace can be rightly regulated and the Roman Emperor not only emerge victorious in war with the enemy but also, extirpating the iniquities of wrongdoers through the machinery of justice, prove as solicitous of the law as he is triumphant over defeated foes' (Thomas 1975: 1).

31. As in various constitutional documents of the Napoleonic era, e.g. *Sénatus-consulte du 14 thermidor an X (1 août 1802)*, 'reconnaissance nationale envers le héros vainqueur et pacificateur' (nominating Napoleon as *Consul à vie*), and see the *Charte constitutionnelle du 4 juin 1814*: 'La divine Providence, en nous rappelant dans nos Etats après une longue absence, nous a imposé de grandes obligations. La paix était le premier besoin de nos sujets.' (Duverger 1971: 119, 121).

32. Cf. Niditch (1997: 43, 86-88) on the symbolic, indeed iconic, functions of monuments.

33. Even the epilogue to the Code of Hammurabi, in proclaiming: 'Let any wronged man who has a lawsuit come before the statue of me, the king of justice, and let him have my inscribed stela read aloud to him, thus may he hear my precious pronouncements and let my stela reveal the lawsuit for him; may he examine

ments in large and busy places. Imagine being a Babylonian judge and having to rely upon the Code of Hammurabi as recorded on the monument now preserved in the Louvre and erected in a public square.

The inscription of laws on stone serves a primarily monumental purpose, as has been recognised in the case of the Laws of Hammurabi. Within the Bible, there are indications that the length of legal texts so inscribed came to increase. The original 'tablets of stone' inscribed by God to Moses (carrying a text, incidentally, that is quite incapable of being applied as law by judges[34]) was of relatively short compass, and Deuteronomy seems to go out of its way to stress that it was only this text that was so inscribed (Deut. 5.22). But by the time we reach Moses' last instructions, and their fulfilment after the crossing of the Jordan, we find that the length and scope of the text inscribed on stone monuments appears to have increased very considerably. Moses commands that when the people have crossed the Jordan, they shall set up 'great stones' (*avanim gedolot*) and 'inscribe on them all the words of this law' (*et kol divre hatorah hazot*), placing them as a monument on Mount Ebal (Deut. 27.2-4). The performance of this obligation is recorded in Josh. 8.32: 'There in the presence of the Israelites he [Joshua] engraved on blocks of stone (*al ha'avanim*) a copy of the law of Moses (*mishneh torat mosheh*).'[35] By this stage, the Israelite tradition appears to have been influenced by the model of the Mesopotamian legal codes, as exemplified by the Code of Hammurabi (which itself was widely copied).[36]

It is noticeable, however, that in the linked narratives of Moses' last days and of Joshua's fulfilment of Moses' instructions, we hear not only of inscribed stones but also of the writing of the law in a *sefer*: Moses

his case, may he calm his (troubled) heart...' (Roth 1995: 134) assumes that the prospective litigant is *not* expected to be able to read the writing himself.

34. Not even Phillips (1970) claims this. For him, the Decalogue was the basis of Israel's criminal law in the sense that it inspired the promulgation of specific criminal offences.

35. The reference is often taken to be to Deuteronomy itself (e.g. Watts 1999: 17-18: 'the mention of blessings and curses indicates that the writer was thinking of the book in more or less its present form'), though this would involve the inscription and then proclamation of a text substantially longer than Hammurabi, itself the most substantial of the ancient Near Eastern 'law codes'.

36. See also Weinfeld (1972: 148-50), arguing that although they overlap, the pattern of the law-code may be preferable to that of the treaty in the explanation of Deuteronomy.

wrote down 'these laws in a book' (Deut. 31.24) for deposit in the Ark of the Covenant (cf. Deut. 31.9), and commanded that there be a septennial reading at the Feast of Tabernacles 'of this law publicly in the hearing of all Israel' (Deut. 31.11).[37] The clear implication here is that it is the text written by Moses in the *sefer* that is to be read out, not the text to be inscribed on the stones. When we reach Joshua's ceremonial at Ebal, the inscribing of the law on stone is followed by a public reading:

> Then Joshua built an altar in Mount Ebal to the LORD, the God of Israel, as Moses the servant of the LORD had commanded the people of Israel, as it is written in the book of the law of Moses, 'an altar of unhewn stones, upon which no man has lifted an iron tool';[38] and they offered on it burnt offerings to the LORD, and sacrificed peace offerings. And there, in the presence of the people of Israel, he wrote upon the stones a copy of the law of Moses, which he had written. And all Israel, sojourner as well as homeborn, with their elders and officers and their judges, stood on opposite sides of the ark before the Levitical priests who carried the ark of the covenant of the LORD, half of them in front of Mount Gerizim and half of them in front of Mount Ebal, as Moses the servant of the LORD had commanded at the first, that they should bless the people of Israel. And afterward he read all the words of the law, the blessing and the curse, according to all that is written in the book of the law. There was not a word of all that Moses commanded which Joshua did not read before all the assembly of Israel, and the women, and the little ones, and the sojourners who lived among them (Josh. 8.30-35).

The phrase ככל הכתוב בספר התורה in v. 34 does not, however, mean necessarily that the text read out was that in the *sefer* (rather than that inscribed on the stones);[39] what may be indicated was that the whole ceremony was carried out in accordance with the instructions given by Moses and recorded in Deuteronomy (cf. v. 31). Certainly, we may assume that a *sefer* with that text was understood to have been available

---

37. On these traditions, see further §9.4 *infra*.

38. Referring to Deut. 27.5-6. Watts (1999: 17) describes this as 'an explicit citation'. It is not, however, a verbatim quotation: the order of phrases has been altered and the second person address has been replaced by a third person formulation. There are also indications elsewhere that 'quotation' was not originally conceived to require verbatim repetition of the original words. See, e.g., the account in Jer. 34 of the slave release law which the Israelites are said to have ignored, and §8.1, *infra*.

39. Contrary to the view I expressed in Jackson (1989: 192).

to Joshua (Deuteronomy 31, above), and to have provided the text
copied on the *avanim*. This, indeed, may be indicated directly, if we
understand v. 32, ויכתב שם על האבנים את משנה תורת משה
אשר כתב לפני בני ישראל to mean: he wrote upon the stones a copy
of the law of Moses, which he (Moses) had written before the children
of Israel'.[40] The narrative thus somewhat uneasily combines the
monumental function of law inscribed on stone with the ritual function
of reading from a holy book—holy in that it had been written by Moses,
at the command (perhaps, dictation) of God. This might be viewed as
reiterating the combination of immoveable monument and portable text
at Sinai itself,[41] though with the difference that the pillars in Exod. 24.4
were uninscribed.

The tradition of the stone tablets, the *luchot*, disturbs any strict correlation between inscriptions as immoveable, the *sefer* as moveable.[42]
Comparison may be made here not with the law code, erected for public
display, but the inscribed contract tablet, a 'private law' document
retained by the parties as evidence of their mutual legal obligations.
That this was indeed the model informing the biblical account is sup-
portable by two aspects of the narrative. First, the very breaking of the
tablets by Moses on being confronted by Israel's disloyalty is commonly seen as reflecting the Babylonian practice of breaking the tablets

40. See further §5.3.2, *infra*. The RSV, quoted above, fails to render לפני
בני ישראל. There is no textual doubt about the phrase, though the preceding
אשר כתב is omitted in LXX Codex Vaticanus. The reference presumably is to the
text Moses wrote according to Deut. 31.9, 24.

41. Exod. 24.4-8; see further §5.3.3, and §9.3-4 for thematic reiteration in the
Moses–Joshua cycle.

42. Moreover, it is not only the *luchot* that were to be lodged in the 'Ark of the
Covenant' (so described in both Deut. 31.9 and Josh. 8.33); the *sefer* that Moses
wrote down (Deut. 31.24) was similarly to be deposited in it, or at least alongside
(*mitsad*) it: Deut. 31.26. The centrality (literally) of the *aron* in the Mount Ebal ceremony indicates that the ark was regarded not as a mere means of transport but as
having a sanctity of its own. Whether Deuteronomy is thus seeking to place this
book on the same level as the second set of *luchot* (themselves written by Moses, at
God's command: Exod. 34.27-28—despite the promise in Exod. 34.1 that God
would personally reinscribe the tablets, making them comparable to the first set,
written with the 'finger' of God: Exod. 31.18) need not be answered in this context.
Nor need the tensions in the accounts of the content of the *luchot* (*hatorah
vehamitsvah*, Exod. 24.12, anticipating the first set; *aseret hadevarim*, Exod. 34.28,
of the content of the second set).

when a contract is discharged (here, by breach).[43] Secondly, the committal of Moses' *sefer* to the Levites for preservation in (or along with) the ark is also expressed in terms of evidence of an obligation, to be preserved in anticipation of its possible breach:

> Moses commanded the Levites who carried the ark of the covenant of the LORD, 'Take this book of the law, and put it by the side of the ark of the covenant of the LORD your God, that it may be there for a witness against you. For I know how rebellious and stubborn you are; behold, while I am yet alive with you, today you have been rebellious against the LORD...' (Deut. 31.25-27).

5.3 *The Uses of the Sefer*

There has been debate as to whether the *sefer* uses the medium of hide or papyrus (Haran 1982: 161-73), but this distinction is relatively unimportant for present purposes. In either case, the medium is less permanent than stone, but more portable. As a result, the *sefer* proved more flexible than the stone inscription, serving a wider variety of purposes. Most of those purposes, however, prove to have associations with the royal court. Here, too, the historical record seems to suggest a growth in the length of the text that might be committed to this medium. We start with the *mishpat hamelukhah* of Samuel, which—from the analogy of the corresponding material in Deuteronomy—seems not to have exceeded a few verses. Ultimately, we come to the text in the book of Ezra, which took from dawn until midday to read out—albeit with a (contemporaneous?) interpretation.[44]

We can classify the uses of the *sefer* under three headings: archival, didactic and ritual.[45]

---

43. See §9.3 n. 46, *infra*, though I argue there that the narrator does not intend to convey the view that the covenant was indeed thus discharged by breach.

44. Between such extremes we may locate the 'intermediate' documents from which the existing biblical collections may, more speculatively, have been compiled. For a preliminary view of this issue in relation to the Covenant Code, see Jackson (1995c: 1778-83, 1801-804).

45. Weinfeld (1972: 164) finds the archival role of writing already in the 'early sources' (Exod. 17.14; 24.4, 7; 34.27-28; Josh. 24.25-26; 1 Sam. 10.25) whereas 'the use of writing for didactic purposes is first met within the book of Deuteronomy', which he identifies with the Hezekian period and later: Deut. 4.7-8, 11 (the *mezuzot*); 17.18-19; 27.2-3; 31.9.

5.3.1 *Archival Uses*

The earliest period, after that narrated in the Pentateuch, to which is ascribed the writing of law in a *sefer,* is that of Samuel (1 Sam. 10.25), where he writes a *mishpat hamelukhah,* and—significantly—deposits it in a sanctuary.[46]

That pattern, of a prophet depositing a particular text in a (now permanent) sanctuary, later the Temple,[47] is repeated in Jeremiah 36. In the fourth year of Jehoiakim's reign, Jeremiah is commanded by God to 'take a scroll'—*megilat sefer*—and write down all his earlier prophecies. Jeremiah cannot do so himself; he seeks the assistance of a court-scribe, Baruch. Baruch is also asked to read the scroll publicly at the Temple. He does so, apparently with the cooperation of the Temple officials, since he reads it 'from the room of Gemariah son of Shaphan the *sofer'*. Gemariah's son Micaiah hears the prophecy, and communicates it to the other officials; he is said to repeat all of its words from memory of what was read out (v. 12). The officials—the *sarim*—thereupon call for Baruch and have him read the scroll to them. They are impressed and decide to inform the king. At the same time, they advise both Jeremiah and Baruch to go into hiding; the scroll is dangerous, the king's reactions may be unpredictable. Nevertheless, they deposit the scroll in the room of the scribe Elishama. Jeremiah's scroll has thus been 'planted'—we might say—in the Temple, with the connivance of the Temple officials. I put the matter in this manner by way of allusion to Blenkinsopp's suggestion (1983: 96; 1995: 113)[48] that the scroll found in the time of Josiah, just a few years earlier, may itself have been 'planted' by the reform party. In fact, Jeremiah has given us a

---

46. On its possible content (1 Sam. 8.9-18), see further §6.2, *infra.*

47. Niditch (1997: 63) claims that there is no archaeologically recoverable evidence of the existence of libraries, or, for that matter, specific reference to them in the Hebrew Bible. But the absence of the institution of a 'library', used systematically for the preservation of documents, does not mean that the archival function was not performed at all. The sources noted in this subsection indicate, at the very least, the ad hoc use of the sanctuary for this purpose. Niditch is hesitant also about accepting the archival function, in the modern sense, in the ancient Near East (65-66), noting studies by oralists in other cultures that suggest that 'archives in ancient cultures tend to serve iconic and memorial purposes rather than modern style record-keeping functions' (at 7).

48. Blenkinsopp raises this only as a possibility, claiming that the questions of historicity regarding this book 'can no longer be unanswered with certainty'. He makes no reference to Jer. 36 in this context.

vivid description of how this might be done. The king then agrees to hear the scroll, but after listening to 'three or four columns' (*delatot*), he cuts the proceedings short,[49] and throws the whole scroll onto the fire.

We may leave the story there. It is, however, worth noting that here, just as in the case of Samuel's deposit of a scroll in the sanctuary, the content of the document is very much concerned with affairs of state: the future of the kingdom and the fate of the king, in the light of God's anger. A point that the inscription and the *sefer* have in common is the fact that, in origin, both appear closely associated with supreme political power.

In this respect, the finding of the *sefer hatorah*[50] in the reign of Josiah (2 Kgs. 22.3-23) perhaps takes us a step further. Though we are not told directly the content of the book, the religious reforms undertaken by Josiah in the wake of its discovery are presented as prompted by its terms. Though this reform is most famously associated with the 'centralization of the cult', a significant part of it is concerned specifically with the practices of the Jerusalem Temple itself, and thus concern the king directly.[51] Thus Josiah orders that all the vessels made for Baal, Asherah, and 'all the host of heaven' be removed from the Temple (23.4); that the Asherah also be removed (23.6); that the premises of the male cult prostitutes, located within the Temple, be destroyed (23.7); that the horses dedicated to the sun be removed from the Temple entrance (23.11); and that the altars erected by Manasseh in the two Temple courts be dismantled and destroyed (23.12).

The archiving practices involving prophet, text and Temple, seen in the narratives of Samuel and Jeremiah, recur also here, in a slightly different form. The ad hoc character of the deposit in the Temple is indicated by the fact that the document is discovered, apparently, in the course of a *financial* audit.[52] Here, the role of the prophet is post hoc: it

---

49. Quite literally: he cut them off 'with a penknife', v. 23.

50. An expression taken to be characteristically Deuteronomic (Widengren 1957: 2 n. 1); see also Josh. 1.8, in §5.3.2, *infra*.

51. See further §6.2, on the relationship of this account to coronation practices and the king's role in the covenant.

52. Shaphan is sent to Hilkiah (the High Priest) at the Temple, to ask him to 'reckon the amount of the money which has been brought into the house of the LORD, which the keepers of the threshold have collected from the people' (2 Kgs 22.4), in order to pay the repairers. Cf. Niditch (1997: 102-104), doubting the

is not known who deposited the *sefer,* but a prophetess, Huldah, is
asked to verify the status of the book, by consulting God, לדרש
את יהוה (2 Kgs 22.13, 18). The verb *darash* is also used elsewhere of
divine consultation on an individual, specific problem, through a
prophet or oracle (Jackson 1972: 24)— for example, in the procedure
used by Moses to adjudicate individual Israelite disputes before he
accepted Jethro's advice that he had better things to do with his time
(Exod. 18.15) and the consultation by Saul of a medium (1 Chron.
10.13-14). In the Josiah story, the effect of such a consultation in
respect of the status of a *sefer* is to claim divine revelation not merely in
respect of the solution of an individual problem, but for the promulgation of an entire corpus of rules.[53]

5.3.2 *Didactic Uses*
Even when we turn to the didactic uses of the *sefer,* this association
with the king retains its prominence. In Deut. 17.14-20,[54] we find (a
version of) the law of the king. It concludes:

> And when he sits on the throne of his kingdom, he shall write for himself
> in a book a copy of this law (*mishneh hatorah hazot*), from that which is
> in the charge of the Levitical priests; and it shall be with him, and he
> shall read in it all the days of his life,[55] that he may learn to fear the
> LORD his God, by keeping all the words of this law and these statutes,

assumption that the book was found in a Temple 'library'.

53. Hezekiah's reform represents an intermediate stage. Here, the focus is entirely on purification of the Temple, the only authoritative source for the ceremonies
being prophetic: the Levitical musicians are posted 'according to the rule prescribed
by David, by Gad the king's seer and Nathan the prophet; for this rule had come
from the LORD through his prophets' (כי ביד יהוה המצוה ביד...במצות דויד
נביאיו (2 Chron. 29.25). Later, when the Temple is reopened to the public, the king
sends out written instructions bidding the people (including Ephraim and
Manasseh) to come and fulfil the passover. When they do, we are told: 'Never
before had so many kept it as it had been written (*kakatuv*)': 2 Chron. 30.5; cf.
Josiah's command (2 Kgs 23.21): 'Keep the passover to the LORD your God, as it is
written in this book of the covenant'; but see also 'Passover letter' from Elephantine (n. 84, *infra*). However, there is no indication in the accounts of the Hezekian
reform of the adoption of a *sefer,* or of the following of written rules other than this.
54. Widengren (1957: 23) compares God's promise to teach David's descendants in Pss. 132.11-12, taking the *edot* there to be written texts entrusted to the
king at his coronation (see further §6.2, *infra*).
55. Greenberg (1995: 18) stresses the 'completely innovative' character of this
emphasis on the lifelong task of royal education.

and doing them; that his heart may not be lifted up above his brethren,
and that he may not turn aside from the commandment, either to the right
hand or to the left; so that he may continue long in his kingdom, he and
his children, in Israel (vv. 18-20).

The identity of the text thus to be written and used is not made explicit.
The expression *mishneh torah* is less likely to be a title for the book as
a whole than a reference to the fact that a 'copy' is being made (as
translations commonly render it): the source of the copy is, indeed,
mentioned—the text in the charge of the Levites.[56] Comparison may be
made with Josh. 8.32, 'He wrote upon the stones a copy of the law of
Moses, which he [Moses] had written before the children of Israel',
where *mishneh* again occurs together with reference to the written
source from which the copy is made (§5.2, *supra*). Deut. 17.18 does
imply that the text is part (*milifne*) of Deuteronomy (*hatorah hazot*):
both the immediate context—imposing restraints on the exercise of
royal power[57]—and the account of Samuel's having written down the
mishpat hamelukhah in a *sefer* and having 'laid it up before the LORD'
(1 Sam. 10.25) suggest that the text here is 'constitutional', concerned
with the royal power itself (cf. Whitelam 1979: 211).[58] We do, indeed,
have a detailed account of what Samuel conceived the *mishpat
hamelekh* to be (1 Sam. 8: 10-18; see §6.2, *supra*). It is not inconceivable that, even within the conception of a *mishneh,* Deut. 17.16-17
might have been supplemented from such a source (see n. 38, *supra*).

Clearly associated with this passage is the charge by God to Joshua at
the opening of that book (Josh. 1.1-8), after the death of Moses, which
includes:

> Only be strong and very courageous, being careful to do according to all
> the law which Moses my servant commanded you; turn not from it to the
> right hand or to the left, that you may have good success wherever you

56. Despite the rendering of מלפני הכהנים הלוים by NEB as 'at the dictation of
the levitical priests'. For the role of the levites as guardians of the written text, cf.
Deut. 31.25-26.

57. Deut. 17.16-17: 'Only he must not multiply horses for himself, or cause the
people to return to Egypt in order to multiply horses, since the LORD has said to
you, "You shall never return that way again." And he shall not multiply wives for
himself, lest his heart turn away; nor shall he greatly multiply for himself silver and
gold.'

58. Niditch (1997:100-102) argues that it is likely to have been a short text,
either the laws pertaining to kingship or the ten Commandments (comparing the
terminology in Deut. 4.44-45).

go. This book of the law [*sefer hatorah hazeh*, see n. 50, *supra*] shall not depart out of your mouth, but you shall meditate on it day and night, that you may be careful to do according to all that is written in it; for then you shall make your way prosperous, and then you shall have good success (vv. 7-8).

Here again, the precise referent of *hatorah hazeh* is unclear. The immediate context is the charge to Joshua to carry out the prescribed conquest of the land. The tradition, however, is clearly related to that of Deuteronomy 17 in that the leader is conceived to be in possession of a written *sefer,* and that *sefer* is presented as a source of meditation/ learning that affects the character in such a way as to lead to success. Though the term *chakhmah* is not used in either source,[59] there is a clear association here with wisdom thinking. Whether the purpose is ultimately juridical is less clear.[60] In the associated sources concerning Jehoshaphat, the judicial and didactic functions are kept quite separate.

The use of a *sefer* in the possession of the king for the purposes of instruction is extended to a popular audience in the account of the 'royal commission'[61] sent out by King Jehoshaphat:[62]

59. Whybray (1974: Ch. 4) considered the influence of the 'intellectual tradition' of the wisdom literature on other parts of Old Testament literature, opting for the presence of the terminology of 'wise' (*chakham*) as his definitional criterion of wisdom. At 113-116, he is critical of the approach of Gerstenberger, as not having dealt adequately with the fact that in the laws the theme of the *chakham* is totally ignored. In my view, Whybray placed too much emphasis on this single criterion, particularly since the term *chakham* is an attribute of a person, while *chokhmah* is an explicit (later) characterization of the possible source of laws; neither term is likely to figure within the content of the laws themselves.

60. Watts (1999: 21) observes of the instruction to study the law daily in both Deut. 17.19 and Josh. 1.8: 'Their positions as leaders (and judges?) of the people suggest that the kind of study intended here is juridical in nature'. He supports this (n.14) with the observation that 2 Kgs. 11.12 suggests that royal authority was represented by possession of the *edut*, which in some texts refers to tablets of law. *Aliter,* Levinson (1997: 138-43), arguing that the omission from Deut. 17.14-20 of any mention of judicial functions, immediately after a passage concerning a Jerusalem-based judicial hierarchy (Deut. 17.8-13), represents a deliberate attempt to restrict royal judicial activity.

61. Watts's phrase: see Watts (1999: 21) for a summary of views on the content/identity of the book here used and the historicity of the account.

62. Viewed as post-exilic and probably unhistorical by Greenberg (1995: 18, 23 n.13); cf. Knoppers (1994: 64-65), relating it to the Chronicler's particular (idealistic) royal ideology. But see also Widengren (1957: 16-17). Dillard (1987:

In the third year of his reign he sent his princes (*sarav*), Ben-hail,
Obadiah, Zechariah, Nethanel, and Micaiah, to teach in the cities of
Judah; and with them the Levites, Shemaiah, Nethaniah, Zebadiah,
Asahel, Shemiramoth, Jehonathan, Adonijah, Tobijah, arfd Tobadonijah;
and with these Levites, the priests Elishama and Jehoram. And they
taught (*vayelamdu*) in Judah, having the book of the law[63] of the LORD
with them (ועמהם ספר תורת יהוה); they went about through all the
cities of Judah and taught among the people (2 Chron. 17.7-9).

As noted earlier, these passages are kept separate from those relating to
the instruction of judges (cf. Knoppers 1994, n. 21, *supra*), which contain no reference to a *sefer*, but require the judges only to act justly and
avoid corruption. But Jehoshaphat's didactic activity appears not to
have been unique: Weinfeld has pointed to a parallel in the Sargon
inscriptions from Assyria: 'to teach them (the natives of Assyria) the
teaching of fearing God and king, I sent officers and overseers' (1972:
163 and n. 3).[64] The implication of 2 Chron. 17.7-9 is that the teaching
was by oral proclamation. The officers and Levites did not leave the
text with their audience for private (or organized, local) study. Given
the low incidence of literacy,[65] this is how things had to be. There is

134) sees it as reflecting Deut. 17.18-20, and notes that the third year of
Jehoshaphat's reign may actually have been the first year of his sole reign, following a presumed coregency necessitated by his father's debilitating disease (2 Chron.
16.12).

63. For views on the identification of the book, see Whitelam (1979: 212), who
argues that it was a book concerned with the cultic measures the king sought to
implement (v.4; Whitelam 1979: 191-92), and is not necessarily of royal origin.

64. Greenberg (1995: 24) is critical of Welch (1990: 118), for following
Weinfeld in seeing here a parallel objective in educating the people about law, and
cites Paul (1969: 74-75) in regarding Sargon's measure as one of 'forced
Assyrianization and religious homogenization' being directed towards foreign
settlers in the newly founded capital. In fact, the point of Paul's observations is to
draw attention to the parallel between the Sargon inscription and the biblical
account (2 Kgs 17.24-28) of the same policy ascribed to Sargon in respect of those
whom he had himself settled in Samaria, namely to familiarize them with the *native*
cult. If anything, this makes more credible the historicity of Jehoshaphat's didactic
activity. We are not told the purpose of Jehoshaphat's educational mission, but a
difference in purpose from that of Sargon would not necessarily destroy the argument for a comparable institution of educational activity sponsored by the king in
the two societies, or, indeed, the possibility of influence.

65. On the definitional issues, see Warner (1980: 81-82); Haran (1988: 83);
Niditch (1997: 39-41). The latter notes studies that suggest that fewer than 10 per

little evidence for any general knowledge of writing in Judah prior to the eighth century (cf. Jamieson-Drake 1991: 147).[66]

cent of the population were literate in ancient Greece, perhaps only 1 per cent in Mesopotamia and Egypt. Both Haran and Warner argue against the inference of widespread literacy on the basis of the presence of the alphabet. The latter, as Warner rightly maintains, is not a sufficient condition: we have to take account of the sociology of innovation and communication. Niditch (1997: 58) concludes: 'The vast majority of texts and letters are pragmatic and brief—military, military–commercial, or commercial in nature. Writing for such purposes appears to be much more common in the second half of the monarchy than in the first, and available to a variety of tradesmen, officials, and others. Even a poor corvée worker could have a message written for him by a local professional. The writing is usually, however, for circumscribed purposes, and the attendant literacy in the modern sense needs to have been only limited in order for such writing to communicate meaningfully to the reader of the text. Indeed, the wide use of sealings in this period is a substitute for the sender's writing while the assumption behind letters is that they are written by scribes and sometimes read by secretaries. Writing that is not for these limited military or commercial purposes has an iconic, symbolic, monumental aspect...' In reviewing her book, Millard (1998: 703-704) takes a more optimistic view: 'Without in any way suggesting that copies of Lady Wisdom's words, or any others, could be bought at every street corner, or that there was a bookshelf in every home, the reviewer maintains that they were not so scarce', but rejects any attribution to him of the view that there existed general literacy in ancient Israel, as opposed to the claim only that writing was not a rare skill and reading was not unusual.

66. Early general literacy is sometimes inferred from Judg. 8.13-14: 'Then Gideon the son of Jo'ash returned from the battle by the ascent of Heres. And he caught a young man of Succoth, and questioned him; and he wrote down for him the officials and elders of Succoth, seventy-seven men.' But we need to know about the youth's background and training; what he is writing is a list, a common early function of writing (see Niditch 1997: 94 for further examples), which need not imply literacy in the full sense. Jamieson-Drake argues against using the Gezer calendar as evidence that tenth-century children there were being taught to read and write (1991: 156-57); see also Haran (1986: 88-89; Millard 1991: 106; Niditch 1997: 45-46). Crenshaw sees the original locus of literacy as within craft guilds (1995: 83); Jamieson-Drake sees it as the preserve of Jerusalem-trained administrators (1991: 148-49). Whybray concludes from Proverbs, Job and Ecclesiastes that 'in the course of a long period in Israel's history there existed an educated class, albeit a small one, of well-to-do citizens who were accustomed to read for edification and for pleasure' (1974: 69). There is a strong consensus, however, that the eighth century saw a strong increase in literacy (Isa. 29.11-12). Jamieson-Drake (1991: 11) assumes it was widespread but not universal; Prov. 25.1 speaks of the 'proverbs of Solomon which the men of Hezekiah king of Judah copied'. But gen-

Jehoshaphat's 'commission' is taken by Watts as just one example of what he sees as the dominant paradigm of the communication of law in the Hebrew Bible. It was designed, he argues, specifically for public readings,[67] the purpose being didactic (Watts 1999: Ch. 3. *et passim*). This, he argues, is reflected in its rhetorical forms[68] and structures,[69] including not only the frequent use of direct address[70] (second-person forms) and motive clauses,[71] but also repetition[72] and the very integra-

eral literacy cannot be claimed before the late seventh century: Deut. 6.9, 11.20, 24.1; Jer. 36.29, 32, though the significance of these sources is also debated. On Deut. 6.9, see Haran (1986: 84); Niditch (1997: 69-70); *aliter*, Lemaire (1981: 58), claiming from this and archaeological evidence that by the seventh century each head of family knew how to read and write (see also Weeks 1994: 152). The principal dissent from this has come from Millard. He speaks of 'written literature existing in the land from at least the tenth century BC onwards' (1995: 207) and claims: 'While some states may have had a higher proportion of scribes than others, few places of any size can have been without someone able to read and write, and the use of writing for tax-collecting and similar purposes will have brought knowledge of the power of writing to every farmer' (1991: 110). Yet this in itself begs questions regarding the nature and 'reach' of the early Israelite state (see Jamieson-Drake 1991: 138-39).

67. Watts (1999: 22, 24 *et passim*). At 15, he argues that the majority of references to reading law in the Hebrew Bible describe a public reading of an entire legal document, such as the reading by Moses of the Book of the Covenant at Sinai. He observes that references to reading are remarkably sparse in the Hebrew Bible, and most references are to the reading of the law, rather than prophecy or hymns or history.

68. E.g. 'hear, listen' (Deut. 5.1; 6.3-4; 9.1); 'keep, observe, take heed' (Deut. 4.1, 9, 15; 27.1; cf. Exod. 34.11-12); 'remember' (Deut. 8.2; 9.7) (Watts 1999: 64).

69. Watts (1999: 36-49), where he adopts a 'narrative-list-sanction' structure (the list often but not necessarily comprising laws). For an evaluation of this approach, see §1.1 n. 18, *supra,* and some applications: §9.3 at n. 38, §9.4 n. 84, *infra.*

70. Watts (1999: 62-65). I am not sure that Alt would have accepted Watts's attribution to him (63) of recognition of the 'rhetorical force of second-person legal address', as implied by his location of 'the original setting of apodictic language in cultic liturgies'. On Alt's account, the apodictic law was recited at a cultic covenant renewal ceremony. We might put the issue in speech act terms: what act was such recitation designed to perform? The answer, for Alt, would surely have been closer to 'promise' than 'persuasion'. Cf. my criticism, below, of Watts's failure to distinguish didactic from ritual readings.

71. Watts (1999: 65-67), stressing motive clauses that link the law to Israel's narrative history.

72. Watts (1999: 68-73). On this aspect of his theory, see further *infra,* §8.1, n. 12.

tion of law and narrative (Watts 1991: 13 *et passim*). That public readings for didactic purposes occurred is indeed the claim made in 2 Chronicles 17—supported, as we have noted, by the Sargon inscriptions. But Watts goes too far in seeking to reduce most communication of law to this model, almost irrespective of the size of the text (1999: 29).[73] He claims that it was this model which also influenced subsequent writing, even where public readings were not envisaged, giving short shrift to those who anticipate any correlation between style and written or oral communication.[74] The difference between preaching and teaching[75] may, indeed, have been less marked in biblical times than it

73. Thus, at 137, he identifies Exod. 19-24 and Deuteronomy as two blocks of material manifesting the pattern of stories followed by lists and then by sanctions. He excepts (at 30) passages showing the results of systematic codification (e.g. Lev. 18) and others that emphasize instructions for specialists (e.g. Lev. 6-7). Watts accepts that it is open to serious question whether the Law of Moses in its final Pentateuchal form was really intended to be read in public at one sitting. Nevertheless, he claims that the Pentateuch follows the rhetorical strategies and generic conventions laid down by the earlier and smaller codes that it incorporates: 'It is my thesis that public reading established the literary forms of Israel's law in the monarchic period, and those forms remained unchanged long after public reading had become a rarity and perhaps an anachronism' (Watts 1999: 30-31).

74. Watts seeks to elide the distinction between readers and listeners (1999: 61 n. 1): 'The distinction between hearers and readers, which has been so fruitful for studies of orality and literacy, is blurred by the practice of reading aloud for aural reception. Since Israel's legal texts and law-reading tradition do not differentiate between readers and hearers, I do not distinguish them either, regarding both as part of the text's "audience".'

75. Watts (1999: 61-62), noting that the presence of rhetorical features in the laws has led to different interpretations—von Rad (1973: 25-36, 60-69) arguing that the hortatory addresses in Deuteronomy and the holiness code reveal the material's origins in the preaching of the Levites, Weinfeld (1972: 51-58, 158-71, 177-78, 244-319) taking the legal rhetoric to be more didactic than sermonic and thus having more in common with wisdom—seeks (at 62) to conflate these two different settings: 'The tradition of public law readings, however, suggests that ancient Israelite law emphasised persuasion *and* instruction... [T]he discovery that the Pentateuch uses a rhetorical strategy that combines and transcends particular genres...also supports the notion that the writers did not limit themselves to the linguistic forms of only one literary tradition.' Similarly, in describing the role of Moses according to Deuteronomy, he conflates the roles of scribe and teacher: the latter reads (and thus repeats) a written text; the former similarly repeats what he has heard, though he also interprets and composes outright (116-22, esp. 117).

is today. But Watts fails to distinguish the non-didactic purpose and setting, when the reading is in a ritual context.[76] To that, I now turn.

5.3.3 *Ritual Uses*

We can identify a third type of use of the *sefer*, which I call 'ritual'. This is a public reading, associated with a festival or some special sacred event, the object of which is fulfilled by the act of public reading itself. It is, of course, the origins of the 'reading' of the Law in the synagogue today[77]—a quite separate function from the teaching of Bible, or the adjudication of cases on the basis of the law in it.

Such a ritual reading is first mentioned in the biblical narrative at the end of the book of Deuteronomy, when Moses gives his final commands[78] to his successor, Joshua:

> And Moses wrote this law, and gave it to the priests the sons of Levi, who carried the ark of the covenant of the LORD, and to all the elders of Israel. And Moses commanded them, 'At the end of every seven years, at the set time of the year of release, at the feast of booths, when all Israel comes to appear before the LORD your God at the place which he will choose, you shall read this law before all Israel in their hearing. Assemble the people, men, women, and little ones, and the sojourner within your towns, that they may hear and learn to fear the LORD your God, and be careful to do all the words of this law, and that their children, who have not known it, may hear and learn to fear the LORD your God, as long as you live in the land which you are going over the Jordan to possess' (Deut. 31.9-13).

The motive of the reading is that of incorporation of the present

---

76. Though I take here a predominantly critical view of Watts's work, there is much of value in the book, particularly his treatment of the different voices and strategies that distinguish Deuteronomy from the rest of the Pentateuch. On this, see further, §§6.2, 9.4 n. 58, *infra*.

77. The 'lesson' of the Christian Church, though it may have its origin in the synagogal reading, is no longer 'ritual' in this sense. In the synagogue, individuals are called on to the *bimah,* and recite blessings before and after the reading of their particular section, the whole (blessings and reading) constituting the performance of a religious act (a *mitsvah*). The church lesson, by contrast, is much closer to Watts's understanding of a public reading for didactic purposes. It is also much shorter than either the weekly reading in the synagogue (though roughly equivalent to the individual 'portion') or the major documents which Watts sees as designed for this purpose (n. 73, *supra*).

78. Interestingly, these are not commands relayed by Moses from God; Moses himself is portrayed as their author (see further §9.4, *infra*).

generation within the covenant (§9.4, *infra*). At the same time, the new adherents to the covenant are put on notice of their obligations. By implication, the adults are taken already to know the rules; it is only the children who are said not to know them.

Such a ritual reading is also attributed to the occasion of the original giving of the law at Sinai (if, indeed, the vital words are original). After the theophany that accompanied the giving of the Decalogue, followed by the communication by God to Moses alone of the '*mishpatim*', Moses ultimately descends from the mountain, and we read of a covenantal affirmation of the law, accompanied by a sacrificial ritual. The literary-historical relations between the elements in this passage are notoriously difficult to disentangle.[79] But for present purposes, it is sufficient to note that a ritual reading from a *sefer* came to be included in it:

> Moses came and told the people all the words of the LORD and all the ordinances; and all the people answered with one voice, and said, 'All the words which the LORD has spoken we will do'. And Moses wrote all the words of the LORD.[80] And he rose early in the morning, and built an altar at the foot of the mountain, and twelve pillars (*matsevah*), according to the twelve tribes of Israel.[81] And he sent young men of the people of Israel, who offered burnt offerings and sacrificed peace offerings of oxen to the LORD. And Moses took half of the blood and put it in basins, and half of the blood he threw against the altar. Then he took the book of the covenant (*sefer haberit*), and read it in the hearing of the people; and they said, 'All that the LORD has spoken we will do, and we will be obedient.' And Moses took the blood and threw it upon the people, and said, 'Behold the blood of the covenant which the LORD has made with you in accordance with all these words' (Exod. 24.3-8).

The central phrase recording the reading, ויקח ספר הברית ויקרא באזני העם (Exod. 24.7), is echoed in the account of the ceremony organized by king Josiah on the occasion of his discovery of the law-book in the Temple:

> Then the king sent, and all the elders of Judah and Jerusalem were gathered to him. And the king went up to the house of the LORD, and with him all the men of Judah and all the inhabitants of Jerusalem, and the priests and the prophets, all the people, both small and great; and he read

---

79. On the *devarim* and *mishpatim*, see *infra*, §9.3, n. 40.
80. At this stage, we are not told on what.
81. See the discussion of this passage *supra*, §5.2 at pp. 122-23.

in their hearing all the words of the book of the covenant which had been
found in the house of the LORD (ויקרא באזניהם את כל דברי ספר
הברית הנמצא בבית יהוה). And the king stood by the pillar[82] and made a
covenant before the LORD to walk after the LORD and to keep his commandments and his testimonies and his statutes, with all his heart and all
his soul, to perform the words of this covenant that were written in this
book; and all the people joined in the covenant (2 Kgs. 23.1-3).

This passage combines the ritual reading, accompanied by covenantal
affirmation, which we find in Exodus, with Deuteronomy's stress upon
the presence of all sections of the population at the public reading. It
may, indeed, have elements of re-enactment of the original acts of reading and affirmation.[83] In none of the sources considered so far do we
hear of any interpretation or discussion of the text accompanying its
public reading.

5.4 *The Ezra Tradition and the Endurance of Law*

It is in the story of Ezra that we find the coalescence of these different
communicational functions. Ezra comes not only as a religious
reformer, but also as a royal administrator, familiar with the practice of
Persian decrees. He wants the words of the law to be put permanently
into the public domain, but not merely to fulfil a monumental function
(as on the stones inscribed at Mount Ebal by Joshua); rather he wishes
to combine the traditional ritual reading of the religious reform with a
didactic function: the words should not only be read out, they should
also be explained. Thus, the famous passage (Neh. 8.7-8) in which Ezra
and his assistants (the Levites)

> helped the people to understand (*mevinim*) the law, while the people
> remained in their places. And they read from the book, from the law of
> God, clearly (*meforash*) and they gave the sense [*vesom sekhel*] so that
> the people understood (*vayaviynu*) the reading (Neh. 8.7-8).

This in itself combines the functions of Jehoshaphat's officers in 2
Chronicles 17 with the ritual of Josiah's reform. But Ezra was not
finished. The next day, he summoned a smaller group to return,
comprising the heads of the families, the priests and the Levites, to
study the text further (ולהשכיל אל דברי התורה, v. 13). The process of

---

82. *Amud,* not *matsevah.* NEB: 'dais'.
83. Cf. Watts (1999: 57), of Deuteronomy.

specialization had begun. Within the one text, there was room for both popular and more specialized audiences.

It is in this context that we should locate the transformation of the biblical legal collections into 'statutory' texts, binding upon the courts and subject to verbal interpretation. Indeed, Crüsemann has argued that it was the new legal framework of the Persian empire that prompted this, since the Persians had a policy not merely of recognizing the traditional laws of their subjects, but also of treating them as being as legally binding as the law of the king.[84] Moreover, he suggests that the author of Est. 8.8 (concerning the 'revocation' of the decree against the Jews) thought there was a 'Persian legal principle' that '[n]ew law can be placed alongside older law without formally canceling the first, even when the second contradicts the first',[85]—a principle which Crüsemann uses in explaining the fact that the redactors of the Pentateuch appear to have been unconcerned by the contradictions between the various documents that they compiled into their work. In fact, there is a hint of a similar idea in the etymology of the Roman verb for 'repeal' of laws: *abrogare* means literally to 'propose something different from...' Some years ago I suggested (of the Roman situation) that '[i]n theory, it

---

84. Crüsemann (1996: 336-37), citing Ezra 7.25, Gunneweg (1985: 139-40) and Frei (1984), for other examples (Egypt, Xanthos). See also Watts (1999: 138-43), including discussion of the 'Passover letter' from Elephantine, which seems to incorporate a Persian Imperial decree regulating the celebration of passover in the Jewish colony there, and arguing that though Persian authorization may well have motivated the editing of the Pentateuch to serve as Judaea's temple law, this does not explain the literary form the redaction took. Interestingly, a juridical motivation has been suggested also for the LXX translation (Modrzejewski 1996: 79-81).

85. Crüsemann (1996: 349-50). See also Watts (1999: 74-75). In 8.8, Ahasuerus authorizes Esther and Mordecai: 'And you may write as you please with regard to the Jews, in the name of the king, and seal it with the king's ring; for an edict written in the name of the king and sealed with the king's ring cannot be revoked.' Earlier, he had delegated such edict-making power to Haman (3.10-11): 'So the king took his signet ring from his hand and gave it to Haman the Agagite, the son of Hammedatha, the enemy of the Jews. And the king said to Haman, "The money is given to you, the people also, to do with them as it seems good to you."' Haman had used the king's ring to promulgate the edict (3.12): 'Then the king's secretaries were summoned on the thirteenth day of the first month, and an edict, according to all that Haman commanded, was written to the king's satraps and to the governors over all the provinces and to the princes of all the peoples, to every province in its own script and every people in its own language; it was written in the name of King Ahasuerus and sealed with the king's ring.'

seems, even a superseded law remained a law just as *dharma, kittum* and *torah* retained their validity despite the absence of enforcement' and pointed to a similar idea in Demosthenes (Jackson 1975b: 509-10).[86]

The unalterable character of the laws of the Persians and Medes is also reflected in another aspect of the Esther story. When Queen Vashti refuses to obey the command of King Ahasuerus to display herself before his guests, the king takes legal advice (Est. 1.13-15). In the interests of men's liberation, he is urged to take a strong line:

> Let a royal order go forth...and let it be written among the laws of the Persians and the Medes so that it may not be altered [*velo ya'avor*], that Vashti is to come no more before King Ahasuerus; and let the king give her royal position to another who is better than she' (1.19).

This, then, is the context in which we hear of the legendary character of the laws of the Persians and the Medes, which changeth not: Vashti is deposed—for ever. An ad hoc, ad personam royal decree is given the status of unalterable law. Why the hyperbole? I take up this question in the next chapter.

---

86. The emergence of the statute—a law whose very wording is binding and whose validity is not limited in time—is itself often associated with the political ideology of Greek democracy. For example, there is a tradition from Locris according to which anyone who proposed an amendment to the law must first explicitly propose the repeal of the previous law, and must do so with a noose placed around his neck (see Vinogradoff 1922: II, 72-75). In fact, the idea seems rapidly to have spread around the mediterranean in the fifth century BCE, this being the period also of the Roman Twelve Tables and the likely editing of the Pentateuch (see further Jackson 1975b: 506-10). Westbrook (1994: 28) has remarked: 'The later biblical codes—the Deuteronomic and Priestly codes—share something of the intellectual ferment of contemporary Greek sources and thus some taste also of their new legal conceptions. The Covenant Code, on the other hand, although it cannot be dated with any confidence, looks back to the cuneiform codes of the second and third millennia.' On this, see Jackson (1995c: 1754-55).

Chapter 6

THE TEMPORALITY OF THE LAW

6.1 *Introduction*

The unalterability of the law—as encountered in the context of the decree of Ahasuerus against Vashti (§5.4, *supra*)—may be regarded as an early response to the problem of the continuity of law. This is a notion so deeply embedded in the modern concept of law that we take it for granted: a law endures until such time as it is repealed (unless an explicit time limit is placed on its duration *ab initio*). In jurisprudence, this was famously expounded by H.L.A. Hart in his argument that the continuity of law—despite changes in the person of the sovereign—is one vital distinguishing feature between the concept 'law' (based on rules) and that of mere 'command' (1994: 50-66, 61-66).

Hart's distinction between 'rule' and 'command' also raises ontological issues. What, precisely, is a law? Is it simply an ongoing command, and if so what precisely is a command? Or is it ontologically different from a command, and if so how? The notion of a command conjures up the image of face-to-face communication, perhaps in a military, perhaps in the domestic setting.[1] It is, essentially, a speech act—an interpersonal interaction that is conventionally regarded as producing an effect in the relationship between the parties (and, perhaps, others). As such, we may regard it in purely semiotic terms—a form of speech behaviour that sociologically can be seen to perform in a certain way. Yet from early times, the performance of speech acts has been viewed with a certain wonder, as if the utterance of the words magically transforms some aspects of existence. Such is the interpretation sometimes offered of the Roman description of a legal obligation as a *vinculum iuris*, an invisible, magic bond that ties together the persons of the obligor and

---

1.   Cf. the view taken of the domestic setting of apodictic law, §2.3.1, *supra*.

obligee (or, by extension, a person and his property).[2] Some such idea may, perhaps, be reflected in the implicit speech act theory of the Bible. Not only does God, in Genesis 1, effect creation by *fiat* (a command expressed in speech):[3] that speech is itself described, in some sources, in terms of the delivery of *chok* to the recipient of the command.[4]

We might conceive of a law as such a speech act of command, extended temporally and in terms of its audience: it is no longer a face-to-face communication, but one directed to an audience that is not present, and that may, indeed, not yet exist. Such a conception of law is not, indeed, incompatible with the argument of Hart, if we understand his 'rule of recognition'[5] as functioning to tell us when the standard speech act of face-to-face communication between individuals is regarded as achieving such extensions. To view the matter in such a way would still be compatible with a semiotic approach, one that views law as a particular form of communication. This is not, however, the standard approach in legal philosophy. There, the view is frequently taken that a law is an abstract entity, often described as a 'norm', which has a logical form and is in principle distinct from its linguistic expressions.[6] This, too, generates questions that may be posed, for Jewish law, in theological terms: Is the *halakhah* a compilation of the 'words' of God, whether transmitted orally or in writing, or do these words simply communicate something else (the *mitsvot,* perhaps) that has an independent, logical, nonlinguistic existence? Biblical theology is not likely to address such a question in the kind of abstract terms in which the issue is discussed in contemporary philosophy. Nevertheless, where in the Bible law is presented as going beyond commands within a face-to-face context, we can at least look for indications as to how the sense of the continuity of law was constructed.

2. See the Scandinavian Realist account, discussed in Jackson (1996a: 129-32).

3. Gen. 1.3: 'And God said, "Let there be light"; and there was light', etc.

4. Job 28.26: '...when he made a decree (*chok*) for the rain, and a way (*derekh*) for the lightning of the thunder'; Jer. 31.34: '...who gives the sun for light by day and the fixed order of the moon and the stars (חֻקֹּת יָרֵחַ וְכוֹכָבִים) for light by night, who stirs up the sea so that its waves roar—the LORD of hosts is his name.'

5. A 'secondary rule', the existence of which distinguishes an advanced legal system from a mere set of primary rules (see Hart 1994: 94-95; Jackson 1996a: 181-83).

6. Classically, in the legal philosophy of Georges Kalinowski, and, with some qualifications, Hans Kelsen (see Jackson 1985b: 256-60; 1988: 140-41 n.13; 1996a: 100-101).

In addressing that issue, two types of approach are possible. The first (§6.2) puts the question in 'constitutional' terms. What was the power of the king in relation to legislation? Is there a difference here between the powers of the king and those ascribed to God? If so, what is the nature of the relationship? Is the role of God modelled upon a conception of royal legislative power, or vice versa?

The second approach (§6.3) poses the issues in semiotic terms: how is the sense of continuity of law constructed? In seeking to answer it, we may be drawn necessarily into the ontological issue: what, precisely, was law conceived to be in biblical literature? Was it an abstract entity, or was it modelled upon interpersonal communication? If we take the latter, more concrete conception as our most likely starting point, we can focus upon the different elements of the communicational model (cf. §5.1, *supra*). For continuity could be ascribed, respectively, to the sender of the message, its receiver, the medium of the message or its referent, where this last is also an object or entitlement which is transferable within human (or even human–divine) interaction.

6.2 *The Legislative Authority of the King*

Consider again the recurrent pattern of ancient Near East legislative practices: the Babylonian king would issue what has come to be known as a '*mišarum*-act' at the beginning of the reign, to be followed several years later by a law code.[7] The *mišarum*-act concerned mostly immediate matters of economic regulation, often directed towards alleviation of the oppressive incidents of debt-slavery. Comparison is sometimes made with the *deror* of King Zedekiah recorded in Jeremiah 34 (*infra*, pp. 150-53). The law code, by contrast, would come several years later (as it did in the case of Hammurabi), and might well repeat material from earlier exemplars.

What is the significance of the recurrent re-enactment of the code, and the fact that it lacked the urgency that apparently attended the *mišarum*-act? The pattern of repetition—which we may compare with the obligation of (apparently) each successive king to have *mishneh hatorah* prepared for his personal use[8]—seems to indicate that the

---

7.   Finkelstein (1961: 91-104). See also Whitelam (1979: 207-208), concluding in favour of 'the ability of the king in Mesopotamia to promulgate law in a real sense'. However, the issue of the temporal duration of such law is not raised.

8.   *Aliter*, Falk (1978: VIII, 37), taking Deut. 17.18 as evidence that 'unlike

authority of the *current* king was always required (even though this was often an ideal statement of the law, not a text which would be used by way of verbal interpretation by the courts). Indeed, the relative lack of urgency in promulgating the law code during each reign itself supports the argument, well-made on other grounds, that the code was not designed as a statutory text in our sense. It was not binding law that continued despite a change in the king.

The *mišarum*-act appears *on its face* to be temporary in nature: it is primarily retrospective in application, granting relief from current debts, etc., rather than regulating transactions which will arise in the future.[9] In the law code, by contrast, a *claim* is impliedly made to the continuity, perhaps even eternity, of the rules it contains. It is important to know when and how such a claim is made. The answer to the question 'how' is to be found partly in the medium—inscription on stone, particularly on a large monument erected in a public place (thus, designed for both temporal and spatial permanence)—and partly in the ideological content, the prologues and epilogues which, even if they do not state explicitly that the rules will subsist in perpetuity, clearly imply such a claim. We then have to ask, quite separately, whether, when and to what extent such claims to continuity were accepted. Indeed, had the debt-relief provisions of the law codes been implemented, there would have been little need for the *mišarum*-acts.[10]

Urnammu, Lipit-Ishtar and Hammurabi, the kings of Israel did not prepare restatements of the law but had it copied from the texts possessed by priests and levites'. Granted this difference between copying and reformulating, the temporal association with the life (and thus reign) of the king remains significant.

9.   Finkelstein (1961: 101, 102), describing the occasional prospective general provisions (as in the Edict of Ammisaduqa) as 'representing for the most part pious hopes and moral resolve rather than effective "law"'. Greenberg (1995: 16-17) mistakenly seeks to distinguish between biblical law and the Laws of Hammurabi (rather than the edicts) along these lines. But the promise in the epilogue of Hammurabi, that anyone who believes he has been wronged may come and read his rights, does not make the laws retrospective: the promise does not apply only to wrongs that occurred before the monument was erected. Greenberg makes a different, and better, point when he argues that Biblical law aims at teaching duties in advance, rather than simply restoring rights after they have been violated. But even here, those who favour an 'ideal' or 'didactic' function for the Babylonian law-codes would not necessarily accept a distinction.

10. Thus practices that Hammurabi condemns on pain of death still fall to be outlawed in the Edict of Ammisaduqa (Finkelstein 1961: 102).

The view is commonly taken that the legislative power of the Israelite kings—at least as depicted by the Bible—was significantly less than that of their ancient Near Eastern counterparts: it is the divinity, in ancient Israel, rather than the king, who is depicted as the source of legislation.[11] However, when we review the sources with particular reference to the question of the continuity of law, and ask whether the king was capable of enacting rules that would survive (in practice, not merely as an ideal or ideological statement—a 'royal apologia') into the reign of his successor(s), the route from ad hoc decree to enduring rule becomes somewhat clearer.[12] For the genesis of the idea of an enduring rule can be associated with two phenomena: first, the use of divine authority in support of even *mišarum*-type activity on the part of the ruler; secondly, in the claim of the king (and the sanctuary) to enduring rights or privileges (§6.3).

Consider first the *mišarum*-type activity. In seeking to dissuade the people from instituting a monarchy, Samuel is told by God to warn the Israelites of *mishpat hamelekh* (1 Sam. 8.9-18). There follows a list of privileges of the king, which we might classify as part of his prerogative.[13] For the most part, these are ad hoc, temporary privileges—almost the converse, we may suggest,of the temporary measures of debt and

11. De Vaux, *Ancient Israel* (1961: 150), noting that the ancient Near Eastern 'codes' were 'at least promulgated by royal authority', observes: 'In Israel, granted the religious nature of the law and its connection with the Covenant, nothing of the sort was possible, and in fact the historical books never allude to any legislative power of the king.' See also Whitelam (1979: 209, 213) for further literature advocating this view. De Vaux (1961: 150) comments on Samuel's *mishpat hamelekh* and Deut. 17: 'It is remarkable that the two "laws of the king" make no allusion to any power of the king to lay down laws.' But this reflects a restricted and particular notion of legislative power. On this criterion, our own annual national budget. which in the UK requires a Finance Act to be implemented, would not involve the legislative power.

12. There may, moreover, have been good political reasons to play down the legislative role of the Israelite king. Watts (1999: 138) takes the view that the Pentateuchal law codes were promulgated in the Persian period, when there was a compelling reason to omit references to royal institutions lest they arouse the suspicion of the imperial overlord.

13. The RSV tries to deny the legitimacy of such privileges by rendering *mishpat* by 'the ways' of the king; but the whole point of Samuel's warning is that by adoption of the foreign model of the monarch, the Israelites will subject themselves to his prerogative rights, not that the king may be predicted to abuse his powers in breach of the law.

and other relief found in the *deror* and its ancient Near Eastern counter-parts (see Weinfeld 1995; Jackson 1998a: 218-62). The king may 'take your sons and appoint them to his chariots and to be his horsemen, and to run before his chariots' (8.11)—in other words, conscription. He may similarly requisition personnel for administrative,[14] agricultural,[15] man-ufacturing[16] and domestic work;[17] he may take 'the best of your fields and vineyards and olive orchards and give them to his servants'—con-fiscation, the closest we come here to a permanent transfer of rights (1 Sam. 8.14); he may take a tithe of grain, vineyards and livestock—tax-ation, here specifically stated (as regards the grain and vineyards) to be for the benefit of the king's civil servants (1 Sam. 8.15, 17); he may requisition slaves and farm animals for labour.[18] The law of the king in Deut. 17.14-20 has a similar flavour. No set of privileges is here stated; rather, they are implied as self-evident, from the fact that imme-diately after the authorization to institute a king, we are told: רק לא ירבה לו סוסים (Only shall he not multiply horses for himself)…etc. The formulation *rak* implies that such a king will have the normal privileges of a king[19]—but subject to (*rak*) the limitations here stated.

I turn now to narratives of the king's activity in matters of econom-ic organization. Weinfeld has argued that the notice that David עשה משפט וצדקה לכל עמו in 2 Sam. 8.15 indicated that he issued an edict in the tradition of the *mišarum*-acts.[20] However this may be, we

14. 1 Sam. 8.12: he may appoint subordinates, שרי אלפים ושרי חמשים—per-haps here an administrative as much as a military structure.

15. 1 Sam. 8.12: he may take people to 'plough his ground and reap his har-vest'.

16. 1 Sam. 8.12: he may take people to 'make his implements of war and the equipment of his chariots'.

17. 1 Sam. 8.13: he may 'take your daughters to be perfumers and cooks and bakers'.

18. 1 Sam. 8.16: 'He will take your menservants and maidservants, and the best of your cattle and your asses, and put them to his work.' The net effect, in conclu-sion: 'and you shall be his slaves' (v. 17), the term *avadim*, in context, referring to debt-slavery, though with little expectation that the protective limits of Exod. 21.2 etc. would be applied.

19. Deut. 17.14, like 1 Sam. 8.20, explicitly ascribes the demand for a king to the desire to emulate foreign nations.

20. Weinfeld (1972: 153), and cf. his view there of Deut. 33.21: further in Weinfeld (1995: 45-48). Cf. Whitelam (1979: 216); at 98-99, he argues tentatively for an association of David's booty law with this tradition.

have two significant sources that relate in some detail the economic measures taken by the king.

Jeremiah 34 records a special covenant (*berit*) entered into by King Zedekiah and the people for the release (*deror*) of their Hebrew slaves. But then the people go back on their undertaking and re-enslave those they had freed. Jeremiah is entrusted with a judgment against them for doing this. Our first question is how the king came to be involved in making such a *berit*. There are a number of rival interpretations. In recounting the event itself, Jeremiah offers no reason for it (vv. 8-9) but in conveying God's judgment he ascribes to Zedekiah's *berit* the motive of fulfilment of an earlier *berit* that God himself had made with their forefathers (v. 14), to set Hebrew slaves free at the end of six (or seven) years.[21] Previous generations had ignored this; Zedekiah and his people had repented, and had made a *berit* to proclaim a *deror*, but had then gone back on it (Jer. 34.13-16). The king is thus presented as taking the initiative in getting the people to commit themselves by *berit* to the fulfilment of an earlier, and still existing, covenantal obligation (God says, 'You recently repented and did what was right in my eyes by proclaiming liberty...', v. 15). Although the parties to the covenant under Zedekiah are the king, the princes and the people, unlike the earlier covenant (said to be between God and the forefathers of the present people), the covenant under Zedekiah also implicates God, who complains, through Jeremiah: '...but then you turned around and profaned my name when each of you took back his male and female slaves, whom you had set free according to their desire, and you brought them into subjection to be your slaves' (v. 16). This covenant, moreover, is said to have been made 'in the house which is called by my Name' (v. 15), thereby implying that God is witness, and perhaps also guarantor.[22] There is some dispute as to whether Jeremiah or a later editor is responsible for interpreting Zedekiah's *berit* as repentance for and

21. The reference in vv. 13-14 appears from the language (*mikets*, cf. Deut. 15.1; *yimakher, akhicha*) to be to the Deuteronomic version of the law of release of debt-slaves (Deut. 15.12-18), although in being formulated only in respect of male slaves (despite Jer. 34.9) it is closer to Exod. 21.2. We need not enter here into the choice in Jer. 34.14 between the apparent *lectio difficilior* of the MT, *mikets sheva,* and the *mikets shesh* of the LXX, which would make the maximum period of debt-slavery conform to both Exod. 21.2 and Deut. 15.12; the issue is complicated by the *mikets sheva* of Deut. 15.1.

22. Cf. §6.3, *infra,* on Esarhaddon's treaties.

restoration of an earlier one (impliedly of continuing validity),[23] the role of the king thus being to take fresh measures (albeit not identical ones[24]) to implement it. But even without the link to the earlier *berit*, Jeremiah presents the *berit* of Zedekiah as supported by divine authority, even though God is not claimed to be a party to it. The permanence of divine sanctions and authority is thus invoked to secure enforcement of a merely temporary, ad hoc economic measure.

An alternative interpretation is based on the practice of ancient Near Eastern kings, in issuing an edict remitting debts, at the beginning of the reign (see Lewy 1958: 21-31; Finkelstein 1961: 91-104; Weinfeld 1995). As in the Bible, we have from the ancient Near East evidence of both ad hoc acts of remission and general norms regarding slavery and debt-remission, such as that in the Laws of Hammurabi (117) which requires a debt-slave to be freed after three years. But whereas in the ancient Near East, with its more developed economies, we have plenty of evidence of such a monarchic practice, in the biblical sources the

---

23. The reference to the earlier *berit* is regarded by several scholars as secondary. See Lemche (1976: 51-52); Westbrook (1991: 16-17 n. 4); Houtman (1997: 100); Chavel (1997: 71-95), arguing that the text reflects editorial activity in or after the time of Nehemiah, seeking to abolish Hebrew debt-slavery altogether. At 74-75, Chavel observes: 'Zedekiah makes no reference to the pentateuchal codes. He simply declares *deror*, similar more to the ancient near Eastern *andurarum* acts than to the law in Leviticus 25.' It is true that the motive of fulfilment of the earlier obligation is not attributed by Jeremiah to Zedekiah in the narrative account of the latter's activity (vv. 8-11) but that is the interpretation placed upon it by God in v. 15 ('You recently repented and did what was right in my eyes by proclaiming liberty'). Lev. 25 (release of debt-slaves in the jubilee year, v. 40) is the least likely of the potential referents of Jer. 34.13-14.

24. Zedekiah uses an immediate, ad hoc measure, comparable to the ancient Near Eastern *andurarum*, rather than reinstituting a regular, time-fixed release. The latter is widely regarded as more likely to have been utopic. Sprinkle (1994: 66-67) takes Jer. 34.14b, 'but your fathers did not obey me or inclined their ears', to indicate that 'the abrogation of the promised release of bondsmen was by that time the norm, not the exception'. But this in itself implies that there was indeed once a real rule (not just, as Sprinkle would prefer, a literary construct), even if that rule was disregarded in practice. Comparable issues arise, of course, in respect of LH 117 (cf. Weinfeld 1995: 156). Marshall (1993: 116-17) agrees with Westbrook (1991: 48) that although a set, universal year of release may be idealistic, as an occasional event the year of release was a practical institution in the ancient Near East from the third millennium onward (referring to the *andurarum* etc. edicts).

incident under Zedekiah stands almost alone.[25] So while the practice of the ancient Near Eastern kings may well have been known, and used on this occasion as a model, we may have to look elsewhere for the particular reasons for this event. Such an explanation is, in fact, available. The incident we are considering is presented, a little incongruously, when Nebuchadnezer is already at the gates of Jerusalem. But Daube has pointed to a pattern of emancipation of slaves in Greece and Rome that he terms 'incorporation by the state' (Daube 1946: 56-75). The state needs to increase the army, and requires slave owners to release their slaves to serve in it. At Rome, the slave once released from the army, would not return to his slavery; in fact, he would become a citizen. In Greece, the battle of Arginusae presents a further example: before it, the citizens of Athens released their slaves. This seems to be the reason why the citizens of Jerusalem at first acceded to the *berit* proposed by Zedekiah. They wanted the slaves to serve in the army,[26] but were not so happy to lose them in perpetuity; when the siege was lifted (temporarily, as it turned out[27]), they wanted the slaves back. There is, perhaps, a hint of such a military background in v. 10, which mentions the *sarim* in the context of the *berit*. Equally, this context explains an otherwise superfluous phrase in v. 10. We have already been told that the slaves are to be emancipated, using the expression *shilach chofshi*, as in Deut. 15.12. But v. 10 still finds it necessary to add that the

25. At least in terms of explicit description of what occurred: Weinfeld (1995) argues that the widespread terminology of *mishpat utsedakah* (which is not used in Jer. 34) alludes to the practice. If Zedekiah's *deror* was unusual for Judaean kings, this may account for its being presented not as the unilateral act of a king but rather as the result of a covenant between the people and the princes on the one hand and the king on the other, impliedly entered into voluntarily (even though once entered into it created an obligation which they were required to 'obey', Jer. 34.8-10). We may suspect, however, that this is a rewriting of a unilateral royal *deror* to make it appear more comparable to the earlier covenantal obligation (also broken). See further Weinfeld (1995: 153-55).

26. Cf. Weinfeld (1995: 152 n.1) ('to facilitate mobilization into the army'); Westbrook (1991: 16-17 n.4) ('resulting from the dire circumstances of the siege', but not referring specifically to conscription). Kessler (1971: 105-108) argues, however, against understanding the release as a purely practical measure (since it affected both male and female slaves), preferring to view it as 'a solemn and sacred act' involving a 'touch of mimetic magic'—to induce God to free the Judaeans from the siege (see also Jackson 1998: 238-42).

27. Jer. 37.5; cf. 34.21; see further Noth (1960: 284-86). For the overall account of the siege (589–87 BCE), see esp. Jer. 39.1-10; 52.3-11; 2 Kgs 25.1-7.

agreement of the people was to emancipate these slaves, 'on terms that they would not be enslaved again'. This seems to be designed to exclude such re-enslavement as might be consistent with economic measures, but would not be consistent with a release to the army, according to the Roman model. If this interpretation is correct, then we see once again the close connection between royal edicts and military matters.

Jeremiah ascribes the earlier slave release rule to a *berit* made not at Sinai, or even Horev, but 'when I brought them out of the land of Egypt'. Could he have been thinking, perhaps, of Exod. 15.25, the *chok umishpat* made at Marah? The *Mekhilta*, the earliest rabbinic commentary on Exodus, dating from the late second or early third century CE, provides surprising confirmation of the existence of such a tradition. Commenting on Exod. 21.1:

> R. Judah says: *And these are the Ordinances* [*ve'eleh hamishpatim*]. These were commanded at Marah, as it is said: 'There He made for them a statute and an ordinance' (Exod. 15.25).

There could hardly be a more suitable topic for a first revelation of divine covenantal obligation, given the narrative context, than one concerning the freeing of slaves. Jeremiah does not appear to regard this earlier covenant as part of a larger set of obligations; moreover, he takes the king to have a special responsibility for its implementation. What historical reality might make such an account intelligible? Could it be that just as the king sought individual divine consultation through prophets and oracles in order to determine individual matters of dispute, so might the development towards continuing statutory law have begun with prophets revealing to the king individual sets of laws, which would claim enduring quality because of the enduring character of their ultimate source (cf. §5.3.1 [end], *supra*)?

The relationship between ruler and divinity may be considered also in the context of Nehemiah's reaction to the economic crisis of his day, apparently prompted by famine (also mentioned in the context of the siege in the time of Zedekiah [Jer. 32.24; 34.17; 52.6; cf. 21.7, 9; 27.8, etc.]). The people were finding it necessary to borrow on interest, mortgage their fields, vineyards and houses in order to buy food (the price impliedly inflated by a famine, Neh. 5.3), and when they no longer had land to serve as security, they were selling their children as debt-slaves to their Jewish brethren. Nehemiah seeks to deal with the matter; he convenes a 'great assembly' (Neh. 5.7) and shames[28] the economic exploiters[29] into both returning the mortgaged property and the (apparently 1 per cent) interest and undertaking to stop such practices in future.[30] (This falls short of remission of the debts themselves, nor is return of the debt-slaves explicitly mentioned, though it may possibly have been included in the package.) The commitment is entered into by an oath, taken in the presence of the priests (Neh. 5.12).[31] Again, we have the pattern of the ancient Near Eastern *deror*, but supported by a religious ceremony.

There are, however, significant differences between the accounts of the activities of Nehemiah and Zedekiah. In the case of Nehemiah, the text makes no direct reference to breach of a divine law, as the basis of complaint; the problem is presented purely as an economic one, reflecting a self-evident injustice. And the role of Nehemiah himself calls for reflection. He is a political leader, but he buttresses this with a moral authority. His own complaint to the creditors echoes a prophetic dispute-speech. He tells us: 'I brought charges against the nobles and the officials' (ואריבה את החרים ואת הסגנים); then follows his speech of condemnation, leading to the agreement on measures to meet the crisis. At the conclusion of the proceedings, not only does he adjure the nobles and officials to do his bidding (Neh. 5.12); he also pronounces a curse, which they accept:

---

28. Neh. 5.8-9: ' "We, as far as we are able, have bought back our Jewish brethren who have been sold to the nations; but you even sell your brethren that they may be sold to us!" They were silent, and could not find a word to say. So I said, "The thing that you are doing is not good. Ought you not to walk in the fear of our God to prevent the taunts of the nations our enemies?" ' A good example of what would later be called *chillul hashem*.

29. With some implication that he himself was complicit: 'Moreover I and my brethren and my servants are lending them money and grain. Let us leave off this interest' (Neh. 5.10).

30. Neh. 5.11-12: '...."Return to them this very day their fields, their vineyards, their olive orchards, and their houses, and the hundredth of money, grain, wine, and oil which you have been exacting of them." Then they said, "We will restore these and require nothing (לא נבקש) from them. We will do as you say." ' Much turns on what is the implied object of *nevakesh*. Most naturally, it refers to the real property and interest which they undertake to return; they will not seek the like in future.

31. We need not decide here whether this constituted a *berit*. For the description of the patriarchal *berit* in some sources as an oath, *shevu'ah*, see §9.2–9.4, *infra*.

> I also shook out my lap and said, 'So may God shake out every man
> from his house and from his labour who does not perform this promise.
> So may he be shaken out and emptied' and all the assembly said 'Amen'
> and praised the LORD.

It is noticeable that it is Nehemiah who takes the initiative in pronouncing this curse; it does not come from the priests. The quasi-regal figure is still centre-stage, here (as in the story of Zedekiah) using divine sanctions to secure enforcement of an immediate, economic measure. We see from this passage further evidence of the intimate connection between political authority on the one hand and the various aspects of divine law on the other. Divine authority is here used in order to support measures of an ad hoc character that might be thought to fall within the special 'secular' interests of the ruler, namely the basic economic welfare of the people. Nehemiah's special responsibilities may well derive from the fact that the economic problems are themselves attributed, in part, to the effects of royal taxation.[32]

The association of royal and divine authority is found elsewhere in a different form: parallel but separate accounts of the creation of a rule, attributed to the king and to God respectively. Take first David's booty law in 1 Sam. 30.21-25, and its Mosaic parallel in Numbers 31. Both passages have some interesting and unusual features. The incident involving David is presented thus:

> Then David came to the two hundred men, who had been too exhausted
> to follow David, and who had been left at the brook Besor; and they
> went out to meet David and to meet the people who were with him; and
> when David drew near to the people he saluted them. Then all the
> wicked and base fellows among the men who had gone with David said,
> 'Because they did not go with us, we will not give them any of the spoil
> which we have recovered, except that each man may lead away his wife
> and children, and depart.' But David said, 'You shall not do so, my
> brothers, with what the LORD has given us; he has preserved us and
> given into our hand the band that came against us. Who would listen to
> you in this matter? For as his share is who goes down into the battle, so
> shall his share be who stays by the baggage; they shall share alike.' And
> from that day forward he made it a statute and an ordinance for Israel to
> this day.

The passage is of interest, as argued above (§2.3.2), for the relationship between decision-making and the promulgation of rules for the future,

---

32. Neh. 5.4: 'And there were those who said, "We have borrowed money for the king's tax upon our fields and our vineyards".'

and the speech forms associated with each. The phrase *chok umishpat*, I suggested, may combine the complementary notions that (a) a general rule has been prompted by an individual decision (*mishpat*); and (b) that individual decision has indeed been elevated to the status of a general rule (*chok*).

But did David have such authority? Falk (1978: 36) argued that he did not.[33] The incident took place while Saul was still king; David was only a military commander. We could, if we wished, avoid this difficulty in one of two ways. We could argue that David as military commander had delegated authority from the king to enact military law. Or we might regard David's 'rule' in v. 24 ('For as his share is who goes down into the battle, so shall his share be who stays by the baggage; they shall share alike') as *not* claiming to extend beyond the immediate occasion, and take v. 25, the comment on the ultimate significance of the incident ('And from that day forward he made it a statute and an ordinance for Israel to this day'), to reflect a later view, that of the narrator, who either is happy to regard David at this stage as if he were already king, or who sought to imply that it was only when David ascended the throne that he then made this ruling into a statute. Neither explanation, however, is really necessary. Moses was never accorded the title of king, but his activities were clearly modelled, in significant respects, on that role (cf. Porter 1963; Whitelam 1979: 214; *aliter*, Watts 1999: 109-111). He issues commands even where not required by God to do so (§9.4, *infra*). He purges the people, after the

---

33.   See also literature cited by Whitelam (1979: 97-98), and his rejection of this view at 213. In fact, the history of the status of this decision of David parallels that regarding David's own status as the head of a hereditary dynasty. We start with a purely private arrangement, between David and Jonathan, made by a *berit* with God as guarantor: 'And Jonathan, Saul's son, rose, and went to David at Horesh, and strengthened his hand in God. And he said to him, "Fear not; for the hand of Saul my father shall not find you; you shall be king over Israel, and I shall be next to you; Saul my father also knows this." And the two of them made a covenant before the LORD' (1 Sam. 23.16-18). When David is in fact appointed king, it is done by a covenant between him and the people, again guaranteed by God, but there is no mention of an hereditary element: 'So all the elders of Israel came to the king at Hebron; and King David made a covenant with them at Hebron before the LORD and they anointed David king over Israel' (2 Sam. 5.3). The hereditary element is found in those sources where David's appointment is conceived as entailing a covenant between him and God, as seen in the royal psalms (see esp. Ps. 132.11-12. n. 55, *infra*) and which Widengren (1957: 22) takes to be implied in 2 Sam. 7.

incident of the golden calf, on his own initiative, and only then goes to seek God's forgiveness for the remainder (Exod. 32.25-29). Joshua, too, acts as a king in significant respects. He too gives *chok umishpat* at Shechem (Josh. 24.25, 35.2, *supra*; §9.4, *infra*). Whitelam argues that the view that David's decision was made as army commander rather than king, 'fails to take into account the evidence from Saul's reign. The whole basis of royal jurisdiction in the early period stemmed from the king's position as head of the army' (Whitelam 1979: 97-98, 248 n. 17).

Whitelam argues that Numbers 31 represents a retrojection back into the Mosaic period of David's ordinance, in order to conform to the 'prevalent legal fiction' that God was the sole source of law, and that this law was immutable.[34] I certainly agree that by reading the general rule back into the Mosaic period, a claim is being made such as may legitimate that continuity of the booty law that 1 Sam. 30.25 itself claims by saying that David's *chok umishpat* continued *ad hayom hazeh*. But continuity from the Mosaic period does not necessarily stem from divine command. And when we turn to Numbers 31, we are in for something of a surprise. Here, too, the instruction occurs in a narrative context in which there is real booty to be divided (women and child captives, livestock, property, Num. 31.9-12), the result of a campaign against the Midianites. Moses orders the death of the captives, other than virgin girls, and the purification of the warriors and their surviving captives (Num. 31.13-20). Attention is then turned to the purification and disposition of the rest. The first instruction is given not by Moses but by Elazar the Priest, introduced however by the description: 'This is the statute of the law (*chukat hatorah*) which the LORD has commanded Moses' (Num. 31.21); this relates to the means of ritual purification of the booty by fire and/or water (Num. 31.22-24). Then God tells Moses to count the booty (Num. 31.26) and divide it into two parts, between the warriors who went out to battle and all the congregation (Num. 31.27)—a wider distribution, we may note, than that ordered by David (either his decision or his rule for the future). This is not introduced as part of the *chukat hatorah* that God was said to have commanded Moses (Num. 31.21); rather, we have a new introduction, with the instruction forming simply a direct command by God to Moses,

---

34. Whitelam (1979: 96-97, 214, 218); at 218, he takes a similar view of the relationship between Jehoshaphat's reform and the Pentateuchal sources on judicial organization (see *infra*, 158-59).

expressed in the second person singular, and with no indication that it is
to have the status of a general rule for the future:

> The LORD said to Moses, 'Take the count (*sa et rosh...*) of the booty that
> was taken, both of man and of beast, you and Eleazar the priest and the
> heads of the fathers' houses of the congregation; and divide (*vechatsita*)
> the booty into two parts, between the warriors who went out to battle and
> all the congregation (Num. 31.25-27).

Various deductions are then required to be made from the two halves,
for the benefit of the priests and the levites (Num. 31.28-30). Moses and
Elazar are said to have carried out these commands (Num. 31.31) and
the chapter concludes by giving the detail of the booty count, and of the
consequent distribution (Num. 31.32-54).

We lack, in Numbers 31, the dispute-decision-rule structure that is
found in both the story of David's booty and the narratives of desert
adjudication. Instead, we have an ad hoc instruction from God to
Moses, and its implementation. There is no hint that the instruction
regarding the division of the booty is to be of continuing validity. It is
only the instruction regarding the means of ritual purification that is
introduced as a *chukat hatorah* that God had commanded Moses. Such
superscriptions elsewhere in the priestly law are often regarded as editorial (see further §6.3 n. 63). Contrary to Whitelam's theory of retrojection (which elsewhere is entirely plausible), the narrator of Samuel
claims a continuing validity for a royal edict on a matter where God is
said to have pronounced only an ad hoc instruction. Should we reverse
the model, and contemplate the possibility that divine legislative power
(sometimes, Mosaic legislative power) is modelled upon that attributed
to the king, the latter being legitimated by other means?[35]

Similar arguments may be applied to another example of the retrojection theory offered by Whitelam: Jehoshaphat's reform of the judicial
system (1979: 190-91, 217). What appears as a royal ordinance in the
historical books, he argues, is ascribed to divine command in the context of the Mosaic narrative. Both judgments require some qualification.
Unlike David's booty law, Jehoshaphat's reform is not described as a
chok, nor does it claim explicitly to possess enduring force. We may
certainly infer that continuity is assumed during the reign of
Jehoshaphat; beyond that is more questionable, nor is there any ques-

---

35. Cf. Whitelam (1979: 213), arguing that the narrator must have assumed that
his audience would be familiar with the legislative authority of the king.

tion of immutability. As for the Mosaic sources, not only does Exodus 18 fail to claim continuing validity for Moses' reorganization;[36] that reorganization is presented as a response not to any command of God, but rather to the advice of Jethro—an aspect of the narrative entirely omitted in the recapitulation of this episode in Deut. 1.9-18, although even there Moses recounts this reorganization as a purely personal initiative, not having been commanded by God.[37]

Even the main body of Deuteronomic laws, including those on judicial organization in Deut. 17.8-13 (which contain the closest Pentateuchal parallel to Jehoshaphat's reform[38]), is presented as the commands of Moses. Their divine status is far from unambiguous. We should pay careful attention to the superscriptions of the various speeches of Moses in Deuteronomy. The first, historical, speech claims no divine inspiration at all: 'These are the words that Moses spoke to all Israel beyond the Jordan in the wilderness, in the Arabah' (Deut. 1.1); indeed, Moses is said to have 'undertook to explain (*be'er*) this law' (Deut. 1.5; see further §8.1 n. 3, *infra*). Nor does the voice change when Moses turns from history to the duty to obey: 'And now, O Israel, give heed to the statutes and the ordinances which I teach you, and do them' (Deut. 4.1).[39] That there is a distinction in status between the covenant

36. The ad hoc character of these arrangements, quite apart from the narrative setting of Exod. 18, is supported by its being based on the military organization, using the 'officers of thousands, officers of hundreds (שרי אלפים שרי מאות שרי חמשים ושרי עשרת, v. 21) etc.

37. In favour of a closer connection between Exod. 18 and the reform of Jehoshaphat, see Knierim (1961: 146-71).

38. Particularly in the phrase *dam ledam* (2 Chron. 19.10/Deut. 17.8; see Levinson 1997:128); the role of the Levitical priests (2 Chron. 19.8/Deut. 17.9); and the apparent division of the Jerusalem jurisdiction between priestly and secular authorities. As for the last, we have in 2 Chron. 19.8 the involvement of *rashe avot* as well as the Levitical priests, and most explicitly in 19.11: 'And behold, Amariah the chief priest is over you in all matters of the LORD; and Zebadiah the son of Ishmael, the governor of the house of Judah, in all the king's matters' (on which see also Whitelam [1979: 202-203]); in Deuteronomy, we have the involvement of *hashofet* along with the Levitical priests in Deut. 17.9, which may correlate with the distinction in 17.11 between 'the instructions [*hatorah*] which they give you, and according to the decision [*hamishpat*] which they pronounce to you, you shall do'). For further comparison of the sources on judicial organization, see Jackson (1995: 1806-26).

39. In Deut. 4.5, Moses says: ראה למדתי אתכם חקים ומשפטים כאשר צוני יהוה אלהי. But the divine command refers not to the content (much less the

and Mosaic commandment is indicated also in Deut. 4.13-14:

> And he declared to you *his* covenant, which he commanded you to per-
> form, that is, the ten commandments; and he wrote them upon two tables
> of stone. And the LORD commanded *me* at that time to teach you statutes
> and ordinances, that you might do them in the land which you are going
> over to possess.

This distinction is compromised, however, in the conclusion to the
speech:

> Therefore you shall keep *his* statutes and *his* commandments, which I
> command you this day, that it may go well with you, and with your chil-
> dren after you, and that you may prolong your days in the land which the
> LORD your God gives you for ever (Deut. 4.40).

Yet the narrator, in his intervention in Deut. 4.41-49, fails to repeat the
possessives: 'This is the law which Moses set before the children of
Israel; these are the testimonies, the statutes, and the ordinances, which
Moses spoke to the children of Israel when they came out of Egypt'
(Deut. 4.44-45). In none of this is there any claim that these *chukim* and
mishpatim are either covenantal or indeed written; as to the form in
which they were communicated to Moses—whether verbally, or by a
more general divine inspiration—the text is (uncharacteristically) silent.
The force of the possessives in Deut. 4.40 (and commonly elsewhere
[Deut. 4.13, 40; 6.2, 17; 7.9; 8.2, 11; 11.1; 13.4, 18; 26.17, 18; 27.10;
28.1, 15, 45; 30.8, 10, 16], therefore, might—compatibly with the clear
distinction in Deut. 4.13-14 (above)—be no more than that of divine
authorization. In many cases, these possessives are accompanied by the
formula 'which I (Moses) command you this day',[40] and elsewhere the
role of Moses is represented as 'teaching' the *chukim* and *mishpatim*.[41]

---

ipsissima verba) but rather the duty of Moses to teach. It is wisdom activity here
that receives divine endorsement, as the following verses make clear.

40. Deut. 4.40; 8.11; 13.19; 27.10; 28.1, 15; 30.8; cf. 6.2 ('I command you',
without *hayom*). The formula also occurs frequently, of course, in other contexts,
both where the *chukim* and *mishpatim* are referred to without the possessive and in
other contexts. Direct commands from God are rare in Deuteronomy: the Decalogue
(Deut. 4.13); 'his testimonies, and his statutes, which he has commanded you' in
the context of Moses' admonition: 'You shall not put the LORD your God to the
test, as you tested him at Massah' (Deut. 6.17); and the threats of curses for dis-
obedience to 'his commandments and his statutes which he commanded you' (Deut.
28.45 (see also §9.4 n. 70, *infra*).

41. Deut. 4.1, 5, 14; 6.1 (all but the first being didactic activity undertaken in

Moses' next speech, in which he recounts the covenant at Horev and the Decalogue, commences: 'Hear, O Israel, the statutes and the ordinances which I speak in your hearing this day, and you shall learn them and be careful to do them' (Deut. 5.2)—again, without attributing divine authority to the *chukim* and *mishpatim*. The direct quotation of God's words in the Decalogue is followed by the insistence that 'he added no more' (Deut. 5.22). Moses then recalls that the people, fearing any further direct divine revelation, ask Moses to serve as intermediary (Deut. 5.23-27). God agrees, orders the people dismissed to their tents, and commands Moses: 'But you, stand here by me, and I will tell you (*va'adabrah*) all the commandment and the statutes and the ordinances which you shall teach them, that they may do them in the land which I give them to possess' (Deut. 5.31). This does claim divine status for the words that Moses is to communicate, and God's command to Moses is itself verbally reiterated when Moses begins to transmit these teachings (thus showing the fulfilment of this task): 'Now this is the commandment, the statutes and the ordinances which the LORD your God commanded me to teach you, that you may do them in the land to which you are going over, to possess it' (Deut. 6.1). Even so, towards the end of this section of the speech,[42] Moses urges: 'You shall therefore lay up these words of mine in your heart and in your soul' (Deut. 11.18). Moreover, the introduction to the next section of the speech, which contains the main body of Deuteronomic laws (chs. 12–26), makes no comparable claim: 'These are the statutes and ordinances which you shall be careful to do in the land which the LORD, the God of your fathers, has given you to possess, all the days that you live upon the earth' (Deut. 12.1). What God has given here is the land, not the law. Nevertheless, a special status—of endurance and immutability, if not divinity—is claimed for these commands: 'All these matters which I hereby command you, you shall keep and observe them; thou shalt not add to them, or detract from them' (Deut. 13.1).

So we have a distinction, according to the Pentateuchal narrative,

---

response to divine command).

42. The narrator appears to intervene at Deut. 10.6-9, but the speech resumes at 10.10 without any new introductory formula. There is no narrative indication of the commencement of a new speech at 12.1, but the original independence of chs. 12–26 is supported, *inter alia*, not only by its introduction but also by the conclusion (11.26-32), including the reference to blessings and curses to be pronounced on Gerizim and Ebal.

between ad hoc measures of judicial organization recommended by Jethro (Exodus 18), and enduring measures (Deut. 17) commanded by Moses, though here without claim of direct divine inspiration. The legitimacy of Jehoshaphat's measures may indeed be buttressed by their association with Mosaic antiquity; at the same time the very description of Mosaic authority in this area may be influenced by the model of royal activity reflected in the account of the reform of Jehoshaphat.

The interaction between models of royal and divine authority (crucially connected in the figure of Moses) appears to provide a basis for explaining the emergence of the idea of enduring law in ancient Israel. We start with the realities of royal power, very much concerned with immediate royal interests (especially, military[43] and the relief of such economic crisis as may threaten law and order[44]). Sometimes, the ruler seeks to use divine authority to buttress the measures he personally seeks to initiate (Zedekiah's *deror*, Nehemiah's measures); there is no claim, however, that the measures themselves have been mandated by God. Such measures are ad hoc; like the Old Babylonian *mišarum*-act, they do not create enduring law. Nevertheless, by the very fact that they use a religious legitimation—specifically, a *berit* with God as guarantor (Jer. 34.15-16) in the case of Zedekiah, a curse in the case of Nehemiah—an element of continuity is introduced, the continuity that attaches to the (divine) person of the guarantor.

A similar pattern is reflected in the narrative of the coronation of Joash, which has elements in common with that of David: first a private pact between the high priest and the army, to instal Joash, made by a *berit* guaranteed by an oath in the Temple;[45] then delivery of the insignia (visible signs of continuity);[46] then the coronation ceremony involving delivery of the *edut*.[47] The king seems to have been standing

43. Measures to relieve the siege (Zedekiah), disposition of booty (David), law and order in the fortified cities (Jehoshaphat). On the restriction to fortified cities, not followed in Deuteronomy, see also Whitelam (1979: 192-94). See also Dillard (1987: 147, 148).

44. Measures to relieve the siege (Zedekiah), Nehemiah's measures in the context of the famine.

45. 2 Kgs 11.4; 2 Chron. 23.1-7, where the king (though aged 7!) is mentioned as a party to the covenant, v. 3; cf. the *berit* between David and Jonathan, made by a *berit* with God as guarantor: 1 Sam. 23.16-18; see n. 33, *supra*.

46. 'And the priest delivered to the captains the spears and shields that had been King David's, which were in the house of the LORD' (2 Kgs 11.4; 2 Chron. 23.9).

47. 'Then he brought out the king's son, and put the crown upon him, and gave

in an elevated place at this time, 'according to the custom',[48] but there is no indication here of a reading of the *edut*.[49] Thereafter, we hear of *two* covenants: 'And Jehoiada made a covenant between the LORD and the king and people, that they should be the LORD's people; and also between the king and the people' (2 Kgs 11.17).[50] The latter echoes the account of the coronation of David in the succession narrative (2 Sam. 5.3; see n. 33, *supra*); the former appears to conflate this with the (bilateral) covenant between God and the David in the royal psalms (see n. 33, *supra*). The covenant involving God is presented as a loyalty treaty. We are not told the nature of that between king and people, but by implication it must involve issues that were *not* included in the tri-partite covenant, or else it would be superfluous. The very juxtaposition of a covenant in which one of the parties is immortal with one in which the parties are all mortal could well have led to the assumption in the latter of some of the connotations of the former—notably, its temporal dimension. If the relationship between king and people is (also) covenantal, then the laws of that king may be expected to endure.

The notion of enduring law is further reinforced by the Mosaic retro-jections. Moses is depicted as taking ad hoc measures (involving the military structure) to resolve the immediate dispute-resolution problems encountered in the new environment of the wilderness (Exodus 18); he

him the testimony; and they proclaimed him king, and anointed him; and they clapped their hands, and said, "Long live the king!" ' (2 Kgs 11.12; 2 Chron. 23.11). On the *edut* in the context of Assyrian coronation ceremonies, see Weinfeld (1972: 85-87), who takes it probably to refer to a covenant document.

48.   2 Kgs 11.14; והנה המלך עמד על העמוד כמשפט. The use of both *hine* and *kamishpat* (the latter omitted in 2 Chron. 23.13) indicates that Athaliah was observ-ing a conventional speech act. Cf. §2.2, *supra*.

49.   Widengren seeks to conflate such readings as we find in the Josianic reform and the law of *Sukkot* (Deut. 31) with the coronation traditions. He thus takes this narrative to establish a custom whereby, at his coronation, the new King 'as the possessor of the law as the book of the covenant, ought to read out to the assembly the commandments of the book of the covenant and then to make the covenant between Yahweh and his people, taking his place by, or on, the pillar at the entrance of the Temple' (1957: 7). But that is not necessary for the present argu-ment.

50.   By contrast, 2 Chron. 23.16 has only one covenant, in which God is replaced as a party by Jehoiada himself: 'And Jehoiada made a covenant between himself and all the people and the king that they should be the LORD's people'. For a possible explanation of the double covenant in terms of a Hittite parallel, see Weinfeld (1972: 87-88).

also has to dispose of booty (Numbers 31). These measures too are ad hoc. They are modelled on the practical role of the (later) king. The coronation practices, as Widengren has persuasively argued, are reflected in Moses' receipt of the *luchot* in an elevated place.[51] But then the model is reversed. The king himself is viewed in Mosaic terms. Like Moses, he is associated with the propagation and teaching of *torah*. But the law propagated by Moses—in his role as mediator of divine law—is enduring law. Thus the idea of the continuity of law comes to be claimed also for royal law. This last stage is reflected most directly in the narrator's attribution of enduring validity *(ad hayom hazeh)* of David's *chok umishpat* (1 Sam. 30.25). But Moses, too, is depicted as fulfilling this role. Not only does he give a series of ad hoc instructions relating to the way the conquest is to be marked;[52] he also gives instructions of enduring validity, without claiming that he does so at God's command.[53]

Of course, the claim to make enduring law was no more guaranteed to be effective in ancient Israel than elsewhere in the ancient Near East. It may be significant in this connection that Nehemiah records (8.13-18) that the law of *Sukkot* itself had not been observed since the days of Joshua, until it was rediscovered in the written law by Ezra (who then read from the book of the law from the first day to the last of that festival).

6.3 *The Construction of Continuity: Chok Olam*

The development proposed in the last section might still be regarded as incomplete. We might still ask: why should divine law itself be conceived as enduring law? I suggested earlier that continuity might be ascribed, in principle, to the sender of a message, its receiver, the medium of the message or its referent. A simple view might be that God is the sender of a covenant, which refers to enduring laws, the laws taking on the continuity of their sender. That, however, begs an impor-

---

51. Widengren (1957: 17-19), where he also associates the Mosaic covenant (esp. Exod. 24.5-8) not only with that of Josiah, but also with 'a typical Mesopotamian royal pattern of ideology, according to which the king ascends to God, is given the tablets of destiny, and gets a special commission as a Messenger or Apostle of God'.

52. On the Mount Ebal ceremony in Deut. 27, see further §9.4, *infra*.

53. On the law of the septennial reading at Sukkot in Deut. 31, see further §9.4, *infra*.

tant questions about the the relationship between covenant and law, and the role of God in the covenant.

The Decalogue threatens future generations with punishment if they do not adhere to the prohibition of idolatry:

> for I the LORD your God am a jealous God, visiting the iniquity of the fathers upon the children to the third and the fourth generation of those who hate me, but showing steadfast love to thousands of those who love me and keep my commandments (Exod. 20.5-6; Deut. 5.9-10).

The love/hate theme is widely seen as originating in ancient Near Eastern treaties, referring to relationships of rebellion or loyalty (Weinfeld 1972: 81-84; Levinson 1992: 46). Levinson cites, as background to the Decalogue, the following clause in the treaties of 672 BCE between Esarhaddon and his eastern vassals, designed to ensure *continuing* loyalty to Esarhaddon's son, Ashurbanipal.[54]

> If, as long as we, our sons and our grandsons live, the Crown Prince designate Ashurbanipal will not be our king and lord, if we place another king, another prince over ourselves, our sons, our grandsons—may all the gods mentioned (here) call us, our offspring, and our descendants, to account.

Levinson comments: 'By transferring the Near Eastern convention of vicarious punishment for breach of treaty loyalty from the political to the theological domain, the biblical text formulates a doctrine which I call the transgenerational consequences of sin' (1992: 47). But two important changes occur in the course of this cultural transfer. First, the role of God is changed from that of guarantor of a treaty to that of a party (the 'sender' in a communicational model) to it. Second, and connected, there is also a subtle shift in the temporal duration of the obligation. I take issue with Levinson's claim that such 'ancient Near Eastern treaties were understood to be made in perpetuity—not only with those immediately signatory to them, but also with succeeding generations' (Levinson 1992: 46-47). The treaty of Esarhaddon puts the issue of temporality in the following terms: '...as long as we, our sons and our grandsons live...' The implication is that the treaty binds the parties and their then living descendants; we are not justified in reading into this an obligation upon an indefinite number of unborn generations. The treaty thus takes account of the mortality of its human partners; God

---

54. Levinson (1992: 47), quoting *ANET* (3rd edn, 1969: 539); and comparing *ANET* (3rd edn 1969: 537).

may be immortal, but God is simply the guarantor. In the Bible, God is transformed into a party to the covenant. If God takes the place of the mortal Esarhaddon and Ashurbanipal as the recipient of loyalty, then, reciprocally, those who owe loyalty[55] maybe conceived as transcending the limits of mortality.[56] And when the covenant comes to be conceived as encompassing laws and not simply (hereditary) blessing and loyalty, the temporality of its sender is naturally ascribed to his message.[57] This, in itself, would prompt a demand for a permanent medium, to ensure that what was obligatory on future generations was indeed the same as in the original act of legislation. Hence the emphasis, traced in the last

55. In the Pentateuch, a covenant between God and the people; elsewhere, however, it may be between God and the king. Widengren (1957: 24-25) notes that in the 'royal Psalms', the covenant between Yahweh and David is conceived in juridical terms. Here, too, the issue of transgenerational obligation arises, the covenant, as Widengren puts it, 'being dependent on the stipulation that the descendants of David keep God's covenant and his witness', citing Ps. 132.11-12: 'The LORD swore to David a sure oath from which he will not turn back: "One of the sons of your body I will set on your throne. If your sons keep my covenant and my testimonies which I shall teach them, their sons also for ever shall sit upon your throne".' See also Ps. 89.4-5, and the comments of Widengren (1957: 22).

56. Though it is *not* clear that this in fact is the implication of 'the third and the fourth generation' in the Decalogue. See Jackson (1975a: 156-60), where I argued for a distinction between 'X *or* (X +1)' and 'X *and* (X +1)', and concluded that the latter was not a form of intensification. If that is correct, then there may be an implied temporal limitation to the living generation even in the Decalogue, as in Esarhaddon's treaty. Moses is presented as sensitive to this issue in introducing the Decalogue to a generation that was *not* alive at the time of its original promulgation: 'The LORD our God made a covenant with us in Horeb. Not with our fathers did the LORD make this covenant, but with us, who are all of us here alive this day' (Deut. 5.2-3). Levinson (1997: 151-52), describes this claim as 'an audacious denial of the facts. The addressees of Moses are actually the new generation that arose after the 40 years of wilderness wandering.' It may be viewed as a legal fiction. Moses is careful not to take the same risk of being vague about the status of future generations in the covenant on the plains of Moab (on which see further §9.4. *infra*): 'Nor is it with you only that I make this sworn covenant, but with him who is not here with us this day as well as with him who stands here with us this day before the LORD our God' (Deut. 29.13-14).

57. For the working out of the problem in the narratives, where the succession of revelations and covenants appear to be prompted by the feeling that—whatever the theory—real commitment was best secured by personal rather than hereditary adherence, see further, §§9.2-4, *infra*.

chapter, upon inscribed stones on the one hand, and an archived *sefer* on the other.

That leaves just one (little explored) aspect of the continuity of law—that of the referent of its rules. I have argued that royal legislation appears to have originated in ad hoc measures: how to distribute *this* booty, whether to release *these* slaves, etc. It may appear natural enough to us to imagine a progression towards continuity merely through a process of generalisation: there should be rules for the distribution of *any* booty, for the release of *any* slaves. In fact, a more specific line of development is apparent, from the semantic range and likely history of the term *chok* (sometimes, *chukah*) itself (see *TDOT*, V, pp. 139-47). Jurisdiction, I have argued, seems to originate (in the Bible as elsewhere) in the interest of the holder of the jurisdiction (Jackson 1995c: 1806-26). The same is true of legislation: *chok* appears to have referred originally not to the abstract entity we call a 'law', but rather to an object or entitlement which is transferable within human (or even human–divine) interaction.[58] It is the continuity of this object or entitlement that lies at the basis of *chok* as a continuing law—*chok olam*. Here, as in some European languages, we have a progression from concrete rights (occasionally, conversely, dues[59]) to the notion of 'the right', or right conduct in general.[60]

Both the concrete and the general meanings are found in the account of Joseph's reform of Egyptian landholding, in order to deal with the famine:

> So Joseph bought all the land of Egypt for Pharaoh; for all the Egyptians sold their fields, because the famine was severe upon them. The land became Pharaoh's; and as for the people, he made slaves of them from one end of Egypt to the other. Only the land of the priests he did not buy; for the priests had a fixed allowance (*chok lakohanim*) from Pharaoh, and lived on the allowance which Pharaoh gave them; therefore they did not sell their land. Then Joseph said to the people, 'Behold, I have this day bought you and your land for Pharaoh. Now here is seed for you, and you shall sow the land. And at the harvests you shall give a fifth to

---

58. I speak here of its use. This is not to deny an etymology in the notion of a physical limit or boundary, produced by cutting.

59. Thus, it is used of the 'quota' of bricks required of the Israelite slaves in Egypt (Exod. 5.13-14), where the Israelite foremen ask: 'Why have you not done all your task of making bricks (מדוע לא כליתם חקכם ללבן) today, as hitherto?'

60. Cf. *TDOT*, V, p. 141, on the likely priority of the more concrete meanings of *chok* to that of ordinances or legal precepts.

Pharaoh, and four fifths shall be your own, as seed for the field and as food for yourselves and your households, and as food for your little ones'. And they said, 'You have saved our lives; may it please my lord, we will be slaves to Pharaoh'. So Joseph made it a statute concerning the land of Egypt, and it stands to this day (וישם אתה יוסף לחק עד היום הזה), that Pharaoh should have the fifth; the land of the priests alone did not become Pharaoh's (Gen. 47.22-26).

The terminology in this last verse is close to that of the narrator's comment on David's booty law (וישמה לחק ולמשפט לישראל עד היום הזה).[61] But the usage in respect of the rights of the Egyptian priesthood is far more concrete: it refers to their right to (at least the use of) their land.

It is hardly surprising that this term should have been used of the entitlements of the Egyptian priesthood, and ultimately of the general, enduring rule giving effect to those rights. For its use in the priestly law is very commonly with reference to the entitlements of the Israelite priesthood, and this is stressed to be permanent. For example:

And you shall take the breast of the ram of Aaron's ordination and wave it for a wave offering before the LORD; and it shall be your portion. And you shall consecrate the breast of the wave offering, and the thigh of the priests' portion, which is waved, and which is offered from the ram of ordination, since it is for Aaron and for his sons. It shall be for Aaron and his sons as a perpetual due (לחק עולם) from the people of Israel, for it is the priests' portion to be offered by the people of Israel from their peace offerings; it is their offering to the LORD (Exod. 29.26-28).

In relation to the *minchah* (cereal offering), the priestly portion is described as חק עולם לדרתיכם (Lev. 6.11 MT; cf. 10.13): a hereditary right of Aaron and his sons. More explicitly still, the wave offering is something which God says: 'I have taken from the people of Israel, out of the sacrifices of their peace offerings, and have given them to Aaron the priest and to his sons, as a perpetual due from the people of Israel' (לחק עולם מאת בני ישראל, Lev. 7.34 MT). In Num. 18.8 (cf. 11) God grants to Aaron (directly) 'whatever is kept of the offerings made to me, all the consecrated things of the people of Israel; I have given them to you as a portion, and to your sons as a perpetual due' (לך נתתים למשחה ולבניך לחק עולם). In Num. 18.21, 23, the Levites'

---

61. Though the collocation of *chok* and *mishpat* is not used in the Genesis narrative. On this, see further §2.3.2, *supra*.

tithe is described as a *chukat olam*, which serves as the *nachalah* of the Levites, since they are deprived of rights of inheritance to the land.

A natural extension of this notion is from the particular entitlements of the priests to the office itself. Thus, we read in Exod. 29.9 that the priesthood (*kehunah*) belongs to Aaron and his sons as a *chukat olam*. In the context of the memorial bread at the Temple, the right to the *chok olam* of the priesthood (Lev. 24.9) is described as a *berit olam*:

> And you shall take fine flour, and bake twelve cakes of it; two tenths of an ephah shall be in each cake. And you shall set them in two rows, six in a row, upon the table of pure gold. And you shall put pure frankincense with each row, that it may go with the bread as a memorial portion to be offered by fire to the LORD. Every sabbath day Aaron shall set it in order before the LORD continually on behalf of the people of Israel as a covenant for ever (ברית עולם). And it shall be for Aaron and his sons, and they shall eat it in a holy place, since it is for him a most holy portion out of the offerings by fire to the LORD, a perpetual due (חק עולם) (Lev. 24.8).

Today, we might be tempted to distinguish, analytically, between the right (*chok olam*) and the legal source of the right (*berit olam*). The parallelism in this text suggests that this distinction is not yet present: the covenant itself, once granted, is a right, an entitlement.

The semantic transition of *chok/chukah* from an entitlement to a divine law may have occurred through the specification, in the cult, of those parts of the sacrifices which did *not* belong to the priests, but rather belonged to God. Thus, in Lev. 3.16-17, of the fat:

> All fat is the LORD's. It shall be a perpetual statute throughout your generations (חקת עולם לדרתיכם), in all your dwelling places, that you eat neither fat nor blood.

The converse of God's entitlement is a human prohibition. The term is then applied to ritual prohibitions which do not have a converse entitlement.[62] The most general usage, 'a statute', is found both in superscriptions and subscriptions[63] to paragraphs of ritual law[64] and elsewhere.[65]

---

62. E.g. Lev. 10.9: wine and strong drink on entering the tent of meeting. See also Lev. 17.7, 23.14.

63. Regarded by *TDOT*, V, p. 144, as secondary, approving Hentschke.

64. See Exod. 12.14, 17 (*passover*); 27.21 (*ner tamid*); 28.43 (priestly clothing); 30.21 (obligatory washing ritual); Lev. 23.21, 41 (festivals).

65. Notably, Lev. 16.29, 31, 34 (*Yom Kippur*); arguably in 24.3 (*ner tamid*); Num. 10.8 (trumpets for summoning the assembly); 19.10, 19 (ritual purity).

It is noticeable that the collocation of *chok* and *mishpat* is not found in these sources dealing with priestly entitlements and ritual law. We have encountered it (§6.2) in the narrator's comment (a narrative subscription) on David's booty law (1 Sam. 30.25). It occurs also in concluding the account of the laws proclaimed in the wake of the decision on the case of the daughters of Zelophehad: והיתה לבני ישראל לחקת משפט כאשר צוה יהוה את משה (Num. 27.11; see further §2.3.2, *supra*). Both sources record an actual dispute and its resolution, followed by the proclamation of law for the future. In the light of the present discussion, the *chok* element might be regarded as much as an entitlement as a law: the entitlement to inherit.[66] But the development towards the general sense of 'statute' is also found in the use of the collocation in the priestly law:

> And these things shall be for a statute and ordinance (לחקת משפט) to you throughout your generations in all your dwellings. If any one kills a person, the murderer shall be put to death on the evidence of witnesses; but no person shall be put to death on the testimony of one witness (Num. 35.29-30).

Here, there is an explicit link with the claim of transgenerational obligation.

Ezra commits himself to the implementation of such statutes. The RSV translates Ezra 7.10:

> For Ezra had set his heart to study the law of the LORD, and to do it, and to teach his statutes and ordinances in Israel.[67]

כי עזרא הכין לבבו לדרש את תורת יהוה ולעשת וללמד בישראל
חק ומשפט

However, it is more natural to take *vela'asot* together with *ulelamed* as referring to *chok umishpat,* rather than the preceding *torat adonai.* Ezra commits himself to study the *torah,* and both to implement and teach it as law. This dual activity echoes that of Jehoshaphat (2 Chron. 17.7-9; 4-11, discussed in §5.1, *supra*). But whereas the written law is mentioned, in the Jehoshaphat tradition, only in relation to teaching and not in relation to adjudication, Ezra appears to have adopted it as *chok,* in the extended sense developed by the priestly writers.

---

66. Cf. Gen. 47.26, of the Egyptian priesthood's landholdings, and the association of *chok* with *nachalah* in relation to the Levites in Num. 18.21, 23, both noted above.

67. *TDOT*, V, p. 143, sees here an allusion to Josh. 24.25.

Chapter 7

'POSTULATES' AND VALUES

7.1 'Postulates' Again

What are values and how are they expressed? Despite the apparent confidence of some biblical scholars, the answers are less than self-evident. If we assume, without further investigation, that values are abstract entities (whether propositions or qualities) that exist in the texts, the minds of the authors or the societies to which they belong, and that their elucidation may proceed by the process of rational inference (from concrete expressions to abstract values), then we may run the risk of applying a modern (some would say modernist) Western post-Enlightenment mode of thought to a quite different culture.[1] This may prove just as hazardous as the application to the biblical texts of modern, Western models of law.

In an attempt to find a model that does not suffer from such cultural contingency, we may seek to apply semiotic approaches to the question. Values are messages transmitted within society, often qualifications of other messages: that such behaviour is good, pleasant, revolting, etc. In the semiotic model derived from Greimas, narratives of behaviour (whether real or fictional) are accompanied by (often tacit) social evaluations (§1.1). The social psychologists Leyens and Codol write: 'Categories are generally not neutral for the individual. Based on their own

---

1. Cf. Douglas (1999: 15), approving a distinction made by sinologists between 'analogical' and 'rational-instrumental' thinking: 'Our logic is based on part–whole relations, the theory of types, causal implications and logical entailments. It organises experience in theoretical terms. Rational construction based upon it always goes in a direction away from the concrete particular towards the universal... For example, rational construction creates contexts in which "human nature", or "human rights", or "equality under the law", can be invoked.' Against this, she contrasts a form of thought variously described as 'correlative', 'aesthetic' or 'analogical' (see further n. 56, infra).

personal experience, or under the influence of social standards, individuals value certain characteristics of objects and thus relate them to *behaviour patterns*' (1988: 93). Indeed, if we adopt a subjective, communicational view of values—values as feelings[2] and evaluations attributed by human beings to objects and behaviour patterns, and communicated to other human beings in ways calculated to make sense to the latter—then we cannot avoid asking about the (semiotic) codes used within any particular society, or discourse group within that society, to make such sense. Equally, we must take account of the distinction, important also in the psychological study of moral development,[3] between moral feeling (the unarticulated sense that something is right or wrong, good or bad, pleasant or unpleasant, etc.) and moral judgment (articulations of the reasons for that sense).[4] Yet even this distinction may not prove adequate for our purposes. We have already encountered two quite different forms of articulation of values in biblical law. On the one hand, a 'diagnosis' (§§2.1, 4.2, 4.7, *supra*) may attribute a moral judgment, without stating the reasons for that judgment.[5] *rotseach hu* (Num. 35.16-18; §§2.1, 4.2, 4.7, *supra*) is not merely an appeal to a *legal* category, even more so, *to'evah*.[6] On the other, 'motive clauses',

2.   There is a close connection in much of the semiotic and psychological literature between values, aesthetics and emotions. For example, Donaldson (1992: 12) defines emotions as 'value feelings'. Frijda (1986: 199, 200) writes: '*Sadness and grief* correspond to the situational meaning structure of emptiness or barrenness; that is, to the explicit absence of something valued…to the extent that absence spreads beyond a specific focus and global emptiness takes over, grief turns into depression.' 'Something valued' here is clearly something desired. For a review of the literature on both the development and structure of the moral sense, stressing the role of narrative in both cognitive psychological and semiotic accounts, see Jackson (1995b: 320-48).

3.   See further Jackson (1995b: 273, 288, 294-99). The overwhelming emphasis of Kohlberg's studies is on articulated moral judgment.

4.   Cf. Donaldson (1992: 12-15) on the distinction between 'value judgments' and 'value feelings'.

5.   The language being in 'restricted code' (pp. 72-73, *supra*), the reasons—or at least the appropriateness of the feeling—may be taken to be self-evident.

6.   'An abomination': e.g. Lev. 20.13, Deut. 18.12; 24.4. It may well be that scholarly interest in identifying abstract ethical reasons for ritual taboos—an activity that necessarily requires the ritual laws to be interpreted as 'symbols'—has prompted the disposition to look for much more abstract values also in the 'civil' laws than either their expression justifies or their understanding requires. Though increasingly popular, this approach to the ritual laws, particularly associated with

frequently referring to the narrative history, set out in an articulated fashion the reasons for adherence to a norm (§4.7, *supra*). More generally, we may ask whether the values of biblical law are expressed in 'restricted' or 'elaborated' code (§3.1, *supra*). Mary Douglas rightly recognizes that different documents of biblical law may articulate their values in different styles. She contrasts Deuteronomy, which 'uses the language of feeling and cause and effect...is political, brilliant at rousing congregations to enthusiasm', with Leviticus, which 'is not given to expatiating on moral values in the abstract, its style is more to do with a concrete logic of positions and objects' (Douglas 1999: 41-42).

In this context we may revisit Moshe Greenberg's famous theory of the 'postulates' of biblical criminal law,[7] in order primarily to identify and assess the model of values he deploys. It is important to place it in the context of the problem for which Greenberg presented it as the solution. The problem, for Greenberg, was that of apparent contradictions in biblical law and the choice between a literary-historical approach, which resolves such contradictions in terms of historical development, and the approach of the 'commentator', whom Greenberg took to be exemplified by Sir John Miles on the Laws of Hammurabi, whose purpose is 'to imagine how this section as it stands can have been interpreted by a Babylonian court'.[8] Greenberg opted for the latter, on the grounds that the distinctions which such a commentator might be obliged to make are not merely

---

Jacob Milgrom (see, e.g., Milgrom [1963: 288-301], commended by Watts [1999: p. 58 n. 80]), and the more recent work of Mary Douglas (notably, Douglas 1999) remains controversial (see Maccoby 1999: 203-208). I do not here seek to enter this controversy. Suffice it to say that it has long been recognized that the 'ceremonial' and the 'judicial' laws may reflect different forms of semiosis (see further Jackson (1984: 25-50).

7.   Greenberg (1960: 5-28). I offered a critique in Jackson (1973a: 8-38) reprinted in Jackson (1975a: 25-63). I stand by the arguments there advanced, with the single qualification that Exod. 21.18-19 does not necessarily stand as a counter-example, given that Greenberg, as he has indicated to me, claims only the incommensurability of money with loss of life (and not with non-fatal human injuries; see, however, n. 43, *infra*). Greenberg has since sought to narrow the area of debate: see Greenberg (1986), discussed further *infra*, pp. 184-87.

8.   Driver and Miles (1952–55: I, p. 99) quoted at Greenberg (1960: 7), where he refers also to Miles's own comparison with the work of Koschaker (Driver and Miles 1952–55: I, 275).

> the recourse of a modern harmonist to escape the contradictions of the text; they are, it would seem, necessary for understanding how an ancient jurist, how the draftsman himself, understood the law. It must be assumed that the laws of Hammurabi were intended as a consistent guide to judges, and had to be interpreted as they stand in as consistent a manner as possible (1960: 7).

The same assumption is adopted in relation to biblical law. Whether it is justifiable in relation to the Laws of Hammurabi has become increasingly controversial (see §5.1, *supra*). Even if it were, any straightforward application of the same model to Biblical law is complicated by the fact that the 'codes' of biblical law have no independence from the text of the Pentateuch. Before we can study the problems of a document that might have provided 'a consistent guide to judges', we have to identify such a document. Greenberg did so, in effect, by stripping away from the Pentateuch everything except those laws whose authorship is attributed to God.[9] That is the document whose contradictions are to be resolved by the art of the commentator. Such, indeed, is the approach of the Rabbis, and there is merit in examining what exegetical approaches are adopted *once* the text is so viewed. Greenberg simply assumed that it was so viewed *ab initio*.[10] His solution was therefore implicit in his very formulation of the problem.

By contrast, I seek to cast light on the processes that led up to this conception of a 'statutory' text—statutory, in that (a) it presented a single, coherent system; (b) its structures are those of literacy rather than orality; and (c) it was to be used as the criterion for resolving disputes in courtroom adjudication. I would claim that my approach is, indeed, closer to the text than that of Greenberg in at least one respect: the Pentateuch presents biblical law *not* as a single document, but as a succession of speeches. For sure, those speeches are largely presented as coming from a single source, God, mainly through the mouth of

9.   Certainly, in Greenberg (1986: 1-17). It is far less clear that this was his position in 1960 (see *infra*, pp. 184-87).

10.   Greenberg (1960: 19) does accept historical development as between the Biblical and Rabbinic positions: '[I]t is legitimate to speak of the law of the Bible as archaic in comparison with postbiblical Jewish law...the jural postulate of the biblical law of homicide reached its fullest expression only later: the invaluableness of life led to the virtual abolition of the death penalty. But what distinguishes this abolition from that just described in the Hittite laws, what shows it to be truly in accord with the peculiar inner reason of biblical law is the fact that it was not accompanied by the institution of any sort of pecuniary compensation.'

Moses—but *not* on a single occasion. The Pentateuch itself is thus clear that we have a number of separate 'texts'. That provides a scholarly basis for the inquiry into the individual histories of these collections of law, distinguishable from the exegetical problems presented by the Laws of Hammurabi. Once this is accepted, it follows that different models of values, and methods for their elucidation, may be appropriate at the various historical stages.

I turn now to the model that Greenberg adopted in order to resolve his problem, that of 'postulates'. He writes:

> Another virtue of the commentator is his insistence on understanding a given body of law in its own terms before leaping into comparisons with other law systems. To do so, however, means to go beyond the individual rules; for it is not possible to comprehend the law of any culture without an awareness of its key concepts, its value judgements (Greenberg 1960: 8).

With this, we need have little dissent.[11] There is, however, a considerable distance between 'individual rules' on the one hand and 'key concepts…value judgements' on the other. What kind of values did Greenberg have in mind? Are they (a) the unarticulated feelings associ-

---

11. As I indicated in Jackson (1975a: 19), my objections to Greenberg were methodological. I had no objection to the search for underlying values as such (though now I would pay closer attention to the range of phenomena that might qualify for such a designation). Originally, I demanded that any principles be explicit (Jackson 1975a: 32). Phillips (1977: 106) responded that we need to be able to make inferences, even in the absence of explicit statements of principle, in order to generate hypotheses, since otherwise we are reduced simply to the activity of cataloguing concrete rules. Cf. Haas (1989: 70), criticizing me for taking the view that: '[a]n individual law is nothing more than an individual law, and imposing any larger meaning on it is already a methodological gamble'. I have since abandoned the form of legal positivism implicit in the demand for explicit principles in favour of the reconstruction of values by semiotic methods, including the conception of narrative meaning advanced in §3.2, *supra*, and the use of structural oppositions such as those discussed in §7.2, *infra*, and first proposed in Jackson (1988a, 1988c). On the need for caution in 'drawing inferences from statements that are not express or unequivocal', cf. Welch (1999b: 115). Haas's own version of the structuralist approach (1989: 76) is one that stresses addressing the values of the text as a whole, but he assumes that this whole text is that of the Pentateuch, and that structuralist oppositions can be derived by extrapolating from quite distinct parts of it; and even when he addresses a particular text (e.g. Num. 35) he fails to consider its literary forms and features, which I take to be an important feature of the literary expression of values in the biblical texts.

ated with the perception of particular behaviour patterns, (b) rules of a certain level of generality (what might be termed 'principles') or (c) the rational justification of relationships between different rules? Greenberg's answer seems to veer between the latter two. Both the talionic formula 'life for life' and Gen. 9.6, which he takes to express the same principle (with equal vagueness, he claims, as to the procedure) are taken to be 'jural postulates'.[12] Elsewhere, however, he appears to view postulates as underlying reasons.[13] He complains that much work comparing biblical with ancient Near Eastern law has been content with comparing individual laws rather than law systems or law ideologies: 'Until the values that the law embodies are understood, it is question whether any individual law can be properly appreciated, let alone profitably compared with another in a foreign system' (Greenberg 1960: 8). The values that he identifies in the course of his study are (a) ideas concerning the origin, purpose and sanction of the law;[14] (b) the famous 'incommensurability' principle: 'In biblical law life and property are incommensurable; taking of life cannot be made up for by any amount of property, nor can any property offence be considered as amounting to the value of a life';[15] and (c) the autonomy principle,

---

12. Greenberg (1986: 16) (of Gen. 9.6): 'For human life taken, life is forfeit: not camels, not money, but life. Surely this is as much a jural postulate as the talion formula "life for life" which Jackson admits is a legal maxim. And, just like the talion formula, it is utterly vague regarding the procedure to be followed in carrying it out.'

13. On this argument, Gen. 9.6a might be regarded as a principle, Gen. 9.6b as a postulate. Greenberg (1986: 16) does indeed take Gen. 9.6's 'exaltation of man as made in God's image' as 'the postulate of the strict biblical law of homicide'.

14. Greenberg (1960: 9-13), ancient Near Eastern law being of royal origin and concerned with, *inter alia*, 'stable government' and other 'political benefits', whereas biblical law, being of divine origin, reflects a stronger notion of 'the idea of the transcendence of the law': 'The very formulation is God's' (at 11). Indeed: 'Not only is Moses denied any part in the formulation of the Pentateuchal laws, no Israelite king is said to have authored a code, nor is any king censured for so doing.' On this latter issue, see §6.2, *supra*. Observance of the law sanctifies and is accounted as righteousness: 'There is a distinctively religious tone here, fundamentally different in quality from the political benefits guaranteed in the cuneiform law collections.'

15. Greenberg (1960: 18), this reflecting a difference in the values implicit in the claims of origin made in biblical and ancient Near Eastern laws respectively, in that 'a basic difference in the evaluation of life and property separates the one from the others. In the biblical law a religious evaluation; in non-biblical, an economic

reflected in the dual (human and divine) standards applied to vicarious punishment (Greenberg 1960: 20-27): 'So far as man is concerned all persons are individual, morally autonomous entities. In this too there is doubtless to be seen the effect of the heightened stress on the unique worth of each life that the religious-legal postulate of man's being the image of God brought about' (Greenberg 1960: 26-27). He describes jural postulates as 'the peculiar inner reason of biblical law'(Greenberg 1960: 19).

Greenberg's stated source of inspiration for 'postulates' is an anthropological/customary model, rather than one that belongs to the sphere of interpretation of written law. He refers enthusiastically to the work of E.A. Hoebel, in support of the proposition (quoted above) that 'it is not possible to comprehend the law of any culture without an awareness of its key concepts, its value judgements'.[16] But Hoebel is not looking for rationalist methods of statutory interpretation;[17] he takes the notion of 'jural postulates' directly from Josef Kohler, a comparative lawyer still influenced to some extent by the German Historical School of Jurisprudence of Savigny (see Jackson 1996a: 58-61). The latter had sought the origins, characteristic features and special value of any body in law in the *Volksgeist* to which it belonged: 'In the general consciousness of a people lives positive law and hence we have to call it people's law (*Volksrecht*)'.[18] Here, legal values were conceived to reside primarily at the level of the popular *unconscious*, and were not to be sought in explicit legal statements:

> The form however in which law lives in the common consciousness of a people is not that of abstract rules but as the living intuition of the institutions of law in their organic connexion, so that whenever the necessity

and political evaluation, predominates' (at 19).

16. Greenberg (1960: 8 n. 5): 'The point is made and expertly illustrated in E.A. Hoebel, *The Law of Primitive Man* (Harvard, 1954), especially chap. 1.' Haas. (1989: 69-70), sides largely with Greenberg on the grounds that anthropologists of law do look for underlying values in a system as a whole. But those underlying values can be sought, in principle, at any stage in the development of a tradition.

17. He does, however, ascribe to postulates a strong determining role within the (unwritten) legal systems with which the legal anthropologist is concerned: 'The particular formulations of specific customs and patterns for behavior that go into a given culture are more or less explicitly shaped by the precepts given in the basic postulates of the specific culture... New patterns are accepted, rejected, or modified with reference to the basic postulates' (Hoebel 1954: 13).

18. Savigny (1867: 12), as quoted in Freeman (1994: 799).

arises for the rule to be conceived in its logical form, this must be first formed by a scientific procedure from that total intuition. That form reveals itself in the symbolical acts which display in visible shape the essence of the jural relation and in which the primitive laws express themselves more intelligibly and thoroughly than in written laws (Freeman 1994: 799-80).

This paragraph expresses a very distinctive view of the forms in which law is expressed. It is, we may say, a historical semiotics of law. Law is first perceived, Savigny argues, not in the form of linguistically expressed rules, but rather in people's subconscious intuitions as to how the institutions of their society work. It is through visible symbols—ceremonies of marriage, transfers of property, etc.—that people originally recognise such institutions. If need be, these institutions can then be expressed in 'logical form' (meaning here linguistic form), but this is the job of experts. Even when it is done, the expression of the legal institutions in linguistic rules will never be as authentic as the popular, intuitive feeling for them.[19]

Hoebel's postulates are also located at a 'deep'[20] level of the social unconscious. He describes the 'basic postulates' as 'too generally hidden; postulates felt, perhaps, by those who live by them, but so much taken for granted that they are but rarely expressed or exposed for examination'.[21] Yet he has also moved significantly away from the German Historical School, not only in eschewing theses of typical historical development (to which anthropological data hardly lends itself) and of the uniqueness of the original cultural values of each *Volk*, but also in his relative indifference, for conceptual purposes, to the manner

19. Cf. Wellhausen (1973: 393): '[a] body of traditional practice should only be written down when it is threatening to die out, and...a book should be, as it were, the ghost of a life which is closed.' This is quoted by Levenson (1980: 17), in the context of the history of scholarship on the relationship between law and covenant. Levenson notes that Greenberg's thesis may be viewed as one form of reaction against this. Yet paradoxically, the origins of Greenberg's concept of 'postulates' is to be found in this very tradition of German romanticism.

20. Such that it becomes necessary, in the quest for a new world order, to engage in 'deep-cutting analysis of the major law systems of the contemporary world in order to lay bear their basic postulates' (Hoebel 1954: 333).

21. Hoebel (1954: 16) quotes with approval Stone (1950: 337): 'The jural postulates...are generalized statements of the tendencies actually operating, of the presuppositions on which a particular civilisation is based...they are ideals presupposed by the whole social complex ...'

of expression of the postulates. This is itself a matter of cultural contingency: societies vary in the degree to which they consciously formalize their behaviour patterns (Hoebel 1954: 40). Thus Hoebel maintains: 'The postulates of a society may or may not be explicitly expressed by its members' (1954: 17). He does, however, accept that postulates may, in some societies, be used consciously in reasoning about law: 'Inasmuch as the members of a society ordinarily accept their basic propositions as self-evident truths and work upon them as if they were truths, and because they do reason from them, if not with perfect logic, they may best be called postulates' (Hoebel 154: 13).

Unlike Hoebel, and for reasons very different from those of Savigny, Greenberg sought to identify the unique values of a particular people. Unlike Hoebel,[22] he assumes that postulates must have a *conceptual* (rather than merely contingent) consistency within the corpus to which they apply. In using the concept of 'postulates' for this purpose, however, he follows Hoebel's drift towards a Western, rationalist model.[23] His values are not those *underlying* the text. They are the explicit value statements of the texts (such as Gen. 9.6[24]) together with rationalist

22. Hoebel (1954: 16): 'Nor are the basic postulates in a culture necessarily perfectly consistent among themselves. However, the measure of consistency between basic postulates, and between the postulates and the specific selected behavior patterns, will be the measure of integration of the culture'.

23. Indeed, Hoebel (1954: 46) commences a chapter arguing for the usefulness of Hohfeld's 'fundamental legal conceptions' in the analysis of primitive law with the statement: 'If there is law in primitive societies in the same sense as in ours, then the basic tools of Western jurisprudence, though originally designed to fit the needs of the student of a system of civilized law, should also, to some degree, serve the needs of the student of primitive law.' The claim that 'there is law in primitive societies in the same sense as in ours' is based by Hoebel on adoption of the following definition: 'A social norm is legal if its neglect or infraction is regularly met, in threat or in fact, by the application of physical force by an individual or group possessing the socially recognized privilege of so acting' (28; see further his discussion in Ch. 2). The argument for the application of modern Western jurisprudence thus takes no account of semiotic difference. As a result, his own claims fall short of clarity. He fails to make clear what distinctions, if any, he intends between rules, principles and precepts. Compare the statement at 13, quoted in n. 17, *supra,* with his reference at 16 to 'the postulates (major and minor) that are used for operation in determination of legal principles'.

24. Thus Gen. 9.5-6 is described as 'a precise and adequate formulation of the jural postulates underlying the biblical law of homicide' (Greenberg 1960: 15). But the meaning of such texts is not unproblematic. Indeed, Greenberg is content to

reconstructions of the supposed reasons for individual laws. Indeed, there is some similarity between Greenberg's methodology in seeking postulates and the approach to legal interpretation by his American near-contemporary, Ronald Dworkin.[25] Dworkin declines to view the legal system as consisting only of 'rules', and insists that it includes also 'principles' (1978; cf. Jackson 1985b: Ch. 9; 1996a: 263-71). In his

---

leave Gen. 9.6b unexplained: '[T]he exact significance of the words [that man was made in the image of God] is not necessary to decide here' (1960: 15). Moreover, Gen. 9.6 itself presents a major exegetical problem relevant to the very issues Greenberg raises: should *ba'adam* be rendered 'by man' (thus referring to human punishment) or 'for man' (thus referring, in context, to divine punishment). For the latter view, see Jackson (1975a: 46), citing LXX, NEB and other usages of the *bet pretii* (cf. Daube [1947: 129-30, 149 n. 17]; Jackson, [1972: 140-41] on Exod. 22.2b, *venimkar bigenevato*); Milgrom (1992: 705), translating: 'For the sake of that person shall his blood be spilled.' The conventional translation ('by man'), moreover, requires dropping the definite article prefix: it should be *be'adam* rather than *ba'adam*) (*aliter*, Sprinkle 1994: 81 n. 1). Greenberg has also now conceded (1986: 15 n. 29) that 'for man' is 'advocated persuasively' by Fokkelman (1975: 34-35). Nevertheless, he still (16) disputes my view that v. 6 refers to divine justice: 'To be precise...the text says two things: (1) God will exact punishment for every homicide, whether committed by beast or man; (2) the punishment will be that the life of any taker of human life will be forfeit, since man is the image of God... But it must count in favour of the view that the agency of a court is implied, that the voice of the verb 'be shed' is passive: in contrast to verse 5, God is no longer the active agent, whence ancient Jewish interpreters inferred that here the obligation of Noachides to institute courts of justice was laid down.' I think that Greenberg has conceded more here than he has gained: he accepts (unlike Sprinkle) that v. 5 does indicate that 'God will exact punishment for...homicide...committed by...man.' Surely that is the immediate context in which the (otherwise) vague passive (leaving aside the assonantal and rhythmic balance of the proverb) is to be interpreted. Moreover, the 'jural postulate' of Gen. 9.6, as we presently find it, is part of the divine promise to Noah and his descendants; it is not a statement of their obligation, of which there is no hint either in the speech of Gen. 9.1-7 or the covenant whose terms are stated in Gen. 9.9-11 (see also Stahl 1995: 42-45). There is also a further exegetical problem in interpreting Gen. 9.6 as creating an 'absolute' obligation in human justice to repay death with death: the distinction between the mandatory and the permissive is not clearly signified in biblical Hebrew. Cf. the same issue regarding *mot yumat* in Exod. 21.12: see Buss (1977: 55-56); Fishbane (1985: 91-92); Westbrook (1988: 53-55, 78), applying the same argument to Laws of Ur-Nammu §1; Sprinkle (1994: 74, 84, 85-86). Cf. the argument of Westbrook (1990: 544), regarding *mot yumat* as applied to adultery in Lev. 20.10.

25. Who, as it happens, was much influenced by Karl Llewellyn, the jurist collaborator of the anthropologist Hoebel.

early account of the matter, 'principles' were *explicit* statements of law, more general in their character than rules, but lacking the 'binding' quality of the latter.[26] But later, Dworkin reformulated his view. A value may exist within the legal system without having been explicitly stated, and such explicit statements as we possess are not necessarily privileged in their formulation. So Dworkin invented a mythical judge, whom he calls 'Hercules'—a judge of *superhuman*[27] ability, who relies not upon his intuition, but rather proceeds on the basis of a critical assessment of the implications in political morality of the *whole* existing set of laws, in relation to that political theory which underlies the constitution and institutions of his particular community. Greenberg, similarly, insists on taking the texts of biblical law as a whole, on finding interpretive means that will make them entirely coherent, and on taking into account, in extrapolating the underlying values, the 'political theory' (here, a theocratic one) that informs it.

How should we understand 'incommensurability', in this context? It has many of the features of a Dworkinian principle, being an inference from a range of different laws and being supported by biblical statements regarding the nature of human life and its place in the divinely created order.[28] Is it, however, too 'abstract' a proposition to be credibly attributed to the biblical sources? In fact, we need not accuse Greenberg of attributing abstractions such as 'incommensurability' or

26. The role of principles was to guide the judge to a decision, particularly in hard cases. An example was the maxim 'A man ought not to profit from his wrong'. There is no statutory rule to that effect, and cases of allowable profiting from one's wrong are to be found. But the law explicitly subscribes to the value of not allowing a man to profit from his wrong, so that this value may be invoked as an argument in deciding fresh cases. To count as a legal principle, as opposed to a merely moral or political principle, Dworkin originally took the view that such a principle must be evidenced by an explicit form of 'institutional support'—typically, for a Common Law system, in the form of statement by previous judges.

27. '...a lawyer of superhuman skill, learning, patience and acumen' (Dworkin 1978: 105).

28. Greenberg's postulates, however, would appear at first sight to differ from Dworkinian principles in that the latter are not binding, but rather have 'weight' in influencing the adoption of rules in conformity with them. Conversely, principles, for Dworkin, may change over time, and may gradually be 'eroded', whereas rules remain static, and have to be 'torpedoed' (1978: 40). However, Greenberg's observation (*supra*, n. 10) that the homicide postulate 'reached its fullest expression' only in the rabbinic period suggests that he does conceive it to have the characteristic of 'weight', or at least of being capable of narrower or wider interpretations.

'autonomy' to the texts. There is a distinction between such abstract *expressions* (which belong to *our* academic discourse) and the concrete correlations of rules to which they are used to refer. When Greenberg wrote: '...[I]n biblical law life and property are incommensurable; taking of life cannot be made up for by any amount of property, nor can any property offence be considered as amounting to the value of a life' (1960: 18), he needed only attribute to the biblical writers the proposition after the semicolon, not the abstract formulation before it.[29] Yet is even the concrete understanding to be expected in biblical times? Very rarely do we find in biblical law comparison of rules. The one instance is Deut. 22.25-26 (see Jackson 1993a: 142-43).

> But if in the open country a man meets a young woman who is betrothed, and the man seizes her and lies with her, then only the man who lay with her shall die. But to the young woman you shall do nothing; in the young woman there is no offense punishable by death, for this case is like that of a man attacking and murdering his neighbor.

Incommensurability, by contrast, is more sophisticated. Instead of two images that evoke similar reactions—murder and rape victims—we have a converse relationship: 'property' should not be given for 'life', 'life' should not be given for 'property'. This sounds, in cognitive developmental terms, like a 'reversible operation' (§1.2, *supra*).

As it happens, one of the best-known experiments in psychological research on moral development involves just such issues. I refer to the

---

29. Cf. Hoebel (1954:17): 'In the study of the social system and its law by the specialist it is his job to abstract the postulates from the behavior he sees and from what he hears. In the analysis and formulation of his report of the postulates the statement is therefore ex post facto'. In relation to the Ifugao, he writes: 'With this general background the basic postulates of legal significance for the Ifugao as they may be abstracted from the Ifugao data are as follows... "The bilateral kinship group is the primary social and legal unit, consisting of the dead, the living, and the yet unborn"' (103-104). Of course, the examples of postulates in Hoebel (1954) are not even those of the field workers; they are in large part abstractions by him from the published research of other field workers. Even where based on his own field research, the postulates commonly reflect the imposition of modern Western thinking. Thus, he writes of the Cheyenne: 'The individual is important and shall be permitted and encouraged to express his potentialities with the greatest possible freedom compatible with group existence, but at the same time the individual is subordinate to the group, and all first obligations are to the maintenance of the well-being of the *tribe*' (123).

'Heinz dilemma'. Kohlberg selected a sample of 84 boys[30] aged 10, 13 and 16 at the time of the original study, and tested them at 6 different times over a period of 20 years. The testing was done by interview, in which subjects were presented with hypothetical moral dilemmas, on which they were asked standardized questions designed to elicit justifications, elaborations and clarifications of the moral judgments initially expressed in response to the dilemmas. The children were told, for example, that a man called Heinz is considering whether or not to steal a drug that he cannot afford to buy in order to save the life of his wife. They were asked: 'Should Heinz steal the drug?' and the reasons for their answers were then explored by further questions. The presentation of the dilemma was designed to elicit subjects' views on value conflicts. Interestingly, this particular dilemma appears to have been designed by the experimenters to present a conflict between the value of preserving life and that of upholding the law; in the event, it was understood by some subjects in terms of a conflict between life and property (1995b: 294-95). Thus, Jake, an 11-year old, regards life as more important, and concludes that Heinz should steal the drug. He says that if Jake got caught the judge should give Jake 'the lightest possible sentence'. Jake describes the dilemma as 'sort of like a math problem with humans' (Gilligan 1982: 26)[31] and justifies his conclusion in such terms:

> 'For one thing, a human life is worth more than money, and if the druggist only makes $1,000, he is still going to live, but if Heinz doesn't steal the drug, his wife is going to die.'

Gilligan notes the social force of such reasoning:

> ...he sets it up as an equation and proceeds to work out the solution. Since his solution is rationally derived, he assumes that anyone follow-

---

30. Girls were not included in the original sample 'because adding gender as a (further) variable would have required doubling the sample. Given the laboriousness of the interviewing and scoring procedures, such a large sample was not feasible'. However, Kohlberg later accepted that 'the omission of girls is regrettable' (1987: 79 n. 3). On the significance of this gender choice, and the 'different voice' identified by Gilligan when she replicated the experiment with girls included (Amy contrasted with Heinz), see Gilligan (1982: Ch. 2); Graycar and Morgan (1990: 50-55); Jackson (1995b: 305-11).

31. Gilligan describes Jake as 'fascinated by the power of logic' and quotes him as opining that math is 'the only thing that is totally logical'. She says at the same time that Jake 'locates truth in math'. It is not entirely clear whence she derives this conclusion.

ing reason would arrive at the same conclusion and thus that a judge would also consider stealing to be the right thing for Heinz to do (1982: 26-27).

Analysing these and other responses in terms of the cognitive developmental schemes of Piaget and Kohlberg, Gilligan assesses Jake thus:

> While this boy's judgments at eleven are scored as conventional on Kohlberg's scale, a mixture of stages three and four, his ability to use deductive logic to bear on the solution of moral dilemmas, to differentiate law from morality, and to see how laws can be considered to have mistakes point toward the principled conception of justice that Kohlberg equates with moral maturity (1982: 27).

If the parallel between cultural development and individual cognitive development is soundly based,[32] we might take this to indicate that the life versus property distinction can be perceived and applied at a relatively young (though developmentally mature) age. Why then doubt the phenomenon that Greenberg described as 'incommensurability' from the earliest period of biblical law? But the parallel is not exact. Jake is contemplating the life and property aspects of a single, concrete situation—a social narrative which evokes an immediate, emotive reaction. Though he can play maths with the variables which might occur in that individual situation, he is not in fact comparing two (or more) situations, in each of which the life/property equation might be presented in a different way. Our initial hesitation about the form of the 'incommensurability' postulate has not been removed. The lesson to be derived from the moral development literature would appear to be that this type of postulate represents a type of value that may not be anticipated before a cognitively advanced stage of cultural development. The present argument serves to indicate the desirability of studies which use such criteria.

In his reply to my 1973/75 critique of his theory, Greenberg insisted that his postulates are confined to 'statements in the law collections— on which alone I base my argument (as a source for inferring legislative 'philosophy')', as opposed to 'stories, proverbs or oracles touching on legal life which may be merely dramatic, or stem from times, sources or practices other than those reflected in the laws'.[33] For example, my

---

32. §1.2, *supra,* discussing Hallpike.

33. Greenberg (1986: 2); cf. 1990: 120: 'In "Postulates" I am concerned with the legislation of the Bible (and with such non-legislative matter as illuminates it)—

argument that the judgment on David for organizing the killing of Uriah subverts Greenberg's claim that homicide is absolute (and incommensurable) only when it is committed 'personally and with intent' is met by: 'To this I protest once again that law cannot be derived from narrative, much less humanly administered law from God's judgments'.[34] Yet the very definition of this 'humanly administered law' is that it claims 'divine authorship'. And though Gen. 20.6 (the prospect of Abimelech's having relations with Sarah, described as 'sinning against God', Greenberg 1960: 12) and Gen. 39.9 (Joseph's protest to Potiphar's wife that adultery with her would be a sin against God), were taken by Greenberg to support his view of the absence of pardon as a legal option in cases of adultery, the discussion of the prospects of acceptance of *kofer* in just such a case in Prov. 6.32-35 is dismissed as having 'nothing to do with law' (1990: 121, 123-24).[35]

Such a strict differentiation was not always fully apparent (to me, at least) in Greenberg's work (though it may have been an underlying postulate of his writing). He concluded his 1959 article on the cities of refuge by observing that although there is no mention of cities of refuge outside of the laws, 'nothing stands in the way of assuming that the laws concerning them reflect the conceptions, perhaps even the custom, of the earliest age of Israel' (Greenberg 1959: 132; 1995: 49). He speaks frequently of 'biblical law' (*simple*), and even of 'the biblical treatment

not with every passage that may have a bearing on legal ideas.' Cf. Greenberg (1995: 18-19), where he observes that in contrast to the ideal picture of the working of the covenant, the 'real' history of Israel, as reflected in the books of Samuel and Kings and the pre-exilic prophets, 'is the story of the failure of the people to realize this ideal'.

34. Greenberg (1990: 121-22) with further examples. At 121 n. 4, he observes: 'Extensive deduction of law from narrative is a hallmark of scholars influenced, as is Jackson, by the work of D. Daube'. I happily accept the characterization. My defence resides in the discursive criterion offered in the text, *infra*.

35. Greenberg (1986: 4) argues that Prov. 6.32-35 is (merely) a 'piece of worldly wisdom' that tells us nothing about the law. But the worldly wisdom would be entirely superfluous if *kofer* were effectively banned in this situation. Greenberg would presumably reply that he does not make claims of effectiveness. Yet Proverbs deals with typical situations, and though any ban on *kofer* might have been evaded on occasion, the attempt to evade it is unlikely to have been as regular as the author here assumes. Greenberg sees the whole passage as reflecting extra-legal institutions (which he views as supported by the usage of *nakam*), including the assumption that the husband is out for 'private revenge'. I take it to reflect a period when such private revenge was still legal.

of the homicide' (1960: 16). And though he has subsequently empha-
sized a footnote in which he indicated that 'our present interest is in the
theoretical postulates of the law systems under consideration' (1960: 18
n. 25; 1986: 2) he does deal with several narrative sources (1960) in
such a way as to imply that he conceives them to belong to, or reflect,
the same system whose postulates he is seeking.[36] For me, the criteria
should be discursive rather than conceptual: not a distinction in principle between 'legislation' and 'narrative', but rather the values of a
particular document. And if the Pentateuch presents itself, or some
major part of it, as a document which integrates law and narrative,[37] are
we not entitled to look for the values of *that* document as a whole? In
this respect, it is Greenberg, by separating the law from the narrative
despite their discursive integration, who is the real adherent of the
literary-historical approach!

However that may be, if we now take on board Greenberg's clear
1986 restriction of his claim regarding postulates, the issues in con-

36. His distinction between 'such non-legislative matter as illuminates' the legislation of the Bible and other passages 'that may have a bearing on legal ideas'
(*supra*, n. 33) is hardly helpful here. Presumably, narrative sources that are consistent with legislative postulates fall into the former category, those which do not into
the latter. Thus Gen. 9.5-6 is taken to shed light on Exod. 21.28 (1986: 2).
Greenberg (1960: 20-27) concludes his treatment of vicarious punishment with the
observation that the study of biblical law 'with careful attention to its own inner
postulates' has as much to reveal 'about the values of Israelite culture' as the study
of Psalms and Prophets, and (at 25) uses Ezekiel in support of the legislative postulate of the 'dual standard of judgement' (human and divine) in this sphere. He also
discusses in this context three narratives (23-24) where vicarious punishment
appears to be applied (the story of Akhan in Josh. 7, the execution of the sons of
Saul, and the punishment of the inhabitants of Yabesh-Gilead in Judg. 21.10-11)
and seeks to explain them compatibly with the postulate of the 'dual standard of
judgement'. I have little difficulty with Greenberg's account of vicarious punishment. But it is difficult to reconcile it with his later restriction of the ambit of his
postulates.

37. This is the answer to the objection of Greenberg (1990: 121-22): 'It is not
known what the relation of the legal portions of the Bible was to the narrative or the
relation of laws to life; nor can it be simply assumed that this or that narrative
statement of a threat (or self-threat) made under duress has legal significance (e.g.,
Joseph's brothers' threat of death to one who stole Joseph's cup, Gen. 44.9).' At the
very least, Greenberg needs to explain why the author/editor of a document should
present narrative accounts of institutions whose values conflict with those of the
law propounded in the same document.

tention become much narrower, and focus on the institution of *kofer*, the case of a slave killed by a goring ox (Exod. 21.32), and the interpretation of Exod. 21.22-23. Even so, the theoretical and methodological problems remain: What type of values is to be expected in sources of this period, and how may they be inferred from the extant material? I still maintain that Greenberg was looking for principles of a degree of abstraction that it would be strange to find in a society only just progressing from orality to literacy.[38] Clearly, for Greenberg, what I have described as a Kantian approach (Jackson 1987: 16-18)[39] was simply a matter of natural inference, but that only demonstrates the degree to which the epistemology of a modern, literate society has been internalized.

To the extent that we can recover the history of transmission of biblical law—even divinely-mandated law, on Greenberg's restriction—we shall be in a better position to consider the shape or form of the values transmitted by the sources at the various stages of development. In the following sections, I offer examples of some alternative approaches to the identification of the underlying values of biblical law.

7.2 The Oppositional Expression of Values

I present here three examples of the search for underlying values, which I claim comply to a greater extent with the discursive criterion suggested above. Their theoretical implications are addressed together, in the concluding section (§7.3).

7.2.1 The Injurious Ox[40]
The sequence of the goring ox laws in Exodus 21 has attracted a certain amount of debate. We have, first, a set of laws regarding an ox that kills a human being (vv. 28-32); secondly, the law of the pit, dealing with

38. This argument was anticipated in outline in Jackson (1984: 35-36; 1987: 16-18).

39. A different kind (substantive rather than methodological) of Kantian parallel is suggested by Levenson (1980: 27), who describes the support of the prohibition of oppression of the resident alien with the motive clause 'because you were resident aliens in the land of Egypt' (Exod. 22.20) as 'a kind of ancient analogy to the Kantian categorical imperative'.

40. See further Jackson (1987: 18-25); and on the goring ox in Exod. 21.28-32, 35-36, Jackson (1975a: 108-52). On the interpretation of Exod. 21.35, see also §3.2, *supra*.

the liability of the owner of the pit when an ox or ass falls therein and is killed (vv. 33-34); third, we revert to the ox as the cause of damage, but here the victim is another ox, not a human being (vv. 35-36). We can ask questions about the history of the text, and the significance of the present arrangement. Daube argued that the whole of the third section, vv. 35-36 (where the ox kills another ox) is secondary, an example of the ancient drafting technique of addition at the end, rather than interpolation in the logical place (1947: 85-88). I have argued that, in literary historical terms, the addition is more likely to have been confined to v. 36, or at least that v. 36 was added later than v. 35 (Jackson 1975a: 141-52). However that may be, we may still ask whether the present arrangement is evidence of underlying conceptions. Finkelstein suggests that it is (1973: 169-290, esp. 269; [posthumously] 1981: 25, 37). He argued that at v. 33, we have a transition that is important for the arrangement of the *Mishpatim* as a whole (Exod. 21.1-22.16).[41] The arrangement of the collection as a whole reflects, in his view, a basic distinction that the authors sought to stress between the 'Law of Persons' and the 'Law of Things'.[42] For them, the ox that gores another ox is a completely different kettle of fish from the ox that gores a human being. That difference is reflected in the arrangement of the section. If vv. 35-36 had followed on immediately after vv. 28-32, we would have naturally regarded them as part of a single conceptual scheme. The pit law interrupts that sequence. It unambiguously belongs to the 'Law of Things'—which Finkelstein argued begins at this point; and so the law of ox against ox also belongs to that grouping.

This argument is part of Finkelstein's wider contention, that the Bible has a different cosmology from the ancient Near Eastern civilizations. In the latter there is a continuum of life forms, with animals differentiated from humans only as a matter of degree, while in the Bible there is a difference in kind, reflected *inter alia* in the nature of the sanctions used to protect the two categories: the protection of human life merits the death penalty; the protection of property does not. But alas, this cosmological version of Greenberg's postulates has to force the evidence, both as regards the sanctions variously applied, but also in

41. Cf., more recently, Otto (1988: 12-31) on Exod. 21.18-32 as 'Körperverletzungsfälle' and Exod. 21.33–22.14 as 'yeshallem-Gesetze'; cf. Otto (1994: 182-83). For my own views, see, for the moment, Jackson (1995c: 1778-83).

42. This reflecting the Bible's (then) unique view of personhood (cf. Levinson 1991: 146).

respect of the arrangement of the collection. We do find monetary sanctions implied in some cases involving human life: the availability of *kofer* in Exod. 21.30; the 30 shekels payable where an ox fatally gores a slave in Exod. 21.32; the compensation for idleness and the duty to secure healing in Exod. 21.19;[43] the compensation in Exod. 21.22, whether it be for miscarriage or premature birth (Jackson 1975a: 95-96).[44] If one regards every one of these cases as 'special', one ends up with a very restricted category of offences against the person. Conversely, Exod. 22.1-2 allows the householder to kill the thief he finds entering by night.[45] Rabbinic interpretation understands this as referring only to a case where the intruder intended to kill;[46] the householder is therefore exercising legitimate self-help in defence of his life. In the biblical period, however, the immunity for killing the nocturnal intruder appears to have been absolute (Jackson 1972: 208-209).

The arrangement of the goring ox laws is, however, explicable in terms of a simple literary pattern. First we have an ox that causes injury, ox versus man; next we have the ox as the victim, man versus ox. Finally, the two roles of the ox are combined, ox versus ox. In the Laws of Hammurabi §§244–52, we encounter the same principle of arrangement, but in reverse order:

244	Ox or ass killed by a lion.
245-249	Ox killed or injured by its hirer (including the case where the hirer may take an exculpatory oath, claiming act of God, 249).
250-252	Ox kills man (free, slave).

But there is also another law in the *Mishpatim* dealing with liability for animals, separated once again from the sequence of ox laws. After ox versus ox, we have the theft laws—cattle theft, I have argued, even in the case of the intruder (Jackson 1972: 49-50)—and then Exod. 22.4,

---

43. It may be argued that there is no loss of life here. But the remedy remains available even if the victim subsequently dies after emerging from his sick-bed (see further Jackson 2000a).

44. The issue is revisited in the light of subsequent comment in my forthcoming *Wisdom-Laws*.

45. Some have taken this to be a death penalty for *furtum manifestum*, but see Jackson (1972: 154-61).

46. With differences of view regarding cases where the intruder's intention was unclear (see Jackson 1972: 209-12).

on depasturation (Jackson 1976: 138-40): ox versus fruit and vegetables.

Stylistically, Exod. 22.4 is far more distinct from the ox laws of ch.21 than are any of the parts of that pericope in relation to each other: the offender is described as a man who sends his animal—*be'iro*, not specifically his ox; the subject of the law is not the animal itself, as in ch. 21. How should we understand the relation between the ox laws and depasturation? I suggest that we can do so at two different levels. We can ask, first, how the distinction was consciously rationalized, and we can ask what made it appear meaningful, even without such conscious rationalization. The first enquiry is akin to Dworkin's rationalist quest for legal values, the second to the semiotic approach. The first is a reflection on the history of interpretation, the second a search for underlying semiotic structures.

We do get conscious rationalizations and conceptualizations of the distinction, both in rabbinic and Roman sources. The Rabbis distinguished between *keren*, literally 'horn', based on the goring ox laws, and *shen* or *regel*, 'foot' or 'tooth', based on depasturation. The former was actionable even when the act took place in the public domain (*Mekhilta ad Ex.* 22.5 (Lauterbach III, 113); Maimonides, *Mishneh Torah, Hilkhot Nezikin* 1.8), the latter only where the animal trespassed into the property of another.[47] 'Foot' and 'tooth', moreover, were actionable only if the owner was to blame,[48] while 'horn' (at least if the animal was *tam*[49]) was actionable irrespective of the owner's fault.[50] But the terminology came to be technical. Not every injury caused with the tooth or foot would be *shen* or *regel:* an animal that ate fruit or

47. *Mekhilta ad Exod.* 22.5 (Lauterbach III, 113); *Mishnah B. Qam.* 2.2 (explicitly for *shen,* but traditionally regarded as applicable also to *regel*); Maimonides, *Mishneh Torah, Hilkhot Nezikin* 3.1. But there is liability for 'benefit' (unjust enrichment) if it occurs in the public domain: *Mishnah B. Qam.* 2.2; Maimonides, *Mishneh Torah, Hilkhot Nezikin* 3.1-2.

48. *Mishnah B. Qam.* 6.1-2; Maimonides, *Mishneh Torah, Hilkhot Nezikin* 4.1. There are indications that early in the tannaitic period there were still some who held to the likely biblical requirement that the depasturization be intentional, stressing the verb *shalach* in Exod. 22.4 (see Jackson 1974: 127-30; 1975a: 255-59).

49. I.e. the owner has not been warned of its vicious propensity, as in Exod. 21.28 and 35 as against Exod. 21.29 and 36. The remedy for *tam* was payment of half damages, this being the rabbinic interpretation of Exod. 21.35.

50. There was early dissent: *Mishnah B. Qam.* 4.9; *Tosefta B. Qam.* 5.7; *Mekhilta ad Exod.* 21.29 (Lauterbach III, 84), but the *halakhah* follows R. Judah (see Maimonides, *Mishneh Torah, Hilkhot Nezikin* 7.1).

vegetables would be *shen* (*Mishnah B. Qam.* 1.4, 2.2; Maimonides, *Mishneh Torah, Hilkhot Nezikin* 1.2, 3.1), but if it ventured to consume clothes or vessels, it was *keren* (*Mishnah B. Qam.* 2.2; Maimonides, *Mishneh Torah, Hilkhot Nezikin* 3.3); similarly, if the animal caused damage through walking, that was *regel* (*Mishnah B. Qam.* 1.4; 2.1; Maimonides, *Mishneh Torah, Hilkhot Nezikin* 1.2), but if it kicked or even slipped, that was *keren* (*Mishnah B. Qam.* 2.1; Maimonides, *Mishneh Torah, Hilkhot Nezikin* 1.5, 3.11). Roman law and English law both adopted similar distinctions. In Roman law, the kicking horse, *equus calcitrosus* ('prone to kick'—apparently a reflection of the biblical *mu'ad*)[51] fell under the *actio de pauperie*, as was the tripping mule, while the animal that strayed into a shop and ate the vegetables gave rise to an action under the *actio de pastu*. English law too had an historic distinction between the *'scienter'* action and 'cattle-trespass', not unconnected historically with the biblical texts (Jackson 1978a: 85-102, xvi; 1978d: 41-56).

These distinctions came to be explained in both Roman and Jewish law. In Roman law, it was the jurist Ulpian in the third century who observed that the test of whether an action lay under the *actio de pauperie* was whether the acts of the animal were *contra naturam* (*Dig.* 9.1.1.7)—not contrary to natural law in general, but contrary to the nature of that species. It is clear that this was not a purely descriptive test of 'nature': if so, the kicking horse or the fighting rams would not be covered, since we know that horses do kick, even if they are not pathologically disturbed, and that rams do fight. Rather, it was a teleological conception of nature, combining a view of the animal's usual behaviour patterns with a conception of what it was appropriate for it to do.[52] The same idea was expressed in the Jewish sources through the concept of *derekh* (Daube 1951: 140-42): where the animal's behaviour

51. *Dig.* 9.1.1.4; cf. *Inst.* IV.9.pr. For the historical connection, see Jackson (1978a: 141-42).

52. On this Aristotelian conception, see Jackson (1996a: 15-19). It was described thus by Hart (1994: 188): 'The doctrine of natural law is part of an older conception of nature in which the observable world is not merely a scene of such regularities, and knowledge of nature is not merely a knowledge of them. Instead, on this older outlook every nameable kind of existing thing, human, animate and inanimate, is conceived not only as tending to maintain itself in existence but as proceeding towards a definite optimum state which is the specific good—or end (*telos* [in Greek], *finis*) appropriate for it.'

was *kedarkah*, according to the usual 'way' of the species, any damage so caused was a matter of *shen* or *regel*; otherwise, the case was one of *keren*.[53] That explains the distinction between the ox that ate fruit and vegetables on the one hand (*shen*) and the ox that ate clothes or vessels on the other (*keren*). Such ideas are still occasionally found in modern law. In an English case of 1964, there was held to be no liability for a 'frolicsome filly' that injured someone in the public highway (in the absence of negligence), since the strict liability remedy of *scienter* was viewed as extending only to cases where there was an 'attack'.[54] And the Animals Act of 1971 reversed a decision of 1954 that allowed recovery for such a friendly injury to a human being, even where the animal had trespassed.[55] Cattle-trespass was for 'natural' offences, like depasturation, not for animals injuring human beings.

This, then, is the way in which these distinctions were consciously rationalized, and I suppose that Ulpian, whatever his origins (there is debate about his Semitisms; he came from Tyre), would be as good an ancient candidate as any to be a Dworkinian Hercules. But these sources are all postbiblical, reflecting the Hellenistic environment. We are entitled to ask also a semiotic question relating to the classifications contained in the biblical texts: what would make them meaningful to the biblical audience? 'What would make them meaningful?' is a different question from 'what did they mean?' The question why certain things are regarded as meaningful—why, despite being particular cultural products, they strike the community as 'natural'—is a function of both general structures of signification and particular social knowledge (see §1.1, *supra*). Classifications appear natural or intelligible where we have a correlation of conventionally associated binary oppositions;[56]

53. *Mishnah B. Qam.* 2.1, 6.2; *Tosefta B. Qam.* 1.5; see further Jackson (1978b: 172-76) on this and Maimonides' modification in favour of a more strictly descriptive conception of *derekh*.

54. *Fitzgerald* v. *E.D. and A.D. Cooke Bourne (Farms) Ltd.* [1964] 1 Q.B. 249; for the position under the Animals Act 1971, see Jackson (1977: 590-96).

55. *Wormald* v. *Cole* [1954] 1 Q.B. 614, reversed by s.4 of the Act.

56. On correlative thinking, cf. Douglas (1999: 16), who contrasts post-Aristotelian Western thinking with 'correlative' or 'aesthetic' or analogical ordering, quoting the sinologists Hall and Ames (1995: 124-25): 'It is based on analogical association, it is…"horizontal", in the sense that it involves the association of concrete experienceable items… Correlative thinking involves the association of image—or concept—clusters by meaningful disposition rather than physical causation.' Though Douglas does not wish to give any concessions to what she regards as

cases appear 'hard' or unusual, where those associations go wrong (cf. Jackson 1996a: 237-45). Here, in the laws relating to animals, there are the oppositions between wild and tame (an opposition that became explicit, in different forms, in Jewish, Roman and English law); between friendship and hostility; between natural behaviour and behaviour related to human culture. Where these binary oppositions are correlated, we have an easy, or 'typical' case. The goring ox laws evoke an image of a normally wild animal acting in a hostile fashion in a natural environment. The depasturation law evokes the three correlated opposites: a domesticated animal (described as a grazer, not an 'ox') acting in a non-hostile fashion (eating), in a cultural context, in that it has been set to eat for agricultural purposes: *veshilach et bei'ro* (Exod. 22.4; Jackson 1976: 138-40). But when we get 'difficult' cases, the ones that delight the jurists (however remote they may be from practice), we find the normal correlations mixed up. Take that famous pile-up on the Capitoline Hill, discussed by Alfenus (*Dig.* 9.2.52.2). Two carts were following each other up the Capitoline Hill, each pulled by mules. The front cart reversed and crashed into the one behind. The latter killed the plaintiff's slave. Alfenus ruled that the owner of the front mules was liable if they had shied (as opposed to slipped). The answer to this problem is less important than the reason it presented itself as a puzzle. Here you had unfriendly behaviour, acts more like wild than domesticated animals, but in the context of human culture, the transport business.

7.2.2 *Eved and Amah in Exod. 21.2-11*
After stating the basic rule of liberation *ex lege* after six years' service (Exod. 21.2), Exod. 21.3-6 deal with the effects upon the slave's family, taking account of two variables: (a) the source of that family (pre-enslavement or post-enslavement, the wife provided in the latter case by the master) and, if post-enslavement, whether the slave is prepared to abandon his new family. The emphasis upon release continues throughout: in each one of the three succeeding clauses, the apodosis prescribes either the terms of release (using the technical term *latset*) or its negation 'and he shall serve forever' (*va'avado le'olam*, v. 6). On

an outdated evolutionary approach, she accepts, in the context of work on the Han dynasty, that 'correlative thinking came first, and remains the basis of the common-sense thinking of daily life, but it gives way when there is a need to criticize the accepted correlations'.

the surface, the compiler is not particularly interested in either the regulation of the circumstances in which slavery arises, or its effects while it subsists. But when we look beyond the manner of formulation of these clauses, to the substance that is implied by them, we find that one important facet of the use that may be made of a debt-slave—his use for breeding purposes—is, indeed, regulated (Exod. 21.3-6):

> If he comes in single, he shall go out single; if he comes in married, then his wife shall go out with him. If his master gives him a wife and she bears him sons or daughters, the wife and her children shall be her master's and he shall go out alone. But if the slave plainly says, 'I love my master, my wife, and my children; I will not go out free', then his master shall bring him to God, and he shall bring him to the door or the doorpost; and his master shall bore his ear through with an awl; and he shall serve him for life.

This aspect, moreover, forms the underlying structure that gives significance to the relationship between the two paragraphs of the *eved* and *amah*, paragraphs which are firmly linked through explicit cross-referencing: 'When a man sells his daughter as a slave, she shall not go out as the male slaves do' (Exod. 21.7).

The first paragraph deals with a male debt-slave (*eved*); the second with a female debt-slave (purchased from a fellow Israelite), termed here an *amah*. There is a clear distinction in the rules applied to these two categories. Seventh year release applies to the *eved* (v. 2), but is explicitly denied for the *amah* (v. 7). Does this mean that there was one form of debt-slavery applicable to men, and quite another for women?[57] From the time of Deuteronomy, commentators have sought to avoid this conclusion. In its version of Exod. 21.2, Deuteronomy includes both the male and the female slave:

> If your brother shall be sold to you, whether a Hebrew man or a Hebrew woman, he shall serve you for six years, and in the seventh you shall send him free from you (Deut. 15.12).

How, then, did Deuteronomy deal with the *amah* of Exod. 21.7-11? Cleverly, the author reconciled the apparent contradiction that he had created, by viewing the case of the *amah* as one where the permanency of slavery was the result of the *voluntary* act of the slave herself, as (for the *eved*) in Exod. 21.5-6. For Deut. 15.17, the verse which reiterates the procedure of piercing the ear-lobe with an awl, so as to create the

---

57. The fullest account of this position is provided by Schenker (1988: 547-56).

status of permanent slavery, is followed by 'and so shall you do to your *amah*'. This is a most striking example of what has come to be known as 'inner biblical exegesis', a clear demonstration of the fact that the interpretation, indeed harmonization, of earlier texts began in the biblical period itself (cf. Fishbane 1985: 211 n. 99).

Despite the artificiality of the interpretation in Deuteronomy, there is evidence that debt-slavery terminable after six years did apply to women as well as men,[58] and that the status of *amah* was a distinct form of dependence, designed to create a permanent sexual relationship (cf. Cardellini 1981: 252-53).[59] The documentary evidence from the ancient Near East suggests that women were actually taken as debt-slaves (for general, not sexual services) more often than were men.[60] In the Bible, Jeremiah refers to the *deror* under King Zedekiah (see further §6.2, *supra*) as involving the setting free of both male and female debt-slaves, the latter here being referred to not by the term *amah*, but rather *shifchah* (Jer. 34.9);[61] the same appears from the complaint made to

58. Such a view is taken in modern times, for example, by Falk (1964: 122); Cassuto (1967: 266-67); Chirichigno (1993: 253-54); Sprinkle (1994: 51); Westbrook (1998: 214, 219 n. 14); Pressler (1998: 149, 167).

59. The precise nature of the status of *amah* is a matter of debate, not least because the institution in the form here described seems to have been superseded by the time of Deuteronomy. Some take it as generating a marriage: Cassuto (1967: 266-67); Fishbane (1985: 210); Sarna (1991: 120), who refers to a seal of Alyah the *amah* of Hananel, who obviously enjoyed superior social rank, and notes that a pre-exilic epitaph of a royal steward from Siloam mentions his *amah*, next to whom he arranged to be buried. Others understand it as concubinage. These include Lipinski (1982: 177); Sprinkle (1994: 51 n. 1), who notes that in Genesis every woman called an *amah* was also a concubine (Gen. 20.17; 21.10, 12, 13 [Hagar]; 30.3 [Bilhah]; 31.33 [Bilhah and Zilpah]; Houtman (1997: 88); Westbrook (1998: 218): 'the relationship is ended by sale or manumission, not by divorce', while noting (228) that Hagar is made a wife, not a concubine, so that she can produce legitimate offspring who will inherit, and as a result has to be divorced.

60. Jackson and Watkins (1984: 418), in relation to distraint. Crüsemann (1996: 157), observes that 'daughters are usually the first to be sold when situations of need arise'. Pressler (1998: 167-68), citing the prologue to Lipit Ishtar and the Edict of Ammisaduqa, as well as Deut. 15, Jer. 34 and Lev. 25, concludes: 'The consistent inclusion of the bondswoman in releases mandated or proclaimed elsewhere in the biblical and cuneiform materials suggests that the burden of proof lies with those who believe that the law of release excludes all women, not just daughters or wives.'

61. It appears from 1 Sam 1.16-18 that the two terms could be used inter-

Nehemiah (5.2, 5; see Weinfeld 1995: 167-74; Jackson 1998a: 242-44; §6.2, *supra*). The existence of a social institution of debt-slavery for women, distinct from the form mentioned in the *amah* paragraph, thus appears certain.

But that does not mean that Exod. 21.2-6 should be interpreted as having female debt-slaves also in mind (despite the fact that *eved*, when used alone, can sometimes include a female slave [Pressler 1998: 168]). Exod. 21.4 cannot apply to such a female debt-slave, since it speaks of an *ishah*[62] given to him, who does not go out with him in the seventh year. And it is this verse that seems to provide the clue to the structural relationship between the two paragraphs. It indicates that a male debt-slave may be used for sexual services—effectively, to breed permanent slaves for his master (Jackson 1988a: 93-94, 236; cf. Sprinkle 1994: 70-71; Matthews 1994: 131-32; Crüsemann 1996: 156 n. 243)[63]—without interference with his status. Sexual services are no different from other services in this respect. Exod. 21.7-11 gives us the opposite side of the coin. A woman debt-slave cannot be used for sexual services unless her status is thereby changed (Jackson 1988a: Chirichigno 1993: 253-54; Matthews 1994: 133; Pressler 1998: 170 n. 52). Sexual activity alters the status of the woman debt-slave, but not that of the male. In part, this may be based upon a perception that the natural bond between mother and child is stronger than that between father and child. For it is self-evident that the mother loves the child and will not wish to be separated from it, whereas in the case of the father it is necessary for him for-

changeably, at least when used in self-description as a mark of deference to a social superior (here: Hannah speaking to Eli).

62.   The status of this woman has been a matter of debate. Being a permanent slave, she is commonly regarded as a foreign bondwoman (e.g. Sarna 1991: 119; Sprinkle 1994: 70). Others suggest that she is an *amah* (vv. 7-11) who is assigned not to the master or his son, but to another member of the household—here the temporary Hebrew debt-slave (see Schenker 1988: 549; Marshall 1993: 119; Crüsemann 1996: 158). But if so, what would her status be once her 'husband' has gone out free, at the end of the six years? Would it be comparable to the status of the *amah* whose husband has taken another wife (or woman), and who must not diminish her basic rights (v. 10)? The *amah* identification is rejected by Houtman (1997: 80) and Van Seters (1996: 541), the latter arguing that Hebrew female slaves purchased for the purpose of marriage could only be the wife/concubine of the owner or his son. But that inference depends upon adopting the *kere* in. v. 8.

63.   Houtman (1997: 90) cites as examples Gen. 17.12-17, 27; Lev. 22.11; Jer. 2.14.

mally to affirm that love, by a speech act[64] required in order to convert his temporary debt-slavery into a permanent (but here voluntary) form of servitude.

The *amah*, by contrast, cannot be retained for simple breeding purposes, on terms that she will either abandon her children after the six years or voluntarily submit to having the slavery made permanent (as Deuteronomy suggests). The woman is passive; she has no will to exercise, no voluntary speech-act to perform.[65] The choices are those of the master. If he wants her as a breeding member of his household, he can only have her on a permanent basis. And if he wants her on a permanent basis, he has to regularize her status.

Thus, female debt-slavery, of the kind referred to in later sources, may well have existed at the time of the *Mishpatim*. But if the analysis here suggested has any plausibility, such ordinary debt-slavery was completely irrelevant to the present text. It is precisely by omitting any mention of the case that was the most common in practice that the message is conveyed that the status of a man is not affected by sexual services, whereas sexual services may not be demanded of a woman without altering her status. The literary connection between the *eved* and *amah* paragraphs is thus not confined to the cross-reference in the apodosis of v. 7.

7.2.3 *The Structure of the Decalogue*

There is an integral relationship between law and narrative in the Bible. One of its manifestations is the use of allusion to narrative history in the context of the justification of particular laws. Two events within that narrative history stand out: the creation of the world (the foundation of universal history) and the exodus of the Israelites from Egypt (the

64. Cf. Viberg (1992: 85), a 'performative utterance'. Since we have the words of the oral declaration, and it makes no mention of swearing, there is no need to interpret it as an oath, even though the ceremony takes place in the 'presence' of the *elohim*. Sprinkle (1994: 60) suggests that the declaration is in effect an adoption formula: made in the presence of the ancestors (*elohim* interpreted as *terafim*), the ancestors of the family are now considered the ancestors of the incoming permanent slave. Yet in accordance with his general thesis, Sprinkle avoids suggesting that this had any historical reality: rather, it shows that the author has shown himself to be a consummate literary genius!

65. Cf. Turnbam (1987: 545-46), though less convincingly in relation to the passivity of her master by comparison with that of the *eved* in the previous paragraph.

foundation of their particular history, and the prelude to the Sinaitic covenant that imposed upon them normative patterns distinguishing them from all others). I suggest that this distinction forms the organizing structure of the Decalogue itself: it speaks of the normative patterns expected of Israelites alone on the one hand, Israelites in common with all human beings on the other.[66]

The name 'Ten Commandments' is, of course, problematic in both its aspects. Different denominational traditions have counted the 'ten' in different ways. In fact, the number 'ten' is not mentioned at all in the Exodus version of the Decalogue; it occurs in the book of Exodus only in Exod. 34.28, the reference to the 'ritual decalogue' of that chapter (see Nielsen 1968: Ch. 1). It is only in Deuteronomy that the tradition of 'ten' is applied, in historical retrospect, to 'the Decalogue' (Deut. 4.13; 10.4). The designation 'commandments', as Carmichael has rightly noted (1985: 313, 340; 1992: 24-25), has even less biblical warrant. The *devarim* are simply 'words'—more accurately, perhaps, in the light of modern linguistic concepts, 'utterances'.

On the other hand, the tradition that there were two tablets is found in the narrative first in Exod. 24.12, where Moses is commanded to ascend the mountain, in order to be given the tablets of stone (here said to contain *hatorah vehamitsvah*, which have been written there for the instruction of the people). After Moses broke the first set of tablets, in anger at the sin of the golden calf, he is ordered to prepare two further blank tablets, on which God himself promises to write 'the words that were on the first tables, which you broke' (Exod. 34.1). What is important for present purposes[67] is that (at least) the original decalogue was clearly conceived to have been written upon two tablets. That implies an internal division of the material into two groups. Where does that division come? Generally, the division has been based on mere inference from the nature of the subject matter and (even more dubious) an assumption that the 'ten' (however identified) should be divided into two groups of five. This view is found already in the *Mekhilta*,[68] and

---

66.   The relationship between Israelite and other cultures is thus conceived not in terms of mutual exclusion: Israelites participate in universal normative culture, but have in addition demands peculiar to themselves.

67.   On the problems of the content and writing of the second set of tablets, see further §9.3 nn. 47-48, *infra*.

68.   *Mekhilta ad Exod.* 20.16 (Lauterbach II, 262): 'How were the Ten Commandments arranged? Five on one tablet and five on the other. On the one tablet

centuries of ecclesiastical and indeed synagogal art,[69] equally premised upon such assumptions, have made us assume that the second group necessarily begins with the prohibition of murder.[70] It is, indeed, easy enough to count five from there, however difficult it may be to compress the preceding material into five commandments. But this division has one very severe disadvantage: the length of the material in the second pentad is very considerably smaller than that in the first, even allowing for a much greater degree of secondary elaboration in the first tablet.[71]

I would suggest that the original conception of the division into two groups is in fact signified by a clue in the text, one whose significance has—to my knowledge—universally been overlooked.[72] There are two historical allusions in the text of the Decalogue. The first occurs at the very beginning, thus at the head of the first group (however one divides

---

was written: "I am the LORD thy God." And opposite it on the other tablet was written: "Thou shalt not murder"... On the one tablet was written: "Thou shalt have no other god." And opposite it on the other tablet was written: "Thou shalt not commit adultery"... On the one tablet was written: "Thou shalt not take." And opposite it on the other tablet was written: "Thou shalt not steal"... On the one tablet was written: "Remember the sabbath day to keep it holy." And opposite it on the other tablet was written: "Thou shalt not bear false witness"... On the one tablet was written: "Honor thy father," etc. And opposite it on the other tablet was written: "Thou shalt not covet thy neighbour's wife".' See Sarfatti (1990: 408-409). Philo, *De Decalogo* 50-51, differs only in reversing the order of adultery and murder.

69. Though not generally taking account of Exod. 32.15, which claims that the writing was on both the front and the back of the tablets. On this latter aspect, see Millard (1994: 49-53, esp. 50-51).

70. For a useful review of the history, see Sarfatti (1990: 365-402, 407-417). He notes (at 410-11) that the Catholic tradition derived from Augustine is opposed to equal division: it groups together nos. 1-3 (though differing as to its internal division) on the first tablet, as manifesting love of God (Mt. 22.36) and the rest on the second tablet, as manifesting love of one's neighbour (see further Nielsen 1968: 33-34).

71. Cf. Nielsen (1968: 33): 139 'verbal units' as against 24. The alternative is very radically to prune the text, so as to reduce each commandment to an equivalent utterance of just a few words (which some biblical scholars have sought to do). For a survey of the older literature, see Stamm and Andrew (1967).

72. A similar division was, however, proposed by Meier (1846), but on the basis of a reconstruction of the original text of the commandments as reduced to the minimum common form (see Nielsen 1968: 13 n. 6).

the text): 'I am the LORD your God, who brought you out of the land of Egypt, out of the house of bondage' (Exod. 20.2).[73] We then have provisions relating to monotheism, idolatry, the divine name and the sabbath day. And then, in v. 11, a second historical allusion, conventionally categorized as a 'motive clause'. But the opening word, *ki*, does not have to be translated 'for' or 'because'. It may be a deictic, rather than a connective expression: '*Behold*, in six days the LORD made heaven and earth...' The Deuteronomic version: we may recall, substitutes a further allusion to the Egyptian slavery:[74] the sabbath is taken as a symbol of freedom, denied the Israelites in Egypt: but now available to them (Deut. 5.15). And the opening injunction of the Exodus Decalogue, 'remember...the sabbath day' is transformed in Deuteronomy into an injunction to 'observe the sabbath day', with the duty of remembrance now presented not as a motive (there is in Deuteronomy no *ki*, or anything comparable), but rather as a supplementary duty, 'you shall remember', *vezakharta*.

My suggestion, therefore, is that the Exodus Decalogue reveals the two groups destined for the two tablets as each headed by an historical allusion:[75] redemption from Egypt in the first, creation of the world in the second.[76] What might be the significance of this literary structure? I suggest that it concerns the opposition between insiders and outsiders, which is a theme also of the surrounding narrative. For it is an outsider, Jethro, who provides advice in Exod. 18 regarding the administration of justice. Next comes the arrival at Sinai (Exod. 19.1), and the immediate

73.   Jewish tradition regards this as the first 'commandment', and not as an historical preamble. For the different views on the overall division taken within the Judaeo-Christian tradition, see the convenient tabulation (the Jewish tradition, Augustine, Lutherans, Roman Catholics, Reformed Christians, Orthodox Christians, Philo and Josephus), provided by Harrelson (1980: 45-48); see also Nielsen (1968: 10-13).

74.   Deuteronomy does, it seems, understand the historical allusion as a motive clause, but it regards the Exodus allusion to the creation as an inappropriate motive for Israel's duty to observe the sabbath. On the parallel reasoning structure in these clauses, see Jackson (1993a: 140-42).

75.   Several sections of the Covenant Code (Exod. 21.2, 28; 22.20; 23.9) are also introduced by (explicit or implicit) historical allusions (see Jackson 1992: 82-84; 1995c: 1781-83; §8.2, *infra*).

76.   Thus the injunction to obey parents opens the second group, rather than concludes the first. In the light of this argument, v. 11b, 'Therefore the LORD blessed the sabbath day and hallowed it', might be regarded as secondary.

offer of a covenant. It too commences with an historical allusion to the exodus: 'You have seen what I have done to Egypt...' (Exod. 19.4). In exchange for Israel's observing the covenant, God promises that 'You shall be my own possession[77] among all peoples...' We are thus to witness the transformation of Israel's identity: from a slave people, entirely subject to the jurisdiction of others, through an independent people, to whom others may give advice on jurisdictional matters, to a people whose identity is defined in terms of its special relationship with God.

The Decalogue continues this concern. The identity of Israel is to be established on two levels: that which is peculiar to it (to be defined in terms of the *ius divinum positivum*), and that which it shares with all mankind.[78] I suggest that the two groups within the Decalogue, according to the division proposed above, reflect just this kind of concept. And the two historical allusions that head the two sections reflect these two dimensions of Israel's identity. The first section is headed by the allusion to Israel's particular history, the exodus from Egypt, and contains *ius civile*—provisions mostly concerning religious practices: monotheism, the ban on images, the ban on idolatry, misuse of the divine name, the sabbath (this last, to this very day, being regarded as a mark of the religious distinctiveness of Jews).[79] Then we have the allusion to universal history, the creation of the world, at the beginning of the second group. What follows within it is *ius gentium*, matters having no connection whatsoever with Israel's religious practices, but reflecting an ethic which may be assumed to have universal claims:[80] honouring parents,

---

77. RSV, *segullah*, more literally translated 'peculiar treasure'—AV.

78. The Romans, we may recall, were very much alive to this distinction. Part of the law of each nation consisted of rules peculiar to itself, its *ius civile*, while the rest was common to all mankind, *ius gentium* (see further Jackson 1995c: 184-93).

79. On this, see further §2.4, stressing the sensory range regulated by these provisions. A somewhat parallel view has been taken by Stahl (1995: 54-55), who argues that the first five deal with God's omnipotence and majesty and his special relationship with Israel, though recognizing that the fifth commandment (the sabbath) lacks this specific focus (and is therefore regarded by Stahl as serving as a transition leading to the second half), while the second half deals with the necessary but mundane functioning of human society (thus reducing the overwhelming impact of the divine immediacy that resonates in the first half). She takes this division to mirror a narrative tension between immediacy and distance in the relationship between God and Israel.

80. This is not to deny the observation of Milgrom (1963: 300): 'The Hebrew Bible was intended for Israel alone—even the Ten Commandments. Only one bibli-

the proscription of murder, adultery, theft, false witness (this last comes close to the concerns already identified with the non-Israelite, Jethro), coveting.

7.3 *Towards a Model of Values in Biblical Law*

The discussion thus far may assist us in formulating a more explicit model for the study of values in biblical law. Such a model would include at least the following elements:

(a) *Form*: the following three broad alternatives may be contrasted:
> (1)   the unarticulated feelings associated with the perception of particular behaviour patterns, i.e. moral feeling (the unarticulated sense that something is right or wrong, good or bad, pleasant or unpleasant, etc.);
> (2)   rules (or combinations of rules) of a certain level of generality (what might be termed 'principles');
> (3)   the rational justification of relationships between different rules ('moral judgment').

(b) *Source*: popular imagery/social experience or literary/cultural[81] sources.

(c) *Concern:* practical (how we should behave) or theoretical (in descending order: the nature of the world order, social identity, status of the individual).

(d) *Expression:* assuming a process of transition from orality to literacy, does the value (for which we now have only literary sources) depend upon a particular form of literary expression?

(e) *Cognition:* what kind of thinking is deployed: concrete/abstract, single situation or situations compared, rules or relationships, 'mental operations'?

gentium was also directed to the Romans, even though there was a realization that it was, as Gaius put it, the product of *naturalis ratio* (*Inst.* 1.1). See also Levenson (1980: 25-26).

81.   Watts (1999: 97-99) argues that the repetition of particular issues elevates them to paradigmatic illustrations of Yahweh's concerns. In terms of semiotic theory, this may be put as a claim that such *literary* means may function as one of the sources of internalization of (new) narrative images of behaviour, accompanied by appropriate evaluations, which in future may be accessed by restricted code. The media today have a similar function.

The examples discussed in this chapter may be summarized in terms of the above model. This is not to assume that the examples, as here argued, are beyond criticism; the purpose, rather, is to develop the model further, by seeking some preliminary correlations of elements within the model, which may in turn allow us to add a developmental aspect: a hypothesis that values in biblical law develop in a particular direction, which can be related to and assessed in terms of other developmental trends within the study of biblical law. My earlier feeling that Greenberg, in his theory of postulates, was seeking too abstract a formulation of values for the period/documents with which we are concerned may itself be analysed more precisely by the use of such means. I commence with my own three examples, and conclude with that of Greenberg.

First, the examples regarding different forms of civil liability for damage and injury caused by animals (§7.2.1). Here, I used both later (rabbinic) sources and comparative material in order to elucidate what I see as the underlying values that distinguish the various paragraphs found in the *Mishpatim*. The Rabbis rationalize what in the biblical text are expressed as opposed images of typical behaviour patterns. But the biblical and rabbinic formulations are not to be regarded as equivalent. The rationalization reflects the discursive world of the Rabbis.[82] Though we may be inclined to regard it as an authentic rationalization of the images presented by the biblical text, it was not an inevitable one—as indeed, the very different modern attempts to explain the arrangement of the biblical text amply demonstrate. We do not need to endorse any Savigny-type claim that the imagistic formulations are more authentic than, or in some sense superior to, the later rational elaborations.[83] But we should still recognise the cognitive differences between such phenomena: in the biblical text, alternations of man and beast as subject and object of the action, and the separation of distinct images of harmful behaviour. We have to await the codification of Maimonides before these issues are fully integrated into a single, articulated rational structure (see Jackson 1978b: 168-76).

Some may object that my argument here is anachronistic. I certainly concede that it is through rabbinic eyes that *shen/regel* on the one hand and *keren* on the other appear as opposed paradigms. But this is no bad starting point. What I read back is not the rabbinic conceptualizations,

82. See Daube (1951: 140-42) on the parallel between *derekh* and *natura*.
83. See *supra*, pp. 177-78.

or their explicit justifications, but rather the elements of the situation (such as *negichah, reshut)* that the Rabbis viewed as significant. Their world-view was far closer to the biblical text than our own. Moreover, in notable respects they incorporated attention to the semiotic features of the text into their own hermeneutics. They concerned themselves with arrangement, inclusion and omission. They attended also to the relationship between parts of the texts. We can use their analysis to help to supply the binary oppositions implicit in the biblical text, even if we do not read back the forms of expression and cognition which the Rabbis deployed.

This means, of course, that the question of values can and ought to be posed separately for the biblical and rabbinic sources. The very fact that similar oppositions are found in other cultures (indeed, the very kind of oppositions for which structural anthropology makes claims of universality) indicates that these values are not dependent upon a particular form of literary expression. Nevertheless, it is the juxtaposition of these paragraphs within a relatively small legal collection that provides us with evidence that they were, indeed, regarded as opposed categories by our writers.[84] As regards the biblical presentation, then, the *form* of the values is the feelings associated with the respective images of the social context in which animals are encountered (wild or tame, in agricultural use or not, behaving 'normally' or aggressively); their *source* is social experience and interaction, though it is not claimed here that this social experience and interaction is unique; the *concern* is practical: how these events of social life should be evaluated (rather than cosmological); their *expression* is implicit: these are the 'tacit social evaluations' which normally accompany the narrative construction of sense in social life (see further §1.1, *supra*), though they have been translated here from orality into the arrangement of the text; their *cognition* is the correlation of simple binary oppositions, this correlation stemming from what is normally encountered in social life.

Much the same may be said of the slavery laws (§7.2.2): the values here may well have originated in social experience, and not be dependent upon a literary formulation. But the literary formulation has made a distinct difference. The two paragraphs are more closely integrated than are those relating to animals: not only are they directly juxtaposed;

---

84.   Thus, the argument of Finkelstein, who saw himself as refining the approach of Greenberg in proposing his 'cosmological' interpretations of the laws of goring oxen, at least has the merit of arguing in part from the arrangement of the text.

there is also a textual[85] cross-reference between them. We therefore advance from correlated evaluations—the temporary male debt-slave may be used for breeding; the temporary female debt-slave may not; breeding is acceptable only in the context of the (permanent) *amah*—to a formula regarding the relationship between gender and status that might be considered cognitively comparable to the incommensurability principle of Greenberg ('property' should not be given for 'life', 'life' should not be given for 'property'). The relationship between gender and status is thus implicitly presented as a mental operation. The form of *expression* of this cognitive construct is not only the direct juxtaposition of the two paragraphs (with correlated oppositions comparable to those in the animals paragraphs) but also the suppression of the case of the temporary female debt-slave, which disturbs those oppositions. She is neither male and temporary (permitted for breeding) nor female and permanent (permitted for breeding). Her omission derives from the fact that the predominant theme of Exod. 21.2-11 is indeed breeding, but the significance of the omission resides in its contribution to the formula, whose *concern* now appears to go beyond the purely practical, and to address the general question of status. The literary formulation thus effects the transformation not only in *expression*, but also *cognition* and *concern*. This may well imply, at the same time, transformations in respect of both *form* and *source*: the value is no longer a tacit social evaluation but rather a theoretical conclusion inferred from those correlated evaluations, a tacit moral judgment; we may assume the involvement here of educated wisdom sources, rather than popular wisdom.

The sense here attributed to the Decalogue (§7.2.3) might appear to be an entirely literary phenomenon. I argued that the correlation of references to narrative history in the Exodus version with the content that follows each such reference suggests a reflection upon norms peculiar to the Israelites and those incumbent also upon the whole (human element in) creation. Its *expression* depends upon relationships in a text of moderate length; its *concern* is not with a practical problem, but rather an issue of identity.[86] Its *form* is not so much that of the moral or

85. In the present context, Exod. 21.7, *kamishpat...*, must be taken as a textual cross-reference; it is not impossible, however, that if the *amah* paragraph ever circulated independently, the cross-reference might have been to a customary rule rather than its literary formulation.

86. Though we may recall the presence of the 'mixed multitude' (*erev rav*) which accompanied the Israelites out of Egypt (Exod. 12.38).

aesthetic connotations of particular social situations, as a classification relating to the scope of application of the rules. In other respects, however, the features of the example are not necessarily dependent upon literacy. In terms of *cognition*, we have here something approaching a 'marked' binary opposition:[87] 'us' versus 'everyone'. In terms of *source*, the narrative cross-references, as they presently stand, are literary, but we need not exclude the possibility that both law and narrative were taught orally in the home (Jackson 2000b), so that the narrative cross-references in the Decalogue might be to the oral presentation of such narratives.

I return, finally, to Greenberg's 'incommensurability'. I hesitate even to designate this as a *form* of values; it approaches an interpretive moral theory.[88] Its *source*, like that proposed for the gender/status formula in relation to the slave laws, must be educated rather than popular; indeed, it makes cross-reference (or, at least, Greenberg claims that it implies such cross-reference) not to a general narrative theme but rather a very specific literary *expression*, Gen. 9.5-6. Its *concern* is not practical (the practicalities are independently established, each with their own associated feelings) but speculative. The very notions of 'life' and 'property'[89] are used by Greenberg as abstractions, in the sense that they are treated as the poles of a binary opposition.[90] But that binary opposition is difficult to sustain in discursive (literary) terms. For Greenberg, the *expression* of such values resides in the 'art of the commentator', which presupposes, as argued above (§7.1), the discursive unity of the entire body of Pentateuchal law, and the legitimacy of making inferences from that entire corpus on the basis of content alone. It is hardly surprising, then, that the form of *cognition* implicit in Greenberg's construction is one of a high level of advance: not only the correlations of oppositions but also their reciprocal reversibility.

---

87. Jackson (1995b: 24-25), though the more inclusive term here, 'everyone', could not logically be used other than including 'us'.

88. This, too, in common with Dworkin in jurisprudence (see further *supra*, pp. 180-81).

89. It may be argued (though not here) that the opposition between 'person' and 'property' is far less stark in the Bible than in our culture, given the considerable range we encounter in different forms of personal dependency.

90. This is not to claim that the biblical texts do not deploy such concepts, though in relation to 'property', general terms such as *melekhet* (Exod. 22.7) are rare, at least in the early stage of the tradition, by comparison with the designation of concrete items of property.

The analysis of these four examples might well be used to generate a hypothetical model for the development of values from orality to literacy:

		Oral	*Literary*
(a)	*Form*	Feelings	Judgments
(b)	*Source*	Popular	Educational élite
(c)	*Concern*	Practical	Speculative
(d)	*Expression*	'Narrative' (sometimes tacit)	Literary structure
(e)	*Cognition*	Binary oppositions	'Operations'

These, of course, are ideal types of the kind of values we might hypothesize in systems located towards the extremes of the orality-literacy spectrum. The examples indicate some points on the transition between them. But this is not the place to take the matter further.

Chapter 8

LAW'S INTERNAL RECOGNITION

8.1 *Introduction*

To what extent might semiotic approaches assist us in understanding relationships between different laws that appear to concern the same theme—for which I use the loose term 'thematic repetition'?[1] Clearly, the basic choice between 'semantic' and 'narrative' conceptions of meaning (§3.2) will have a direct impact: a 'more general' formulation will not, in fact, 'contradict' a 'less general' formulation if the former is understood as 'restricted code' for a typical situation which differs sufficiently from that of the latter. However, the choice between 'semantic' and 'narrative' approaches is not inherent in a particular text; it is the application to the text of a conventional epistemology. The same 'text', originating in an oral culture, may move from being understood 'narratively' to a 'semantic' interpretation, when the text itself moves into a social setting (often, one of literacy) in which the operative epistemology is different.

Less obvious is the application of narrative semiotics to thematic repetition of the content of law. I argue in Chapter 9 that repetition commonly functions as 'Recognition' (in the Greimassian sense) in the narratives of the law, as applied both to the roles of particular subjects (Abraham, Moses, Joshua), and to the communicative acts that they perform (testing, promising, covenanting, incorporating, saying farewell, etc.). To what extent, if at all, can such notions be applied also to the content of the messages? If a law is 'repeated', does that recognize the validity of the earlier expression only in so far as the original is repeated exactly, without change? Where there is a change, what modality does that introduce into the form of recognition? This raises, of course, some very fundamental questions—of the very conception of

1. Not an unproblematic notion, however (see Dozeman 1989: 147-50).

identity and difference, and of the evaluation of 'accuracy' in the transmission of tradition. Here, as elsewhere, it is all too easy to assume that our own epistemological notions are natural, inevitable or even the most progressive, and to impose them upon a culture whose assumptions in these areas are quite different. This section commences, therefore, by noting some of the more explicit indications that biblical authors themselves give of their views on such matters, before introducing a number of models offered in the modern, scholarly literature.

A striking comment on the force of repetition is found in a source not commonly noted in this connection: Joseph's interpretation of Pharoah's dreams. First Pharoah dreams about the seven thin cows consuming the seven fat ones, then (a separate dream: we are told, 'And Pharaoh awoke. And he fell asleep and dreamed a second time') he dreams about the seven thin ears of corn swallowing up the seven fat ears (Gen. 41.1-7). Joseph is ultimately summoned to interpret them. He commences by saying: 'The dream of Pharaoh is one; God has revealed to Pharaoh what he is about to do' (Gen. 41.25). Two quite different dreams—presented explicitly as forms of divine revelation—with a single (very specific) message. Why were two dreams required? Joseph addresses the question directly: 'And the doubling of Pharaoh's dream means that the thing is fixed by God (כי נכון הדבר מעם האלהים), and God will shortly bring it to pass' (Gen. 41.32). The effect of the doubling is a metamessage, a message about the force or status of the message: it is firmly determined, and to be implemented immediately.

Of course, pairs of dreams occur also elsewhere in the Joseph narrative: we may well regard them as a narrative theme. But within that theme, there are subtle variations. Consider first Joseph's own apparent megalomania. First, he tells his brothers: 'We were binding sheaves in the field, and lo, my sheaf arose and stood upright; and behold, your sheaves gathered round it, and bowed down to my sheaf' (Gen. 37.7). This dream is not symbolic; it is directly representational: Joseph and his brothers themselves figure in it. No need for any interpretation here; the brothers immediately get the message and are not best pleased. But Joseph is not finished. He has a second dream: 'the sun, the moon, and eleven stars were bowing down to me' (Gen. 37.9). This is not directly representational, but again needs no interpretation. The force of the repetition here is *not* that the dream is to be implemented immediately. There may, indeed, be an implication (again) that repetition of the message validates the communication as a divine revelation—even though the content here does add a new element: the relationship of Joseph not only to his brothers but also to his parents. But the repetition here also has another function. The second dream, though not directly representational, is nevertheless transparent in its meaning precisely because of its relationship to the first dream (which was directly representational). The two dreams, it may be added, are not here presented as 'one'. Not only is there a new element in the second. The temporal relationship between the two is not clear. Unlike Pharoah, who wakes after the first dream, then falls asleep again and has the second dream, Joseph tells his brothers the dream about the sheaves of corn and receives their reaction (Gen. 37.8) before we are told that he dreams again. Nevertheless, the first dream provides the interpretive framework for the understanding of the second.

A similar structure informs the account of the third pair of dreams, though these are simultaneous messages received by different people: Pharoah's chief butler and chief baker, with whom Joseph is incarcerated (Gen. 40.1-19). And though they concern the same theme—the future prospects of the respective dreamers—their interpretations are radically different. The text is interested in this issue. Even before Joseph offers his interpretation, we are told that the two prisoners dreamed 'each his own dream, and each dream with its own meaning' (Gen. 40.5). The two had, according to the narrative, sought interpretations of the dreams, without success. Again before hearing and interpreting the dreams, Joseph tells them: 'Do not interpretations belong to God?' (Gen. 40.8). The dream of the butler is directly representational in that the butler's restoration is depicted: 'Pharaoh's cup was in my hand; and I took the grapes and pressed them into Pharaoh's cup, and placed the cup in Pharaoh's hand' (Gen. 40.11); Joseph's insight is required only in interpreting the three branches in temporal terms, as three days. The baker's dream, by contrast, is far less directly representational: the birds eating out of the top (third) basket on his head (Gen. 40.16-19) are taken to represent birds eating his flesh after Pharoah has him hanged. The narrative stresses, however, a unity between the dreams: we are told at the outset that the two dreams occurred on the same night (Gen. 40.5). The relationship between them is similar to that between Joseph's own pair of dreams: the first is more transparent than the second, and the symbolism of the second is decoded by reference to the transparency of the first. The thematic reiteration here is thus not concerned merely with the force, or content of the message, but also with the very means of ascribing meaning to it.

In this set of narratives concerning 'Joseph's dreams', there is thus no single meaning attached to the reiteration: we have to attend carefully to the indications provided by the text itself, indications that derive from the narrative framework, the story of the pragmatics of the dream: its perception, telling and interpretation. These are issues with which the texts are clearly interested: the dreams are revelations from God, who does not speak twice merely for literary effect; repetition may signify the force of an utterance, or it may contribute to the very process of interpretation, whether the message is the same, the same with supplementation, or different.

Are we to regard such issues as irrelevant when we turn from dreams to law? I doubt it. What is striking about the accounts of 'Joseph's dreams' is simply the explicitness with which these issues are raised. At the very least, they provide us with models or hypotheses for the consideration of other forms of thematic reiteration of divine messages, where the texts are less explicit. Is the reiteration that is represented by Deuteronomy (in the Decalogue, if not more generally) an indication of the 'immediacy' of the coming-into-force of the laws (like Pharoah's dreams, according to Gen. 41.32) in the context of the imminent entry into the land? The reiteration of the giving of the tablets of the law—despite the uncertainties in the text as to whether the two sets carried the same text and whether the second was inscribed by God or Moses (see further §9.3, at nn. 47-48, *infra*)— may be taken to indicate that the second still carries the force of the first, notwithstanding the circumstances of the latter's destruction. We also have the account of the destruction by Jehoiakim of Jeremiah's scroll, as it was being read, by cutting it off column by column and casting the pieces in the fire.[2] Jeremiah is told: 'Take another scroll and write on it all the former words that were in the first scroll' (Jer. 36.27). He does so, dictating to Baruch not only 'all the words of the scroll which Jehoiakim king of Judah had burned in the fire' but also 'many similar words...added to them' (Jer. 36.32). Indeed, there is a hint of a further addition; God tells Jeremiah, immediately after instructing him to write the second scroll:

---

2.   Jer. 36.23; Niditch (1997: 104-105) notes that although the first scroll is destroyed, its words remain in the mind and mouth of Jeremiah, who is able to dictate a second copy. In fact, even the contents of the first scroll are not said to have been dictated to Jeremiah at the time he is told to write them down; he is assumed to remember all the previous oracles that God has given to him.

And concerning Jehoiakim king of Judah you shall say, 'Thus says the
LORD, You have burned this scroll, saying, "Why have you written in it
that the king of Babylon will certainly come and destroy this land, and
will cut off from it man and beast?" Therefore thus says the LORD concerning Jehoiakim king of Judah, He shall have none to sit upon the
throne of David, and his dead body shall be cast out to the heat by day
and the frost by night. And I will punish him and his offspring and his
servants for their iniquity; I will bring upon them, and upon the inhabitants of Jerusalem, and upon the men of Judah, all the evil that I have
pronounced against them, but they would not hear' (Jer. 36.29-31).

It is not clear whether this further judgment on Jehoiakim, for having
burned the scroll, is to be written into the second scroll. That the second
scroll, which replaced the first, was a supplemented version, is not
however in doubt. No *bal tosif* for Jeremiah: ועוד נוסף עליהם דברים
רבים כהמה (Jer. 36.32). If anything, the supplemented text gains in
force from its relationship to the original. It is not merely a replacement, regrettably required because of unfortunate events; it has the status of the original, its production being ordered by God, and it has a
supplementary text, the latter perhaps reflecting the very circumstances
of its initial rejection. There are striking similarities here to the history
of the stone tablets.

Deuteronomy's self-presentation also has much in common with this.
The first revelation may not here have been rejected, but the covenant
in the land of Moab is explicitly described as additional to that at
Horeb—מלבד הברית אשר כרת אתם בחרב (Deut. 29.1; see further
§9.4, *infra*). Moreover, the narrator introduces the first speech of Moses
by saying that he 'undertook to explain [*be'er*] this law' (Deut. 1.5).[3]
Hatorah hazot can hardly be taken to refer to anything other than the
speeches in Deuteronomy itself. So this additional covenant is also different in its pragmatics: it is explicitly expository—not only the laws
but the reasons for their observance. Commenting on this passage,
Watts observes: 'Ironically, awareness of change creates concern for
the tradition's integrity within Deuteronomy itself, which contains the
only Pentateuchal injunctions against modifications' (1999: 120).

Certainly, Deuteronomy, which was concerned to indicate that God

---

3.   Cf. Levinson (1997: 151): 'Deuteronomy consistently asserts its derivative
status by presenting itself as either mere application of preceding legislation (Deut
1.5) or legislative codicil to the original covenant at Sinai/Horeb (Deut 28.69).' On
the latter claim, see further §9.4, pp. 258-59, *infra,* in the context of Deut. 7.7-11.

did not add anything to the Decalogue at the Horeb revelation (Deut. 5.22), seeks to stress (Deut. 4.2; 13.1, MT) that there should be no further addition to what is now being revealed.[4] It does not follow, however, that the supplement represented by Deuteronomy itself was conceived as a 'change', any more than the inclusion of Joseph's parents in his second dream changed the meaning of the first.[5] Here again, repetition of the message validates (recognizes) the communication of the first as a divine revelation, albeit in a different 'voice'.[6] In one respect, however, the relationship of Deuteronomy to the earlier revelation reverses that between Joseph's two dreams: here, it is the second that is the more transparent, being presented as containing its own explanation—a feature that many modern commentators, in remarking upon its hortatory and didactic character, effectively confirm.

Modern commentators address the significance of 'thematic repetition' of laws through a range of inferred models.[7] Repetition is commonly viewed as a device particularly appropriate in oral literature, partly to assist the memorization and transmission of the tradition.[8] Such repetition is not necessarily exact: the words, the whole words and nothing but the words. When the tradition is first written down, such repetitions are not eliminated simply because their mnemonic function is no longer required, but their very character may appear different in their new literary form: repetition may then come to appear as textual

---

4.   Quite possibly in reaction to a prophetic practice of supplementation, as indicated in Jer. 36.

5.   This continued to be reflected in the use made in rabbinic Judaism of Deuteronomy's *mishneh hatorah hazot* (Deut. 17.18; cf. Josh. 8.23; and see further §5.2, *supra*). A term used in the biblical text to refer to a direct copy (of Deuteronomy, or part of it), became a title—*mishnah*—indeed *mishneh torah* in the case of Maimonides—applied to texts that represented vast supplements on the originals, without being conceived to change them.

6.   Cf. Watts (1999: 79-80, 129), arguing that the laws of Exodus, Leviticus and Numbers are presented by the anonymous narrator as what God told Moses to command the Israelites; in Deuteronomy, the narrator has Moses voice the commands of God (as well as his own: *infra*, §9.4).

7.   This is not to imply any criticism of the exercise of inferring models for this matter. It is not always clear, however, that full use has been made of explicit indications (which fall to be evaluated, for sure) in the texts themselves.

8.   Jackson (1995b: 65, 79), and see the different possible interpretations of repetition in the analysis of 'behavioural style' (including style of speech behaviour), at 66.

quotation (Niditch 1997: 10-11, 18-19).[9]

Particular attention has been paid of late to thematic reiterations of pentateuchal laws that include contradictions between the two versions. Reference has been made to the view that it was the policy of the Persian empire, in granting limited legal autonomy, which may have prompted the collation of the disparate texts that generated such contradictions, since Persian royal edicts were claimed to be irrevocable (§5.4, *supra*).[10] Whatever the historical stimulus, it is no longer assumed that this process of collation of contradictory texts proceeded without any attempt to resolve such contradictions in the course of the editing process. Bernard Levinson, developing Michael Fishbane's notion of 'inner biblical exegesis', has pointed to some literary techniques (more systematic and sophisticated than those long claimed by the 'interpolationist' literary-historical tradition), that involve the partial repetition of the 'old' text, with elements that then transform its meaning.[11]

Differences of approach to these matters reflect, of course, a basic ideological choice: must the model we choose account for all the data? Put differently, must we assume that our ancient authors and editors were capable of applying their own methods perfectly, almost seamlessly (though not, of course, without leaving sufficient clues for us to detect their activities!)? There are versions of both the literary-historical and the literary-holistic approaches that do appear to attribute such per-

---

9.   Watts (1999: 72) notes the view of Savran (1988: 116) that the authenticity of the quotations in Deuteronomy depends not upon comparison with prior speech but upon the authoritative voice who quotes them—that is, Moses.

10.   Watts (1999: 75) seeks to convert this into a rhetorical theory: 'From a rhetorical perspective, this theory can be rephrased to suggest that Persian-period readers and hearers would not accept the alteration of written law.' That assumes, to my mind, an unwarranted convergence between an ideological, constitutional claim and popular perceptions. How many people really think of the Queen as Head of the Church of England?

11.   See esp. Levinson (1992) for the striking example of the modification within Deuteronomy of the Decalogue principle of intergenerational vicarious punishment (on which see §6.3, *supra*). Levinson compares Deut. 7.9-10, which 'quotes' but adapts the Decalogue teaching, with Ezek. 18.1-4, concluding (at 56): 'This radically revisionist textual voice of Moses in Deuteronomy, despite appearances, in fact voices the concerns of Israelite authors roughly contemporary with the prophet Ezekiel' (see also Levinson 1997: 20; cf. Watts 1999: 118). On Jer. 31.29-31, see §9.1 n. 5, *infra*.

fection to the human authors. On the one hand, some literary-historical approaches appear to assume that every change made in a text is deliberate, motivated; on the other, some literary-holistic approaches seek to apply a single model, irrespective of the (at times) relative inappropriateness of that model.[12] Such different forms of perfectionism necessarily run the risk of imposition of theory upon the evidence. The search for perfectionism, however, may derive from current ideological positions (whether secular or religious). Without such an assumption, we are in a better position to evaluate the application of models to particular texts on the basis of the merits of the individual case concerned. This allows both for pluralism in the choice of models applied to different texts, and for what may be termed semiotic errors and accidents. Or should we seek a psychoanalytical explanation for every scribal error?

8.2 *Chiasmus and Thematic Repetition: From Orality to Literacy*

Repetition commences within short, oral texts,[13] such as the parallelism in Pharoah's dreams. Within the oral context it can already acquire a form of 'reversibility', that which we find in the basic chiastic structure: for example, Gen. 9.6, שפך דם האדם באדם דמו ישפך (cf. Welch 1990a: 7). From there, chiasmus within a single sentence, we proceed to the arrangement of sentences within a paragraph based upon the same principle,[14] and thence to larger structures. Consider the following from

---

12. Cf. Levinson (1991: 136) in his review essay of Sternberg (1985). Watts (1999: 74-84) seems to me to fall into the same trap, despite being sensitive to the problem. Repetition is viewed as a rhetorical, instructional device (68-73), a form of re-emphasis (at 78), whatever the distribution of the material (e.g. the twelvefold repetition of the sabbath command in the Pentateuch, noted at 68). Where contradictions cannot be explained as variations for re-emphasis, he has recourse to different audiences anticipated within the text (comparing speeches by politicians and court decisions that frequently address individuals or social groups in conflict with each other) (cf. Stahl 1995: 20). By the time of the pentateuchal redaction, he claims (at 84, cf. 137), 'the idea of Mosaic law has become even more important than its contents; so long as the idea is accepted, the contradictions in detail can be reconciled later'.

13. See Douglas (1999: 46-48) on the basic parallelism underlying the chiasmus.

14. See the examples provided by Welch (1990), including the claim that of 19 units identified in Exod. 21.2-23.17, 'fifteen of the 19 segments can be described as being chiastically balanced to some degree' (17). However, six of these are no more than A-B-A patterns, and even these are sometimes achieved with some artificiality (e.g. unit 8, taken to comprise Exod. 21.33-36, although this combines two inde-

the homicide laws as presented in Numbers 35:

A1	v. 17	And if he struck him down with a stone (*be'even yad*) in the hand, by which a man may die, and he died, he is a murderer; the murderer shall be put to death.
B1	v. 20	And if he stabbed him from hatred, or hurled at him, lying in wait (*bitsediyah*), so that he died
C1	v. 21	or in enmity (*be'eyvah*) struck him down with his hand, so that he died, then he who struck the blow shall be put to death; he is a murderer; the avenger of blood shall put the murderer to death, when he meets him.
C2	v. 22	But if he stabbed him suddenly without enmity (*belo eyvah*)
B2	v. 22	or hurled anything on him without lying in wait (*belo tsediyah*),
A2	vv. 23-25	or used a stone (*bekhol even*) by which a man may die, and without seeing him cast it upon him, so that he died, though he was not his enemy, and did not seek his harm; then the congregation shall judge between the manslayer and the avenger of blood, in accordance with these ordinances; and the congregation shall rescue the manslayer from the hand of the avenger of blood...

The chiasmus here has been slightly obscured by some elaborations and being embedded into a larger structure. But its presence is clearly indicated by the nature of the repetitions: not simply the same theme, but direct negation in the second series of the situations contemplated in the first. This is done by both linguistic negation (vv. 21, 22: with or without enmity, with or without 'lying in wait'), and by reversing the situation: from deliberate casting a stone (v. 17) to casting it without seeing (v. 23). The literary chiasmus is thus here combined with operations we more traditionally associate with logic: negation and classification. The latter is reflected in what unites the two sets internally: the first is a set of cases with one legal result: the court (by implication) must hand over the murderer to the *go'el hadam*; the second is a group where the court is bade protect the killer, if these facts are established after an adjudication. These differing legal consequences are stated at the *end* of each of the two sets, thus in C1 and A2, since they apply to 'all the foregoing'.

Given the availability of these two opposed legal outcomes, it may appear natural to organize the cases in binary oppositional terms

pendent casuistic paragraphs [Welch 1990: 14]). This does not detract from the strength of some of Welch's other examples.

(though this would not account for its chiastic arrangement). There is, however, a further factor involved. The binary oppositional structure mirrors that of the homicide laws in earlier sources, both the *Mishpatim* and Deuteronomy. Indeed, it combines themes from those two sources: the paradigm case of premeditated homicide (ambush) is here taken up, using the terminology of the *Mishpatim* (though here in nominalized form);[15] that very image (though in different language) is explicitly linked with previous hatred in Deuteronomy.[16] This is all the more striking since Numbers takes up an intermediate case that was not contemplated in the earlier sources: v. 22 deals with intentional but unpremeditated homicide, while both the *Mishpatim* and Deuteronomy opposed premeditated with accidental homicide (cf. Jackson 1975a: 90-92).[17] By uperimposing upon the situational opposition one based upon legal outcomes, the author of Numbers 35 is able to place this new case within a seemingly traditional oppositional structure. The institutional concern has taken precedence over the social understanding, just as the language has become more abstract and the presentation more logical.[18]

15. In Exod. 21.13 *va'asher lo tsadah,* in Num. 35.20 *bitsdiyah* (see further §4.2, *supra*).

16. 'But if any man hates his neighbour, and lies in wait for him (*ve'orav lo*) and attacks him, and wounds him mortally so that he dies...' (Deut. 19.11).

17. This has been contested by Phillips (1977: 114 n. 34): 'But Jackson is mistaken in regarding Numbers 35.22 as referring to "intentional but unpremeditated homicide" and verse 23 as governing "accidental homicide," for verse 23 merely illustrates by a particular precedent what is envisaged by verse 22b.' But the two cases in 22b and 23 are quite different: 22b is 'hurled anything on him without lying in wait'; v. 23 is 'used a stone, by which a man may die, and without seeing him cast it upon him, so that he died'. Greenberg (1990: 122 n. 8) argues that my 'claim that Num 35.22-23 provides asylum for intentional homicides is not supported by the final hypothetical circumstance: "or without seeing [him] dropped on him any deadly stone object"'. But I clearly distinguished between vv. 22 and 23: the fact that both are 'unpremeditated' does not mean that both are 'intentional': what it does mean is that they are comparable in their legal consequences (Jackson 1975a: 91; cf. Jackson 1985a: 663). Neither Phillips nor Greenberg is able to deny that the offender in v. 22a ('if he stabbed him suddenly without enmity') is entitled to protection at the city of refuge.

18. Contrast the *Mishpatim*, where the two poles of such oppositions are presented together within a single narrative context (e.g. Exod. 22.6-7: if the thief is found ... if the thief is not found), rather than as part of an opposed list spanning several different narrative contexts.

The binary oppositions have moved from the sphere of orality to that of literacy.

I have argued that the first major component of the *Mishpatim* may be identified (inter alia) by the presence of a chiasmus (Jackson 1995c: 1779).

A1	Exod. 21.2-11	Liberation of male and female slave
B1	21.12-17	Capital provisions[19]
C1	21.18-19	Injuries from a brawl
D	21.20-21	Fatal assault on one's own slave
C2	21.22-23	Brawl affecting a pregnant woman
B2	21.24-25	Talionic provisions
A2	21.26-27	Liberation of male or female slave.

Mary Douglas has argued for a further elaboration of chiastic structures into a 'ring' device for structuring entire books.[20] However, in comparing repetitive textual units larger than a chapter, a linear repetitive sequence (without this form of reversibility) seems more likely. Even with the possibility of the 'backward scanning' available from a written text, the reader will need to indulge in a great deal of to-ing and fro-ing to grasp the structure.[21]

The same issue can arise in thematic repetitions in a linear sequence.

19. Before the widely acknowledged addition of vv. 13-14. The two B elements are correlated not (or not primarily) in terms of their content, but rather in terms of their form: they are the only sets of provisions that digress from the standard casuistic form. But literary forms of comparability are a feature of biblical law, as argued in §§7.2–3 above. There may also be an element of thematic correspondence, in the sense that the first of the participial provisions invokes the death penalty for murder, which can be understood as an application of the talionic principle.

20. Both Leviticus and Numbers, though with differences (see Douglas 1993, 1999). In the latter, at 52, she contemplates the use of such devices at two levels: 'The whole book [of Numbers] presents itself as a macro-ring of major rings: law and narrative set in alternating rings, and these decomposable into minor rings again.'

21. Niditch (1997: 127-30), regards the relationship between the Deuteronomic history and Chronicles as the one fairly certain example of composition in a literary mode, involving the use of a manuscript to produce another written work. Even here, however, the earlier history is not discarded or replaced: 'Rather in good oral-traditional style, variants are allowable and accommodated' (at 130).

The following 'double series' has been identified by Carmichael in the Covenant Code (1972:19-25; 1974: 62-65).[22]

(1) 22.20 You shall not wrong a stranger or oppress him, for you were strangers in the land of Egypt.

23.9 You shall not oppress a stranger; you know the heart of a stranger, for you were strangers in the land of Egypt.

22.21 You shall not afflict any widow or orphan.

22.22 If you do afflict them, and they cry out to me, I will surely hear their cry;

22.23 and my wrath will burn, and I will kill you with the sword, and your wives shall become widows and your children fatherless.

(2) 22.24 If you lend money to any of my people with you who is poor, you shall not be to him as a creditor, and you shall not exact interest from him.

23.10 For six years you shall sow your land and gather in its yield;

22.25 If ever you take your neighbour's garment in pledge, you shall restore it to him before the sun goes down;

23.11 but the seventh year you shall let it rest and lie fallow, that the poor of your people may eat; and what they leave the wild beasts may eat. You shall do likewise with your vineyard, and with your olive orchard.

22.26 for that is his only covering, it is his mantle for his body; in what else shall he sleep? And if he cries to me, I will hear, for I am compassionate.

23.12 Six days you shall do your work, but on the seventh day you shall rest; that your ox and your ass may have rest, and the son of your bondmaid, and the alien, may be refreshed.

22. The proposal is supported by the argument that the Deuteronomic reworking of some of these laws shows that the author 'was quite aware of the way in which laws in the *Mishpatim* were set down in correspondence with other laws there': (1972: 22). Carmichael argues that this technique of internal repetition was also used in Deuteronomy itself.

(3)   22.27   You shall not revile God, nor curse a ruler of your people.

(4)   22.28   You shall not delay to offer from the fulness of your harvest and from the outflow of your presses. The first-born of your sons you shall give to me.

(5)   22.29   You shall do likewise with your oxen and with your sheep: seven days it shall be with its dam; on the eighth day you shall give it to me.

(6)   22.30   You shall be men consecrated to me; therefore you shall not eat any flesh that is torn by beasts in the field; you shall cast it to the dogs.

23.13   Take heed to all that I have said to you; and make no mention of the names of other gods, nor let such be heard out of your mouth.

23.14   Three times in the year you shall keep a feast to me.

23.15   You shall keep the feast of unleavened bread; as I commanded you, you shall eat unleavened bread for seven days at the appointed time in the month of Abib, for in it you came out of Egypt. None shall appear before me empty-handed.

23.16   You shall keep the feast of harvest, of the first fruits of your labor, of what you sow in the field. You shall keep the feast of ingathering at the end of the year, when you gather in from the field the fruit of your labor.

23.17   Three times in the year shall all your males appear before the LORD GOD.

23.18   You shall not offer the blood of my sacrifice with leavened bread, or let the fat of my feast remain until the morning.

23.19   The first of the first fruits of your ground you shall bring into the house of the LORD your God.
You shall not boil a kid in its mother's milk.

He concedes that the correspondence is 'fairly loose' (Carmichael 1972: 21; 1974: 64). In its favour is the fact that these two units are clearly marked as such by formal and substantive differences with what immediately precedes and succeeds them[23] (though that may speak more to their respective literary histories rather than their literary relationship). Each (1) begins with the same historical allusion,[24] to the Israelite experience in Egypt, in connection with the admonition not to oppress strangers. For the rest, the connections are thematic rather than substantive, and depend in part upon the classification system we use in order to infer the respective themes. Thus in (2), Carmichael pairs protection of the poor from loans at interest and from oppressive pledging with seventh-year release of the land's produce for the poor and sabbath rest for the bondmaid's son and for the sojourner. These may appear rather different matters. If we apply modern forms of legal classification, we might put (2) from the first list under some rubric such as 'creditor and debtor', or perhaps 'security, pledge', while we would regard the latter as 'agricultural law' and 'labour law'. Such technical legal concepts, however, are inappropriate here. The pairing is justifiable if we take as the basis of classification not substantive rules or concepts, but rather the underlying purpose, namely the protection of the poor, based upon an evaluation of the social imagery of the poor man facing the elements (negatively in Exod. 22.26, positively in Exod. 23.11). That is evident enough in the first sequence, where the rules concern loans at interest and oppressive pledging. But it also appears from the face of the corresponding item of the second sequence, where the field is to lie fallow in the seventh year 'that the poor of your people may eat' (Exod. 23.11); similarly, the reason given for the cessation of work on the seventh day is not that 'you' (the free Israelite) shall be refreshed by the rest, but rather that 'your ox and your ass may have rest, and the son of your bondmaid, and the alien, may be refreshed' (Exod. 23.12) (Carmichael 1974: 64). In (3), Exod. 23.13 appears to respond to a question arising from Exod. 22.27: Does the ban on cursing (*tekalel*) *elohim* permit the cursing of *elohim acherim*? The answer

---

23. Before the first: the short, apodictic, capital provisions of Exod. 22.17-19 (MT), after: the 'litigation' pericope discussed below; before the second: the 'litigation' pericope discussed below; after: the angel pericope (commencing 'Behold, I send an angel before you...', Exod. 23.20).

24. On historical allusions as markers of sections in the Decalogue, see *supra*, §7.2.3 and n. 75 (in relation to other collections of laws).

is negative: even though cursing them would not be an offence comparable to the prohibition, you should not even mention them (in effect, a
measure of respect, if expressed in a manner perhaps suggesting
defilement of the lips). (4) and (5) (which I would not necessarily
divide up in the way that Carmichael does) relate, in both cases, to agricultural offerings: the first fruits of the harvest, the vine, oxen, sheep
and indeed the first-born son (Exod. 22.28-29); agricultural offerings in
the context of the three pilgrimage festivals (Exod. 23.14-19a). In both
lists, the series concludes with a dietary law: the ban on torn animals,
terefah, in the first series, the ban on seething a kid in its mother's milk
in the second.

Carmichael takes this double series structure to result from 'the
scribal practices of the sages' but regards the technique as having
'mnemonic advantages useful in instruction. The M scribe's concern
with mnemonic technique may reflect classroom experience'
(Carmichael 1974: 65). He compares the arrangement of proverbs, and
suggests that the compiler of the *Mishpatim*

> came to his task familiar with, and influenced by, the compilation of the
> kind of material now found in the present book of Proverbs... This
> would explain...the mnemonic element in the method, because the
> scribal activity in the preceptive, proverbial literature directly reflects
> classroom instruction where mnemonic aids are fundamental (Carmichael
> 1972: 25).

The list, on this account, has effected a transition from orality to literacy. I find this rather implausible,[25] at least for the double series as a
whole. Lists are associated with literacy, rather than oral transmission.
Here, moreover, the structure is in part a matter of inference from
theme: not the most immediately recognizable form of connection.[26] Of
course, one could use literary-critical scissors to reduce each list to
something that would correspond more simply and directly to the other.
Even so, only (1)-(3) present immediately recognizable connections.

25. Comparison may be made with the work by psycholinguists in the
Chomskyan tradition on the cognitive limits of the acceptability of embedding (see
§4.5, *supra*).

26. Carmichael (1972: 24) maintains: 'If you already know a list of things and it
is desired that you learn another list, it is an aid to memory to set the things in the
second list in a sequence which corresponds as closely as possible with the things in
the first list.' At the same time he stresses the 'loose' status of the connections here
(Carmichael 1974: 64).

Further evidence of the imposition of literary sophistication upon thematic reiteration may be found in the passage that intervenes between the two parts of Carmichael's double series:

A1	23.1	You shall not utter a false report. You shall not join hands with a wicked man, to be a malicious witness.
A2	23.2	You shall not follow a multitude to do evil; nor shall you bear witness in a suit, turning aside after a multitude, so as to pervert justice;
A3	23.3	nor shall you be partial to a poor man in his suit.
B	23.4	If you meet your enemy's ox or his ass going astray, you shall bring it back to him.
	23.5	If you see the ass of one who hates you lying under its burden, you shall refrain from leaving him with it, you shall help him to lift it up.
C3	23.6	You shall not pervert the justice due to your poor in his suit.
C2	23.7	Keep far from a false charge, and do not slay the innocent and righteous, for I will not acquit the wicked.
C1	23.8	And you shall take no bribe, for a bribe blinds the officials, and subverts the cause of those who are in the right.

This seems, at first sight, a curious collection. Its main theme is the perversion of justice. The first three verses prohibit false testimony, whether as a result of conspiracy, popular pressure, or partiality to the poor, while the last three verses seem directed towards the judge, counselling him to do justice to the poor and to take no bribes.[27] But between those two groups of injunctions, we have what are sometimes categorized as 'humanitarian' provisions: the duty to bring back an enemy's straying ox or ass, and to assist him in lifting up an ass that is lying down under its burden (Exod. 23.4-5).[28] There are thus two literary questions to be answered in respect of this passage. First, what internal principle, if any, gives it its unity? Secondly, what is the rela-

27. One might just argue for a chiastic arrangement, as I have implied in designating the verses A1-3, C3-1 respectively.

28. One might think that this is a literary unit crying out for the application of Daube's theory of amendment by addition at the end, what he calls the *lex clausulae finalis* (1947: Ch. 3), indicating that the unit originally comprised the two elements regarding false testimony and the humanitarian provisions, while the third, thematically far closer to the first, was subsequently added. But we are here concerned with the final literary structure, rather than the preceding literary history.

tionship of the unit as a whole to the wider literary structure?

As regards the first, the passage once again shows the non-necessary status of those classifications that often strike us as most natural. The 'humanitarian' provisions have that significance only if we focus upon the interests of the animals, to the exclusion of other elements of the text. What is remarkable, in this context, is the fact that both apparently 'humanitarian' provisions posit a context of enmity between the owner of the animal and the person upon whom the duty is imposed. The command is not to return *any* straying ox or ass, or to assist with the uplifting of *any* overburdened animal: it is, in the first case, 'your enemy's ox or his ass'; in the second, 'the ass of one who hates you'. We are not to conclude that the author of the text would have restricted the duties to those cases. Nevertheless, the selection of that particular instance of humanitarian behaviour to animals as the one for inclusion, as opposed to the class in general, is significant. And this supplies the clue to the internal structure of the unit. Enmity is presupposed also in the context of litigation. The message of the literary structure, taken as a whole, is that enmity must neither subvert the administration of justice, nor interfere with the observance of ethical behaviour. As argued in an earlier chapter (§3.4), litigation is not conceived as the normal manner of resolving disputes: the typical situation in which it is envisaged is one not merely of dispute, but of enmity. Enmity, we might say, is here conceived as the source of litigation; in our society, it is the result.

What of the relationship of Exod. 23.1-8 to the literary structure as a whole? Two views are possible: either it has been inserted into an already existing double series, or it originally concluded the Covenant Code, the second sequence of Carmichael's second series (as well as the angel pericope) being added at a later stage.[29] The issue is not easy to decide. Carmichael thinks Exod. 23.1-8 was already in the text when Exod. 23.9-19 was added, applying the Daubean principle of *lex clausulae finalis* (1972: 23 n. 7; 1974: 64 n. 14).[30] I am inclined to view

29. The fact that there is one thematic element in common to all three sections, the concern with the poor, does not really assist in deciding this question, though it may be noted that this passage is not unequivocably 'pro-poor' in the same sense as the double series: the case of the poor man is not to be perverted (Exod. 23.6) but at the same time no partiality is to be shown to him (Exod. 23.3).

30. For the *lex clausulae finalis*, see n. 28, *supra*.

Exod. 23.1-8 as late,[31] though this does not necessarily detract from Carmichael's argument. Whatever the answer to this question of literary history, the final literary structure involves the application of an A-B-A sequence at two different levels, both within Exod. 23.1-8, and in the relationship between that passage and what surrounds it (the two elements in the double series). This is surely literary artifice rather than oral instruction.

8.3 *Law and Narrative*

Can reiteration cross 'genres', so that the relationship between law and literature can also admit of it? In one sense, a positive answer has already been implied to this question, through the comparability claimed in the last section between reiteration in the narratives of 'Joseph's dreams', Jeremiah's prophecies and both the narratives and the content of the laws. This is hardly remarkable, if the literature is one that equally ascribes the dreams, prophecies and laws to divine revelation, and which emanates from editors who endorse that belief in the accounts that they provide of these different media of divine revelation.

As for law and literature, there is increasing recognition of the importance of their interrelation for the understanding of each. We may distinguish a number of different dimensions of this relationship. Allusion to narratives in laws, whether as motive clauses or historical introductions, has already been noted (§7.2.3, pp. 200-201, *supra*). Another is the impact of the narrative frame on our conception of the nature or force of the laws, discussed at some length in the next chapter. But narrative framing may also influence our view of substantive legal developments. When we consider the (first) case of the daughters of Zelophehad (Num. 27.1-11; §2.3.2, *supra*), it would appear at first sight that the daughters are protesting against a purely *customary* set of rules (on intestate distribution). Certainly, the daughters refer to no legal source for the rule against which they are protesting, nor do we have

---

31. Jackson (1995c: 1804): the litigation theme does not fit well with the *Mishpatim* and is related to that of another passage on the margins of the collection, namely the narrative of Jethro's advice to Moses on the administration of justice (Exod. 18.13-26), which immediately precedes the narrative of the arrival of the Israelites at Sinai (Exod. 19.1). It may thus have been the same hand that added both the Jethro story and Exod. 23.1-8 to the Sinaitic pericope. But that would not explain why it was added in the present place.

records of any such. Moreover, the relative ease with which the daughters succeed in achieving change might be easier understood if it is assumed that they are not asking for a change in divine law, but merely in current custom.[32] (For sure, the argument might be reversed: could not Moses authorise a mere change in, or departure from, customary law without having to consult God?) However, the narrative framework in which we find the dispute, and the resultant law, must be taken into account.[33] In the previous chapter, Moses and Aaron are asked to take a census of the male adult Israelites ('from twenty years old and upward, by their fathers' houses, all in Israel who are able to go forth to war', Num. 26.2), and they do so. This is preparatory to the entry to the land: it is done 'in the plains of Moab by the Jordan at Jericho' (Num. 26.2). After the census is complete and recorded (for us, as for them), God commands: 'To these the land shall be divided for inheritance (*benachalah*) according to the number of names' (Num. 26.53). Throughout the lists of the descendants of Jacob's sons (including the two eldest sons of Joseph whom he had adopted for this purpose [§2.2, *supra*], Ephraim and Menasseh), we encounter only male names, with just three exceptions: Miriam and her mother Yocheved (Num. 26.59)—who do not count for this purpose anyway, being of the tribe of Levi (Num. 26.62)—Serah the daughter of Asher (Num. 26.46),[34] and the daughters of Zelophehad, whose anomalous position (better, that of Zelophehad himself) is already noted: 'Now Zelophehad the son of Hepher had no sons, but daughters: and the names of the daughters of Zelophehad were Mahlah, Noah, Hoglah, Milcah, and Tirzah' (Num. 26.63; cf. Sakenfeld 1988: 38). Thus it is clear from the narrative

---

32. Levinson (1992: 43-44) finds only one example of an explicitly acknowledged legal change in the Bible, comparable to those in the Hittite Laws, Ruth 4.7: 'Thus formerly (*lifnim*) it was done in Israel in cases of redemption or exchange: to validate any transaction, one man would take off his sandal and hand it to the other. Such was the practice in Israel.' He comments (44-45) that the custom thus said to have been modified does not derive from the revelation of a law at Sinai; it is an unwritten common law or custom, not a formal statute.

33. Cf. Watts (1999: 77 n. 61): 'The case of Zelophehad's daughters and their inheritance rights…is an example of an isolated ruling developed in close dependence on narrative.'

34. Her inclusion is strange. She did have brothers (Num. 26.44), who are mentioned. It cannot be assumed that there were no other families who had both sons and daughters, even if it can be assumed (at a pinch) that Zelophehad was the only one blessed with daughters alone.

framework that the daughters of Zelophehad are protesting in ch. 27 not against customary law, but against a specific divine command allocating the promised land to the sons of Jacob *in the male line*. The outcome of the divine consultation is that the *nachalah* (the same term as that used in Num. 26.53, commanding the allocation of the land) of Zelophehad is indeed to be transferred to his daughters—at least in part.[35] Sadly, perhaps, the narrative context of this decision was later discarded for halakhic purposes, with the result that a set of rules designed explicitly to determine distribution of landholdings in the promised land has been taken as a general law of intestate distribution.[36]

This very topic presents us also with a different type of relationship between law and narrative: one in which the law may be understood in terms not of its surrounding narrative framework but rather in the context of a quite distinct narrative preserved elsewhere. Consider the law of primogeniture in Deut. 21.15-17:

35. There appears to have been conflict over this. Num. 27.7 records the decision in two clauses: 'you shall give them possession of an inheritance among their father's brethren' (נתן תתן להם אחזת נחלה בתוך אחי אביהם) 'and cause the inheritance of their father to pass to them' (והעברת את נחלת אביהן להן). There is no need for both clauses, and in fact they are in conflict. The meaning of בתוך אחי אביהם in the first is that the daughters *share* with their uncles (a compromise decision), as is shown by the use of the same phrase in the account of the disposition of Job's estate: 'He had also seven sons and three daughters. And he called the name of the first Jemimah; and the name of the second Keziah; and the name of the third Keren-happuch. And in all the land there were no women so fair as Job's daughters; and their father gave them inheritance among their brothers' (Job 42.13-15): ויתן להם אביהם נחלה בתוך אחיהם. Nevertheless, the conflicting tradition, that the daughters of Zelophehad inherited to the exclusion of their uncles (from Zelophehad's share) is supported in the sequel, where the interested members of the family complain against the potential alienation of Zelophehad's land outside the tribe, referring to the oracular decision as: '...and my lord was commanded by the LORD to give the inheritance of Zelophehad our brother to his daughters' (Num. 36.2): לתת את נחלת צלפחד אחינו לבנתיו, and certainly this was the decision for the future. For ancient Near Eastern parallels to both Num. 27.8 and Job 42.15, see Ben-Barak (1980: 22-31), who suggests (28) that בתוך אחיהם in Job 42.15 'does not necessarily mean that their rights were equal to those of the sons' (but does not notice that the same expression is used in the decision regarding the daughters).

36. Of *de'orayta* status, so that it cannot be overriden in principle (i.e. by using words of inheritance) by will. For the problem and its avoidance by the use of words of gift, see Grunfeld (1987).

> If a man has two wives, the one loved and the other disliked, and they
> have borne him children, both the loved and the disliked, and if the first-
> born son is hers that is disliked, then on the day when he assigns his pos-
> sessions as an inheritance to his sons, he may not treat the son of the
> loved as the first-born in preference to the son of the disliked, who is the
> first-born, but he shall acknowledge the first-born, the son of the dis-
> liked, by giving him a double portion of all that he has, for he is the first
> issue of his strength; the right of the first-born is his.

The law of primogeniture is not phrased, as we might have expected, in
general terms: the first-born shall have a double portion. Rather, it is
formulated in terms of a contest between the sons of different wives,
where the oldest son happens to be the son of the wife in disfavour. On
one reading, all the law is saying is: do not discriminate against that son
for that reason. Moreover, nowhere else in the Hebrew Bible do we
hear of a 'double portion'[37]—except in the narrative of the succession
to Jacob, where the two sons of Joseph take his place, thus effectively
giving his line just such a double portion (on Gen. 48.5; see §2.2,
supra). That Joseph, the son of the favoured Rachel, is given the
birthright in preference to Reuben, the (oldest) son, who happens to be
the son of Leah (the unfavoured wife), is indeed stated explicitly in 1
Chron. 5.1:

> The sons of Reuben the first-born of Israel (for he was the first-born; but
> because he polluted his father's couch, his birthright was given to the
> sons of Joseph the son of Israel, so that he is not enrolled in the geneal-
> ogy according to the birthright...)

Carmichael has very plausibly argued that the Deuteronomic law has
the patriarchal narrative in mind (1974: 61-62; 1979: Ch.3; 1985: 142-
45); indeed, that it was probably composed as a criticism of Jacob's
behaviour.[38] It is difficult to imagine what else might have prompted the

37. More generally, there is a narrative theme of preference of the *younger* son.
Stahl (1995: 17) comments on this as the paradigmatic example of law being
undermined by narrative (referring to Abel/Cain, Isaac/Ishmael, Jacob/Esau): 'This
reversal so embodies the nomos, the normative discursive practice of biblical narrative, that one might even say it becomes a necessary condition for the protagonist
who would transform himself into a hero and achieve his divinely ordained mission.'

38. Cf. Stahl (1995: 17): '...not only can narrative undercut law, but law can
also reverse the ideological and ethical import of biblical narrative'. The story of
Reuben's 'anticipation' of his inheritance with Bilhah, referred to both in 1 Chron.
5.1 and Gen. 49.4, might well be viewed as a later reaction to this criticism.

formulation of the primogeniture law in this way. And even if it does have an independent, customary origin, the law, thus written, could hardly be read—or listened to—by anyone familiar with the patriarchal narratives without evoking such associations.

In what context might such a relationship between law and narrative have developed? Carmichael locates it in a literary setting, of courtly scribes pondering and reacting to the tradition (1992: 15-21). His argument is based in part on what he sees as the systematic character of this activity. Increasingly, he has extended his argument from an aid to the understanding of some Deuteronomic laws to a general theory of much of pentateuchal law.[39] He places great reliance upon the arrangement of the laws as reiterating the narrative sequence of themes.

This is not the place to enter into the merits of particular examples.[40] Suffice it here to contest the principle and context. Watts argues that 'the narrative setting seems decisive for the interpretation of law only when the laws are relatively isolated from each other'.[41] He is referring to the relationship between laws embedded in a narrative framework. I would argue that the same applies to the form of relationship that Carmichael has identified. To me, it makes far more sense in a domestic setting of oral instruction,[42] in which the connection can be pointed out as the story is told. Wisdom, in my view, begins at the popular, oral level: it is not to be regarded as a purely literary (foreign-inspired) importation, notwithstanding the influence which such models may have had when the transition was made from orality to literacy. But even then, it would be difficult to find the kind of law-narrative parallels, linked systematically in their arrangement (or otherwise), that Carmichael claims. The rewriting of Samuel–Kings by the Chronicler is one thing; this is quite another. For Carmichael, the arrangement of a whole list of laws takes on meaning by reference to a narrative

39. Extending to the Decalogue and the *Mishpatim* (Carmichael 1992). Dare I ask now (see Carmichael 1992: ix) whether he contemplates the systematic application of the theory to the priestly laws?

40. See the review of Levinson (1990: 227-37) and Carmichael's reply (1994: 240-45).

41. Watts (1999: 77), following Alt (1989: 81-82) (though Alt there gives 'the Deuteronomic law' as an example of a 'smaller collection').

42. In Jackson (2000b) I argue that individual proverbs, too, may allude positively or negatively to the narrative tradition. See further, §10.3, *infra*, for the example of talio.

sequence in a different document, leaving a minimum of clues by which it can be decoded. A truly sophisticated parlour game. I could just about imagine, in an age of genteel leisure, such a game in a particular kind of Senior Common Room. I cannot imagine it in Whitehall: our own civil servants might doubtless wish they had the time for such pursuits!

Laws do not have a single origin or relationship to narrative. In some cases, it may indeed have been a narrative that prompted the evaluation (positive or negative) expressed in a law. In others, the law may originate in domestic instruction informed by purely social (rather than cultural) knowledge.[43]

43. E.g. the judicial bribery theme (Exod. 23.8; Deut. 16.19; cf. Prov. 17.23; see further Jackson 2000b). Yet even here there are narrative sources that could be connected, but are not necessarily even evoked. Schiffman (1998: 156-58) refers to the practice of the sons of Samuel reported in 1 Sam. 8.1-3, as well as Isa. 1.23; 5.23; 33.15; Ezek. 22.12; Mic. 3.11; 7.3; cf. Pss. 15.5; 26.9-10. On the other hand, he notes, Prov. 17.8 and 21.14 simply indicate that bribes are given with the expectation of their influencing ruling parties.

Chapter 9

'COVENANT RENEWAL' AND NARRATIVE STRUCTURE

9.1 *Introduction*

It is widely acknowledged today that the approach to Old Testament law by Christian theologians has often reflected a Christian anti-nomianism based on opposition to Jewish 'legalism', the latter itself reflecting a Christian opposition between law and grace.[1] Less common is the recognition that readings of the Hebrew Bible that stress covenant renewal may equally stem from the same interfaith dispute.[2]

I believe that much of the talk of covenant renewal in the Old Testament, and all of the talk about a regular covenant renewal ceremony,[3] is the product of a largely (but not exclusively [Weinfeld 1973: 71-72]) Christian reading.[4] As a concept, it hangs on one text, Jer. 31.31-34,

---

1.   Although it is not so frequently appreciated that the term 'legalism' itself was coined in the context of internal Christian disputes over justification by works (see Jackson 1979a: 4-6).

2.   On the Wellhausian view of covenant, and later reactions to it, see Levenson (1980: 17-21).

3.   Cf. Booij (1984: 2 and literature cited n. 3); Nicholson (1986: 54-69); and the comments of Watts (1999: 34). The classical account of Alt (1989: 126-32) may be criticized on methodological grounds (see §2.3.1 n. 22, *supra*).

4.   Alt's own characterization of the apodictic law (which played a central role in his theory of the covenant renewal ceremony) itself has considerable overtones of Christian antinomianism: e.g. on Exod. 21.12: 'The outlook of the whole Old Testament leaves us in no doubt of the answer: it is Yahweh who demands a stern retribution for every drop of blood that is spilt' (1989: 110); the 'unmitigated application of the *lex talionis*...never takes into account...the subjective guilt of the offender—it only looks at the outward consequences of the deed and exacts accordingly a purely external retribution' (106); '...the apodeictic law of Israel displays an unrestrained power of aggression which seeks to subject every aspect of life without exception to the unconditional domination of the will of Yahweh, and can therefore recognize no secular or neutral region' (132); cf. van Houten (1991: 11), observing

which projects a future 'new covenant', *berit chadashah*.[5] But there is no phrase found in the Bible for 'to renew a covenant', *lachadesh berit*; the verbal form, which one might expect in the historical and legal sources, simply does not exist.[6] Indeed, in several passages commonly interpreted as reflecting covenant renewal, even the term *berit* is not found. The error results from not attending sufficiently to the narrative line of the biblical texts, and to the contexts in which *berit* is used.

Let me begin with a point of semantics. Great subtlety attaches to the semantic field of old versus new, and the morphology of terms within it.[7] What is meant by talk of covenant 'renewal'? Our term 'renewal', out of context, is ambiguous. If it is a matter of a periodic ceremony, involving a public reading—the mythical 'covenant renewal ceremony'—then clearly we are talking of confirmation (often to ensure the personal commitment of the next generation or cohort: a matter of

that the study of Old Testament law in the tradition of de Wette, Wellhausen, Alt and Noth, though still the starting point for contemporary discussion, has 'also bequeathed to us a tradition which denigrates a law-centered religion'.

5.   Levinson (1992: 51), has rightly pointed to the connection with the future (he contrasts Ezek. 18 and Deut. 7.9-10; see §8.1 n. 11, *supra*) rejection of trans-generational punishment in vv. 29-31. That is the new element in the covenant (for the earlier doctrine, see §6.3, *supra*). A different view is taken by Greenberg (1995: 18-19): 'The new covenant will not be different in content, but it will be inscribed on the hearts and on the minds of the future Israel. This is a counsel of despair. There is no hope that humans in their present nature can observe the Torah. Salvation will come only when God intervenes and makes observing the Torah natural, so that it will no longer be necessary to learn it.' He cites in support (at 19-20) Ezek. 36.24-27. My preference for Levinson's view on Jer. 31 does not, of course, entail rejection of Greenberg's reading of Ezek. 36.

6.   We do find *lehakim berit*, *Deut*. 8.18: 'You shall remember the LORD your God, for it is he who gives you power to get wealth; that he may confirm his covenant which he swore to your fathers, as at this day' (RSV). But even 'confirm' may go beyond what is required here. It is a matter of fulfilment to a later generation of obligations under the *berit* undertaken to their forefathers. It is an issue of incorporation into the covenant, rather than confirmation of the status of the covenant itself (see text, *infra*).

7.   Some years ago I reviewed the English edition of the late Ze'ev Falk's book on Second Commonwealth Halakhah. I was puzzled that he kept on referring to certain laws as 'novelties'. I turned up the original Hebrew; in fact, he had used the term *chiddushim*. I concluded that he had not been well served by his translator. Laws require the due seriousness and permanency of innovation, not the short-term entertainment value of novelties. (Or so I thought at the time.)

incorporation[8]). The very *regularity* of the ceremony implies that it has not been ordained because there is special reason to doubt commitment, much less to substitute something new for something old. Why, then, talk of 'renewal'? If there is anything new, it is not the covenant but those committing themselves to it. Elsewhere, we do find ceremonies where there was reason to doubt the strength of the previous commitment (e.g. Jer. 34, regarding release from slavery [§6.2, *supra*]). The content of the covenant is not being altered; rather those subject to it are becoming penitents, *ba'ale teshuvah*. Parties to a covenant who recognize that they are already bound by it reaffirm their commitment to it. There is a third context, where the content of a covenant is indeed being revised (as in Jer. 31.31) or supplemented by reference to a new text, and where this explains the need for a new act of affirmation. We have, then, three essentially different situations, both analytically and theologically, which we might call confirmation/incorporation, recommitment and revision. It is highly significant that a single term, renewal, has become conventional in respect of all of them.

In §§9.2–9.4, I review in outline the biblical accounts of covenant from patriarchal times up to Joshua, in the light of the Greimassian conception of narrative,[9] based on a sequence of the setting of goals ('Contract'), acting in furtherance of those goals ('Performance') and evaluation of their purported accomplishment ('Recognition')[10]—and

8.   See, e.g. n. 6, *supra*. This is a recurrent theme of the narratives (see §§9.2–9.4, *infra*).

9.   §1.1, *supra*, though not, compatibly with the theory itself, in a reductionist manner: there is no need to argue that every aspect of the narrative reflects the *structures élémentaires de la signification*. Rather, the object here is to see what contribution such structures may make to our understanding of the final literary compilation, and particularly the relations between the various narrative segments. The result should be regarded as no more than an hypothesis, that calls for evaluation in the light of a full scholarly analysis of each individual segment, something beyond the scope of the present essay. In what follows, the terms Subject, Performance and Recognition etc. are capitalized where the intention is to allude to their use in Greimassian theory.

10.   The conceptual structure adopted by Stahl (1995: 18-26) may be contrasted. She sees at the heart of the narratives concerning biblical law a Bakhtinian dialogic tension—between the optimistic fulfilment of divine will and the inevitable failure/rebellion against it (cf. Greenberg [1995: 18-19], observing that in contrast to the ideal picture of the working of the covenant, the 'real' history of Israel, as reflected in the books of Samuel and Kings and the Pre-exilic prophets, 'is the story of the failure of the people to realize this ideal'). The act of communication of law

the understanding it suggests of the phenomenon of narrative reiteration. In particular, I suggest that thematic reiteration in the narratives
concerning communication of law and covenant functions in narrative
terms as a form of Recognition of previous action.[11] Thematic reiteration, I argue, is a most significant form of Recognition found in the
Bible. Though the traditions of the patriarchal covenant and that at
Sinai appear quite different, there are parallels between the stories of

---

is not complete, in her view, 'until the listeners fulfill the instructions, injunctions,
etc. that constitute those laws' (at 21). I do not think this necessarily follows from
the statement she quotes from Todorov: 'The utterance is not the business of the
speaker alone, but the result of his or her interaction with a listener, whose reactions
he or she integrates in advance'. The meaning of an act of communication may
indeed take account of the sender's anticipation of the receiver's reaction, but that
anticipated reaction is not the same as the actual, subsequent reaction (which may
turn out to be quite different). In the Greimassian account, the act of communication and the response of the audience can be analysed separately (the sender and
receiver, respectively, as Subjects of their own narrative syntagms, with corresponding changes in the actantial position of the other party). In short, there is an
independent narrative analysis of the act of communication (referred to in §1.2 as
the 'narrativisation of pragmatics'). Applied to the position of Moses, on Stahl's
account he has to emerge (I think he does emerge) as a tragi-hero, one of the least
successful leaders depicted in the Bible. But is that the image that the biblical texts
endorse? Deut. 34.10-11 provides the following explicit Recognition of Moses
(*pace* Watts 1999: 113): 'And there has not arisen a prophet since in Israel like
Moses, whom the LORD knew face to face, none like him for all the signs and the
wonders which the LORD sent him to do in the land of Egypt, to Pharaoh and to all
his servants and to all his land.' The implication would appear to be that the Contract of Moses was not to ensure that his audience 'fulfill the instructions, injunctions, etc. that constitute those laws'; rather, it was to be an instrument of communication between God and humanity, including the communication of the authority
of God, through *otot umofsim* (a requirement of prophetic status, cf. Deut. 13.2,
applicable even to the 'false prophet'), to the Egyptians. Stahl's position is not, in
fact, supported by Searle's concept of a constitutive rule (invoked at 21 n. 18):
indeed, the speech act tradition distinguishes between the performative force of an
utterance (the meaning of an act of communication, which does indeed depend
upon the social understanding of what it purports to do) and its perlocutionary
effects (in the minds and behaviours of its audience, once it—the speech act—has
been performed). A promise is still a promise even if it is not fulfilled. Otherwise,
the notion of a broken promise would be a contradiction in terms.

11. That does not detract from the recurrent theme of incorporation in the
covenant, which is located at the 'thematic' and 'surface' levels of the narrative,
and forms part of the instantiation of the 'structural' level.

the relationship with God of Abraham on the one hand, Moses on the other. Recognition through reiteration, it may be argued, is also the significance of the book of Deuteronomy within the narrative framework of the Pentateuch. The law was given in Exodus to Numbers. Now Moses starts a speech of his own; he tells us, once again, that it was given. Reiteration of themes can also proceed on a personal level. Moses commissions Joshua to be his successor. He gives him certain immediate commands, to be performed on entry to the promised land. Joshua performs those commands. Later in the book, in the last two chapters, we have a further set of connections between Moses and Joshua, in the form of reiteration for Joshua of the various elements that made up the valedictory scene of Moses himself. This has important implications for the status of both Joshua and Moses (and those who, in the minds of the author and audience) may be modelled upon them.

Such an approach, of course, involves a literary reading of the final text, and in particular the macro-narrative it tells; its compositional history is a quite different matter. There is much in the accounts of the monarchy that, if reliable, might be taken to have provided historical models for the covenants in the ancestral history. My purpose here[12] is not to argue for (or against) such theories of sources; suffice it to indicate that the typology of confirmation/incorporation, recommitment and revision, used here to distinguish different functions of *berit,* is also found there. Thus, the *berit* in favour of the succession of Joash (2 Kgs 11.4)[13] may be taken as a model of confirmation/incorporation, comparable, inter alia, to those in favour of Isaac (Gen. 17.19-20) and those about to enter the land in Deuteronomy 29; those under Asa (2 Chron. 15.13, in the context of a victory celebration[14]), and Hezekiah (2 Chron. 29)[15] may be taken as a model of recommitment, comparable to

12. See §6.2, *supra,* for arguments regarding the role (and its transformation) of God as guarantor of covenants (including royal covenants), and the role of the covenant doctrine in the emergence of an understanding of the continuity of law.

13. On the covenants in the coronation of Joash, see *supra,* §6.2, and n. 49, for Widengren's attempt to connect these traditions with covenant renewal.

14. Cf. Josh. 24. Ancient Near Eastern treaties frequently followed military confrontations.

15. The story commences with Hezekiah's speech to the priests and the Levites, recognising the previous neglect of the temple, and pledging himself to its restoration. Using the familiar pattern of historical prologue followed by commitment, he announces that 'I intend that we should pledge ourselves to the LORD God of Israel' (עתה עם לבבי לכרות ברית...), 2 Chron. 29.10). But that is the last we hear of this

that in Exodus 34; that under Josiah[16] may be taken as a model of revision, comparable to the general tenor of Moses' activity in Deuteronomy[17]—though there is also here a strong element of recommitment.[18] There is also an example of covenant as a loyalty pledge,[19] comparable both to the Abrahamic covenant and that in Exod. 19.5.

9.2 *The Patriarchal Covenants*

The patriarchal covenant is recounted in Genesis 15. God appears to the childless Abram in a vision. Abram complains that he has no children of his own, and that Eliezer of Damascus, 'a slave born in my house' will be his heir.[20] In response God points to the stars as a visible sign[21] that Abram's children will be numerous as the stars (Gen. 15.3-4). Abram recognizes the promise: 'Abram put his faith in the LORD' (והאמן ביהוה, Gen. 15.6). Then God reveals himself as the one who had directed Abram from Ur, and further promises that the land will be an inheritance for his children. Abram asks: 'How can I be sure that I shall occupy it?' (Gen. 15.8). It is in response to that request for reassurance—an example early in the narrative of the theme of seeking

particular covenant. The ceremonies in the temple are not described as such; they represent no more than restoration of the cult, without any formal act of commitment. Of course, it can be argued that the Chronicler would have us take it for granted that Hezekiah actually fulfilled his stated intention to enter into a covenant. But biblical narrative does not shy away from recording the implementation of a promised action, not least when we are concerned with a significant performative act. We can certainly say that Hezekiah accomplished a huge feat of religious restoration, the record of which is preserved for us in great detail by the Chronicler. As for any covenant that may have been involved, we, like the Chronicler, can only decline to speak.

16. 2 Kgs 23.2-3; cf. the terminology of Exod. 24.7.

17. E.g. on transgenerational punishment, as argued by Levinson: see §8.1 n. 11; more generally, Moses' activity as explaining and supplementing the covenant at Horeb, §9.4, *infra*.

18. Moreover, the burning of the Asherah and the scattering of its dust (2 Kgs. 23.6) may be compared to Moses' actions in Exod. 32.20.

19. 2 Kgs 11.17; 2 Chron. 23.16 (stated in v. 18, but not in 2 Kgs, to be *kakatuv betorat mosheh*).

20. Gen. 15.2-3. Why such a slave should have the designation 'of Damascus' is not clear (cf. Skinner 1930: 279).

21. Cf. Gen. 1.14, where the *me'orot* are described as having the function, *inter alia*, of serving as *otot*.

evidence, preferably supernatural, in support of theological claims—
that what Jewish tradition has wrongly called the *berit beyn habesarim*
is recounted (Gen. 15.9-11, 17). As presented by the text, the animals
that are halved are not presented as part of a *berit* ceremony; they are
produced on God's command directly in response to Abram's request
for reassurance, before any further promises and well before any mention of *berit*.[22] They are the instrument of the proof that Abram is seeking. God effects a miracle, what elsewhere is described as an *ot*, a
'sign', by miraculously causing 'a smoking fire pot and a flaming torch'
to pass between the pieces. (We are not told whether the animals are
consumed.) However, between the laying out of the pieces and the
appearance of the divine fire, God speaks again to Abram, in a dream:

> Know of a surety that your descendants will be sojourners in a land that
> is not theirs, and will be slaves there, and they will be oppressed for four
> hundred years; but I will bring judgment on the nation which they serve,
> and afterward they shall come out with great possessions. As for your-
> self, you shall go to your fathers in peace; you shall be buried in a good
> old age. And they shall come back here in the fourth generation; for the
> iniquity of the Amorites is not yet complete (Gen. 15.13-16).

Abram's need for reassurance, in respect of God's (seemingly more
immediate) promise of the land in v. 7, is answered, but he pays a price
for his doubt: his descendants will not inherit until the 'fourth generation' and in the meantime will suffer the Egyptian servitude.[23] Only
thereafter do we hear of a *berit*. But it is introduced explicitly as referring to the promise that follows, not to the sacrifice (if that it be) that
preceded:

> That very day the LORD made a covenant with Abram, saying: 'To your
> descendants I give this land, from the river of Egypt to the great river,
> the river Euphrates, the land of the Kenites, the Kenizzites, the
> Kadmonites, the Hittites, the Perizzites, the Rephaim, the Amorites, the
> Canaanites, the Girgashites and the Jebusites' (Gen. 15.18-21).

This is so explicit as an *hereditary* blessing that one finds it difficult to

---

22. They may be understood as a sacrifice: God commands Abram to 'bring'
them, and it is Abram who, without further instruction, kills them by cutting them
in two (except the birds), and lays them out for God.

23. The reference to the 'fourth generation' supports the view that this is a
(transgenerational) punishment for Abram's doubt. See Daube (1947: Ch. 4) on the
relationship of 'ruler punishment' to collective responsibility. And see 179 on the
place of hereditary blessing in this complex.

understand interpretations of God's relations with Isaac and Jacob as covenant renewals. Whereas, later in the narrative, the issue of hereditary *obligations* undertaken under a covenant arises, here we are dealing with an hereditary benefit. Yet even here, a problem of continuity arises (cf. Ch. 6, *supra*). Modern English lawyers might understand this in terms of the doctrine of 'privity of contract', under which 'third party' beneficiaries cannot enforce a benefit promised to them in a contract to which they are not parties. Here, the problem may reside with the underlying model of the royal grant (see Weinfeld 1970: 184-203; 1995: 242), exemplifying the original ad hoc character of royal 'legislation'. Hence, the need to reaffirm the covenant to successive generations of beneficiaries.[24] Such 'confirmation' is hardly 'renewal' in a theological sense.

The next covenant (Gen. 17) is associated with Abram's (and Sarai's) name changes. Again, the narrative context is a threat to Abram's (authorized) successors: we have just been told of the birth of Ishmael. On this occasion, Abram voices no complaint or doubt: Ishmael is not the obvious threat to his posterity that 'Eliezer of Damascus' was. But there is a doubt, in the minds at least of the story's audience, and it is this which the narrator addresses. God offers renewed confirmation: despite all appearances, the original promise (in effect, to them) will be fulfilled. So the new promise to Abram takes account of the fact that his descendants are not confined to the (as yet, unconceived) Israelites. At first, the confirmation is in general terms:

> When Abram was ninety-nine years old the LORD appeared to Abram, and said to him, 'I am God Almighty; walk before me, and be blameless. And I will make my covenant between me and you, and will multiply you exceedingly' (Gen. 17.1-2).

At that, we are told, 'Abram fell on his face' (Gen. 17.3). Is this a gesture of respect? Then it should have been performed as soon as God appeared, and before he began to speak. If it is a reaction to the speech, what kind of reaction? Gratitude? Silent, embarrassed scepticism? When God speaks again, it is as if in reply to the obvious objection: I have one son, and he is Ishmael:

> Behold, my covenant is with you, and you shall be the father of a multitude of nations. No longer shall your name be Abram, but your name

---

24. Clauses reaffirming previous treaties are found in the treaty texts of the ancient Near East, e.g., the treaty between Ramses II and Hattusilis, in both Egyptian and Hittite versions (*ANET*: 200, 202).

shall be Abraham; for I have made you the father of a multitude of nations. I will make you exceedingly fruitful; and I will make nations of you, and kings shall come forth from you. And I will establish my covenant between me and you and your descendants after you throughout their generations for an everlasting covenant, to be God to you and to your descendants after you. And I will give to you, and to your descendants after you, the land of your sojournings, all the land of Canaan, for an everlasting possession; and I will be their God.

Taken literally, the answer is only partially satisfactory: Abraham will be the father not of just one nation but several; God's covenant will thus be not with Ishmael (alone) but with (all) his descendants—both to be their God (and thus protector) and to give them the land of Canaan. The audience, however, will not understand the covenant literally: the intended beneficiaries of the covenant will come from the line of Isaac, to the exclusion of Ishmael. But now, for the first time in the narrative,[25] the promise/blessing is accompanied by a reciprocal obligation, which in turn is hereditary:

As for you, you shall keep my covenant, you and your descendants after you throughout their generations (*ledorotam*). This is my covenant, which you shall keep, between me and you and your descendants after you: Every male among you shall be circumcised. You shall be circumcised in the flesh of your foreskins, and it shall be a sign of the covenant (*le'ot berit*) between me and you. He that is eight days old among you shall be circumcised; every male throughout your generations, whether born in your house (*yelid bayit*), or bought with your money from any foreigner who is not of your offspring, both he that is born in your house and he that is bought with your money, shall be circumcised. So shall my covenant be in your flesh an everlasting covenant (*berit olam*). Any uncircumcised male who is not circumcised in the flesh of his foreskin shall be cut off from his people; he has broken my covenant (Gen. 17.9-14).

This first covenantal obligation is hardly arbitrarily chosen. The very first covenantal promise had also been accompanied by visible proof, the rainbow, described as *ot haberit* (Gen. 9.12). Similarly, a visible sign is to distinguish those descendants of Abraham who are the hereditary beneficiaries of the promises from those who are not.[26] That estab-

---

25. Cf. the observation of Stahl (1995: 47), on the unilaterality of the Noahide covenant (Gen. 9.8-11).

26. Cf. Levenson (1980: 23-24), comparing also the sabbath in Exod. 31.12-17 (and assigning all three to P). He rightly observes that 'circumcision and the Sab-

lished, God promises that Sarah will conceive (Gen. 17.16). Abraham falls on his face again,[27] and this time we are told explicitly that it is in scepticism, which he expresses first to himself, then to God:

> Then Abraham fell on his face and laughed, and said to himself, 'Shall a child be born to a man who is a hundred years old? Shall Sarah, who is ninety years old, bear a child?' And Abraham said to God, 'O that Ishmael might live in thy sight!' (Gen. 17.17-18)

Abraham is (again?) willing to settle for succession by Ishmael. The audience, and its narrator, is not. God's final response maintains the inclusiveness implicit in the preceding speech (where the covenant of circumcision is not restricted to these *yelid bayit*), but makes the required distinction between the lines of Ishmael and Isaac:

> No, but Sarah your wife shall bear you a son, and you shall call his name Isaac. I will establish my covenant with him as an everlasting covenant (*livrit olam*) for his descendants after him. As for Ishmael, I have heard you; behold, I will bless him and make him fruitful and multiply him exceedingly; he shall be the father of twelve princes, and I will make him a great nation. But I will establish my covenant with Isaac, whom Sarah shall bear to you at this season next year.

Here, the older son, Ishmael, still gets the blessing, but it is the younger, Isaac, who gets the *berit* (impliedly, of the land). The two concepts are used here in opposition.

The story of the *akedah,* the countermanded instruction to Abraham to sacrifice Isaac, already exhibits the phenomenon of thematic reiteration which is a feature not only of relationships between the various patriarchal narratives, and between those of Moses and Joshua (described below) but also in some respects between the two sets of narratives.[28] It commences by characterizing what is to follow: 'After

---

bath in P are indeed covenantal obligations, although it is important not to confuse them with stipulations. The rainbow, circumcision, and the Sabbath testify to the existence of a covenantal relationship. They are clearly demarcated from the laws or norms the body of the Covenant might impose.'

27. Is this simply a further turn in the same conversation between the same parties (as in the interchange over Sodom and Gemorrah), with Abraham still not satisfied that the promise can be fulfilled in respect of (what the audience knows to be) its true target? Very likely. But there may also be a hint that this is a new persona, Abraham not Abram, who is reiterating the behaviour of his predecessor.

28. E.g. the meeting at the well, leading to the marriages of Isaac (Gen. 24.15), Jacob (Gen. 29.9-11), and Moses (Exod. 2.15-16).

these things God tested Abraham' (Gen. 22.1). Isaac is threatened with
being sacrificed as a burnt offering (Gen. 22.2), echoing the animals
that Abram did *not* set to the flame in Gen. 15. Abraham is again
depicted as subject to conflicting loyalties: he utters, successively, *hineni*,
in response to God's initial summons (Gen. 22.1), Isaac's expression of
anxiety (Gen. 22.7), and the angel's interruption of the sacrifice (Gen.
22.11). After Abraham sacrifices the ram in substitution for Isaac (Gen.
22.13), the angel speaks again:

> And the angel of the LORD called to Abraham a second time from
> heaven, and said, 'By myself I have sworn, says the LORD, because you
> have done this, and have not withheld your son, your only son, I will
> indeed bless you, and I will multiply your descendants as the stars of
> heaven and as the sand which is on the seashore. And your descendants
> shall possess the gate of their enemies, and by your descendants shall all
> the nations of the earth bless themselves, because you have obeyed my
> voice' (Gen. 22.15-18).

The angel reports that God has sworn an oath in response to Abraham's
behaviour. It is not described as a *berit*, and its content is not new. It
reiterates Gen. 15.3-4 (above), the promise that (the then) Abram's
posterity would be as numerous as the stars. What is the point of it?
One might see it as the equivalent of God's promise after the flood: I
will never *again* destroy mankind. Yet in the *akedah*, the whole story
was presented *ab initio* as a test: there was never any intention to kill
Isaac. Abraham's posterity was never seriously in question. If we ask,
then, *why* Abraham was tested, the answer would appear to reside in the
talionic principle, found also elsewhere in the patriarchal narratives
(Jacob, the deceiver, deceived): here, Abraham, the tester of God (Gen.
15), is in turn tested. We might conclude that the angel's second speech
is an appropriate conclusion to the narrative, in that it reiterates, and
thus recognizes the continuing validity of, the initial promise to Abram.
But there is in fact one new element in the situation: the presence of
Isaac. Now, for the first time, the promise is repeated, confirmed to the
second generation.

After the death of Abraham, God appears to Isaac during a time of
famine, and tells him to remain in Gerar and not go to Egypt, adding:

> I will be with you, and will bless you; for to you and to your descendants
> I will give all these lands, and I will fulfil the oath which I swore to
> Abraham your father. I will multiply your descendants as the stars of
> heaven, and will give to your descendants all these lands; and by your
> descendants all the nations of the earth shall bless themselves; because

> Abraham obeyed my voice and kept my charge, my commandments, my
> statutes, and my laws (Gen. 26.3-5).

We have an explicit reference back to the promise to Abraham, and a
promise that reiterates its content (as an hereditary blessing). The new
promise, reiterating the old, constitutes Recognition of it. If there was
any doubt about the status of Isaac, at the time of the *akedah*, to be the
next direct recipient of the hereditary blessing, it is resolved here. It is
repeated in similar terms in Gen. 26.24, where God appears to Isaac at
night and says: 'I am the God of Abraham your father; fear not, for I am
with you and will bless you and multiply your descendants for my servant Abraham's sake'.

Just as there is a repetition of the blessing to Isaac, as if the first (Gen.
22.15-18) is problematic (being communicated in Abraham's lifetime,
when Isaac is still a dependent), so too with Jacob. Here, indeed, there
is a double problem—not only whether there has to be an independent
communication of the blessing by God to Jacob, but also whether, if the
blessing is capable of *human* transmission, Jacob can succeed to it by
unworthy means? To this latter question, the answer is clearly negative.
Neither the 'birthright' (*bekhorah*) that he induces the exhausted Esau
to buy by fraud[29] (Gen. 25.29-34), nor the 'blessing' that he later
obtains by impersonation (Gen. 27), mentions the promise of the land.
It is only thereafter, with Jacob about to leave for Laban's household in
order to escape Esau's wrath, that Isaac—no longer deceived as to his
identity—communicates the divine hereditary blessing:

> God Almighty bless you and make you fruitful and multiply you, that
> you may become a company of peoples. May he give the blessing of
> Abraham to you and to your descendants with you, that you may take
> possession of the land of your sojournings which God gave to Abraham
> (Gen. 28.3-4).

But even this is not enough. The first night after Jacob leaves for Haran,
he apparently has a dream in which he sees God at the top of a ladder to
heaven (Gen. 28.10-13). God here communicates the blessing directly
to Jacob:

---

29. Following Daube (1947: 194-200), who argues that Esau thought he was
getting a blood-broth, while the soup was actually lentils. But even without this
interpretation, Jacob takes advantage of Esau's state of (at least) exhaustion to
impose a deal which otherwise (despite the narrator's attempt to avoid this conclusion: 'Thus Esau despised his birthright', Gen. 25.34) he may be expected to have
declined.

And behold, the LORD stood above it and said, 'I am the LORD, the God
of Abraham your father and the God of Isaac; the land on which you lie
I will give to you and to your descendants; and your descendants shall
be like the dust of the earth, and you shall spread abroad to the west and
to the east and to the north and to the south; and by you and your descendants shall all the families of the earth bless themselves...' (Gen. 28.13-
14).

The stars of the heaven may have become the dust of the earth, but the
message is explicitly one of Recognition of the earlier promise and
incorporation of Jacob and his descendants in it. But why was it necessary, when Isaac had already communicated that blessing? What the
two accounts have in common is an assumption that the hereditary
blessing does not descend *automatically*; wherein they differ is the
means by which the next generation is to be incorporated in it—
whether by a (speech) act of succession or by reiteration of the promise
by God himself. But some form of explicit incorporation, at this stage,
there has to be. In the next generation, the children of Jacob (including
Ephraim and Menasseh) again receive blessings from their father on his
death bed, and are explicitly identified with 'the twelve tribes of Israel',
who by now (the time of the narrator and his audience) have indeed
taken possession of the land.

In short, the hereditary blessing is sometimes, but far from always,
described as a *berit;* where it is so described, it is in response to a threat
or doubt as to succession (Gen. 15, 17); it is usually unilateral, the one
exception being the (self-interested) acceptance of a sign of being its
beneficiary (circumcision); the function of its repetition is Recognition
of its continuing validity—particularly with reference to succeeding
generations of beneficiaries who are to be incorporated within it.

9.3 *Covenant Renewal in Exodus*

The theme of the patriarchal promise, now consistently presented in
terms of an hereditary covenant, links the narratives in Genesis and
Exodus. It becomes relevant immediately on the change of king:

In the course of those many days the king of Egypt died. And the people
of Israel groaned under their bondage, and cried out for help, and their
cry under bondage came up to God. And God heard their groaning, and
God remembered his covenant with Abraham, with Isaac, and with
Jacob. And God saw the people of Israel, and God knew their condition
(Exod. 2.23-25).

If we take the stories from Abram as a macro-narrative of the relations between God and the people, what we have observed thus far is the institution of a 'Contract' (in the Greimassian sense) in which God becomes the Subject of an hereditary obligation. At this point, an Opponent is presented, who threatens to impede Performance. The attitude of the new pharoah is presented not simply as an incident in the changing fortunes of the Israelites, but as directly relevant to the Contract God has undertaken.

In speaking to Moses from the burning bush,[30] God recognizes this, without prompting:

> I am the God of your father, the God of Abraham, the God of Isaac, and the God of Jacob... I have seen the affliction of my people who are in Egypt, and have heard their cry because of their taskmasters; I know their sufferings, and I have come down to deliver them out of the hand of the Egyptians, and to bring them up out of that land to a good and broad land, a land flowing with milk and honey (Exod. 3.6, 7-8).

Moses is commissioned to effect the delivery, but he doubts his capacity (Exod. 3.10), to which God responds (as to the doubts of Abram in Gen. 17) with a visible sign.[31] God stresses, moreover, that he should be identified to the Israelites not only by the 'name' vouchsafed to Moses (Exod. 3.14) but also as the God of the patriarchs, thus the one who made the hereditary promise to them (Exod. 3.13, 15, 16). Indeed, he is to report the words of God thus:

> I have observed you and what has been done to you in Egypt; and I promise that I will bring you up out of the affliction of Egypt, to the land of the Canaanites, the Hittites, the Amorites, the Perizzites, the Hivites, and the Jebusites, a land flowing with milk and honey (Exod. 3.16-17).

---

30. Burning but not consumed. The relationship with the story of the *akedah* (Gen. 22: §7.2 *supra*) deserves exploration. Note that Moses responds to the initial summons in the same language as Abraham: *hineni* (Exod. 3.4; cf. Gen. 22.1). With God's manifestation in fire, cf. also Exod. 19.18.

31. Exod. 3.12, 'and this shall be the sign for you, that I have sent you': by implication, the reference is to the burning bush itself. The theme of the visible manifestation of authority continues in Exod. 4.1-9. Moses may have had his own *ot* (the burning bush), but the suffering Israelites will also require one (or more). Even if they continue to believe in the hereditary promise, how will they know that Moses speaks in the name of the God who gave that promise? Moses is provided with three visible *otot* in order to convince them. The same theme is repeated, of course, in his interactions with Pharoah.

Again, we have reconfirmation of the promise to a new generation. God anticipates the (self-imposed) difficulties ahead, but nevertheless promises ultimate success:

> I know that the king of Egypt will not let you go unless compelled by a mighty hand. So I will stretch out my hand and smite Egypt with all the wonders which I will do in it; after that he will let you go (Exod. 3.19-20).

But Moses soon has cause to doubt the promise. At the darkest hour of the Israelite sojourn in Egypt, when, in response to the first approach of Moses and Aaron, Pharoah withdraws the provision of straw for the making of bricks, the Israelite foremen appeal unsuccessfully to Pharoah, and then complain to Moses, who in turn complains to God:

> They met Moses and Aaron, who were waiting for them, as they came forth from Pharaoh; and they said to them, 'The LORD look upon you and judge, because you have made us offensive in the sight of Pharaoh and his servants, and have put a sword in their hand to kill us.' Then Moses turned again to the LORD and said, 'O LORD, why hast thou done evil to this people? Why didst thou ever send me? For since I came to Pharaoh to speak in thy name, he has done evil to this people, and thou hast not delivered thy people at all' (Exod. 5.20-22).

Moses, like Abraham before him, voices (reasonable) doubt that God is going to perform his Contract. Moses is referring here not to the patriarchal promise, but to the promise made to him personally at the burning bush. In response, however, God reconfirms, first to Moses personally and then, through him, to the people, not only the promise to Moses to deliver the people but also the patriarchal promise, here described as made under oath:

> I am the LORD. I appeared to Abraham, to Isaac, and to Jacob, as God Almighty, but by my name the LORD I did not make myself known to them. I also established my covenant with them, to give them the land of Canaan, the land in which they dwelt as sojourners. Moreover I have heard the groaning of the people of Israel whom the Egyptians hold in bondage and I have remembered my covenant. Say therefore to the people of Israel, 'I am the LORD, and I will bring you out from under the burdens of the Egyptians, and I will deliver you from their bondage, and I will redeem you with an outstretched arm and with great acts of judgment, and I will take you for my people, and I will be your God; and you shall know that I am the LORD your God, who has brought you out from under the burdens of the Egyptians. And I will bring you into the land which I swore to give to Abraham, to Isaac, and to Jacob; I will give it to you for a possession. I am the LORD' (Exod. 6.2-8).

Once again, confirmation by God is required in the light of the new, severe threat to Performance of the Contract. But the reassurance was not sufficient: 'Moses spoke thus to the people of Israel; but they did not listen to Moses, because of their broken spirit and their cruel bondage' (Exod. 6.2-9). God would have to do more.

Though the narrative in Exodus frequently (but again, not universally) presents the relationship between God and Israel in covenantal terms, the focus is on redemption from slavery as a prelude to inheritance of the land. There is no hint in these sources that reciprocal, 'legal' obligations will be imposed on Israel.[32] That changes when we reach the Sinaitic pericope,[33] but even there the picture is mixed.

Immediately on arrival at Sinai (Exod. 19.1), Moses goes up to God,[34] who tells him to convey to the Israelites the following very general, conditional covenant, backed up by a historical prologue designed to show the power of the proposer and thus the desirability of acceding to his offer:

> You have seen what I did to the Egyptians, and how I bore you on eagles' wings and brought you to myself. Now therefore, if you will obey my voice and keep my covenant, you shall be my own possession among all peoples; for all the earth is mine, and you shall be to me a kingdom of priests and a holy nation (Exod. 19.4-6).

The ('priestly'[35]) covenant here is reciprocal, though the content of the obligations of the people is not stated: in its narrative context (provided 'my covenant' is understood as a reference to the existing one, not the covenant to be entered into *after* the revelation of the law), it may be understood as an exchange of loyalty/adherence for protection.[36] The

32. The imposition of law *after* redemption, however, is hardly unexpected, either in terms of ancient Near Eastern treaties or the biblical account of the Noahide laws and covenant after rescue from the flood.

33. Indeed, the immediately preceding narrative is that of Jethro's response to the perceived litigiousness of the people (Exod. 18.13-27).

34. For a semiotic analysis of Exod. 19.1-8, see Rivard (1981: 335-56).

35. Contrary to the common view that while the JE source recognizes two covenants, one made with the patriarchs and the other with all Israel at Sinai-Horeb, P knows of a Noahide and a patriarchal covenant, but not a Sinaitic one. For this view, which he sees as reflecting scepticism as to the continuing viability of covenantal law, perhaps influenced by the theology of Ezekiel, see Blenkinsopp (1976: 280-81).

36. On the applicability of the ancient Near Eastern *mišarum*-act and covenant of grant models to different aspects of the biblical narrative, see Jackson (1998a:

fact that there is no mention in it of the land is sometimes taken to indicate an exilic source. This may well be correct, but the promise of the land may still (in the present context) be implicit, if (as seems most likely) the reference to 'my covenant' does indeed refer to an existing covenant—which it is now time for the current generation to reconfirm.

Moses comes down and performs his task (v. 7): the statement וישם לפניהם את כל הדברים האלה serves not only as a record of the making of the offer to the people, but also as performance by Moses of his task. The people accept. Moses returns and tells God of the acceptance by the people. God then tells Moses that he will come in a cloud so that the people themselves should hear God talking to Moses, 'that the people may hear when I speak with you, and may also believe you for ever' (וגם בך יאמינו לעולם, Exod. 19.9). This is not an anticipation of the Decalogue, but of a prior exchange between God and Moses (Exod. 19.19). Here, an auditory sign is provided for the continuity, indeed permanence, of the authority of Moses. Again, there is reiteration of themes from Gen. 15: only after Abram has 'believed' the promise that he will have descendants as numerous as the stars does God reveal his name, and does Abram seek and receive a sign, in the form of the miraculous offering; only after the people has accepted the covenant recognizing the redemption from Egypt is a sign given of the enduring status of Moses.

224-27). There is no necessary conflict between claims of such historical connections and the 'rhetorical' approach adopted by Watts. He himself cites (1999: 59 n. 84) Nohrnberg (1995: 69-95), for 'the literary effect of the Pentateuch's adaptation and expansion of the ancient genres of treaty, law and grant'. Watts (1999: 40-45) reviews a range of ancient sources, including the Hittite treaties and some of the law codes, in which instructions and laws are presented in a narrative context, rejects the view that it should be regarded as a distinguishing feature of a particular genre ('though in Israel's culture it did become a typical feature of Torah'), and claims that it occurs in too many cultures to generate theories of literary dependence, or to help in dating a document's composition: 'Instead, it indicates the rhetorical setting of the literature and the persuasive goals motivating its composition' (45). 'Rhetorical setting', in my view, goes too far, if Watts thereby implies anything like the public reading he identifies for pentateuchal law. Elsewhere (40) he speaks of 'rhetorical strategy'. There is a fine borderline here between 'rhetorical' approaches, which focus upon 'persuasion' and semiotic approaches, which focus on sense construction, since (a) the latter is a precondition of the former, and (b) semiotics often views persuasion as making sense of the act of enunciation.

The function attributed to direct auditory perception of God's voice, in pronouncing the Decalogue, is different. When, after the event, the people indicate that they no longer want to hear God directly, Moses explains that the frightening direct speech was to test them, and instil the fear of God (Exod. 20.18-20)—a reversal of the earlier theme in which sceptical humans test God by seeking a perceptual sign to confirm their belief. Moses now approaches the cloud. We have a reversion to God's commands recorded in the form of messages that he is to convey to the Israelites. Then follows the altar law, and the Covenant Code, introduced with a formula echoing the enunciation of the offer in ch. 19: ואלה המשפטים אשר תשים לפניהם.[37]

The Covenant Code, as we now have it, concludes with the angel pericope (Exod. 23.20-33), although the latter, in both form and content, is clearly distinct, being divine speech expressed in the first person, tied to the particular historical context, and commencing with an introductory *hineh*. Watts sees it as manifesting the 'sanction' element (in respect of the preceding 'list' of laws) in his story-list-sanction structure.[38] But it is more complicated than that:

> (20) Behold, I send an angel before you, to guard you on the way and to bring you to the place which I have prepared. (21) Give heed to him and hearken to his voice, do not rebel against him, for he will not pardon your transgression; for my name is in him. (22) But if you hearken attentively to his voice and do all that I say, then I will be an enemy to your enemies and an adversary to your adversaries. (23) When my angel goes before you, and brings you in to the Amorites, and the Hittites, and the Perizzites, and the Canaanites, the Hivites, and the Jebusites, and I blot them out, (24) you shall not bow down to their gods, nor serve them, nor do according to their works, but you shall utterly overthrow them and break their pillars in pieces. (25) You shall serve the LORD your God, and I will bless your bread and your water; and I will take sickness away from the midst of you. (26) None shall cast her young or be barren in your land; I will fulfil the number of your days. (27) I will send my terror before you, and will throw into confusion all the people against whom you shall come, and I will make all your enemies turn their backs

37. Rashi seizes upon the conjunctive *vav* to stress that these laws were from Sinai just as the Decalogue.

38. Watts (1999: 51-52, 107), arguing that the role of the angel reiterates that in Exod. 14.19 at the time of the crossing of the *yam suf* (Exod. 13.18; 15.22): 'Then the angel of God who went before the host of Israel moved and went behind them', so that the story 'ground[s] the promise of future success in the experience of past deliverance'.

to you. (28) And I will send hornets before you, which shall drive out Hivite, Canaanite, and Hittite from before you. (29) I will not drive them out from before you in one year, lest the land become desolate and the wild beasts multiply against you. (30) Little by little I will drive them out from before you, until you are increased and possess the land. (31) And I will set your bounds from the Red Sea to the sea of the Philistines, and from the wilderness to the Euphrates; for I will deliver the inhabitants of the land into your hand, and you shall drive them out before you. (32) You shall make no covenant with them or with their gods. (33) They shall not dwell in your land, lest they make you sin against me; for if you serve their gods, it will surely be a snare to you.

We have here a self-contained set of reciprocal promises—described as a *berit* not directly, but by inference: it includes a ban on the future making of any *berit* 'with them or with their gods' (v. 32): Israel is already committed. The reciprocal obligations are clear enough: explicit reconfirmation of the promise of the land (vv. 23, 28-31), protection (v. 27) and well-being (vv. 25-26) on the one hand, general loyalty and obedience (vv. 21-22, 25) plus abstention from and suppression of the idolatry they will encounter in the land (v. 24) on the other. There is no reference to the preceding laws of the Covenant Code as incorporated within these reciprocal obligations. We need not here speculate upon the compositional history. Suffice it to note that this is the first explicit reference within the Sinaitic pericope to the promise of the land (with a warning, seemingly, that the conquest will take time: vv. 29-30).

The voice of the narrator resumes in ch. 24.[39] In v. 3, Moses comes (down) and relates (orally) both the *mishpatim* and the *devarim* to the people (see §5.3.3, *supra*).[40] They proclaim their acceptance (v. 3). Moses writes down the text (v. 4). He builds an earthen altar, thus performing the command given in Exod. 20.24. There are then sacrifices (v. 5), and the *sefer haberit* is read and accepted (orally[41]) in between

39. The first two verses must be misplaced. Moses is now commanded to ascend the mountain again, but he was last located approaching the cloud. The first two verses belong with verses 9-11 (cf. Nicholson 1974: 78-80).

40. There is a strong case for regarding *ve'et kol hamishpatim* in Exod. 24.3 as secondary: the immediate response of the people to the oral account refers only to the *devarim;* Moses writes only the *devarim* in 24.4 and when the *sefer haberit* is read to them, their acceptance is phrased, again, in terms only of the *devarim* (24.7) (cf. Kutsch 1973: 80 n. 161; Childs 1974: 502).

41. Niditch (1997: 90), contrasts the acceptance of the covenant in Neh. 10.1 (where we have a long list of those who 'set their seal' on the covenant) with that in

two parts of a blood ritual in which the blood is formally designated 'the blood of the covenant which the LORD has made with you in accordance with all these words' (v. 8).[42] This is certainly revision of the covenant, though without any suggestion of withdrawal of earlier promises or obligations: whether circumcision or loyalty. Then the text continues with the theophany to Moses, Aaron, Nadav, Avihu and the elders (Exod. 24.9-11).

Not only does the structure of the initial dialogue at Sinai echo that with Abram, as argued above. Within the Sinai pericope itself, we also have a further reiteration of that structure, before and after God's enunciation of the Decalogue: first God's command to Moses to convey the offer (Exod. 19.3; 21.1), then Moses' performance of that task (Exod. 19.7; 24.3), then the people's response (Exod. 19.8 and 24.3), then a theophany (Exod. 19.9-11; 24.1-2, 9-11) (cf., in part, Childs 1974: 502-503; Nicholson 1982: 83). Through reiteration of the pattern *at Sinai itself*, the validity of God's promise to make Israel a special people is already recognized.

After the laws of the sanctuary, the narrative structure resumes with the story of the golden calf (Exod. 32, 34). Ch. 32 is commonly viewed as manifesting the breaking of the covenant (in the sense of a breach of its terms so serious that the covenant itself is automatically abrogated) and ch. 34 as its 'renewal'. But the matter is not put in this way in ch. 32. Certainly, there has been a serious breach of the loyalty pledged to God before the Decalogue, and of the commandments against idolatry.

Exod. 19.8: in the former 'the makers of the covenant...participate in a legal, written agreement' whereas in the latter 'the people agree only orally'. The contrast is even stronger, in my view, here in Exod. 24, in that there is here a written document which is recited. Nevertheless, its acceptance is oral, just as it was in response to the offer of a non-written covenant in Exod. 19.8. This would appear to reflect a stage (superseded by the time of Nehemiah) when the written document was regarded merely as evidence of the covenant, rather than constitutive of it. There is a similar pattern in relation to promulgation. Greenberg (1995: 17) writes: 'From the very first, the covenant stipulations must have been proclaimed publicly by the lawgiver'. Finkelstein (1961: 92) endorses the view of Kraus that the *mišarum* act was probably proclaimed orally (cf. *likro deror*, Jer. 34.15, 17) and that documents like the edict of Ammisaduqa are subsequent literary compilations that 'had no particular official status, but served rather as a guide for local officials for the execution of the royal decree' (see also Niditch 1997: 96-98).

42. See further Widengren (1957: 18) on the parallel with Josiah's covenant; Nicholson (1982: 74-86).

Adding insult to injury, the new deity[43] is proclaimed the redeemer from Egypt (Exod. 32.4). God tells Moses that the people have 'corrupted themselves' and 'turned aside quickly out of the way which I commanded them' (vv. 7-8), and threatens to destroy them (v. 10). Moses argues that such a destruction would constitute (what might later be termed) a *chillul hashem*,[44] and reminds God of his oath (Gen. 22.16; 26.3; see §9.2, *supra*) to the patriarchs, combining the promises of posterity multitudinous as the stars (Gen. 15.3-4; 22.17; 26.4; see §9.2, *supra*) with the land:

> Remember Abraham, Isaac, and Israel, thy servants, to whom thou didst swear by thine own self, and didst say to them, 'I will multiply your descendants as the stars of heaven, and all this land that I have promised I will give to your descendants, and they shall inherit it for ever' (v. 13).

Moses here reverses his role, and becomes the spokesman of the people to God, rather than that of God to the people, successfully reminding God that the oath he swore to the patriarchs was hereditary.

God relents (v. 14) and Moses descends the mountain with the two inscribed tablets,[45] but on seeing the golden calf he shatters them (v. 19). This has been interpreted in legal terms: in Babylonia, when a debt was discharged, the tablets were broken.[46] But here the narrator

---

43. On the problem of the plural in Exod. 32.4 and a possible connection with Jeroboam's calves in 1 Kgs 12.28, see Childs (1974: 566).

44. 'Why should the Egyptians say, "With evil intent did he bring them forth, to slay them in the mountains, and to consume them from the face of the earth"?' (v. 12).

45. See §6.2 n. 51 for Widengren's interpretation of this as manifesting an ancient Near Eastern royal ideology.

46. See, e.g., Sarna (1991: 207): 'This was not an impetuous act; rather, it quite deliberately signified the abrogation of the covenant. In Akkadian legal terminology to 'break the tablet' (*tuppam ḫepû*) means to invalidate or repudiate a document or agreement. Moses is no longer the intercessor but the decisive, energetic leader.' This, in fact, is the strongest argument that the covenant was conceived as abrogated (not merely breached) by the golden calf incident, and so falls to be 'renewed' in ch. 34 (Sarna heads his treatment of the latter section: 'Renewal of the Covenant'). But the argument is based on a questionable methodology. A (genuine) ancient Near Eastern legal usage is imposed in a way that actually conflicts with what the biblical text tells us. Despite Sarna's characterization of Moses' action as a deliberate legal act, the text itself tells us: 'Moses' anger burned hot (ויחר אף משה), and he threw the tables out of his hands and broke them at the foot of the mountain' (Exod. 32.19). Secondly, the statement that 'Moses is no longer the intercessor but

provides his own explanation of Moses' act: it is an expression of anger (v. 19). He accuses Aaron of bringing a 'great sin' on the people (v. 21; cf. 30). Moses purges the people (vv. 26-29) and asks God for forgiveness for the rest. God promises to punish only the (remaining) sinners (v. 33), and sends a plague to do so (v. 35). Thereupon, the promise of the land—and an instruction to proceed to it—is reaffirmed for the rest. God says to Moses:

> Depart, go up hence, you and the people whom you have brought up out of the land of Egypt, to the land of which I swore to Abraham, Isaac, and Jacob, saying, 'To your descendants I will give it.' And I will send an angel before you, and I will drive out the Canaanites, the Amorites, the Hittites, the Perizzites, the Hivites, and the Jebusites. Go up to a land flowing with milk and honey; but I will not go up among you, lest I consume you in the way, for you are a stiff-necked people (Exod. 33.1-3).

Once again, a question has arisen as to who are the legitimate heirs of the promise. There is a reconfirmation to the survivors. What is reconfirmed is not any Sinaitic covenant but—again—the oath (this time promising the land, cf. Exod. 6.8) made to the patriarchs. The only aspect of the Sinaitic relationship that is referred to is a reiteration of a promise to send an angel to lead the people to the promised land (Exod. 33.2, cf. 23.16).

In ch. 34 Moses is told to cut stone tablets like the first, on which God will rewrite[47] the contents of the first set (v. 1),[48] and to ascend the

---

the decisive, energetic leader' only prompts the question: On whose authority did he revoke the covenant? When he functions as 'intercessor', it is on behalf of the people, not God. It is surely inconceivable that the covenant would be abrogated, in the light of the people's breach, by anyone other than God, and of this there is no hint.

47. The first set had been written with 'the finger of God' (Exod. 31.18); see Niditch (1997: 79-82), placing this in the context of other examples of 'special writing' that may exist in an oral culture and are rooted ultimately in 'what the illiterate think of writing'. Despite Exod. 34.1, the command *after* God's speech (which includes the 'ritual Decalogue') is for Moses to do the writing (Exod. 34.27), which he does (Exod. 34.28).

48. This is quite explicit: 'the words that were on the first tables, which you broke'. Similarly, in Exod. 34.28: 'And he wrote upon the tables the words of the covenant, the ten commandments,' *aseret hadevarim* being the name of the Decalogue also in Deut. 4.13, 10.4 (this leading Ibn Ezra to suggest that the second set of tablets was indeed inscribed with the Deuteronomic version). For the biblical writers, however, the matter is less clear. In context, Exod. 34.28 is simply the

mountain. There, he pleads again for forgiveness (v. 9).[49] God responds, and here for the first time in the golden calf narrative do we hear of a *berit* :

> Behold, I hereby make a covenant. In full view of all your people I will do miracles [*nifla'ot*][50] as have never been performed in all the world or in any nation; and all the people among whom you are shall see the work of the LORD; for it is a terrible thing that I will do with you (Exod. 34.10).

The concern here is neither the patriarchs' posterity nor the land. It is simply the converse of the *chillul hashem* that Moses had warned against in Exod. 32.12, a concern for the reputation of Israel's God in the eyes of others. Much depends, however, on whether, or how much of, the continuation of this speech is regarded as part of this same covenant. The speech continues:

> Observe what I command you this day. Behold, I will drive out before you the Amorites, the Canaanites, the Hittites, the Perizzites, the Hivites, and the Jebusites. Take heed to yourself, lest you make a covenant with the inhabitants of the land whither you go, lest it become a snare in the midst of you. You shall tear down their altars, and break their pillars, and

fulfilment of God's instruction in the preceding verse: 'Write these words; in accordance with these words I have made a covenant with you and with Israel' (where 'these words' refer most naturally to the immediately preceding 'ritual decalogue' of Exod. 34.17-26), unless we accept (with Jewish tradition) that the juxtaposed, apparently co-referential, expressions, *divre haberit* and *aseret hadevarim* in Exod. 34.28, do in fact have different referents. If so, we need to understand Exod. 34.27 as commanding some form of communication *other than* inscription on the tablets. Sarna (1991: 22) suggests a parallel with Exod. 24.4, which would imply that the immediately foregoing laws are written in a *sefer* rather than on *luchot;* he refers also to an early rabbinic tradition stressing *al pi* in Exod. 34.27, so as to suggest that (despite the instruction to 'write' these laws), the reference in fact is to the Oral Torah (he cites Jerusalem Talmud *Pe'ah* 2.6 [17a], *Meg.* 4.1 [74d] and Babylonian Talmud *Gitt.* 60b). Watts (1999: 69) notes the view of Johnstone (1987: 28), that the ritual decalogue 'picks up the beginning of the Decalogue and the end of the Book of the Covenant to mark by a kind of merismus (in this case, totality indicated by extremes) the entire contents of Decalogue and Book of the Covenant on the conjoint basis of which the Covenant was made'.

49. In the preceding speech (words that have become a central feature of the Yom Kippur liturgy: vv. 6-7), it is unclear whether the subject of *vayikra* in v. 6 is Moses or God. The RSV takes it to be God (see also Childs 1974: 611-12).

50. Again here, we have an association of *berit* with proof of status by miraculous means (cf. Gen. 9.12; 17.9-14; §9.2, *supra*).

cut down their Asherim (for you shall worship no other god, for the LORD, whose name is Jealous, is a jealous God), lest you make a covenant with the inhabitants of the land, and when they play the harlot after their gods and sacrifice to their gods and one invites you, you eat of his sacrifice, and you take of their daughters for your sons, and their daughters play the harlot after their gods and make your sons play the harlot after their gods (Exod. 34.11-16).

We then have the so-called 'ritual decalogue' (Exod. 34.17-26), followed by God's instruction to Moses: 'Write these words; in accordance with these words I have made a covenant with you and with Israel' (Exod. 34.27), and Moses' action (apparently) in compliance: 'And he was there with the LORD forty days and forty nights; he neither ate bread nor drank water. And he wrote upon the tables the words of the covenant, the ten commandments' (Exod. 34.28).[51] Since God's speech commences in v. 10 with reference to—indeed a performative of —a covenant, and the speech concludes (subject to the narrator's interjection, v. 27a) with an instruction to write down these very words, on the basis of which the covenant is made,[52] it might seem reasonable to regard the whole of vv. 10-26 as incorporated in this covenant. That, no doubt, is the sense intended by the redactors. But the passage seems to combine two quite distinct elements (Stahl 1995: 66): vv. 10-16 echo the themes of the 'angel' pericope appended to the Covenant Code,[53] and indeed fulfils a similar narrative function, as a 'departure speech'. The 'ritual decalogue', on the other hand, does not anticipate a particular temporal context and is not concerned with relations between Israelites and others.[54] What would be the significance of regarding all this as incorporated in a covenant? In what sense would this be 'covenant renewal'?

The function of the covenant, I suggest, is the formal resolution of a dispute. The terminology הנה אנכי כרת ברית (Exod. 34.10) makes no allusion back to an earlier *berit* that is being renewed or replaced. It is,

---

51. On the difficulties of the relationship of these two verses, see n. 48, *supra*.

52. No hint here, incidentally, of the consent of the people, much stressed in the Sinai pericope.

53. Exod. 23.20-33, discussed *supra*. Both open with a performative, address the problems of idolatry anticipated on entry to the land, and ban covenanting with its inhabitants.

54. Other than Exod. 34.24: 'For I will cast out nations before you, and enlarge your borders; neither shall any man desire your land, when you go up to appear before the LORD your God three times in the year.'

however, comparable to that used in Gen. 9.9, after the cataclysm of the flood, where God proclaims: הנני מקים את בריתי אתכם. A *berit* is used to formalize the settlement of disputes between Abraham and Abimelech in Gen. 21.27, Isaac and Abimelech in Gen. 26.28, and Jacob and Laban in Gen. 31.44. The settlement of a dispute may, indeed, revise the relationship between the parties, taking account of the dispute itself: it is thus hardly inappropriate that the first provision of the 'ritual decalogue' is 'You shall make for yourself no molten gods' (Exod. 34.17). That does not mean abrogation of the previous relationship: it may mean supplementing it with additional terms.[55] The golden-calf incident nowhere suggests that the Sinaitic covenant had been *abrogated* and was now to be *renewed*.[56] Rather, it tells us of a dispute consequent on that covenant. The dispute concerned a significant breach of the Sinaitic covenant—one, no doubt, that might have entitled God to regard it as abrogated—followed by a further distinct covenant designed to settle the dispute and to state the terms of its settlement. To use a legal analogy, breach of the Sinaitic Contract led to damages and a settlement, not to discharge of the Sinaitic Contract itself.

9.4 Covenant Renewal in Deuteronomy and Joshua

The reports of the impending death of Moses in the book of Numbers proved greatly exaggerated. Deuteronomy is cast mainly in the form of Moses' speech—in fact, speeches—at the end of the 40 years in the desert, before the entry to the promised land. Taken as a whole, it serves as a Recognition—through reiteration in the speeches of

---

55. Thus, it should not necessarily be inferred that the covenant relationship here established dispenses with the Decalogue, an issue that concerns Stahl (1995: 65-66). At 51-53, she views the Sinai narratives as reflecting the conflicting themes of intimacy (direct revelation) and alienation (golden calf). This would exemplify my suggestion (§9.2) that we view the stories from Abram as a macro-narrative of the relations between God and the people. But Stahl is committed, in my view, to too postmodernist a reading. It is certainly true that 'operating...as the conduit between the voice of God and the voices of the people, Moses repeatedly goes up and down the mountain delivering messages' but does that really make him 'polyphony incarnate' (at 52)?

56. Watts (1999: 77) denies that Exod. 34 contains a 'new' covenant for a different reason: the continuity implicit in the relationship between chs. 25–31 and 35–40.

Moses—of the significance of the acts that are recounted, the Performances of God and of Moses himself.[57]

Compared with the bulk of the laws in Exodus-Numbers, introduced through the anonymous narrator telling us that God had instructed Moses to transmit the laws that follow to the people (e.g. the opening verse of the *Mishpatim*, Exod. 21.1), we have in Deuteronomy a reversal of relationships. Deuteronomy is truly *torat mosheh*, in that the narrator tells the story of the speeches that Moses delivers, in the course of which it is Moses who himself narrates both the story of God's relationship to Israel[58] and the laws that have been given. However, we should also pay attention to the divisions the background narrator makes between the various speeches attributed to Moses.

In the first speech, largely devoted to historical narrative, Moses expresses clearly what he conceived the *berit* to be:

> And he declared to you his covenant, which he commanded you to perform, that is, the ten commandments; and he wrote them upon two tables of stone. And the LORD commanded me at that time to teach you statutes and ordinances, that you might do them in the land which you are going over to possess (Deut. 4.13-14).

The 'that is' of the RSV is not found in the Hebrew, but it is an accurate representation of the force of the apposition. Moses contrasts the status of the *aseret hadevarim* that were inscribed on the tables from the *chukim* and *mishpatim* that he was commanded to teach (no claim here that the latter were written down, or even that God dictated them rather than authorized Moses to formulate them: there is no definite article attached to 'statutes and ordinances'). The distinction, however, turns out to be of a largely theoretical character. Breach even of this non-covenantal, but still divinely authorized, law entails the risk of significant sanctions, extending even to loss of the land (*infra*, p. 258).

In the second speech, Moses' quotation of the Decalogue is introduced thus:

---

57. On its significance as a thematic repetition of the content of the previous revelation, see §8.1, *supra*.

58. See further Watts (1999: 79-80, 90, 109, 122-24, 129); Levinson (1992: 56), on the 'radically revisionist textual voice of Moses in Deuteronomy'. McConville (1985: 3) notes 'the occasional lapse from speech of Moses to Israel to narrative about Moses and Israel', as in ch. 27, but regards this as an integral part of the treaty structure of the book, which 'ultimately...is cast in the third person.'

Hear, O Israel, the statutes and the ordinances [*hachukim ve'et hamishpatim*] which I speak in your hearing this day, and you shall learn them and be careful to do them. The LORD our God made a covenant with us in Horeb. Not with our fathers did the LORD make this covenant, but with us, who are all of us here alive this day. The LORD spoke with you face to face at the mountain, out of the midst of the fire, while I stood between the LORD and you at that time, to declare to you the word of the LORD; for you were afraid because of the fire, and you did not go up into the mountain. He said... (Deut. 5.1-5).

If there is any suggestion from 5.1 that the *berit* includes *chukim* and *mishpatim*, it is dispelled by Moses' remark immediately following his recitation of the Decalogue: 'These words the LORD spoke to all your assembly at the mountain out of the midst of the fire, the cloud, and the thick darkness, with a loud voice; and he added no more' (5.22).[59]

The Decalogue is here unambiguously related to the *berit* at Horev, but Moses is concerned to stress its continuing validity for the present generation. This is achieved in two ways: on the one hand by a fiction (much emphasised in later Jewish writings) that this first (and all future) generations were in fact (in some sense) present at the original revelation; secondly (which we might consider otiose if the fiction were really taken seriously) by Moses' repeating the *devarim* to the present generation. The question whether incorporation into the covenant requires direct divine address to the new adherents—an issue encountered in the covenant stories of both Isaac and Jacob (§9.2)—still appears not to have been resolved. However, the theme of continuity in respect of the patriarchal promise is now transferred to that of a covenant incorporating 'legal' obligations.

The status of the promises to the patriarchs, as conceived in Deuteronomy, is itself of some interest. The promise of the land is *never* explicitly ascribed in Deuteronomy to a covenant; normally it is referred to as a divine gift (Deut. 1.21, 25, 36; 2.24, 29, 31; 3.1, 18, 20; 4.1, 21, 38; 5.16 [cf. Exod. 20.12, Decalogue], 9.22; 11.29, 31; 12.10;

---

59. Described by Levinson (1997: 152-53) as a 'deliberate textual polemic... [an] attempt to divest the Covenant Code of its authority by rejecting its Sinaitic pedigree... By circumscribing Sinai and silencing the Covenant Code, the redactors of Deuteronomy sought to clear a textual space for Moab as the authentic—and exclusive—supplement to the original revelation.' However, by a 'major irony... Second Temple editors incorporated both the Covenant Code and the legal corpus of Deuteronomy into the Pentateuch. In doing so, they preserved Deuteronomy alongside the very text that it sought to replace and subvert.'

15.4, 7; 17.14; 18.9; 19.1-3, 10, 14; 21.1, 23; 24.4; 25.15, 19; 26.1, 2; 26.9; 27.1, 3; 28.8; 32.52)—frequently as one with continuing validity: an 'inheritance'.[60] Where the origins of that gift are mentioned, they are normally[61] identified as an 'oath' sworn by God to the patriarchs (Deut. 1.35; 6.10, 18, 23; 7.13; 8.1; 10.11; 11.21; 19.8; 26.3, 15; 30.20; 31.7, 20, 21, 23; 34.4). This may well be a shorthand: in Deut. 4.31 the patriarchal covenant is itself said to have been 'sworn' to them.[62] Even so, there must have been a reason for the shorthand. Though a patriarchal covenant to give the land may be presupposed (indeed, may be thought in large measure to have been discharged by performance), Deuteronomy reserves the terminology of *berit* for the Decalogue on the one hand and, as we shall see, some subsequent commands of Moses on the other.

The theological significance of the land for Deuteronomy is not that it is the benefit to Israel of a unilateral covenant given to the patriarchs. Rather, it is one side of a bilateral relationship, of which the other is Israel's observance of both covenant (the Decalogue) and divinely authorized law. Thus, the land is conceived as the place where the commandments are to be performed (Deut. 5.31; 6.1; 12.1). Continuing possession of the land (or at least the prosperity and long life derived from it [Deut. 11.17; 15.4; 23.20; 25.15; 28.11; 30.16, 32.47]) is now taken to be conditional upon observance of particular laws (Deut. 4.26; 16.20), law in general (Deut. 4.40; 11.8; 28.63; 30.18) and (less commonly) covenant (Deut. 29.24-25). More controversially, it is viewed as a reward for their observance.[63]

Deuteronomy 7.7-11, later in this speech, may be taken as encapsulating a number of claims regarding the interrelationship of previous elements in the story:

60. Variously described as *nachalah, yerushah, lerishtah*: Deut. 3.18; 4.21, 38; 5.31; 11.8; 12.9-10; 15.4; 19.2-3, 10, 14; 21.1, 23; 24.4; 25.19; 26.1.

61. Occasionally as a simple promise, using *diber* (Deut. 6.3).

62. The same combination is found in Deut. 29.12, 14 (29.11, 13, MT), the 'additional' covenant sworn in the 'land of Moab', discussed below, though the terminology is not that of *shava* but rather a conjunction of *berit* and *alah*.

63. In Deut. 8.5-10, where the promise of the land is introduced with a comparison to domestic pedagogy ('Know then in your heart that, as a man disciplines his son, the LORD your God disciplines you'). Contrast Deut. 9.4-6, where the Israelites are urged not to consider possession of the land the result of their own merit, but rather of the wickedness of (the conquered) nations on the one hand and fulfilment of the patriarchal promise on the other.

(7) It was not because you were more in number than any other people that the LORD set his love upon you and chose you, for you were the fewest of all peoples; (8) but it is because the LORD loves you, and is keeping the oath which he swore to your fathers, that the LORD has brought you out with a mighty hand, and redeemed you from the house of bondage, from the hand of Pharaoh king of Egypt. (9) Know therefore that the LORD your God is God, the faithful God who keeps covenant and steadfast love with those who love him and keep his commandments, to a thousand generations, (10) and requites to their face those who hate him, by destroying them; he will not be slack with him who hates him, he will requite him to his face. (11) You shall therefore be careful to do the commandment, and the statutes, and the ordinances, which I command you this day.

The reference to paucity of numbers in v. 7 naturally refers to the clan of Abraham at the time of making the patriarchal covenant. In context, that to the exodus therefore impliedly claims fulfilment of the promise to make the descendants of the patriarchs as numerous as the stars, as well as the promise (soon to be fulfilled) of the land. The covenant in v. 9 is the Decalogue, as shown by the formulation in terms of those who love and hate God (cf. Deut. 5.9-10).[64] Given Deuteronomy's insistence that God did not add to the words of the Decalogue (Deut. 5.22; see further n. 59, *supra*), v. 11 might appear surprising, in requiring adherence to *hamitsvah ve'et hachukim ve'et hamishpatim*. But note the change of subject of the verb 'command': 'You shall therefore be careful to do the commandment, and the statutes, and the ordinances, which *I* command you this day.' The RSV's 'therefore' is more explicit than the Hebrew, which has merely *veshamarta*. However, it is justified. Moses is presented at the outset as having set out to 'explain' this *torah* (Deut. 1.5; see further §8.1 at n. 3, *supra*). Here, he claims that he will do so by personally issuing *hamitsvah ve'et hachukim ve'et hamishpatim*. This corresponds to Moses' introduction to the main body of laws in Deuteronomy:

> These are the statutes and ordinances (*hachukim vehamishpatim*) which you shall be careful to do in the land which the LORD, the God of your fathers, has given you to possess, all the days that you live upon the earth (Deut. 12.1).[65]

64. For Levinson's interpretation of this as revising the Decalogue's threat of transgenerational punishment, see §8.1 n. 11, *supra*; on the love/hate terminology, see §6.3 at p. 165, *supra*.

65. See further §6.2 at p. 161, *supra,* in the context of a review of the divisions

Moses will issue non-covenantal law in order to ensure adherence to the covenant.[66] A biblical anticipation of *seyag latorah*?

Deuteronomy provides a version of the story of the golden calf (Deut. 9.8-21; 10.1-5, 10-11), presented as one (if the major) instance of the continuing stubbornness and rebelliousness of the people. The sin is not described as a breach of covenant and there is no mention of any covenant entered into in settlement of that dispute.

After the speech that contains the main body of Deuteronomic laws (in chs.12–26), there follows a sequence of smaller speeches containing instructions directly related to the entry into the land. It is these speeches that form the crucial link between the books (and stories) of Moses and Joshua, and introduce a new cycle of narrative reiteration.

First, large plastered stones[67] are to be set up on the day of the crossing the Jordan, on which should be written 'all the words of this law'; the stones are to be erected on Mount Ebal, where a stone altar is to be built, on which sacrifice should be made, as an act of rejoicing (Deut. 27.2-8).[68] We may note that this is an instruction that Moses does *not* claim that God has given him; the narrator simply tells us that Moses and the elders of Israel commanded the people to do it. Between this and the instruction regarding the blessings and curses on Gerizim and Ebal, there is an interruption:

> And Moses and the Levitical priests said to all Israel, 'Keep silence and hear, O Israel: this day you have become the people of the LORD your God. You shall therefore obey the voice of the LORD your God, keeping his commandments and his statutes, which I command you this day' (Deut. 27.9-10).

This can hardly be in its proper place. 'This day you have become the people of the LORD your God' implies an act of incorporation of the current generation into the covenant, but that does not come until Deut. 29.10-15 (below): Moses has been recounting previous history, sermonizing on it and providing further *chukim* and *mishpatim* (whatever their status, see §6.2, at pp. 159-61, *supra*). Moses next commands the

of the speeches in Deuteronomy, and their superscriptions.

66. Especially the septennial *Sukkot* reading in Deut. 31 (see p. 264, *infra*).

67. See further, on the traditions of inscribed and uninscribed stones, §5.2, *supra*.

68. Note the parallel with the incident of the golden calf. Rejoicing in the presence of the deity is not itself objectionable; it depends on the form it takes, and the deity with whom one rejoices.

people to perform the ceremony of blessings and curses, on Gerizim and Ebal, when they have crossed the Jordan.[69] The text of the curses is relayed in the form of the *oratio directa* to be pronounced by the Levites, while the blessings (and further threats) follow not as the *ipsissima verba* of blessings and curses that are to be formally pronounced, but as a continuation of Moses' speech in which he relays God's promises and threats. There is no explicit mention of *berit* in chs. 27 or 28, but the long (*tochakha*) speech containing the blessings and curses (Deut. 27.11–28.68) threatens reversal of those covenantal promises which had already been fulfilled: 'Whereas you were as the stars of heaven for multitude, you shall be left few in number; because you did not obey the voice of the LORD your God' (Deut. 28.68); 'And the LORD will bring you back in ships to Egypt, a journey which I promised that you should never make again' (Deut. 28.62). The narrator's context has, by this stage, intervened in the presentation. This is part of a concluding passage dealing with punishment for an *existing* breach of obligation:

> All these curses shall come upon you and pursue you and overtake you, till you are destroyed, because you did not obey the voice of the LORD your God, to keep his commandments and his statutes which he commanded you (Deut. 28.45).

Ch. 29.1 opens in the voice of the narrator:

> These are the words of the covenant (*eyleh divre habrit*) which the LORD commanded Moses to make with the people of Israel in the land of Moab, besides the covenant which he had made with them at Horeb. And Moses summoned all Israel and said to them... [*oratio directa*] (Deut. 29.1-2).

There is not the slightest suggestion that this covenant 'in the land of Moab' either replaces or renews an earlier *berit*. It is clearly stated to be additional to that at Horeb: מלבד הברית אשר כרת אתם בחרב.[70]

What is the point of this additional covenant? Despite the Masoretic

---

69. Repeating Deut. 11.29 though not, here, 'on the day that they crossed'.

70. Cf. Watts (1999: 72), who notes that statements like Deut. 6.1, 'Now this is the commandment, the statutes and the ordinances that Yahweh your God commanded [me] to teach you...' are relatively rare. The book more often emphasizes the present moment of lawgiving: '...that I command you today': Deut. 11.8, 26; 12.28; 13.19; 28.69, which 'casts the laws of Moab as additional to, rather than a repetition of, the laws of Sinai'. Cf. §6.2 n. 40, *supra*.

chapter division, Deut. 29.1[71] must surely refer to what follows in ch. 29, rather than what precedes. Chapter 29 begins with a normal historical prologue ('You have seen all that the LORD did before your eyes in the land of Egypt...'), commencing with אתם ראיתם as in Exod. 19.4. Then the people are formally commissioned as parties to this additional covenant (Deut. 29.10-15):

> (10) You stand this day all of you before the LORD your God; the heads of your tribes, your elders, and your officers, all the men of Israel, (11) your little ones, your wives, and the sojourner who is in your camp, both he who hews your wood and he who draws your water, (12) that you may enter into the sworn covenant of the LORD your God, which the LORD your God makes with you this day; (13) that he may establish you this day as his people, and that he may be your God, as he promised you, and as he swore to your fathers, to Abraham, to Isaac, and to Jacob. (14) Nor is it with you only that I make this sworn covenant, (15) but with him who is not here with us this day as well as with him who stands here with us this day before the LORD our God.

The whole emphasis is upon the identification of those who are parties to the covenant (whatever their rank, gender and age, vv. 10-11; even, in v. 15, those not present—probably an attempt to make the covenant prospective for future generations *without* the need for further ceremony) and their status as the successors to the patriarchal covenant is stressed (v. 13). Later in the speech Moses calls heaven and earth to witness that he has set before the people a choice between life and death, good and evil. He urges them to choose life, so that they should be the people who will inherit the benefit of the patriarchal promise: 'That you may dwell in the land which the LORD swore to your fathers, to Abraham, to Isaac, and to Jacob to give *them*' (Deut. 30.20)—*latet lahem*. He does not say, 'to give to you'. The implication is that the patriarchal covenant was indeed irrevocable, in the sense that some descendants of Abraham, Isaac and Jacob would inherit the promised land. It did not follow that all, or any particular group, of the patriarchs' descendants would qualify—an issue which, as argued above (§9.2),

---

71. Deut. 28.69 according to the Masoretic chapter division. This might be a grounds for regarding Deut. 28.69/29.1 as a colophon referring back to the preceding material. See Levenston (1984: 141) for other examples. But this would be very difficult to sustain, given the absence of covenant terminology in the preceding speech and its complete concentration on rewards and punishments. By contrast, what follows has the structure of a covenant, as the present analysis seeks to show.

informs the covenant narratives in Genesis. This particular group, the generation of the children of the survivors of the golden calf incident (who themselves had been reconfirmed as beneficiaries of the covenant in Exod. 34), is given that privilege in exchange for entering into a further *berit*.

The fact that this covenant is said to be 'additional to' (*milvad*) that at Horeb suggests an important distinction, in the thought of the Deuteronomist, between the 'Sinaitic' and patriarchal covenants: the former is regarded as continuing, and we have observed already Deuteronomy's fiction that the unborn generation were already present there. Hitherto, the patriarchal sworn promise did not automatically descend to future generations, even if now, on the point of entry to the land, when the first real beneficiaries are known, it does become hereditary (vv. 14-15). But there is also a further change. For Deuteronomy, the covenant at Horeb had included only the Decalogue; now, in this additional covenant, the choice of life and death depends upon observance also of 'the commandments of the LORD your God which I command you this day...and by keeping his commandments and his statutes and his ordinances' (Deut. 30.16). A detailed body of 'legal' instruction is thus added to the covenant. Whereas the redactors of the Sinaitic pericope did this by incorporation of the *Mishpatim* into the account of the covenant in Exod. 24.3 (see n. 40, *supra*), Deuteronomy uses the story of an additional *berit* to do so.

Chapter 31 commences an independent speech, separated from what precedes by the narrator's short continuation passage (Deut. 31.1-2). But the sequence that begins in ch. 31 has a different narrative function from what precedes. Here we get Moses' valedictory. He tells the Israelites that he is now 120 years old and that God has told him that he will not cross the Jordan. The Israelites are not to fear; God will lead them into battle against their enemies. Then he summons Joshua, and charges him in similar fashion (Deut. 31.7-8). Next he writes down *hatorah hazot* (Deut. 31.9)[72] and gives it to the priests to carry in the

---

72. Whereas the Sinaitic account has Moses write down the *sefer haberit* immediately on coming down from Sinai, the Deuteronomic presentation assumes, in so far as it maintains that Moses is transmitting material directly revealed to him by God, that he first teaches it orally and only now (before his death) writes it down. There is, however, one inconsistency in this account. According to Deut. 28.58, Moses already threatens: 'If you are not careful to do all the words of this

ark of the covenant.[73] It is at this stage that he gives them (his last) general command, again, *without* claiming to do so at God's command, that every seven years, on the occasion of the *shemitah*, at the festival of *Sukkot*, they are to read publicly *hatorah hazot*:

> At the end of every seven years, at the set time of the year of release, at the feast of booths, when all Israel comes to appear before the LORD your God at the place which he will choose, you shall read this law before all Israel in their hearing. Assemble the people, men, women, and little ones, and the sojourner within your towns, that they may hear and learn to fear the LORD your God, and be careful to do all the words of this law, and that their children, who have not known it, may hear and learn to fear the LORD your God, as long as you live in the land which you are going over the Jordan to possess (Deut. 31.10-13).

It is clear why, for narrative purposes, such a law of septennial reading has to come in its present place; only then, when Moses has written down the whole of the law, can the instruction to read it every seven years refer unambiguously to the whole written *torah* (or even to the whole of the Mosaic instructions in Deuteronomy). Though there is no explicit suggestion that such septennial readings are for anything other than instructional purposes, the institution fits with the theme of what immediately precedes: those who are (now) bound for the future to this covenant should have regular exposure to its content. It is thus, at the same time, a 'ritual' reading (§5.3.3, *supra*). Incorporation in the covenant entails knowledge (or at least being put on notice of) of the content of its obligations.[74]

To summarize: from ch. 27, we have a number of quite separate instructions offered by Moses himself, of which two—the erection of monumental law, and the ceremony of blessings and curses—are designed for one particular historical occasion, while the third—the septennial reading of the law—is presented as having continuing valid-

---

law which are written in this book...', even though no *sefer* has, according to the narrative, yet been written.

73. Along with the second tablets (Deut. 10.5).

74. Greenberg (1995: 18) compares modern adult education 'retreats'! I am not sure I would chose Jerusalem at *Sukkot* for such. A more serious point of dispute is his adoption of a 'dramaturgical' model, in describing the purpose of the gathering as a 'public re-enactment of the covenant-ceremony'. I argue in §5.3.3, *supra*, for a 'ritual' function of the reading. But there is nothing to suggest a re-enactment (which implies reiteration of the original speech act, not simply the content of the *sefer*).

ity. Additionally, and quite separately, we have a *berit* which Moses says God commands him to make, there and then, in the plains of Moab. This *berit* confirms the present Israelites as the successors to the patriarchal covenant, before the entry to the promised land. The fact that God commands Moses to make this covenant may be viewed, additionally, as functioning to recognize both the performance by Moses of his task,[75] and to adumbrate the performance by God of his: he has brought the people to the promised land, even if it has not yet been conquered.

Immediately thereafter, the narrator tells us that God announces to Moses his imminent death, and we have the traditions regarding the Song of Moses, his viewing of the promised land from Mount Nebo,[76] and Moses' blessing of the Israelites. Moses dies. The first chapter of Joshua takes up the theme of a written law, now in connection with Joshua, even before the crossing of the Jordan. God's charge to Joshua puts him on the same footing as Moses, explicitly as far as military conquest is concerned (Josh. 1.5). In return, Joshua is required to perform 'all the law which Moses my servant commanded you' (Josh. 1.7)—that is, what we may call the 'direct commands of Moses'. Then follows a reference to written law: 'This book of the law shall not depart out of your mouth, but you shall meditate on it day and night...' (Josh. 1.8). This does not reiterate either the instruction regarding monumental law, or that of a septennial reading; it does, however, echo the 'law of the king' in Deut. 17.18.[77] In short, Joshua is being charged not

75. This is recognized in several different ways. On the viewing of the land from Mount Nebo, see n. 76, *infra*. There is also the explicit epitaph in Deut. 34.10-12, on which Tigay (1996: 137-38) remarks (though with a different intent: he sees it as directed against proponents of syncretistic Yahwism): 'As the final statement about Moses in a markedly ideological book, and as the book's own conclusion, the passage is likely to have a significance that serves the ideological aims of the book as a whole.' Whatever the historical sources of the viewing and the epitaph, they amount to Recognition both of the fulfilment of Moses' task and indeed of God's promise to the patriarchs.

76. Deut. 32.49. Daube (1947: 25-36) argued that this may originally have denoted legal acquisition of the land, parallel to the Roman *traditio* by *fines demonstrare*: see esp. *Dig.* 41.2.18.2: 'If my vendor from my tower points out neigbouring land to me who have bought it, and says that he delivers vacant possession, I begin to possess no less than if I had set foot within its boundary' (Daube's translation, at 28).

77. See further §5.3.2 (beginning), *supra*. On the monarchic status attributed to

only to follow the instructions of Moses, but also to act like him. The two themes converge in the association of Joshua with the monarchical tradition. Throughout the book of Joshua, both themes are frequently reflected, in the narrative parallels between Joshua and Moses (Wenham 1971: 145-46; Childs 1979: 245-46), and in the qualification of various actions as having been performed *kakatuv*.

The ceremony at Gilgal, immediately after the crossing of the Jordan, does not correspond to anything Moses commanded; rather, it is a direct command from God (on Josh. 4.1-7, see §5.2, *supra*). However, immediately after the conquest of Jericho and Ai, Joshua fulfils Moses' instructions regarding Mount Ebal. Josh. 8.30-35 echoes Deut. 27.2-8 in considerable detail,[78] but with a couple of significant variants. In case the significance of Joshua's actions might be lost on the audience, the narrator explicitly refers, three times in the course of six verses, to the authorities for Joshua's actions—these being a written book of *torah* twice, and a command of Moses, here unattributed to a written source (v. 33), on the third occasion. The elements which the passage shares with Deuteronomy 27 are clear enough: Mount Ebal, an altar of unhewn stones (*avanim shelemot*), burnt offerings and peace offerings, the act of inscribing the stones.[79] But there is more. What Joshua does in this passage also evokes other Deuteronomic instructions. The positioning of half the people on Mount Ebal and the other half on Mount Gerizim (v. 33) refers back to the next, but separate instruction given by Moses in Deuteronomy 27, that related to the blessings and the curses, and these latter are proclaimed in v. 34. Josh. 8.30-35 thus seeks to show fulfilment of the two separate but consecutive instructions given in Deuteronomy 27. The reading of the law[80] (not, apparently, just the blessings and curses) and the stress on the inclusion within the ceremony of 'the women, and the little ones, and the sojourners' apparently

Joshua, stressing the parallel obligations in studying the *sefer* in Josh. 1 and Deut. 17, see Widengren (1957: 15-16), who suggests also that the location of the *berit* of Josh. 24 at Shechem (*infra*) may have been especially significant for the Northern Kingdom, Joshua being a member of the tribe of Ephraim.

78. Cf. Weinfeld (1972: 70-71); less plausibly de Vaux (1965: 143).

79. Josh. 8.32: *mishneh torat mosheh*; see further §5.2 at n. 35, §5.3.2 at p. 133, *supra*.

80. Its identity is not explicit: see Watts (1999: 17-18), arguing for Deuteronomy in more or less its present form.

also conflates elements of the *Sukkot* reading (Deut. 31.11-12).[81]

What, then, is the evidence that Josh. 8.30-35 is either intended to signify, or reflects, the institution of a covenant renewal ceremony?[82] I see none whatsoever. The passage is fully explicable in terms of a narrative pattern (quite explicit in the texts) of Mosaic instruction and Joshuan fulfilment. It makes narrative sense in Greimassian terms as the story of Joshua, receiving a 'Contract' from Moses and performing it.

That leaves us with Joshua's own valedictories, in chs. 23 and 24, which turn out to be the only remaining evidence for the covenant renewal ceremony. Let us admit right away that there is here something worth discussing. Josh. 24.25 tells us that Joshua made a *berit* with the people and gave them *chok umishpat* at Shechem. Before we interpret this in terms of cultic history, we are entitled to ask what narrative sense it makes. Chapter 24 is, as Gordon Wenham has described it, 'a fitting climax to the whole book'.[83] Just as Moses has more than a single valedictory at the end of Deuteronomy, so too with Joshua in chs. 23 and 24. But Joshua 24 forms a climax in a double sense. On the one hand, it is the end of Joshua's personal story, and manifests 'Recognition'—what Greimas calls the 'glorifying test'. But at the same time, it represents a narrative form of recognition of the fact that the patriarchal covenant had itself now been fulfilled: God had promised to give the land to Abraham's descendants; the land had now been duly conquered; and the people assemble to recognize that fact. Dare I say that it is pure Hollywood? Those who proposed the Hexateuchal thesis had more narrative sense than most of the directors of Old Testament epics, in taking the story this far, and making this the final scene.[84] Can't you see

81.   Though the range of participants might also reflect the 'additional' covenant on the plains of Moab (Deut. 29.11).

82.   E.g. Blenkinsopp (1983: 82), referring to it simply as a 'covenant ceremony', but almost discarded (for other reasons) in the 1995 edition, at 94.

83.   Wenham (1971: 148), although even he describes it in terms of 'renewal of the covenant at Shechem'.

84.   Watts (1999: 153-54) differs, supporting the pentateuchal view, on the grounds that the Pentateuch as a whole exemplifies his story-list-sanction structure: the history of Israel's origins (Gen. 1–Exod. 19), lists that specify Israel's obligations (Exod. 22–Num. 36), and sanctions that spell out Israel's possible futures (Deut.). He defends himself against an anticipated criticism: 'In contrast to the literary complaint that the narrative plot has not been concluded, the persuasive rhetoric of the Pentateuch suggests that this story never ends. One may certainly supplement it...but whether one continues to the climax of Joshua, or to the nadir of the Exile,

the final credits go up as the people shout their acclamation, and Joshua reiterates Moses' final covenantal act, that act which he could only make at the plains of Moab but which his successor makes there in the promised land, now joyously celebrating the fulfilment of the patriarchal promise?

Well, now that you have seen the film, it's time to read the critics. Let us look at some of the details that contribute to this recognition scene. Already in ch. 23, the first of the two valedictory speeches, Joshua uses the terminology of the charge to him in ch. 1 of not deviating to the right or the left from the book of the law of Moses (Josh. 23.6). The end of that speech is as explicit a recognition of the performance of God's promise as one could imagine:

> You know in your hearts and souls, all of you, that not one thing has failed of all the good things which the LORD your God promised concerning you; all have come to pass for you, not one of them has failed (Josh. 23.14).

But the next cycle of covenantal history is anticipated. Israel is warned not to transgress its own obligations under the existing covenant by committing idolatry, for fear of God's removal of them from the land. In ch. 23, there is no covenant confirmation, recommitment or revision, simply a recognition that God has done his part, and that Israel's continued success depends upon its fulfilment of the existing covenantal relationship. And that, in this chapter, is understood as no more and no less than the ban on idolatry.

The second valedictory ceremony, this time located specifically at Shechem, is more complex. In ch. 24, Joshua's speech commences with his quoting God in *oratio directa*;[85] the account of Israelite history from Terah down to the conquest, in Josh. 24.2-13, is formulated as God's first person account of what he had done.[86] After reporting God's speech, Joshua personally provides the lesson: 'Now therefore fear the

or further still to the reform of Ezra, the essential question of Deuteronomy's sanctions always remains unresolved: will Israel live by this Torah or not?...the Pentateuch's inconclusive plot reinforces its rhetorical strategy of making readers decide its ending by their own actions.'

85. Cf. Moses in Deuteronomy, e.g. Deut. 1.6-8, 35-36; 37-40, 42, etc.

86. It has been noted that in this account, there is no mention of the giving of the law, or of any covenant, at Sinai (Booij 1984: 3). However, there is no mention of the patriarchal covenant either. What we have is a list of God's actions, mainly of a military character.

LORD...put away the gods which your fathers served beyond the River, and in Egypt ...' (Josh. 24.14). He challenges them, however, to 'choose this day whom you will serve' (Josh. 15-16), thus echoing the theme of choice in one of the valedictory addresses of Moses (Deut. 30.19). The people reply that they would not dream of forsaking the LORD for other gods, and in their response they explicitly recognize what God has done for them: 'It is the LORD our God who brought us and our fathers up from the land of Egypt', etc. (Josh. 24.16-18). But Joshua is not satisfied with any pat response. He warns the people that they may not be up to the standards demanded by the LORD; he is a jealous God who will not forgive their transgressions if they do dissent (Josh. 24.19-20). The people respond a second time: 'Nevertheless, we will still serve the LORD' (v. 21).[87] Joshua then calls the people to witness against themselves, and there follows a solemn declaration by the people: 'The LORD our God we will serve, and his voice we will obey' (v. 24). Only then, and most summarily, do we hear of a covenant, and of the giving of law at Shechem (v. 25); and equally of the writing by Joshua of *hadevarim ha'eleh* in *sefer torat elohim*.

There are those who talk of a reading of the law in the context of this covenant at Shechem; even a purported identification of the Covenant Code of Exodus 21–23 with 'the law book read by Joshua during (this) covenant ceremony at Shechem' (Blenkinsopp, *supra* n. 82). But there is no hint whatsoever in this chapter of a reading. It is only by conflating ch. 24 with the proceedings of Mount Ebal in ch. 8 (which Blenkinsopp does) and then further conflating the two with the command of a septennial reading in Deuteronomy 31, that the mythical institution of the covenant renewal ceremony at Shechem is produced.[88] But neither of these traditions regarding a reading make any mention of covenant, nor does the covenant story at Shechem make any reference to a reading. I would suggest that our own reading, taking the story in its temporal sequence, makes quite adequate narrative sense. The *entry* into the promised land is a significant event, but not in itself the fulfilment of the patriarchal covenant. Its significance lies in part in the recognition of Joshua as the successor of Moses, by his fulfilment of

87.   Cf. the double acceptance of the covenant in Exod. 24.3, 7.

88.   Watts (1999: 164) not only adopts the covenant renewal interpretation but sees this as manifesting the 'sanction' part of his story-list-sanction structure for the book: 'Joshua moves from stories of conquest to lists of occupied territory to the promises and threats of Joshua's covenant renewal.'

Moses' last testament, his ad hoc and immediate commands. At the *end* of Joshua's life, there is a need for a different kind of recognition, but this proceeds at two levels. There is the explicit recognition of the fulfilment of the covenant—both the patriarchal promise of the land (Josh. 24.8) and an allusion to the battle-angel promise at Sinai;[89] there is the implicit mutual recognition of the significance of the two leaders, Moses and Joshua, through reiteration of the details of their valedictory scenes: the charge to the people, challenging them to choose; the covenant, the writing, the issuing of non-divinely dictated commands. In fact the *chok umishpat* of Joshua—a phrase associated elsewhere with law-giving[90] not in the context of covenant—seems to demand such an explanation. Why, otherwise, does Joshua, when about to die, start legislating?

---

89.   Josh. 24.12, 'And I sent the hornet before you', cf. Exod. 23.28; more generally: Josh. 23.10, 'One man of you puts to flight a thousand, since it is the LORD your God who fights for you, as he promised you'.

90.   On Exod. 15.25, see §6.2 at p. 153; on Ezra 7.10, see §6.3 at pp. 169-70.

Chapter 10

TALION

10.1 *Introduction*

In the Introduction to this book, talion was put forward as an example
of the kind of debate in comparative legal history that provoked my dis-
satisfaction with contemporary methodology and my quest for new
interdisciplinary models that might provide more soundly based alternatives.[1] In the previous chapters, I have given an account of what that
quest has yielded, with examples of possible applications to biblical
law. I return now to the initial example.[2] Many of the issues raised in
previous chapters find applications to this problem. In fact, talion
proves a good case study for the identification of the semiotic features
of the transition of biblical law from orality to literacy.

10.2 *The Oral Formulae*

We tend to speak of 'an eye for an eye' as '*the* talionic formula'. However, in Deut. 19.16-21, it is combined with another:

1.   Mary Douglas may be thought to have been engaged in a parallel quest.
Whereas I have sought diachronic as well as synchronic models, she has largely
avoided the former and concentrated upon the cognitive features of the final literary
products. Her approach is now applied to talion in Ch. 10 of her innovative and
stimulating *Leviticus as Literature* (1999); some points of difference are noted
below, §§10.5–10.7, and may assist in further sharpening the underlying theoretical
and methodological issues.
2.   Some aspects of the present chapter are more fully explored in Jackson
(1996b; 107-23; 1997: 127-49). My original literary-historical analysis is in Jackson
(1973b: 273-304). I revisit the issue in greater detail in my forthcoming *Wisdom-
Laws*.

> If a malicious witness rises against any man to accuse him of wrong-
> doing, then both parties to the dispute shall appear before the LORD,
> before the priests and the judges who are in office in those days; the
> judges shall inquire diligently, and if the witness is a false witness and
> has accused his brother falsely, then *you shall do to him as he had meant
> to do to his brother*; so you shall purge the evil from the midst of you.
> And the rest shall hear, and fear, and shall never again commit any such
> evil among you. Your eye shall not pity; it shall be *life for life, eye for
> eye, tooth for tooth, hand for hand, foot for foot*.

I have myself previously referred to 'you shall do to him as he had
meant to do to his brother' as 'the talionic *principle*', by contrast with
'the concrete formula' (Jackson 1997a: 134-35). Closer inspection of
the narrative sources, however, reveals that there were *two* oral formulae in circulation. It is possible, moreover, to distinguish their respective usages.

I take first the *tachat* formula. There are good reasons to suppose that
it had an independent, oral existence:[3] its very form (not paralleled in
the ancient Near East[4]) suggests this, with its formulaic repetitions;
each one of the three contexts in which we find it in biblical law fails to

---

3.   Cf. Prévost (1977: 624); Lafont (1994: 117-18). Alt (1989:105) argues that
the formula 'had its own origin, and followed its own peculiar course of development, before it was put into its present position', without specifying whether that
origin was oral or written. On Alt's 'cultic' interpretation of the formula
('Talionsformel'), based on a second-century BC votive inscription (*anima pro
anima, san(guine) pro san(guine), vita pro vita*) from North Africa, see
Schwienhorst-Schönberger (1990: 85-86, 96). Otto (1994:184 and n. 77) sees in this
inscription support for the view that *nefesh tachat nefesh* was originally independent of the talion-formula (as in Exod. 21.24), and did indeed have a cultic origin.
Others (e.g. Prévost 1977) take the whole of Exod. 21.23b-25 to be a single, stereotypical formula, such that vv. 24-25 were incorporated along with v. 23b, even
though only the latter was really relevant.
4.   Jackson (1975a: 103-104; 1997: 143-44). *Aliter* Doron (1969: 26-27), who
argues that while the Laws of Hammurabi do not use a formula where talion is prescribed, 'where compensation is provided, the Code of Hammurabi too, uses a formulaic statement not unlike our formula', quoting LH 263: *alpam kima alpim
immeram kima immerim*. But the latter is part of a grammatically complete apodosis
within a casuistic law, governed by the verb *iriab*, comparable to *shor tachat
hashor* in Exod. 21.35 etc. In Exod. 21.23-24, the formula is similarly integrated
(though in a second person formulation). But it is clear that it circulated without
such grammatical integration. There is nothing in the Hebrew of Deut. 19.21 corresponding to the RSV's 'it shall be'.

provide an adequate explanation of its possible origin;[5] moreover, we find many concrete applications of the idea (expressed in a range of termonology) both in biblical narratives[6] (the theme, for example, of the deceiver deceived, as in the Jacob cycle) and in accounts of divine justice.[7] Indeed, Houtman suggests that talion played a significant role

5.   All three statements of talion in the laws appear to be independent of the context in which they were inserted: cf. Cazelles (1946: 55-56); Phillips (1970: 96-99); Sarna (1991: 126): 'the talion list is a citation from some extra biblical compendium of laws and has been incorporated intact into the Torah'. Loewenstamm (1977: 355-56) noted that even in Deut. 19 the formula itself is almost redundant, and out of context: the punishment for the 'deceitful witness' is stated in Deut. 19.19a: 'You should do to him as he intended to do to his fellow-man.' Much the same argument can be made for Lev. 24.19-20, on which see further §10.5, *infra*. Thus, the law of physical injuries in Leviticus, like that of the malicious witness in Deuteronomy, would be substantively complete without the formula (cf. Jackson 1997: 135).

6.   E.g. Boogaart (1985: 45-56) on Judg. 9 (and see Welch 1990a: 10); Carmichael (1986: 25-27) on aspects of the story of Ahab; Carmichael (1992: 120): 'Judah emerged as the leader among the brothers in disposing of Joseph. As their father later commented sarcastically, he was the wild beast, a lion, that had preyed upon his son Joseph (Gen 49.9). His destiny in turn was to experience the loss of sons. Indeed, he almost destroyed his own children conceived by Tamar. Judah's story is told as part of Joseph's—indeed the Judah–Tamar story is embedded within the Joseph story—because of the narrator's belief in an inexorable law of retribution that requires that wrongdoing be visited with its appropriate penalty'. (On the Judah-Tamar story, see also Nel [1994: 23].) Acceptance of such an interpretation does not require us to accept Carmichael's application of his theory of the narrative inspiration of the laws—here, as alluding to a series of events that were thought to have happened (or at least to have been contemplated) in the case of Tamar: not only burning, but also corpse mutilation (the various injuries in the formula referring not to the absence of death, but to mutilation of a corpse after execution) (Carmichael 1992: 124; 1986: *passim*, esp. 34). Carmichael takes the Tamar story to have inspired also Deut. 25.11-12 and regards the entire paragraph of Exod. 21.22-25 (unified in terms of allusions to this narrative) as a probable Deuteronomic insertion in the book of the Covenant. This is one of the less persuasive of Carmichael's arguments. It is worked out in a fashion such as to deny that the formula had an existence prior to its use (on Carmichael's view) to allude to narrative sources: Carmichael argues (1986: 36) that 'the formula [in Deut. 19.15-21] as such is original to the Deuteronomic law about false testimony. This claim is based on the observation that the detailed concern with what happened to the bodies of Ahab and Jezebel is the primary inspiration for its composition.'

7.   For the earlier literature on this, see Jackson (1975a: 84 n. 58); see also

in interpersonal relationships.[8]

If so, what would the formula have meant as transmitted orally?[9] It is better to ask: How would the formula have been used? The Bible itself is familiar with the idea that self-help preceded institutional dispute resolution[10]—in my view, a far more appropriate focus for any attempt to locate the history of talion within evolutionary schemes than claims for the priority of financial or physical remedies as such. [11] The boast of Lamech (Gen. 4.23-24)—'I have slain a man for wounding me (*lefits'i*), a young man for striking me (*lechavurati*). If Cain is avenged seven-fold, truly Lamech seventy-sevenfold'—whose terminology indeed

Jackson (1996b: 108); cf. Nel (1994: 22). *Aliter*, Koch (1955) discussed by Boogaart (1985: 47-48).

8.   Houtman (1997: 166), citing Gen. 4.23; Exod. 12.29; Judg. 1.6-7; 15.10-11; 1 Sam. 15.33; 1 Kgs 21.19; 2 Kgs 10.24; Ezek. 16.59; Obad. 15-16; Hab. 2.8; Job 2.4; Houtman (2000: 166-67).

9.   Though it is difficult to conclude that, semantically, *ayin tachat ayin* has anything other than its 'literal' meaning, the notion of 'restricted code' itself requires that we take account of what would have been understood as the typical use (the pragmatics) of the formula, as argued *infra*, at pp. 280-81, in relation to *kofer*. Nevertheless, there is still support in the literature for a purely 'literal' meaning: see Alt (1989: 106); Daube (1947: 107-108, 111); Cardascia (1979: 175) (but metaphorical by the time of Deuteronomy); Otto (1994: 184-85) (though impliedly abrogated, he argues, by the redactional technique of being framed by compensatory laws); Crüsemann (1996: 148-49).

10.   Westbrook (1988a: 45-46) describes the stories of Lamech and Samson as 'evidence of psychological history'.

11.   For the earlier debate on substantive evolutionary models, see Diamond. (1957: 151-55; 1971: 98-101, 398-99); Jackson (1975a: 101-102, 104); Prévost (1977: 623); Cardascia (1979: 169-70) (a five-stage model, but with attention given to the impact of increasing institutionalization and the concurrence of talion and compensation in the form of voluntary composition); Frymer-Kensky (1980: 230-34) (following Diamond and Finkelstein in the evolutionary model, but with a dif-fusionist gloss: talion within Mesopotamian law reflects West Semitic influence, following Loewenstamm [1957: 194] and Lambert [1965: 289]); Sarna (1991: 126); Houtman (1997: 166-67). Paul (1970: 75-77), under the influence of the Diamond/Finkelstein evolutionary model, is led to conclude from LH 196, 197, 200 that 'any physical offence against the awelutum would now be much more severely prose-cuted and could not be composed by a mere financial settlement', even while stressing that Hammurabi (unlike biblical law, following Greenberg) does accept composition in cases of homicide (LH 207)! See also the critique of evolutionary models by Westbrook (1988: 41-47), who provides the best account of the matter as a function of institutional development.

reflects (or anticipates?) two of the three terms used in Exod. 21.25,[12] is often cited as an example of unregulated (unlimited) revenge for bodily injury and/or insult (Boecker 1980: 174: Blenkinsopp 1995: 91; Westbrook 1988a: 45-46). Of the pre-monarchic settlement period, we hear the refrain: 'In those days there was no king in Israel; every man did what was right in his own eyes.'[13] The talionic formula may thus be seen as a restriction upon such unlimited revenge as we find in the case of Lamech: only one eye for an eye, etc (Boecker 1980: 174; Blenkinsopp 1995: 91).

This appears to be the point also of the story regarding the captured Canaanite king, 'Adoni-Bezek'—the only biblical source that mentions the actual infliction[14] by human institutions of ('literal') talion for (non-fatal) bodily injuries—even though the talionic formula we find used there is the more general formulation, what I shall call the *ka'asher* formula:

12. This is taken by some to suggest that Exod. 21.25, even if it circulated separately, is also old (see Cazelles 1946: 56; Daube 1947: 147 n. 22). It may well be, however, that the writer is seeking to contrast the illegitimate, excessive boast of Lamech with what is seen as the proper application of the principle of talion, where only a proportionate *petsa* or *chaburah* (and certainly not death) would be permitted. Cf. Schwienhorst-Schönberger (1990: 118-19), arguing that Exod. 22.20-26 contains literary allusions to Exod. 1-3 and that both stem from the editor who integrates the Covenant Code into the Sinai pericope. In Jackson (1975a: 107) I argued for a priestly author of Exod. 21.25. Its terminology is not found in the versions at either Deut. 19.21 or Lev. 24.20. Daube (1947: 113), suggested that the *shever* of Lev. 24.20 may represent the *petsa* and *keviyah* of Exod. 21.25. More likely, I would suggest, is the view that it replaces *yad* and *regel* (cf. *shever regel* and *shever yad* in Lev. 21.19), indicating that talion applies not only for severance of a limb but also the breaking of a bone. Eye, tooth and bone, we may note, are the parts of the body mentioned in the talionic provisions of Hammurabi (LH 196, 197, 200).

13. Judg. 17.6; cf. 21.25 (the concluding verse of the book) and 19.1, the introduction to the story of the Levite and his concubine. Cf. Westbrook (1988a: 46), citing also Samson's excessive revenge on the Philistines for depriving him of his betrothed bride.

14. *Pace* Sprinkle (1993: 242), who suggest that 'it may be more 'poetic justice' than an application of the original, intended meaning of this law'. But though the story does not use the *tachat* formula as it appears in Exod. 21.24, there is (as argued in the text below) a close terminological connection with the '*ka'asher* formula' in Deut. 19 and Lev. 24, both of which also include versions of the *tachat* formula.

[T]hey pursued him, and caught him, and cut off his thumbs and his
great toes. And Adoni-bezek said, 'Seventy kings with their thumbs and
their great toes cut off used to pick up scraps under my table; as I have
done, so God has requited me' (Judg 1.6-7; Jackson 1975a: 83-84).

Although Adoni-Bezek had mutilated 70 kings, punishment—in a form
he is made to attribute to divine justice[15]—is restricted to him. The language attributed to the king (כאשר עשיתי כן שלם לי אלהים[16]) is
comparable to the general, *ka'asher* + *asah l'*, form found in both Deut.
19.19 (ועשיתם לו כאשר זמם לעשות לאחיו) and Lev. 24.19 (באשר
עשה כן יעשה לו). Indeed, the structural similarities here are such as to
make it likely that they are all reflections of an alternative, more general
version of the oral formula. The restriction of the punishment to the
king (rather than inflicting it also on 69 other captured Canaanites) is
also consistent with the ideology of personal responsibility reflected in
Deut. 24.16.[17]

Though primary attention has been directed, hitherto, to the oral origins of the *tachat* formula,[18] it is clear that the more general *ka'asher*
formulation[19] also circulated orally, and indeed was used independently
of the *tachat* formula. In addition to the remark attributed to Adoni-
Bezek, it occurs in the story of Samson, who explains his actions
against the Philistines with the words 'as they have done to me so I did
to them' כאשר עשו לי כן עשיתי להם (Judg. 15.11). Doron has argued,

15. Piattelli (1995: 68) regards this as one of the first cases that 'transferred to
divine justice a punishment of already human application' (see also Jackson 1975a:
84, 102-103).

16. The use of the verb here appears to have been overlooked by Daube (1947:
134-44), even though it provides further support for his general thesis, of 'the part
played by the principle of compensation in that law which, at first sight, belongs as
exclusively as any to the province of criminal law, the law of retaliation' (at 103, cf.
146).

17. Though the latter is expressed in terms of liability for the death penalty, the
punishment of Adoni-Bezek led to his death and was no doubt anticipated to do so.
Daube (1947: Ch. 4) has explored the relationship between different forms of collective responsibility and 'ruler punishment'. There is no need to invoke here
notions of 'vicarious punishment' (which assume that the offender receives no
direct, personal punishment at all).

18. Or formulae: Daube (1947: 129), noting the *b'* variant in Deut. 19, suggests
that 'the law of retaliation existed in several slightly different forms from a very
early time'.

19. Despite its greater generality, I have argued that it, too, should be understood as 'restricted code' (Jackson: 1997: 142).

in support of the view that the (*tachat*) talionic formula refers to compensation, that even the *ka'asher* formula is not to be taken literally, since Samson's 'act of revenge does not correspond exactly to the Philistines' provocation of him by having set his wife and father-in-law on fire'.[20] But this calls for a closer examination of the course of events.[21]

Samson's father-in-law gives his wife to his companion (Judg. 14.20), after Samson had gone back to his own father's house (Judg. 14.19), thus seemingly deserting/divorcing her.[22] Samson takes revenge through the blazing foxes (Judg. 15.4-6), a purely property-oriented response.[23] The Philistines clearly recognize that this act is in response to the loss of his bride (Judg. 15.6). They then burn the bride and her father (Judg. 15.6). Samson swears further revenge for this: '"If this is what you do, I swear I will be avenged upon you, and after that I will quit". And he smote them hip and thigh with great slaughter' (Judg. 15.7-8). The Philistines then attack Lehi, claiming that they want to take Samson prisoner and 'to do to him as he did to us' (לעשות לו כאשר עשה לנו, Judg. 15.10). The Judaites send 3000 men to Samson, to ask him to explain his actions.[24] Samson does so by using the same *ka'asher* formula that the Philistines had used in justifying their own actions: 'And he said to them, "As they did to me, so have I done to them"' (כאשר עשו לי כן עשיתי להם, Judg. 15.11). The reference, in context, is surely to Samson's 'great slaughter' (מכה גדולה) in response (explicitly: 'If this is what you do...', Judg. 15.7) to the killing of his wife and father-in-law (Nel 1994: 26), rather than to his destruction of their fields by the foxes (or, if it is that as well, the latter is in response to the deprivation of his bride—and her 'fruits' [Nel

20. Doron (1969: 25), following Ibn Ezra (cf. Sprinkle 1993: 242).

21. See also Nel (1994: 26), and earlier literature there cited, on talion in the overall structure of the Samson story.

22. As her father claims when Samson later goes back to reclaim her: 'I really thought that you utterly hated her; so I gave her to your companion' (Judg. 14.2).

23. Which some see as based on the metaphor that Samson had himself used when he found out that his wife had revealed the riddle to her people: 'If you had not plowed with my heifer, you would not have found out my riddle' (Judg. 14.18).

24. Their purpose at first appears to be ambivalent. Is it to warn and protect him, as the numbers involved might suggest, or is it to seek an explanation from him and, failing an adequate response, to hand him over, as their comments to him might suggest: 'Do you not know that the Philistines are rulers over us? What then is this that you have done to us?' (Judg. 15.11).

1994: 26, citing Gese 1990]). Clearly, that explanation does not satisfy the Judaites—or, if it does, they fear that it will not satisfy the Philistines—and they carry out their mission to take Samson prisoner and hand him over to the Philistines (Judg. 15.12-13).

The following conclusion may be drawn from the narrative: the *ka'asher* formula implies *qualitatively* equivalent retribution, but there is no concern for *quantitatively* equivalent retribution.[25] Samson's uses of the foxes may have devastated the produce of many Philistine farmers, even though only his own 'produce' had been prejudiced by the removal of his wife; he engages in an (unquantified) 'great slaughter' in response to the killing of his wife and father-in-law; the Philistines, if we may judge by the three thousand men marshalled by the Judaites in response, may wreak unquantified revenge on the town of Lehi if their demand is not met. The same concern for qualitative rather than quantitative equivalence, we may recall, was true of Adoni-Bezek: he applies the *ka'asher* formula, despite the fact that he had mutilated 70 royal victims, while only he is mutilated (but in precisely the same way) in return.[26] It is this opposition between the qualitative and the quantitative which makes the boast of Lamech in Gen. 4.23 so outrageous: 'I have slain a man for [merely] wounding me, a young man for [merely] striking me. If Cain is avenged sevenfold, truly Lamech seventy-sevenfold.' He sees in purely quantitative terms what is in fact a qualitative difference—between non-fatal and fatal injuries.

The *tachat* formula is also found in two narratives. The first is the parable of the guardsman, used to reproach Ahab for not carrying out his obligation to execute the defeated Ben-Hadad. A disguised prophet pretends to be a soldier who has been commanded to guard a prisoner, in the following terms: 'Guard this man! If he is missing it will be your

25. *Aliter*, Nel (1994: 26-27), who describes Samson's subsequent killing of 1000 Philistines with a jawbone as an 'equal military retaliation'. But this only highlights the source of the difficulty: in so far as (this type of) talion derives from vengeance practices against foreigners, retaliation, precisely because it is military, can hardly be exact.

26. And, again like the story of Adoni-Bezek, the principle is *not* regarded as exclusively or peculiarly Israelite: it is attributed (at least at this stage of the story) to the Philistines as well as Samson, using virtually identical terminology. As regards the sequel, however, Nel (1994: 27) maintains that 'the actions of the Philistines were not governed by the same principle and cumulatively led to their destruction'; indeed, that 'the narrator tries to demonstrate with his symbolic story that the Yahwistic judicial order was superior to that of the Philistines'.

life for his life (והיתה נפשך תחת נפשו) or you must weigh out silver.'
The prisoner, however, escapes. Ahab pronounces judgment against the
soldier. The prophet thereupon reveals himself, and turns the judgment,
using precisely the same words, against Ahab: והיתה נפשך תחת נפשו
(1 Kgs 20.39-43). In the second narrative, Jehu, having enticed the Baal
worshippers into the temple of Baal, tells the guards whom he places
outside: 'The man who allows any of those whom I give into your
hands to escape shall forfeit his life' (נפשו תחת נפשו, 2 Kgs 10.24).[27]
Daube has argued that in both these cases the guard's liability to lose
his life is expressed in terms of his liability personally to replace the
escaped prisoner. The latter was doomed to execution, so the guard,
now standing in his stead, is equally doomed to execution.[28]

On the basis of these narratives, we may compare the incidence of the
two formulae. First, it is noticeable that though their 'talionic' effect
may be the same, the fact that in the *tachat* sources it is the offender
who must *personally* replace the lost prisoner has precisely the quantitatively limiting effect that we have seen the *ka'asher* formula to lack.
Second, it is the *ka'asher* sources that deal with the effects of physical
harm (death[29] and mutilation); the *tachat* sources, dealing with escaped

27. Schwienhorst-Schönberger (1990: 100) notes that, by contrast with
Exod. 21.23, we have here a 'Nominalsatz im Rahmen einer Pendenskonstruktion'.
This merely illustrates the flexibility of use of the formula in oral transmission.

28. Daube (1947: 117-21), discussing also the relationship of these sources to a
possible original understanding of *nefesh tachat nefesh* in the law of homicide,
where the offender had to replace the dead victim with *live* members of his own
family, to enter the service of the family of the deceased. That is excluded in the
present context: Jehu's Baal worshippers are 'destined to destruction' from the start
(though the instruction to execute them is given to the guards only later). The parable told to Ahab is slightly different. We would not know, from it alone, that the
prisoner was 'destined to destruction' (Daube's phrase), rather than slavery. If it
were the latter, then *vehayta nafshekha tachat nafsho* could mean (as I have argued
for *nefesh tachat nefesh* in Exod. 21.23 (1975a: 96-98; §10.4 at nn. 52-53, *infra*)
that the guard must take the escapee's place as a slave. What appears to exclude this
interpretation, here, is the fact that the parable is designed to lead to the conclusion
that Ahab, having spared a prisoner who was 'destined to destruction', is thereby
himself doomed to death. Even so, it is not difficult to envisage the phrase being
used of the liability of a guard to take the place of an escaped prisoner (as a slave)
in other circumstances.

29. The death penalty for homicide is sometimes described as an example of
talion (e.g. Marshall [1993: 122] on Exod. 21.12). Although it may be correct, for
analytical and legal historical purposes, to distinguish talion from the regulation of

prisoners, are concerned with (in effect, property) losses:[30] whether the escapees are prisoners of war or prisoners of conscience (the Baal worshippers), they are completely at the disposal of the ruler, to be enslaved or killed at will. Thirdly, the *ka'asher* sources deal with intentional offences, committed in cold blood; in the *tachat* sources, the unfortunate guards are probably no more than negligent. Certainly, there is no suggestion that they must stand in the place of the escapee only if they have deliberately connived at the prisoner's escape.

10.3 *A 'Wisdom-Law'?*

I argued in §3.3 for a concept of 'wisdom-laws' at the beginning of the Israelite legal tradition: a concept of laws based in orally transmitted, sometimes 'arbitrary' rules that can be used for immediate, rough-and-ready dispute resolution, without the need to involve third parties or formal institutions. This may apply not only to the availability of self-help but also to its restrictions. It is not necessary to see any such restrictions as depending upon either institutional proclamation or institutional enforcement: a customary restriction, expressed in the form of the talionic formula, may very well have come first. Moreover, the context of self-executing customary norms[31] is one that, as may be seen

homicide, the Bible clearly associates them, in the use here of the *ka'asher* formula. The juxtaposition of *nefesh tachat nefesh* with *ayin tachat ayin*, etc., in the legal sources is more problematic: Lev. 24.18-20, *nefesh tachat nefesh* does *not* indicate a death penalty for homicide (that is expressed by *mot yumat*); in Deut. 19.21 the form *nefesh b'nefesh* again does not refer to a penalty for an actual death (unless one takes the Sadducean view); and in Exod. 21.23-24, the meaning of *nefesh tachat nefesh* is also problematic.

30. Boecker (1980: 175), and Cardascia (1979: 172-73), in stressing that talion was limited to cases of bodily injury, ignore the narrative sources and are thus led to a simplified account, even though they may be correct in denying that talion had the status of an 'overriding principle' of Old Testament law (Boecker) or a 'general principle of punishment' (Cardascia).

31. Among members of the *same* community. Some view the application of talionic penalties on a collective basis as stemming originally from inter-group relations between nomadic tribes (Boecker 1980: 174) or as a form of self-help between members of different (tribal?) communities who did not share a common local jurisdiction (Otto 1994: 185-86). However this may be, there is no reason to restrict talion from the period of the settlement to 'outsiders' (however defined), though clearly it could apply to them: indeed, the context in Lev. 24 is a dispute between 'an Israelite woman's son, whose father was an Egyptian', who quarrelled

also in the context of homicide, admits of negotiation: if homicide long remained a matter for purely private remedies (pursuit, blood vengeance, ransom,[32] refuge), it is hard to imagine that courts regularly intervened in matters of non-fatal injuries.[33] Josephus, in my view, reflects the original realities (even though he may also have been aware of the parallel in the Roman XII Tables[34]), when he writes:

> He that maimeth a man shall undergo the like, being deprived of that limb whereof he deprived the other, unless indeed the maimed man be willing to accept money; for the law empowers the victim himself to assess the damage that has befallen him and makes this concession, unless he would show himself too severe.[35]

The view that talion should be understood as subject to *kofer* has attracted significant support in modern scholarship.[36]

with 'a man of Israel' (Lev. 24.10, see Jackson 1996b: 118-19).

32. David offered *kofer* to the Gibeonites (2 Sam. 21.3); indeed, in the case of murder such 'ransom' appears to have been banned only at a late stage in the history of biblical law (Num. 35.31-32), and in the case of adultery it does not appear to have been banned in biblical times at all (Prov. 6.32-35, on which see further Ch. 7 n. 35, *supra*). These are all, however, matters of some controversy (see Jackson 1975a: 41-50, 59-62; *Wisdom-Laws*, forthcoming).

33. Cf. Paul (1970: 76), at least as regards Exod. 21.24-25; *aliter*, Boecker (1980: 175): '...talion...was valid only as the official sentence of a properly constituted court'; Otto also associates the introduction of talion with the work of the local courts (1988: 30-31; 1991: 183: cf. Nel 1994: 21-22). We may note that Deut. 19 can hardly be used to argue for court enforcement for talion in general, since the very context of the offence is the judicial process (cf. Jackson 1996b: 110). Westbrook, in my view, seeks too uniform a picture of the ancient Near Eastern (including the biblical) position in so far as he presents the 'dual right—to revenge or ransom' as 'a legal right—that is to say, one enforceable with the aid of the machinery of the legal system' (1988a: 45). According to the biblical sources, even homicide appears to have remained largely a private matter long after the establishment of the monarchy.

34. VIII.2, *Si membrum rup(s)it, ni cum eo pacit, talio esto*, reflecting a similarly early stage in Roman institutional history. We need not go as far as Westbrook (1998: 71; cf. 1988b: 103 on VIII.4) in claiming that the Roman provision actually reflects ancient Near Eastern influence, though the possibility is not excluded.

35. *Ant.* 4.8.35.280; Daube (1956: 256); Jackson (1996b: 109-10). The explanation offered by Josephus presupposes that the dispute is settled privately, rather than before a court (unlike his understanding of Exod. 21.22, which he presents quite separately: *Ant.* 4.278).

36. Cassuto (1967: 276-77); Jackson (1975a: 85, 86); Sprinkle (1993: 238-39;

We may relate this issue to a more traditional debate in biblical scholarship, the relationship between 'law' and 'wisdom' (Jackson 2000b). The origins of the apodictic law have long been argued by some to be located within domestic instruction, and the arguments from speech forms are, in my view, strong (§2.3.1). But domestic instruction on 'law' may also take the form of comment on knowledge communicated in narrative form.

Such narratives may be ordinary social experience, the narratives that provide the cultural context of that social experience, or, indeed, the interaction of the two[37] (the relationship between ordinary social experience and TV drama—even 'soaps'—is the modern counterpart). Storytelling, and even our knowledge of stereotypical social situations, with their narrative structures,[38] are accompanied always by forms of evaluation (§1.1), often tacitly expressed through the very language in which they are told. Sometimes, such evaluations may generate proverbs. Talion is a case in point:

> Do not say, 'I will do to him as he has done to me;
> I will pay the man back for what he has done.'
>
> (Prov. 24.29) אל תאמר אשר עשה לי כן אעשה לו אשיב לאיש כפעלו

We might well be tempted to interpret this simply as a comment upon forms of everyday social interaction. But the language in which it is expressed is the very *ka'asher* formula which we have encountered in the narratives of Adoni-Bezek and Samson. In Adoni-Bezek's case, the narrator has him attribute the principle to divine justice. No such justification is found in Samson's invocation of the principle. As noted above, Samson's invocation of the principle did not satisfy the Judaites. What apparently made Samson's justification problematic was its quantitative rather than its qualitative disproportion—a characteristic of those expression of talion where we find the *ka'asher* rather than the *tachat* formula. It may well be just such unacceptable connotations of this use of the *ka'asher* formula in narrative sources that our proverb is seeking to target. At any rate, the implicit criticism of Samson's action

---

1994: 94); Westbrook (1988a: 45-47, 71-77, 80-81). Also in support of the availability of *kofer* in respect of talion, Houtman (1997: 166) cites 1 Kgs 20.39, but that is a case of compounding a (supposed) *capital* liability by payment of money. However, the *capital* liability is expressed in terms of the formula of Exod. 21.23: נפשך תחת נפשו או כבר בסף תשקול.

37. For a classic exposition of this theme, see Daube (1963).

38. I here use the term in the technical, semiotic sense (§1.1, *supra*).

within the narrative, combined with the explicit criticism in the proverb, may be combined to illustrate the didactic setting and function of 'wisdom-laws', an important element in the internalization necessary for their self-executing character.

10.4 *Semantic and Narrative Readings*

Consider, next, the type of meaning to be attributed to the formulae. When we find them in the narratives, we have the context in which they are to be understood. What about the social context? As in the case of homicide, the nature of the intention with which the blow was struck is not determinative of legal categories: the law does not operate through legal categories at this stage; rather, it focuses upon the social experience of typical situations[39] such as ambush, brawl, the wood-chopping accident. Intention is part and parcel of what makes such situations appear significantly different, but it is not utilized as a necessary condition (an 'element' of a crime) as in the modern, positivist model. The perceived intention of the offender might well influence the moral outrage felt by the victim, and thus his willingness to compromise. Thus, payment of *kofer* is that much more likely in practice the less the moral outrage felt by the victim, just as much as in the case of homicide. Conversely, the greater the moral outrage—whether in terms of the perceived intention of the offender or the gravity of the result of his activity[40]—the more likely that talion will have been demanded.

The situation does not necessarily change, I would argue, as soon as the formula is incorporated into a written text. The phenomenon of 'oral residue' requires us to consider whether the text should be read 'literally' (semantically) or by reference to the typical narratives it evokes (§3.2). Take the *tachat* formula in Exod. 21.24-25:

> eye for eye, tooth for tooth, hand for hand, foot for foot,
> burn for burn, wound for wound, stripe for stripe.

39. This, of course, begs the question: '*whose* social experience'? Different social groups have different foci. Thus, Daube (1947: 110-14) distinguishes the approach to talion by the priestly writer: given the priestly doctrine of atonement for the shedding of blood, retaliation here may well not be restricted to intentional wrongdoing, as, Daube implies, it is in Exodus.

40. E.g. the 70 victims of Adoni-Bezek. In Jackson (1996b: 108) I note that a link is here made between discretionary talion and divine justice.

24 עין תחת עין שן תחת שן יד תחת יד רגל תחת רגל
25 כויה תחת כויה פצע תחת פצע חבורה תחת חבורה

It is partly through the Sermon on the Mount[41] that this provision has been taken as representative of a crude and cruel legalism attributed to Jewish law. Whether Matthew was indeed referring to physical retaliation for loss of a limb has indeed been doubted.[42] Suffice it to say that readers of the New Testament have adopted such a 'literal' reading of it, which makes, *inter alia*, the following assumptions: (a) it applies whatever the circumstances of the injury (deliberate or accidental); (b) it applies whatever the relative bodily conditions of offender and victim; (c) the remedy is mandatory: you have to apply it (see further Jackson 1997).

In what circumstances may talionic punishment be demanded? Are we to take a 'literal' (semantic) view, and say that because the formula does not address the circumstances of the offence, the latter are irrelevant, so that the provision 'applies' whether the injury was inflicted deliberately or accidentally?[43] Or are we to understand it narratively,[44] in terms of the typical image of the infliction of bodily injury, which is a deliberate[45] attack? As we have seen, there is only one mention of the actual *practice* of talion as a measure of human justice (though there the *ka'asher* formula is used): the story of the king Adoni-Bezek. His offence was clearly deliberate. By contrast, the *tachat* formula occurs in narratives where the wrongdoer is acting negligently. Whether talionic punishment could ever have been applied where the injury was caused accidentally is a matter for speculation. If the text is read narratively,

41. 'You have heard that it was said, 'An eye for an eye and a tooth for a tooth.' But I say to you, Do not resist one who is evil. But if any one strikes you on the right cheek, turn to him the other also' Mt. 5.38-39.

42. Daube (1956: 255-59) argues from the antithetical examples Jesus provides that he is arguing not against mutilation for bodily injury but rather against suing for damages for insult.

43. The immediate context of this occurrence of the formula is indeed accidental injury (Exod. 21.22-23). But it is probable that this context is not original: on the interpolation of these verses, see Jackson (1975a: 96-107).

44. Finkelstein (1981: 34-35) wrote that talion should be regarded as a 'paradigm'.

45. Cf. Philo's rendition (*De Specialibus Legibus* 3.195): 'If, then, anyone has maliciously (ἐπιβεβουλευκώς) injured another in the best and lordliest of senses, sight, and is proved to have struck out his eye, he must in his turn suffer he same' (Colson's translation, Loeb edition).

we do not have to assume that it was intended for application way beyond the scope of the typical narrative images it evoked. That would be a matter for debate.

Similar considerations apply to the relative bodily conditions of offender and victim. Arguing that *ayin tachat ayin* refers to compensation rather than bodily retaliation, the Rabbis asked:

> What then will you say where a blind man put out the eye of another man, or where a cripple cut off the hand of another or where a lame person broke the leg of another. How can I carry out in this case [the principle of retaliation of] *'eye for eye'*, seeing that the Torah says, *Ye shall have one manner of law,* implying that the manner of law should be the same in all cases (*B. Qam.* 84a [Soncino translation]; see also Aristotle, *Nik. Eth.* 5.5; Cohn 1973b: 741).

Since the biblical text stated no limitations on the relative bodily conditions of offender and victim, the Rabbis understand that no such limitations can apply. But such a 'literal' application of talion would mean that the eye of the offender must be taken, notwithstanding the fact that he will thereby be rendered completely blind etc., whereas his victim was left half-sighted. Such a conclusion is rejected as self-evidently[46] impossible. The range of the biblical provision cannot however be restricted to exclude such cases (while preserving it for the 'normal' case), in the light of the 'one law' principle. If we cannot modify the range of the principle, we must then seek an alternative meaning for the penalty, one where the blind, crippled or lame offender will suffer no more than the able-bodied offender. *Ayin tachat ayin* must therefore mean compensation rather than retaliation.

This rabbinic argument, we may note, depends upon two aspects of the literary presentation of talion. First, the range of application of the formula is given a 'literal' reading: since no limitations on the relative bodily conditions of offender and victim have been stated, no limitations apply. Secondly, the justification for not making an exception for the atypical (blind, crippled, lame) offender is taken from the literary association (§10.6, *infra*) between the talionic formula as it appears in Lev. 24.20 and the (closely juxtaposed) 'one law' principle (Lev. 24.22), even though the latter is actually used in the biblical text for a quite different purpose: to stress that the law of blasphemy applies

---

46. Unless we take the 'one law' principle to refer to equivalence between offender and victim. But this does not appear to be its function in the talmudic argument.

equally to the *ger,* here the son of an Israelite woman and an Egyptian man. If, by contrast, we ask what would have been the meaning of the talionic formula as transmitted orally, and thus replace a literal by a narrative reading, we can hardly suggest that the image of the typical offender was that of the blind, crippled or lame! The exception to which the Rabbis objected would have been implicit: physical retaliation (subject to the argument below) could be applied to the typical case; it need not be applied to the atypical case, notwithstanding the unqualified range of the words.

The argument thus far might appear to endorse what is generally viewed as a 'literal' approach to the penalty: bodily retaliation rather than monetary compensation. But there is a further issue to be considered: whether such a sanction was mandatory or not. The view that talionic punishment is here presented as mandatory cannot in fact be based upon any notion of literal meaning, since there is no linguistic expression in the text on which it can be based. The Hebrew formula has no verb at all.[47] Without a verb, there is nothing explicit to indicate which modality—prescription or permission—is intended. It is simply the assumption of a (modern, positivist) reader that 'an eye for an eye' means 'you *must* give/take an eye for an eye', rather than 'you *may* give/take an eye for an eye'.[48] In short, the mandatory character of talionic punishment derives from discourse assumptions, not literal meaning. And the particular discourse assumption here made turns out to be unjustified. As argued in §10.3, *kofer* appears always to have been an option.

10.5 *Developmental Aspects*

The self-executing nature of talionic punishment gives way in later sources to institutional regulation. The comparison, however, is not straightforward, since the context of wrongdoing also changes. In Deut. 19.16-21 (quoted in §10.2, *supra*), the very context of the offence is the

47. That is clear in Deut. 19.21 and Lev. 24.20, in the light of which any argument that the formula in Exod. 21.24-25 was originally governed by the verb in the previous verse (ונתתה נפש תחת נפש) is much weakened.

48. In fact, even where (as normal) verbs are present, biblical Hebrew grammar does not have any clear or regular way of distinguishing these modalities. The attribution of the correct modality is a matter of 'restricted' rather than 'elaborated' code'. On this issue in relation to *mot yumat*, see §7.1 n. 24 (end), *supra*.

judicial process. It is noteworthy that here, where the talionic punishment is expressed in the apodosis by the *ka'asher* formula,[49] it is applied to an offence involving a premeditated wrong: the offence of the 'malicious' witness, *ed chamas* (in rabbinic terms: *ed zomem*). The third occurrence of the talionic formula also occurs in an institutional context: the laws commanded by God in the context of resolving the case of the 'blasphemer'. But this case is presented not as a premeditated offence, but rather as one that occurred on the spur of the moment:

> Now an Israelite woman's son, whose father was an Egyptian, went out among the people of Israel; and the Israelite woman's son and a man of Israel quarreled in the camp, and the Israelite woman's son blasphemed the Name, and cursed. And they brought him to Moses. His mother's name was Shelomith, the daughter of Dibri, of the tribe of Dan. And they put him in custody, till the will of the LORD should be declared to them. And the LORD said to Moses, 'Bring out of the camp him who cursed; and let all who heard him lay their hands upon his head, and let all the congregation stone him' (Lev. 24.10-14).

The case itself is resolved by oracular consultation (perhaps because of doubt whether the offence extended to the son of an Egyptian). This is not the only indication of priestly interest. In the homicide laws, it is only when we reach the priestly account that we find regulation of intentional but unpremeditated killing. The earlier sources—Exod. 21.13-14 and Deut. 19.4-5, 11—had confined themselves to an opposition between premeditated killing on the one hand and pure accident on the other. The priestly writer supplies the missing case, in terms that allude to the criteria of the earlier sources (Num. 35.22-25; see further §8.2, *supra*). Daube drew attention (in this very context) to the systematizing tendencies of the priestly lawgivers.[50] Perhaps this may be regarded as part of the 'bureaucratisation' that Mary Douglas observes also in the context of purity:

> The systematisation of sin in Leviticus makes all human creatures unavoidably liable to defilement. Regardless of good intentions defilement in one form or another is going to happen to everyone and any one at any time (1996: 93).

49. The *tachat* formula appears in what might be regarded as a colophon, added to the end of the paragraph, v. 21.

50. Daube (1947: 111-12) on the use of *hikah nefesh* in vv. 17 and 18 of both the killing of a man and the killing of a beast, and noting the priestly capacity for 'comprehensive schemata'.

To this extent, the priestly treatments of both homicide and talion are comparable to the priestly laws of contagion. Nor was such 'bureaucratisation' a matter merely of completion of a system of legal dogmatics. It is in the priestly law that we find the strongest movement away from self-executing laws, not only in the case of premeditated homicide, but also for those entitled to the 'protection' of the city of refuge:

> Moreover you shall accept no ransom for the life of a murderer, who is guilty of death; but he shall be put to death. And you shall accept no ransom for him who has fled to his city of refuge, that he may return to dwell in the land before the death of the high priest (Num. 35.31-32).

As in contagion, the law here 'brings sin within the control of the priests'; the priestly remit, moreover, is extended to cover the whole range of mental states.

To what extent is this institutional development paralleled in terms of (more developed) expression? The principal argument relates to the form in which the talionic formula appears in Leviticus 24, in the context of an elaborate, literary chiasmus (§10.6, below). But there are also other features of the modes of representation of talion in the legal sources which perhaps deserve more attention than they have hitherto received.[51] Jerome Bruner (1966) identified a threefold sequence of forms of representation in the development of the language of children: enactive, ikonic, symbolic. The notion of 'enactive' representation is, in a sense, pre-linguistic (Jackson 1995b: 254-55): the infant senses a need and learns that certain actions regularly serve to fulfil that need. Later, we encounter a second stage, that of 'ikonic representation', characterized by the capacity 'to represent the world to himself by an image or spatial schema that is relatively independent of action' (Bruner 1966: 21). That form of representation is based on visible resemblance. Only later do we encounter 'symbolic' representation, where the means of representation bears no visible relationship to what is represented.

Does this have any application to the modes of expression of talion? In one respect, it does. The formula in Exodus can be divided, for both formal and substantive reasons, into two: 'a life for a life' on the one hand, 'an eye for an eye...etc'. on the other. In fact, the translation 'a life for a life' is an interpretation, the Hebrew (*nefesh tachat nefesh*) being translatable either as 'a person for a person' or (making some

---

51. For a fuller version of the argument in the rest of this section, see Jackson (1997: 139-145).

anachronistic assumptions) 'a soul for a soul'. There is, I have argued, strong evidence both from other biblical sources[52] and the ancient Near East[53] that 'a life for a life' in Exod. 21.23 in fact refers to substitution of persons. Many of the laws of the *Mishpatim* are, as I have argued, 'self-executing' (§§3.2, 10.3). In the context of Exod. 21.22-23 we may assume that any initiatives are taken by the victims themselves, not the State authorities. Perhaps the unusual second person expression in the apodosis of v. 23, 'and *you* shall give', reflects not so much 'pathos',[54] but rather an understandable recommendation that the family of the offender should take the initiative in providing the substitute, and not wait for the distressed woman and her husband to have to come forward and make demands. At any rate, the form of representation could be described as 'enactive': it is through the performance of the action of taking a substitute that the lack is recognized and met. In due course, no doubt, the presence of the substitute in the household of the victim may be seen as an iconic representation of the lost person; ultimately, the situation may be translated into forms of symbolic representation: loss, remedy, rights, compensation.

The version of talion that we find in Deuteronomy stresses the iconic aspect. It uses first the *ka'asher* formula for the punishment of the *ed chamas*, but then reverts to the *tachat* formula. Notice, however, how it introduces the latter: 'Your eye shall not pity; it shall be life for life, eye

---

52. Lev. 24.18 uses the same expression, *nefesh tachat nefesh*, to reiterate the principle of compensation in respect of animals: 'He who kills a beast shall make it good, life for life.' This clearly means that he substitutes a live animal for the one whose death he has caused, not that an animal of the offender is killed in exchange. On the guardsman narratives, see §10.2, *supra*.

53. Jackson (1975a: 97-98), arguing from the similar terminology in MAL §A50. The idea was mooted already by Daube (1947: 116), noting Hittite Laws §§1–4 (which provides for substitution of persons, the number depending on the status of the victim, in cases of homicide resulting from either a quarrel or an accident) but without reference to MAL §A50; cf. Prévost (1977: 624, 626) (suggesting direct literary borrowing); Cardascia (1979: 171-72); Schwienhorst-Schönberger (1990: 84 n. 26); Isser (1990: 32, 44), citing also the use of *nefesh* in Lev. 27. In supporting this view, Weingreen (1976: 5) commented: 'There are many instances in the text of the Hebrew Bible where phrases are used in specific contexts which are not meant to convey their literal meanings but to denote certain implications and these are immediately understood by those to whom the words are directed.' This is very close to Bernstein's conception of 'restricted code' (§3.1, *supra*).

54. As has been suggested by Loewenstamm (1977: 359).

for eye, tooth for tooth, hand for hand, foot for foot' (Deut. 19.21). The offence of the perjurer must be *visually manifest* on his body. No doubt this serves as a punishment for the offender, but the stress is laid upon the effects on the observer. They will continually be reminded of the offence, both of its iniquity and of the consequences of performing it. The immediacy of the visual representation of talion has been powerfully expressed by the semiotician, Roberta Kevelson:

> In the ancient *lex talionis* that which was emphasized was not a compensatory remedy but a representational response to an intended injury, such that the offence in its vivid, imagistic actuality could not be euphemized and that the punishment—the apparent punishment conveyed by a deterrent law—could be seen in the mind's eye and so acutely apprehended that it was, virtually, significantly, experiential (1994: 170).

Yet the Bible, as already observed, embeds two of the three uses of the talionic formula within a more general principle, one couched in terms of symbolic representation. It was as if to say that neither form is sufficient in itself; we need both the emotive immediacy of vision and (what is here presented as) the rational symbolism of abstract principle. Yet it would be wrong, in my view, to impose a strictly 'semantic' reading even upon the *ka'asher* principle: 'then you shall do to him as he had meant to do to his brother' (Deut. 19.19); 'as he has done it shall be done to him' (Lev. 24.19). These should still be viewed as retaining some oral residue of 'restricted code', such that some cases would be regarded as more typical and appropriate for application of the formula than would others.

The biblical texts do not stand in relation to each other in a clear developmental sequence. In particular, one 'stage' does not disappear to make way for the next. All that is here claimed is that there is a developmental sequence in their appearance. Iconic representation is not likely to appear before there has been a stage of enactive; symbolic is not likely to appear before there has been a stage of iconic. But earlier stages may leave traces in later stages.

10.6 *Literary Reiteration*

The talionic principle, as found in narrative, is almost by definition an expression of thematic reiteration: two separate incidents related to each other by a form of reciprocity. We have seen several examples already in sketching the narrative structure of the stories of the covenant.[55] In the patriarchal narratives Jacob is a deceiver (of Isaac) himself deceived (by Laban); the kidnapped Joseph turns, effectively, kidnapper (of Benjamin); his brothers, who put him into a *bor* (Gen. 37.22, 28, 29) are themselves threatened by him with imprisonment in a *bor*.[56] And many other examples could be cited.[57]

Such paired narratives may or may not make use of common language to make their point. Very often, the narrative line is in itself sufficient. We may have little doubt that such manifestations of talion in the narratives derive ultimately from oral storytelling. There is also, however, a literary[58] chiasmus based on talion. After the decision in the case of the blasphemer, God issues a series of commands that appear at first sight quite disparate *inter se* and unconnected with the dispute that prompted the proclamation.[59] That this is not, however, a purely adventitious accumulation of interpolations is shown by the chiastic structure of the passage.[60]

A1	13	And the LORD said to Moses,
B1	14	'Bring out of the camp him who cursed; and let all who heard him lay their hands upon his head, and let all the congregation stone him.
C1	15	And say to the people of Israel, Whoever curses his God shall bear his sin.
D1	16	He who blasphemes the name of the LORD shall be put to death; all the congregation shall stone him; the sojourner as well as the native, when he blasphemes the Name, shall be put to death.
E1	17	He who kills a man shall be put to death.
F1	18	He who kills a beast shall make it good, life for life.

55. E.g. Abraham as tester and tested (§9.2, *supra*).

56. Gen. 42.16, though ultimately only Shimon suffers this fate (Gen. 42.18, 24); the Egyptian dungeon where Joseph was himself imprisoned is itself described as a *bor* (Gen. 41.14).

57. See, e.g., the literature cited in n. 6, *supra*.

58. Chiasmus does not appear to have been confined, however, to the purely 'literary' sphere: there is a remarkable example of its use in one of the legal practice documents from Elephantine, Cowley 13 (see Porten 1981b: 172; Jackson 1992b: 90).

59. On the relationship between dispute resolution and laws proclaimed in that context, see §2.3.2, *supra*.

60. Cf. Welch (1990a: 7-9), citing Thomas Boys, 1825, as having first identified (the major part of) this structure.

G1	19	When a man causes a disfigurement in his neighbour, as he has done it shall be done to him,
H	20	fracture for fracture, eye for eye, tooth for tooth;
G2		as he has disfigured a man, he shall be disfigured.
F2	21	He who kills a beast shall make it good;
E2		and he who kills a man shall be put to death.
D2	22	You shall have one law for the sojourner and for the native; for I am the LORD your God.'
C2	23	So Moses spoke to the people of Israel;
B2		and they brought him who had cursed out of the camp, and stoned him with stones.
A2		Thus the people of Israel did as the LORD commanded Moses.

Chiasmus, it has been suggested, is 'a practice not uncommon when quoting, or adverting to, well-known established texts'.[61] This passage is closely connected, thematically, to the first section of the Covenant Code. Many of the individual topics are common, as indeed may be the common underlying theme: that of the possible forms and legal consequences of quarrels. It is this, we may recall, which provides the narrative setting of the case of the blasphemer, which commences:

> Now an Israelite woman's son, whose father was an Egyptian, went out among the people of Israel; and the Israelite woman's son and a man of Israel quarreled in the camp (Lev. 24.10).

The term 'quarreled' (*vayintsu*) is the same as that which provides the narrative setting in the *Mishpatim* for the case of the pregnant woman (Exod. 21.22), the context of the talionic formula which is at the centre of the present chiasmus. Indeed, this explains why a seemingly unconnected series of norms is promulgated in the wake of the decision on the blasphemer: in narrative (if not in semantic, or conceptual) terms quarrels are apt to lead to cursing and blasphemy (vv. 14, 16), and all sorts of injuries, including fatal injuries to human (v. 17) and animal (v. 18) bystanders, and non-fatal injuries (vv. 19-20). The thematic parallels with the Covenant Code are close. There too we find the regulation of cursing (Exod. 22.28, in addition to the Decalogue ban on misuse of the divine name), concern for the legal position of strangers (Exod. 22.21; 23.9), homicide (Exod. 21.12-14), both fatal and non-fatal injuries arising from a quarrel (Exod. 21.18-19, 22-25), and fatal injuries to animals (Exod. 21.33-36). And of course, the talionic formula—the centre of the Levitical chiasmus—is the closest *verbal*

61. Weinfeld (1990: 12), citing Zeidel. I have not had access to the latter.

parallel to the Covenant Code. In short, the Levitical passage gains immensely in coherence if we view it as a literary reworking of themes from the Covenant Code.

Mary Douglas has recently offered a different explanation (1999: 205-208, 211-15). She too sees talion as central to the passage, and seeks to interpret the punishment of the blasphemer as an application of it. She concedes the difficulty in doing so in practical terms, and proposes instead that the talionic principle here resides in the form of expression (a semiotic talion, we might say): the blasphemer, in one notice, 'hurled' (*nakav*) insults at God, and so stones are hurled at him. There is also a play on words ('a grim playfulness') in the names of the maternal family of the blasphemer: Shelomit (suggesting retribution), Dibri (suggesting lawsuit), Dan (suggesting judgment). Citing similar punning in the stories of Pinchas and Susanna,[62] she observes: 'The victims of injury find something peculiarity gratifying in the malefactor being requited poetically as well as practically' (Douglas 1999: 215). She anticipates some scepticism on this:

> It is probably right this linguistic level of retaliation should sound unconvincing to the lawyers. It really belongs in the context of oracles, on which information is short. One can suppose that the speech of an oracle should not be in the same register as everyday speech; it is oxymoronic, its enigmatic sayings enhance the impression of tapping into deep resources or wisdom (Douglas 1999: 215).[63]

It is true that the use of the verb *nakav* is attributed to God's oracular reply to Moses (Lev. 24.16), but the rest of that speech of the oracle is indeed 'in the same register as everyday speech'. Suppose, however, that we accept Douglas's argument. What purpose is the oracle seeking

---

62. She argues for a similar phenomenon in the story of the punishment meted out by Pinchas in Num. 25.1-5 (Douglas 1999: 208-11) and compares the explicit punning on the names of the trees in the story of Susannah: 'Daniel's judgement, which makes a verbal matching of crime and penalty, illustrates the law of retaliation in Leviticus' (214-15).

63. But even granting that, I am not sure that the comparison she makes to the speech of Daniel ('His verbal wit contributed to Daniel's reputation as a brilliant judge' [215]) is apt. Daniel is certainly presented as inspired, but he does not function as an 'oracle' (notwithstanding the lawyers' attempt to appropriate that form of authority in the expression 'the oracles of the law': see the book of John Dawson of that title [1968]): he speaks in public, and his rhetoric is one of humiliation. See also §2.2, pp. 53-55.

to achieve? She suggests that the narrative is here being used in a subtle fashion as a form of softening or even criticism of the earlier principle (which she understands as crude and literal):

> This reading suggests that Leviticus 24 is less vengeful and angry than Exodus 21 and Deuteronomy 19. Is it possible that the Leviticus writer is taking a different line on the enigma of divine justice and compassion? He is more of a visionary and poet than a lawgiver, he does not deserve to share in the odium that attaches to the law of talion as a primitive and violent system. By quoting it in a jingly form, in a peculiar circumstance where its fit is not clear at all, surrounded with funny names, where it only makes sense as a play upon words, he may be trying to say something else about the measure-for-measure principle. Leviticus is possibly making an opening here for the complex view of retribution celebrated in the Book of Job. What is being tested is the universal validity of the principle of retribution (Douglas 1999: 212).[64]

Indeed:

> This study argues against taking the story of the blasphemer punished by stoning too legalistically. It is not teaching the letter of the law but making a literary comment on the letter of the law (Douglas 1999: 214).

I have no conceptual quarrel with the argument either that oracles may be expected to operate in a different 'register' to that of everyday speech or even that the author of Leviticus is a visionary and poet as well as a lawgiver. Douglas's argument, however, unfortunately resurrects the old stereotypes of biblical law in general and talion in particular, in the very act of claiming that the priestly writer seeks to oppose them. Part of the argument of this chapter has been that we can get, historically, behind 'the letter of the law', to the oral origins of the formula, and its use in a context of weak institutionalization, one where talion was not mandatory but rather an option which would normally be negotiated away by *kofer*.[65] At the same time, the writer undoubtedly

---

64. Douglas (1999: 212). Cf. at 213: 'Surely the idea of exact repayment for injury is against the spirit of Torah, which enjoins forgiveness and compassion', and Douglas (1996: 86), where she takes support for this from Drai (1991).

65. Sadly, the same has to be said in reply to those who regard talion as a concrete norm motivated by the desire for equality between all possible defendants (e.g. Paul 1970: 76; Childs 1974: 471). Indeed, Crüsemann (1996: 161-63) identifies a precise social context for talion, as part of an eighth-century campaign for social justice. These arguments, however, fail once it is realized that the alternative to a compensation tariff (such as is found in some ancient Near Eastern

deploys sophisticated literary means to convey his message. I would suggest that the chiasmus noted above has stronger claims than Douglas's punning. The latter technique, in my view, is more likely to belong to an earlier oral stratum of storytelling. The priestly writers may not have been a lawyers, but they were (often deadly) serious.

10.7 *Talion as a 'Principle'*

In fact, Douglas tries to have it both ways. Despite the jokiness, there is a serious purpose: talion is held out as the justification of the punishment of the blasphemer, but the principle is now a covenantal one, encompassing good for good as well as harm for harm (Douglas 1996: 87; 1999: 205, 216), and stressing its compensatory as well as retaliatory character. As regards the blasphemer:

> God's words from the oracle, 24.17-23, explain that the particular case demonstrates the general principle of equivalence, that is the basic principle on which the curser of the living God must be cursed to death (Douglas 1999: 208).

One may agree that talion is presented in Lev. 24 as a 'general principle of equivalence', but on different grounds: talion occurs at the centre point of the chiasmus—a literary means of signalling its importance—but the chiasmus is based upon a collection of rules from Exodus (where talion is also found). The priestly writer is thus seeking to integrate under a common principle a series of rules stated separately in the *Mishpatim*. The compensatory element was there from the beginning (see esp. Daube 1947: Ch. 3). But that beginning is oral, contextual, pragmatic.

The talionic formula should not be regarded, from the beginning, as the manifestation of an abstract principle of equivalence.[66] Such a

---

sources) is not simple bodily retaliation but retaliation subject to the possibility of negotiated *kofer*. Under this system, the rich still have the advantage of buying themselves out of trouble: they can make the victim an offer he cannot afford to refuse.

66. *Pace* some commentators on its occurrence in the *Mishpatim*, e.g. Sarna (1991:126): 'the list is actually a general statement of legal policy that formulates the abstract principle of equivalence and restitution in concrete terms'; Sprinkle, (1993: 242; 1994: 92 ['expressing a general principle in a poetic/proverbial manner'], 94 ['the principle of proportionality: the punishment should be proportional with the damages caused by the offence', though he accepts that the practice was

principle is quite out of place within the cognitive structures of the *Mishpatim*. When biblical law wishes to express the talionic principle in more general terms, it had the concrete[67] *ka'asher* formula with which to do so. As in the argument regarding 'Postulates' (§7.1), we must not impose upon biblical law the cognitive levels and discursive styles of the post-Renaissance West. There are, of course, devices found within the Bible for the communication of general, underlying principles and values. Such devices, as I have argued (§§7.2–7.3, *supra*), utilize literary relationships rather than inference from the particular to the general or from the concrete to the abstract. Talion provides a further example (§10.6).

It would, indeed, be possible to accommodate the interpretation of Douglas's view of talion in Leviticus as a reaction against a 'legalistic', 'letter of the law' conception, but only on the basis that the process of transformation from orality to literacy had already produced the target at which she sees Leviticus as aiming. In fact, there is no evidence of that target (unless, indeed, we so characterize its operation as a principle of divine justice), until we get to postbiblical times. And even there, the picture is mixed. Can we even be certain that the target of the Rabbinic reinterpretation was mandatory literal retaliation, rather than an entitlement to such with the additional option of acceptance of *kofer*?

The analysis here suggested assists us in understanding the historical development of the talion text in Exod. 21.22-25. There, it is widely regarded as an addition to the original text, fitting ill with the circumstances of the accidental injury to the pregnant bypasser (Jackson 1975a: 78):[68] the formula of vv. 24-25 is placed there, as we have seen, quite out of context (see n. 5, *supra*). At best, we might argue, it is attracted by the *tachat* formula at the end of v. 23 (*nefesh tachat nefesh*). Its very decontextualization is a form of abstraction, despite the concrete imagery in which it is expressed. The 'eye' here functions neither as the eye which sees the talionic punishment (Deut. 19.21), nor

talion subject to *kofer*]).

67. Cf. Douglas (1999: 216): 'The sense is that the priestly writer is in the habit of using the logic of the concrete'.

68. In my forthcoming *Wisdom-Laws*, I argue that even Exod. 21.22-23 does not belong originally to the *Mishpatim*, being a 'secondary' type of problem, unlike the rest of the *Mishpatim*'s rules. The present argument, however, does not depend upon this.

as the absent eye taken in retaliation. It now functions as part of a formula: whatever damage has been suffered, you are entitled to seek comparable damage in return. It presupposes the form of symbolic representation found in both Deut. 19.19 and Lev. 24.19. Indeed, vv. 24-25 may be taken, in another sense, to represent the culmination of the scribal tradition of talion. They collect together not only the four parts of the body listed in Deut. 19.24, but also that different form of representation found in Lev. 24.20: 'fracture for fracture' (*shever tachat shever*).[69] Here the emphasis shifts from a distinct part of the body to the form of injury suffered by a range of possible limbs. The term *shever* is not repeated in Exod. 21.25, but the form of representation is: burn,[70] wound, stripe (or bruise). This represents not simply a change from the location of the injury (its material place, susceptible to indexical representation) to the diagnosis of a generic condition; we may well view the burn, wound or stripe as nominalizations, only barely suppressing the iconicity of the act of burning, the act of wounding, the act of bruising. The identification of the priestly writer as the source of this further symbolization is supported by Lev. 24, where the argument is presented in chiastic form (§10.6).

69. I argued in Jackson (1975: 106-107) for a two-stage interpolation.

70. There may well be narrative allusions in all three items: with 'burn for burn', cf. the fate of Nadav and Abihu (Lev. 9.24; 10.1-2), as discussed by Douglas (1999: 200-202). The other two items share terminology with Lamech's boast, Gen. 4.23-24 (§10.2, *supra*).

BIBLIOGRAPHY

Alt, A.
    1989   'The Origins of Israelite Law', in *Essays on Old Testament History and Religion* (repr.; Sheffield: JSOT Press; Oxford: Basil Blackwell [1966]): 81-132.

André-Vincent, Ph.
    1974   'Le langage du droit dans la Bible', *Archives de philosophie du droit* 19: 89-102.

Austin, J.L.
    1975   *How to Do Things with Words* (Oxford: Oxford University Press, 2nd edn [1962]).

Barkun, M.
    1968   *Law without Sanctions* (New Haven: Yale University Press).

Barr, J.
    1961   *The Semantics of Biblical Language* (Oxford: Oxford University Press, 1961).

Bartlett, F.C.
    1932   *Remembering: A Study in Experimental and Social Psychology* (Cambridge: Cambridge University Press).

Beard, R.M.
    1969   *An Outline of Piaget's Developmental Psychology* (London: Routledge & Kegan Paul).

Ben-Barak, Z.
    1980   'Inheritance by Daughters in the Ancient Near East', *JSS* 25: 22-33.

Bernstein, B.
    1971   *Class, Codes and Control* (3 vols.; London: Routledge & Kegan Paul).

Bisharat, G.
    1989   *Palestinian Lawyers and Israeli Rule: Law and Disorder in the West Bank* (Austin: University of Texas Press).

Bix, B.
    1995   *Law, Language and Legal Determinacy* (Oxford: Clarendon Press).

Blakemore, D.
    1992   *Understanding Utterances: An Introduction to Pragmatics* (Oxford: Basil Blackwell).

Blenkinsopp, J.
    1976   'The Structure of P', *CBQ* 38: 275-92.
    1995   *Wisdom and Law in the Old Testament* (Oxford: Oxford University Press, rev. edn [1983]).

Boden, M.A.
  1979   *Piaget* (Brighton: Harvester Press).
Boecker, H.J.
  1980   *Law and the Administration of Justice in the Old Testament and Ancient East* (trans. J. Moiser; London: SPCK).
Boogaart, T.A.
  1985   'Stone for Stone: Retribution in the Story of Abimelech and Shechem', *JSOT* 32: 45-56.
Booij, Th.
  1984   'Mountain and Theophany in the Sinai Narrative', *Biblica* 65: 1-26.
Bourcier, D.
  1978   'Le procès des narrations: Notes sur le système narratif du droit', *La narration nouvelle* (March): 135-49.
Boyer, G.
  1965   *Mélanges d'histoire du droit oriental* (Paris: Sirey).
Brin, G.
  1994   *Studies in Biblical Law* (Sheffield: Sheffield Academic Press).
Brown, R.
  1958   'Is the Child's Thinking Concrete or Abstract?', *Psychological Review* 65: 18-21.
Bruner, J.
  1990   *Acts of Meaning* (Harvard: Harvard University Press).
Bruner, J.S.
  1964   'The Course of Cognitive Growth', *American Psychologist* 19: 1-15.
  1974   *Beyond the Information Given* (London: George Allen & Unwin).
Bruner, J.S., R.R. Olver and P.M. Greenfield
  1966   *Studies in Cognitive Growth* (New York: John Wiley & Sons).
Buckland, W.W. and P. Stein
  1963   *A Text-Book of Roman Law from Augustus to Justinian* (Cambridge: Cambridge University Press).
Burkes, S.
  1999   'Wisdom and Law: Choosing Life in Ben Sira and Baruch', *JSJ* 30: 253-76.
Buss, M.
  1977   'The Distinction between Civil and Criminal Law in Ancient Israel', *Proceedings of the 6th World Congress of Jewish Studies* (Jerusalem: World Union of Jewish Studies): I, 51-62.
Carasik, M.
  1999   'To See a Sound: A Deuteronomic Rereading of Exodus 20:15', *Prooftexts* 19: 257-65.
Cardascia, G.
  1979   'La place du talion dans l'histoire du droit pénal à la lumière des droits du Proche-Orient ancien', in *Mélanges offerts à Jean Dauvilliers* (Toulouse: Université des sciences sociales de Toulouse): 169-83.
Cardellini, I.
  1981   *Die biblischen 'Sklaven'-Gesetze im Lichte des keilschriftlichen Sklavenrechts* (Bonn: Königstein/Taunus).

Carmichael, C.M.
    1972   'A Singular Method of Codification of Law in the Mishpatim', *ZAW* 84: 19-25.
    1974   *The Laws of Deuteronomy* (Ithaca: Cornell University Press).
    1979   *Women, Law, and the Genesis Traditions* (Edinburgh: Edinburgh University Press).
    1985   *Law and Narrative in the Bible: The Evidence of the Deuteronomic Laws and the Decalogue* (Ithaca: Cornell University Press).
    1986   'Biblical Laws of Talion' (Oxford: Oxford Centre for Postgraduate Studies): 21-39 (published together with D. Daube, 'Witnesses in Bible and Talmud').
    1992   *The Origins of Biblical Law: The Decalogues and the Book of the Covenant* (Ithaca: Cornell University Press).
    1994   'Laws of Leviticus 19', HTR 87.3: 239-56.
Cassuto, U.
    1967   *A Commentary on the Book of Exodus* (trans. I. Abrahams; Jerusalem: Magnes Press).
Cazelles, H.
    1946   *Etudes sur le Code de l'Alliance* (Paris: Letouzey & Ané).
    1986   'משה', *ThWAT* V: 28-46.
Chavel, S.
    1997   "Let my People go!' Emancipation, Revelation, and Scribal Activity in Jeremiah 34.8-14', *JSOT* 76: 71-95.
Childs, B.S.
    1974   *Exodus: A Commentary* (London: SCM Press).
    1979   *An Introduction to the Old Testament as Scripture* (London: SCM Press).
Chirichigno, G.C.
    1993   *Debt-Slavery in Israel and the Ancient Near East* (Sheffield: JSOT Press).
Chomsky, N.
    1980   *Rules and Representations* (Oxford: Basil Blackwell).
Cohn, H.H.
    1973a   'Homicide', *Encyclopedia Judaica* (Jerusalem: Keter): VIII, 944-46.
    1973b   'Talion', *Encyclopedia Judaica* (Jerusalem: Keter): XV, 741.
Crenshaw, J.L.
    1995   *Urgent Advice and Probing Questions: Collected Writings on Old Testament Wisdom* (Macon, GA: Mercer University Press).
Crüsemann, F.
    1996   *The Torah: Theology and Social History of Old Testament Law* (Edinburgh: T. & T. Clark).
Crystal, D. and D. Davey
    1969   *Investigating English Style* (London: Longman).
Daube, D.
    1936   'On the Third Chapter of the *Lex Aquilia*', *Law Quarterly Review* 52: 253-68.
    1941   'Codes and Codas in the Pentateuch', *Juridical Review* 53: 242-61.
    1944   'Some Forms of Old Testament Legislation', *Proceedings of the Oxford Society of Historical Theology*: 36-46.

| 1946 | 'Two Early Patterns of Manumission', *Journal of Roman Studies* 36: 56-75. |

1947   *Studies in Biblical Law* (Cambridge: Cambridge University Press, repr. New York: Arno Press, 1969).

1951   'Negligence in the Early Talmudic Law of Contract (Peshi'ah)' (Festschrift Fritz Shulz; Weimar: H. Bohlaus Nachfolger): 124-47 (reprinted in C.M. Carmichael [ed.], *Collected Works of David Daube*. I. *Talmudic Law* [University of California at Berkeley: Robbins Collection, 1992]: 305-32).

1953   *The New Testament and Rabbinic Judaism* (London: Athlone Press, repr. New York: Arno Press, 1973).

1961   'Direct and Indirect Causation in Biblical Law', *VT* 11: 249-69.

1963   *The Exodus Pattern in the Bible* (London: Faber & Faber).

1969   *Roman Law, Linguistic, Social and Philosophical Aspects* (Edinburgh: Edinburgh University Press).

1973   'The Self-Understood in Legal History', *The Juridical Review* (NS) 18: 126-35.

1981   *Ancient Jewish Law: Three Inaugural Lectures* (Leiden: E.J. Brill).

Dawson, J.P.

1968   *The Oracles of the Law* (Ann Arbor: University of Michigan Law School).

de Vaux, R.

1965   *Ancient Israel: Its Life and Institutions* (trans. J. McHugh; London: Darton, Longman & Todd, 2nd edn).

Diamond, A.S.

1957   'An Eye for an Eye', *Iraq* 19: 151-55.

1971   *Primitive Law, Past and Present* (London: Methuen).

Dillard, R.B.

1987   *2 Chronicles* (Waco, TX: Word Books).

Donaldson, M.

1992   *Human Minds* (London: Allen Lane).

Doron, P.

1969   'A New Look at an Old Lex', *JANESCU* 1.2: 21-27.

Douglas, M.

1975   *Implicit Meanings* (London: Routledge & Kegan Paul).

1993   *In the Wilderness: The Doctrine of Defilement in the Book of Numbers* (Sheffield: JSOT Press).

1996   'Sacred Contagion', in J.F.A. Sawyer (ed.), *Reading Leviticus: A Conversation with Mary Douglas* (Sheffield: Sheffield Academic Press): 86-106.

1999   *Leviticus as Literature* (Oxford: Oxford University Press).

Douzinas, C., R. Warrington and S. McVeigh

1991   *Postmodern Jurisprudence* (London: Routledge & Kegan Paul).

Dozeman, T.B.

1989   *God on the Mountain: A Study of Redaction, Theology and Canon in Exodus 19–24* (Atlanta: Scholars Press).

Drai, R.,

1991   *Le mythe de la loi du talion* (Aix-en-Provence: Alinea).

Driver, G.R. and J.C. Miles
    1952, 1955   *The Babylonian Laws* (2 vols.; Oxford: Clarendon Press).
Driver, S.R.
    1911   *Exodus* (Cambridge: Cambridge University Press).
Duverger, M.
    1971   *Constitutions et documents juridiques* (Paris: PUF, 6th edn).
Dworkin, R.
    1978   *Taking Rights Seriously* (London: Duckworth).
Falk, Z.W.
    1964   *Hebrew Law in Biblical Times* (Jerusalem: Wahrmann Books).
    1967   'Hebrew Legal Terms: II', *JSS* 12: 241-44.
    1978   'Addenda to "Hebrew Law in Biblical Times" ', *Diné Israel* 8: 33-48.
Fensham, F.C.
    1962   'Widow, Orphan and the Poor in Ancient Near Eastern Legal and Wisdom Literature', *JNES* 21: 129-39.
Fernandez, J., I. Karp and C.S. Bird (eds.)
    1980   *Explorations in African Systems of Thought* (Bloomington: Indiana University Press).
Figulla, H.H.
    1951   'Lawsuit Concerning a Sacrilegious Theft at Erech', *Iraq* 13: 95-101.
Finkelstein, J.J.
    1961   'Ammisaduqa's Edict and the Babylonian "Law Codes"', *JCS* 15: 91-104.
    1973   'The Goring Ox: Some Historical Perspectives on Deodands, Forfeitures, Wrongful Death and the Western Notion of Sovereignty', *Temple Law Quarterly* 46: 169-290.
    1981   'The Ox That Gored', *Transactions of the American Philosophical Society* 72.2: 1-89.
Fishbane, M.
    1985   *Biblical Interpretation in Ancient Israel* (Oxford: Clarendon Press).
Fitzpatrick-McKinley, A.
    1999   *The Transformation of Torah from Scribal Advice to Law* (Sheffield: Sheffield Academic Press).
Fletcher, G.
    1976   'The Metamorphosis of Larceny', *Harvard Law Review* 89: 469-530.
    1978   *Rethinking Criminal Law* (Boston: Little, Brown).
Fokkelman, J.
    1991   *Narrative Art in Genesis* (Assen: Van Gorcum, 1975; Sheffield: JSOT Press, 2nd edn).
Francis, H.
    1975   *Language in Childhood* (London: Paul Elek).
Freeman, M.D.A.
    1994   *Lloyd's Introduction to Jurisprudence* (London: Stevens, 6th edn).
Frei, P.
    1984   'Zentralgewalt und Lokalautonomie im Achämenidenreich', in P. Frei and K. Koch (eds.), *Rechtsidee und Reichsorganisation im Persererreich = Orbis Biblicus et Orientalis* 55: 7-43.

Frick, F.S.
1985   *The Formation of the State in Ancient Israel* (Sheffield: Almond Press).
Frijda, N.H.
1986   *The Emotions* (Cambridge: Cambridge University Press).
Frymer-Kensky, T.
1980   'Tit for Tat: The Principle of Equal Retribution in Near Eastern and Biblical Law', *BA* 43: 230-234.
Fuller, R.
1982   'The Story as the Engram: Is it Fundamental to Thinking?', *Journal of Mind and Behavior* 3: 127-42.
Gemser, B.
1953   'The Importance of the Motive Clause in Old Testament Law', *SVT* 1: 50-66.
Gergen, K.J. and M.M. Gergen
1986   'Narrative Form and the Construction of Psychological Science', in T.R. Sarbin (ed.), *Narrative Psychology: The Storied Nature of Human Conduct* (New York: Praeger): 22-44.
Gerstenberger, E.
1965   *Wesen und Herkunft des 'apodiktischen Rechts'* (Neukirchen–Vluyn: Neukirchener Verlag).
Gese, H.
1990   'Die altere Simsonüberlieferung (Richter c. 14-15)', in *idem, Alttestamentliche Studien* (Tübingen: J.C.B. Mohr): 52-71.
Gilligan, C.
1982   *In a Different Voice* (Cambridge, MA: Harvard University Press).
Gilmer, H.W.
1975   *The If-You Form in Israelite Law* (Missoula, MT: Scholars Press).
Ginsburg, H. and S. Opper
1969   *Piaget's Theory of Intellectual Development: An Introduction* (Englewood Cliffs, NJ: Prentice-Hall).
Goody, J.
1977   *The Domestication of the Savage Mind* (Cambridge: Cambridge University Press).
1986   *The Logic of Writing and the Organization of Society* (Cambridge: Cambridge University Press).
1987   *The Interface between the Written and the Oral* (Cambridge: Cambridge University Press).
Graycar, R. and J. Morgan
1990   *The Hidden Gender of Law* (Leichhardt, NSW: Federation Press).
Greenberg, M.
1959   'The Biblical Conception of Asylum', *JBL* 78: 125-32.
1960   'Some Postulates of Biblical Criminal Law', in M. Haran (ed.), *Yehezkel Kaufman Jubilee Volume* (Jerusalem: Magnes Press, 1960): 5-28 (reprinted in his *Studies in the Bible and Jewish Thought* [Philadelphia: The Jewish Publication Society, 1995]: 25-41).
1962   'Crimes and Punishments', in *IDB*: I, pp. 733-44.
1986   'More Reflections on Biblical Criminal Law', in S. Japhet (ed.), *Studies in Bible* (Scripta Hierosolymitana, 31; Jerusalem: Magnes Press): 1-17.

1990   'Reply to the Comments of John Welch', in E.B. Firmage, B.G. Weiss
        and J.W. Welch (eds.), *Religion and Law: Biblical-Judaic and Islamic
        Perspectives* (Winona Lake: Eisenbrauns): 120-25.

1995   'Three Conceptions of the Torah in Hebrew Scriptures', in *idem, Studies
        in the Bible and Jewish Thought* (Philadelphia: Jewish Publication Soci-
        ety): 11-24 (reprinted from 1990 Rendtorff Festschrift).

Greengus, S.
1994   'Some Issues Relating to the Comparability of Laws and the Coherence
        of the Legal Tradition', in B.M. Levinson (ed.), *Theory and Method in
        Biblical and Cuneiform Law* (Sheffield: Sheffield Academic Press): 60-87.

Greimas, A.J.
1982   *Semiotics and Language: An Analytical Dictionary* (trans. L. Crist *et al.*;
        Bloomington: Indiana University Press).
1989   'On Meaning', *New Literary History* 20: 539-50.

Greimas, A.J. and E. Landowski
1976   'Analyse sémiotique d'un discours juridique', in A.J. Greimas, *Sémio-
        tique et sciences sociales* (Paris: Editions du Seuil): 79-128 (now trans-
        lated in *The Social Sciences: A Semiotic View* [trans. P.J. Perron and F.H.
        Collins; Minneapolis: University of Minnesota Press, 1990]: 102-38 [=
        Narrative Semiotics and Cognitive Discourses (London: Pinter, 1990)]).

Gruber, H.E. and J.J. Vonèche
1977   *The Essential Piaget* (London: Routledge & Kegan Paul).

Grunfeld, I.
1987   *The Jewish Law of Inheritance* (Oak Park, MI: Targum Press).

Gudjonsson, G.
1992   *The Psychology of Interrogations, Confessions and Testimony* (New
        York: John Wiley & Sons).

Gulliver, P.H.
1969   'Dispute Settlement Without Courts', in L. Nader (ed.), *Law in Culture
        and Society* (Chicago: Halbe): 24-68.

Gunneweg, A.H.J.
1985   *Esra* (*KAT* 19.i; Leipzig: Gütersloh).

Haas, P.
1989   ' "Die He Shall Surely Die": The Structure of Homicide in Biblical Law',
        Semeia 45: 67-87 (= D. Patrick [ed.], *Thinking Biblical Law* [Atlanta:
        Scholars Press]).

Hägerström, A.
1953   *Inquiries into the Nature of Law and Morals* (trans. C.D. Broad; Uppsala:
        Almquist; Wiesbaden: Harrassowitz).

Hall, D. and R. Ames
1995   *Anticipating China* (Albany: State University of New York Press).

Hallpike, C.R.
1979   *The Foundations of Primitive Thought* (Oxford: Clarendon Press).

Haran, M.
1982   'Book Scrolls in Israel in Pre-Exilic Times', *JJS* 33: 161-73.
1988   'On the Diffusion of Literacy and Schools in Ancient Israel', in J.S.
        Emerton (ed.), *Congress Volume, Jerusalem 1986* (Leiden: E.J. Brill): 81-
        95.

Harrelson, W.
1980 *The Ten Commandments and Human Rights* (Philadelphia: Fortress Press).

Harris, R.
1975 *Ancient Sippar* (Leiden: Nederlands Historisch-Archaeologisch Instituut).

Hart, H.L.A.
1958 'Positivism and the Separation of Law and Morals', *Harvard Law Review* 71: 593-629 (reprinted in *idem, Essays in Jurisprudence and Philosophy* [Oxford: Clarendon Press, 1983]: 49-87).
1994 *The Concept of Law* (Oxford: Clarendon Press, 2nd edn [1961]).

Havelock, E.A.
1963 *Preface to Plato* (Cambridge, MA: Belknap Press).

Hoebel, E.A.
1954 *The Law of Primitive Man: A Study in Comparative Legal Dynamics* (Cambridge: Harvard University Press).

Houtman, C.
1997 *Das Bundesbuch: Ein Kommentar* (Leiden: E.J. Brill).
2000 *Exodus*, III (Leuven: Peeters).

Inhelder, B. and J. Piaget
1969 *The Early Growth of Logic in the Child* (trans. E.A. Lunzer and D. Papert; New York: W.W. Norton).

Isser, S.
1990 'Two Traditions: The Law of Exodus 21:22-23 Revisited', *CBQ* 52: 30-45.

Jackendoff, R.
1993 *Patterns in the Mind: Language and Human Nature* (Hemel Hempstead: Harvester Wheatsheaf).

Jackson, B.S.
1968 'Evolution and Foreign Influence in Ancient Law', *American Journal of Comparative Law* 16: 372-90.
1972 *Theft in Early Jewish Law* (Oxford: Clarendon Press).
1973a 'Reflections on Biblical Criminal Law', *JJS* 24: 8-38.
1973b 'The Problem of Exod. xxi.22-25 (Ius Talionis)', *VT* 23: 273-304 (reprinted in Jackson [1975a]: 75-107).
1974 'The Goring Ox Again', *Journal of Juristic Papyrology* 18: 55-93.
1975a *Essays in Jewish and Comparative Legal History* (Leiden: E.J. Brill).
1975b 'From *Dharma* to Law', *American Journal of Comparative Law* 23.3: 490-512 (partially reprinted in H. Goodman [ed.], *Between Jerusalem and Benares* [Albany: State University of New York Press, 1994]: 181-93, 325-31).
1976 'A Note on Exodus 22:4 (MT)', *JJS* 27: 138-41.
1977a 'Cave Canem', *Modern Law Review* 40: 590-96.
1977b 'Susanna and the Singular History of Singular Witnesses', *Acta Juridica*: 37-54 (= *Essays in Honour of Ben Beinart*).
1978a 'Liability for Animals in Roman Law: An Historical Sketch', *The Cambridge Law Journal* 37: 122-43.
1978b 'Maimonides' Definitions of *Tam* and *Mu'ad*', *Jewish Law Annual* 1: 168-76.

1978c	'On the Origins of *Scienter*', *Law Quarterly Review* 94: 85-102, xvi.
1978d	'Travels and Travails of the Goring Ox: The Biblical Text in British Sources', in Y. Avishur and J. Blau (eds.), *Studies in Bible and the Ancient Near East Presented to S.E. Loewenstamm* (Jerusalem: Rubinstein): 41-56.
1979a	'Legalism', *JSS* 30: 1-22.
1979b	*Structuralism and Legal Theory* (Liverpool: Liverpool Polytechnic Press).
1980a	'Historical Aspects of Legal Drafting in the Light of Modern Theories of Cognitive Development', *International Journal of Law and Psychiatry* 3: 349-69.
1980b	'Towards a Structuralist Theory of Law', *Liverpool Law Review* 2: 5-30.
1982a	'Legal Drafting in the Ancient Near East in the Light of Modern Theories of Cognitive Development', in *Mélanges à la mémoire de Marcel-Henri Prévost* (Paris: PUF): 49-66.
1982b	'Structuralisme et "sources du droit" ', *Archives de philosophie du droit* 27: 147-60.
1982–1983	'Structuralism and the Notion of Religious Law', *Investigaciones Semióticas* 2.3: 1-43 (Carabobo, Venezuela).
1984	'The Ceremonial and the Judicial: Biblical Law as Sign and Symbol', *JSOT* 30: 25-50 (reprinted in J.W. Rogerson [ed.], *The Pentateuch: A Sheffield Reader* [Sheffield: Sheffield Academic Press]: 103-27).
1985a	'Murder', in P.J. Achtemeier (ed.), *Harper's Bible Dictionary* (San Francisco: Harper & Row): 663-64.
1985b	*Semiotics and Legal Theory* (London: Routledge & Kegan Paul; repr. Liverpool: Deborah Charles Publications, 1997).
1987	'Some Semiotic Questions for Biblical Law', in A.M. Fuss (ed.), *The Oxford Conference Volume* (Jewish Law Association Studies, 3; Atlanta: Scholars Press): 1-25.
1988a	'Biblical Laws of Slavery: A Comparative Approach', in L. Archer (ed.), *Slavery and Other Forms of Unfree Labour* (London: Routledge): 86-101.
1988b	*Law, Fact and Narrative Coherence* (Merseyside: Deborah Charles Publications).
1988c	'Some Literary Features of the Mishpatim', in M. Augustin and K.-D. Schunck (eds.), *Wünschet Jerusalem Frieden: Collected Communications to the XIIth Congress of the International Organization for the Study of the Old Testament, Jerusalem 1986* (Frankfurt: Peter Lang): 235-42.
1989	'Ideas of Law and Legal Administration: a Semiotic Approach', in R.E. Clements (ed.), *The World of Ancient Israel: Sociological, Anthropological and Political Perspectives* (Cambridge: Cambridge University Press): 185-202.
1990	'Legalism and Spirituality: Historical, Philosophical and Semiotic Notes on Legislators, Adjudicators, and Subjects', in E.B. Firmage, B.G. Weiss and J.W. Welch (eds.), *Religion and Law: Biblical-Judaic and Islamic Perspectives* (Winona Lake: Eisenbrauns): 243-61.
1992a	'Law and Language: A Metaphor for Maine, Model for his Successors?', in A. Diamond (ed.), *The Victorian Achievement of Sir Henry Maine* (Cambridge: Cambridge University Press): 256-93.
1992b	'Practical Wisdom and Literary Artifice in the Covenant Code', in B.S.

Jackson and S.M. Passamaneck (eds.), *The Jerusalem 1990 Conference Volume* (Jewish Law Association Studies, 6; Atlanta: Scholars Press): 65-92.

1992c   'The Prophet and the Law in Early Judaism and the New Testament', *Cardozo Studies in Law and Literature* 4.2: 123-66 (reprinted in S.M. Passamaneck and M. Finley [eds.], *The Paris Conference Volume* [Jewish Law Association Studies, 7; Atlanta: Scholars Press, 1994]: 67-112).

1992d   'The Wisdom of the Inessential', *Legal Studies* 12: 103-117.

1993a   'On the Nature of Analogical Argument in Early Jewish Law', *The Jewish Law Annual* 11: 137-68.

1993b   'Piaget, Kohlberg and Habermas: Psychological and Communicational Approaches to Legal Theory', in V. Ferrari and C. Faralli (eds.), *Laws and Rights* (Milan: Giuffrè): II, 571-92.

1994   'Envisaging Law', *International Journal for the Semiotics of Law* 7.21: 311-34.

1995a   'The Literary Presentation of Multiculturalism in Early Biblical Law', *International Journal for the Semiotics of Law* 8.23: 181-206.

1995b   *Making Sense in Law: Linguistic, Psychological and Semiotic Perspectives* (Liverpool: Deborah Charles Publications).

1995c   'Modelling Biblical Law: The Covenant Code', *Chicago–Kent Law Review* 70.4: 1745-1827.

1996a   *Making Sense in Jurisprudence* (Liverpool: Deborah Charles Publications).

1996b   'Talion and Purity: Some Glosses on Mary Douglas', in J.F.A. Sawyer (ed.), *Reading Leviticus: A Conversation with Mary Douglas* (Sheffield: Sheffield Academic Press): 107-123.

1996c   'Thematisation and the Narrative Typifications of the Law', in D. Nelken (ed.), *Law as Communication* (Aldershot: Dartmouth): 175-94.

1997   'An Aye for an I?: The Semiotics of Lex Talionis in the Bible', in W. Pencak and J. Ralph Lindgren (eds.), *New Approaches to Semiotics and the Human Sciences: Essays in Honor of Roberta Kevelson* (New York: Peter Lang): 127-49.

1998a   'Justice and Righteousness in the Bible: Rule of Law or Royal Paternalism?', *ZABR* 4: 218-62.

1998b   ' "Law" and "Justice" in the Bible', *JJS* 44.2: 218-29.

2000a   '*Exodus* 21:18-19 and the Origins of the Casuistic Form', *Israel Law Review* 33 (Falk memorial volume; forthcoming).

2000b   'Law, Wisdom and Narrative', in G.W. Brooke and J.-D. Kaestli (eds.), *Narrativity in the Bible and Related Texts* (Leuven: Peeters): 31-51,

2000c   'The Original "Oral Law" ', in G.W. Brooke (ed.), *Jewish Ways of Reading the Bible* (*JSS* Supplement X; Oxford: Oxford University Press, forthcoming).

2002   *Wisdom-Laws: A Study of the Mishpatim* (Oxford: Clarendon Press, forthcoming).

Jackson, B.S. and T.F. Watkins

1984   'Distraint in the Laws of Eshnunna and Hammurabi', *Studi in onore di Cesare Sanfilippo*, V (Rome: Giuffrè): 411-19.

Jamieson-Drake, D.W.
    1991   *Scribes and Schools in Monarchic Judah* (Sheffield: Almond Press).
Johnstone, W.
    1987   'Reactivating the Chronicles Analogy in Pentateuchal Studies, with Special Reference to the Sinai Pericope in Exodus', *ZAW* 99: 16-37.
Jori, M.
    1993   'Legal Performatives', in *The Encyclopedia of Language and Linguistics* (Oxford: Pergamon Press): IV, 2092-97.
Kenny, A.J.P., J.R. Lucas, C.H. Waddington and H.C. Longuet-Higgins
    1973   *The Development of Mind* (Edinburgh: Edinburgh University Press).
Kernéis, K.
    1991   'Vol de nuit: L'abrogation de l'ancien article 382-3 du Code Pénal ou la fin d'un "document de droit primitif"', *Revue historique de droit français et étranger* 77: 281-309.
Kessler, M.
    1971   'The Law of Manumission in Jer 34', *BZ* 15: 105-108.
Kevelson, R.
    1994   '*Lex Talionis*: Equivalence and Evolution in Legal Semiotics', *International Journal for the Semiotics of Law* 7: 155-70.
King, L.W.
    1912   *Babylonian Boundary Stones and Memorial Tablets in the British Museum* (London: British Museum Publications).
Knierim, R.
    1961   'Exodus 18 und die Neuordnung der mosaischen Gerichtsbarkeit', *ZAW* 73: 146-71.
    1989   'The Problem of Ancient Israel's Prescriptive Legal Traditions', *Semeia* 45: 7-26 (= D. Patrick [ed.], *Thinking Biblical Law* [Atlanta: Scholars Press].
Knoppers, G.N.
    1994   'Jehoshaphat's Judiciary and "The Scroll of YHWH's Torah"', *JBL* 113: 59-80.
Koch, K.
    1955   'Gibt es ein Vergeltungsdogma im Alten Testament?', *ZTK* 52: 1-42.
Kohlberg, L.
    1971   'From Is to Ought: How to Commit the Naturalistic Fallacy and Get Away with It in the Study of Moral Development', in T. Mischel (ed.), *Cognitive Development and Epistemology* (New York: Academic Press, 1971): 151-235.
    1987   'Theoretical Introduction to the Measurement of Moral Judgment' (with Kelsey Kauffman), in A. Colby and L. Kohlberg (eds.), *The Measurement of Moral Judgment*, I (Cambridge: Cambridge University Press): 1-61.
Kraus, F.R.
    1960   'Was ist der Codex Hammurabi?', *Genava* 8: 283-96.
Kress, G.
    1989   *Linguistic Processes in Sociocultural Practice* (Oxford: Oxford University Press).

Kurzon, D.
1986   *It is Hereby Performed... Legal Speech Acts* (Amsterdam: John Ben-
            jamins).
Kutsch, E.
1973 ·   *Verheissung und Gesetz: Untersuchung zum sogenannten 'Bund' im Alten
            Testament* (Berlin: W. de Gruyter).
Lafont, S.
1994   'Ancient Near Eastern Laws: Continuity and Pluralism', in B.M. Levin-
            son (ed.), *Theory and Method in Biblical and Cuneiform Law: Revision,
            Interpolation and Development* (Sheffield: Sheffield Academic Press):
            91-118.
Leemans, W.F.
1991   'Quelques considérations à propos d'une étude récente du droit du
            Proche-Orient ancien' (review of Westbrook 1988a), *BO* 48: 409-37.
Lemaire, A.
1981   *Les écoles et la formation de la Bible dans l'ancien Israël* (Göttingen:
            Vandenhoeck & Ruprecht).
Lemche, N.P.
1976   'The 'Manumission of Slaves—the Fallow Year—the Sabbatical Year—
            the Yobel Year', *VT* 26: 38-59.
Levenson, J.D.
1980   'The Theologies of Commandments in Biblical Israel', *HTR* 73: 17-33.
Levenston, E.A.
1984   'The Speech-Acts of God', *Hebrew University Studies in Literature and
            the Arts* 12: 129-45.
Levinson, B.M.
1990   'Calum M. Carmichael's Approach to the Laws of Deuteronomy', *HTR*
            83.3: 227-37; Carmichael's reply at *HTR* 87.3 (1994): 240-45.
1991   'The Right Chorale: From the Poetics to the Hermeneutics of the Hebrew
            Bible', in J.P. Rosenblatt and J.C. Sitterson, Jr (eds.), *'Not in Heaven':
            Coherence and Complexity in Biblical Narrative* (Bloomington: Indiana
            University Press): 129-53, 241-47.
1992   'The Human Voice in Divine Revelation: the Problem of Authority in
            Biblical Law', in M.A. Williams, C. Cox, and M.S. Jaffee (eds.), *Inno-
            vations in Religious Traditions* (Berlin: W. de Gruyter): 35-71.
1997   *Deuteronomy and the Hermeneutics of Legal Innovation* (New York:
            Oxford University Press).
Lewy, J.
1958   'The Biblical Institution of *deror* in the Light of Akkadian Documents',
            Eretz Israel 5: 21-31.
Leyens, J.-P. and J.-P. Codol
1988   'Social Cognition', in M. Hewstone, W. Stroeber, J.-P. Codol and G.M.
            Stephenson (eds.), *Introduction to Social Psychology* (Oxford: Basil
            Blackwell).
Liedke, G.
1971   *Gestalt und Bezeichnung alttestamentlicher Rechtssätze: Eine formge-
            schichtlich terminologische Studie* (Neukirchen–Vluyn: Neukirchener
            Verlag).

Limber, J.
    1973   'The Genesis of Complex Sentences', in Timothy E. Moore (ed.), *Cognitive Development and the Acquisition of Language* (New York: Academic Press): 169-85.
Lipinski, E.
    1982   'Sale, Transfer, and Delivery in Ancient Semitic Terminology', in H. Klengel (ed.), *Gesellschaft und Kultur im alten Vorderasien* (Berlin: Akademie Verlag): 173-85.
Locher, C.
    1986   *Die Ehre einer Frau in Israel* (Freiburg: Universitätsverlag).
Loewenstamm, S.E.
    1957   Review of Goetze, *The Laws of Eshnunna, IEJ* 7: 194.
    1980   'Exodus 21:22-25', in *idem, Comparative Studies in Biblical and Ancient Oriental Literatures* (Neukirchen–Vluyn: Neukirchener Verlag): 517-25 (repr. from *VT* 27 [1977]: 352-60).
Luria, A.R.
    1976   *Cognitive Development: Its Cultural and Social Foundations* (ed. M. Cole, trans. M. Lopez-Morillas and L. Solotaroff; Cambridge, MA: Harvard University Press).
Lyke, L.L.
    1997   *King David with the Wise Woman of Tekoa* (Sheffield: Sheffield Academic Press).
Maccoby, H.
    1999   *Ritual and Morality* (Cambridge: Cambridge University Press).
Maimonides
    1954   *The Book of Torts* (trans. H. Klein; New Haven: Yale University Press).
Mandler, J.M.
    1984   *Stories, Scripts and Scenes: Aspects of a Schema Theory* (Hillsdale: Lawrence Erlbaum Associates).
Mandler, J. and N.S. Johnson
    1977   'Remembrance of Things Parsed: Story Structure and Recall', *Cognitive Psychology* 9: 111-51.
Marshall, J.W.
    1993   *Israel and the Book of the Covenant: An Anthropological Approach to Biblical Law* (Atlanta: Scholars Press).
Matthews, V.H.
    1994   'The Anthropology of Slavery in the Covenant Code', in B.M. Levinson (ed.), *Theory and Method in Biblical and Cuneiform Law* (Sheffield: Sheffield Academic Press): 119-35.
Mays, W.
    1994   'Popper, Durkheim and Piaget on Moral Norms', *Journal of the British Society for Phenomenology* 5: 233-42.
McConville, J.G.
    1985   *Law and Theology in Deuteronomy* (Sheffield: JSOT Press).
McKeating, H.
    1975   'The Development of the Law of Homicide in Ancient Israel', *VT* 25: 46-68.

Meier, E.
1846   *Die ursprüngliche Form des Dekalogs* (Mannheim: Friedrich Basser-
            mann).
Mettinger, T.
1971   *Solomonic State Officials* (Lund: C.W.K. Gleerup).
Mey, J.L.
1993   *Pragmatics: An Introduction* (Oxford: Basil Blackwell).
Milgrom, J.
1963   'The Biblical Diet Laws as an Ethical System', *Interpretation* 17: 288-
            301.
1992   *Leviticus* (Garden City, NY: Doubleday).
Millard, A.
1991   'The Uses of the Early Alphabets', in C. Baurain, C. Bonnet and V.
            Krings (eds.), *Phoinikeia Grammata* (Liège: Société des Etudes
            Classiques): 101-14.
1994   'Re-Creating the Tablets of the Law', *Bible Review* 49: 49-53.
1995   'The Knowledge of Writing in Iron Age Palestine', *Tyndale Bulletin* 46:
            207-17.
1998   Review of Niditch 1997, *JTS* 49: 699-705.
Modrzejewski, J.M.
1996   'Jewish Law and Hellenistic Legal Practice in Egypt', in N. Hecht, B.S.
            Jackson, S,M. Passamanech, D. Piattelli and A.M. Rabello (eds.), *An
            Introduction to the History and Sources of Jewish Law* (Oxford: Claren-
            don Press): 75-99.
Nel, P.J.
1994   'The Talion Principle in Old Testament Narratives', *JNSL* 20: 21-29.
Nicholson, E.W.
1974   'The Interpretation of Exodus XXIV 9-11', *VT* 24: 78-80.
1982   'The Covenant Ritual in Exodus XXIV 3-8', *VT* 32: 74-86.
1986   'Covenant in a Century of Study since Wellhausen', *OS* 24: 54-69.
Niditch, S.
1997   *Oral World and Written Word: Orality and Literacy in Ancient Israel*
            (London: SPCK).
Nielsen, E.
1968   *The Ten Commandments in New Perspective* (London: SCM Press).
Nohrnberg, J.
1995   *Like unto Moses: The Constituting of an Interruption* (Bloomington:
            Indiana University Press).
Nöth, W.
1990   *Handbook of Semiotics* (Bloomington: Indiana University Press).
O'Banion, J.D.
1992   *Reorienting Rhetoric: The Dialectic of List and Story* (University Park,
            PA: Pennsylvania State University Press).
Olson, D.R.
1994   *The World on Paper* (Cambridge: Cambridge University Press).
Ong, W.
1982   *Orality and Literacy* (London: Methuen).

Otto, E.

1881   *Wandel der Rechtsbegründungen in der Gesellschaftsgeschichte des antiken Israel: Eine Rechtsgeschichte des 'Bundesbuches' Ex XX 22– XXIII 13* (Leiden: E.J. Brill).

1991   *Körperverletzungen in den Keilschriftrechten und im Alten Testament* (Neukirchen–Vluyn: Neukirchener Verlag).

1993   'Town and Rural Countryside in Ancient Israelite Law: Reception and Redaction in Cuneiform and Israelite Law', *JSOT* 57: 3-22 (reprinted in J.W. Rogerson [ed.], *The Pentateuch: A Sheffield Reader* [Sheffield: Sheffield Academic Press]: 203-21).

1994   'Aspects of Legal Reforms and Reformulations in Ancient Cuneiform and Israelite Law', in B.M. Levinson (ed.), *Theory and Method in Biblical and Cuneiform Law* (Sheffield: Sheffield Academic Press): 160-96.

Patrick, D.

1985   *Old Testament Law* (London: SCM Press).

Paul, S.M.

1969   'Sargon's Administrative Diction in II Kings 17 27', *JBL* 88: 73-74.

1970   *Studies in the Book of the Covenant in the Light of Cuneiform and Biblical Law* (Leiden: E.J. Brill).

1978   'Adoption Formulae', *Eretz Israel* 14: 31-36.

Phillips, A.

1970   *Ancient Israel's Criminal Law* (Oxford: Basil Blackwell).

1977   'Another Look at Murder', *JJS* 27: 105-26.

Piaget, J.

1932   *The Moral Judgment of the Child* (London: Routledge & Kegan Paul).

1965   *Etudes sociologiques* (Geneva: Libraire Droz).

1971   *Structuralism* (trans. C. Maschler; London: Routledge & Kegan Paul).

1980   *Six Psychological Studies* (ed. D. Elkind; Brighton: Harvester).

Piaget, J. and B. Inhelder

1958   *The Growth of Logical Thinking: From Childhood to Adolescence* (London: Routledge & Kegan Paul).

Piattelli, D.

1984   'Effetti giuridici dell'affrancazione degli schiavi alla luce dei documenti aramaici di Elefantina', *Atti del XVII Congresso Internazionale di Papyrologia* (Napoli: Centro Internazionale per lo Studio dei Papiri Ercolanesi): 1233-44.

1995   'Zedaqà: Pursuit of Justice and the Instrument of "Ius Talionis" ', *Israel Law Review* 29: 65-78.

Polkinghorne, D.E.

1988   *Narrative Knowing and the Human Sciences* (Albany: State University of New York Press).

Porten, B.

1981   'Structure and Chiasm in Aramaic Contracts and Letters', in J. Welch (ed.), *Chiasmus in Antiquity* (Hildesheim: Gerstenberg): 169-82.

Porter, J.R.

1963   *Moses and Monarchy* (Oxford: Basil Blackwell).

Pospisil, L.
1971   *Anthropology of Law: A Comparative Theory* (New York: Harper & Row).
Power, R.P.
1981   'The Dominance of Touch by Vision: Occurs with Familiar Objects', *Perception* 10: 29-33.
Pressler, C.
1998   'Wives and Daughters, Bond and Free: Views of Women in the Slave Laws of Exodus 21.2-11', in V.H. Matthews, B.M. Levinson and T. Frymer-Kensky (eds.), *Gender and Law in the Hebrew Bible and the Ancient Near East* (Sheffield: Sheffield Academic Press): 147-72.
Prévost, M.-H.
1976   'Formulation casuistique et formulation apodictique dans les lois bibliques', *Revue historique de droit français et étranger* 54: 349-60.
1977   'A propos du talion', in *Mélanges dédiés à la mémoire de Jacques Teneur*, II (Lille: Université du droit et de la santé): 619-29.
Redish, J.C.
1985   'The Plain English Movement', in S. Greenbaum (ed.), *The English Language Today* (Oxford: Pergamon Institute of English): 125-38.
Ritchie, I.D.
2000   'The Nose Knows: Bodily Knowing in Isaiah 11.3', *JSOT* 87: 59-73.
Rivard, R.
1981   'Pour une relecture d'Ex 19 et 20: Analyse sémiotique d'Ex 19. 1-8', *Science et esprit* 33: 335-56.
Roberts, S.
1979   *Order and Dispute: An Introduction to Legal Anthropology* (Harmondsworth: Penguin Books).
Rock, I. and C.S. Harris
1967   'Vision and Touch', *Scientific American* 216: 96-104.
Rofé, A.
1986   'The History of the Cities of Refuge in Biblical Law', in S. Japhet (ed.), *Studies in Bible* (Scripta Hierosolymitana, 31; Jerusalem: Magnes Press): 205-39.
Ross, A.
1957   'Tu-Tu', *Harvard Law Review* 70: 812-25.
Roth, M.T.
1995   *Law Collections from Mesopotamia and Asia Minor* (Atlanta: Scholars Press).
Sakenfeld, K.D.
1988   'Zelophehad's Daughters', *Perspectives in Religious Studies* 15: 37-47.
Sarbin, T.R., (ed.)
1986   *Narrative Psychology: The Storied Nature of Human Conduct* (New York: Praeger).
Sarfatti, G.B.
1990   'The Tablets of the Law as a Symbol of Judaism', in B.Z. Segal (ed.), *The Ten Commandments in History and Tradition* (Jerusalem: Magnes Press): 383-418.

Sarna, N.M.
1991   *The JPS Torah Commentary: Exodus* (Philadelphia: The Jewish Publication Society).

Savigny, F.C. von
1867   *System of the Modern Roman Law* (trans. W. Holloway; Madras: J. Higginbotham).

Savran, G.
1988   *Telling and Retelling: Quotation in Biblical Narrative* (Bloomington: Indiana University Press).

Sbisà, M. and Fabbri, P.
1981   'Models (?) for a Pragmatic Analysis', *Journal of Pragmatics* 4: 301-19.

Schenker, A.
1988   'Affranchissement d'une esclave selon Ex 21,7-11', *Biblica* 69: 547-56.
1998   'Die Analyse der Intentionalität im Bundesbuch (Ex 21-23)', *ZABR* 4: 209-17.

Schiffman, L.H.
1988   'The Prohibition of Judicial Corruption in the Dead Sea Scrolls, Philo, Josephus and Talmudic Law', in J. Magnes and S. Gitin (eds.), *Hesed ve'Emet: Studies in Honor of Ernest S. Frerichs* (Atlanta: Scholars Press): 155-78.

Schiffrin, D.
1994   *Approaches to Discourse* (Oxford: Basil Blackwell).

Schulz, F.
1946   *History of Roman Legal Science* (Oxford: Clarendon Press).

Schwartz, B.
1983   Review of R. Soncino, *Motive Clauses in Hebrew Law, JSS* 28: 161-63.

Schwienhorst-Schönberger, L.
1990   *Das Bundesbuch (Ex 20,22-23,33): Studien zu seiner Entstehung und Theologie* (BZAW, 188: Berlin: W. de Gruyter).

Searle, J.R.
1969   *Speech Acts* (Cambridge: Cambridge University Press).

Segert, S.
1973   'Form and Function of Ancient Israelite, Greek and Roman Legal Sentences', in H.A. Hoffner (ed.), *Orient and Occident: Essays presented to C.H. Gordon* (Neukirchen–Vluyn: Neukirchener Verlag, 1973): 151-59.

Sekuler, R. and R. Blake
1990   *Perception* (New York: McGraw-Hill, 2nd edn).

Sherwin, R.K.
1994   'Law Frames: Historical Truth and Narrative Necessity in a Criminal Case', *Stanford Law Review* 47: 39-83.

Skinner, J.
1930   *Genesis* (Edinburgh: T. & T. Clark, 2nd edn).

Sprinkle, J.M.
1993   'The Interpretation of Exodus 21:22-25 (*Lex Talionis*) and Abortion', *WTJ* 55: 233-53.
1994   *The Book of the Covenant: A Literary Approach* (Sheffield: JSOT Press).

Stahl, N.
1995   *Law and Liminality in the Bible* (Sheffield: Sheffield Academic Press).

Stamm, J.J. and M.E. Andrew
1967 *The Ten Commandments in Recent Research* (London: SCM Press).
Starr, J.
1992 *Law as Metaphor: From Islamic Courts to the Palace of Justice* (Albany: State University of New York Press).
Steinmetzer, F.X.
1922 *Die babylonischen Kudurru (Grenzsteine) als Urkundenform* (Paderborn: Schöningh).
Sternberg, M.
1985 *The Poetics of Biblical Narrative: Ideological Literature and the Drama of Reading* (Bloomington: Indiana University Press).
Stone, J.
1950 *The Province and Function of Law* (Sydney: Maitland Publications).
Szlechter, E.
1970 'L'interprétation des lois babyloniennes', *Revue internationale des droits de l'antiquité* 17: 81-115.
Tannen, D.
1986 *That's Not What I Meant! How Conversational Style Makes or Breaks Your Relations with Others* (New York: Ballantine).
Thomas, J.A.C.
1975 *The Institutes of Justinian* (Amsterdam: North-Holland).
Tigay, J.H.
1996 'The Significance of the End of Deuteronomy', in M.V. Fox *et al.* (eds.), *Texts, Temples and Traditions: A Tribute to Menahem Haran* (Winona Lake, IN: Eisenbrauns): 137-43.
Trankell, A.
1972 *The Reliability of Evidence: Methods for Analyzing and Assessing Witness Statements* (Stockholm: Beckmans).
Turiel, E.
1983 *The Development of Social Knowledge: Morality and Convention* (Cambridge: Cambridge University Press).
Turnbam, T.J.
1987 'Male and Female Slaves in the Sabbath Year Laws of Exodus 21:1-11', in K.H. Richards (ed.), *SBL Seminar Papers 1987* (Altanta: Scholars Press): 545-49.
Ulrich, D.R.
1998 'The Framing Function of the Narratives about Zelophehad's Daughters', *Journal of the Evangelical Theological Society* 41: 529-38.
van der Sprenkel, S.
1962 *Legal Institutions in Manchu China* (London: Athlone Press).
van Houten, C.
1991 *The Alien in Israelite Law* (Sheffield: Sheffield Academic Press).
Van Seters, J.
1996 'The Law of the Hebrew Slave', *ZAW* 108: 534-46.
Viberg, A.
1992 *Symbols of Law: A Contextual Analysis of Legal Symbolic Acts in the Old Testament* (Stockholm: Almqvist & Wiksell).

Vinogradoff, P.
  1922   *Outlines of Historical Jurisprudence* (2 vols.; Oxford: Clarendon Press).
von Rad, G.
  1953   *Studies in Deuteronomy* (London: SCM Press).
Warner, S.
  1980   'The Alphabet: An Innovation and its Diffusion', *VT* 30: 81-90.
Watson, A.
  1974   *Legal Transplants* (Edinburgh: Scottish Academic Press).
Watts, J.W.
  1999   *Reading Law: The Rhetorical Shaping of the Pentateuch* (Sheffield: Sheffield Academic Press).
Weeks, S.
  1994   *Early Israelite Wisdom* (Oxford: Clarendon Press).
Weinfeld, M.
  1970   'The Covenant of Grant in the Old Testament in the Ancient Near East', *JAOS* 90: 184-203.
  1972   *Deuteronomy and the Deuteronomic School* (Oxford: Clarendon Press).
  1973   'The Origin of the Apodictic Law: An Overlooked Source', *VT* 23: 63-75.
  1977   'Judge and Officer in Ancient Israel and the Ancient Near East', *IOS* 7: 65-88.
  1990   'The Uniqueness of the Decalogue and its Place in Jewish Tradition', in B.Z. Segal (ed.), *The Ten Commandments in History and Tradition* (Jerusalem: Magnes Press): 1-44.
  1995   *Social Justice in Ancient Israel and in the Ancient Near East* (Jerusalem: Magnes Press; Philadelphia: Fortress Press).
Weingreen, J.
  1976   'The Concepts of Retaliation and Compensation in Biblical Law', *Proceedings of the Royal Irish Academy* 76/C/1: 1-11.
Weinreich-Haste, H.
  1983   'Kohlberg's Theory of Moral Development', in H. Weinreich-Haste and D. Locke (eds.), *Morality in the Making* (Chichester: John Wiley & Sons): 5-18.
Welch, J.W.
  1990a   'Chiasmus in Biblical Law', in B.S. Jackson (ed.), *The Boston Conference Volume* (Jewish Law Association Studies, 4; Atlanta: Scholars Press): 5-22.
  1990b   'Reflections on Postulates: Power and Ancient Laws. A Response to Moshe Greenberg', in E.B. Firmage, B.G. Weiss and J.W. Welch (eds.), *Religion and Law: Biblical-Judaic and Islamic Perspectives* (Winona Lake, IN: Eisenbrauns): 113-19.
Wellhausen, J.
  1973   *Prolegomena to the History of Ancient Israel* (Gloucester, MA: Peter Smith).
Wenham, G.J.
  1971a   'Legal Forms in the Book of the Covenant', *Tyndale Bulletin* 22: 95-102.
  1971b   'The Deuteronomic Theology of the Book of Joshua', *JBL* 90: 140-48.
Westbrook, R.
  1985   'Biblical and Cuneiform Law Codes', *RB* 92: 247-64.

1988a   *Studies in Biblical and Cuneiform Law* (Paris: Gabalda).

1988b   'The Nature and Origins of the Twelve Tables', *Zeitschrift der Savigny-Stiftung für Rechtsgeschichte (Rom. Abt.)* 105: 74-121.

1989   'Cuneiform Law Codes and the Origin of Legislation', *Zeitschrift für Assyriologie* 79: 201-222.

1990   'Adultery in Ancient Law', *RB* 97: 542-80.

1991   *Property and the Family in Biblical Law* (Sheffield: JSOT Press).

1994   'What Is the Covenant Code?', in B.M. Levinson (ed.), *Theory and Method in Biblical and Cuneiform Law* (Sheffield: Sheffield Academic Press): 15-36.

1998   'The Female Slave', in V.H. Matthews, B.M. Levinson and T. Frymer-Kensky (eds.), *Gender and Law in the Hebrew Bible and the Ancient Near East* (Sheffield: Sheffield Academic Press): 214-38.

Whitelam, K.

1979   *The Just King: Monarchical Judicial Authority in Ancient Israel* (Sheffield: JSOT Press).

Whybray, R.N.

1974   *The Intellectual Tradition in the Old Testament* (Berlin: W. de Gruyter).

Widengren, G.

1957   'King and Covenant', *JSS* 2: 1-32.

Williamson, H.G.M.

1982   *1 and 2 Chronicles* (Grand Rapids: Eerdmans).

Wilson, R.R.

1993   'The Role of Law in Early Israelite Society', in B. Halpern and D.W. Hobson (eds.), *Law, Politics and Society in the Ancient Mediterranean World* (Sheffield: Sheffield Academic Press): 90-99.

Yaron, R.

1961   *Introduction to the Law of the Aramaic Papyri* (Oxford: Clarendon Press).

1969   *The Laws of Eshnunna* (Jerusalem: Magnes Press; 2nd edn, 1988).

INDEXES

INDEX OF REFERENCES

HEBREW BIBLE

INDEX OF AUTHORS

JOURNAL FOR THE STUDY OF THE OLD TESTAMENT
SUPPLEMENT SERIES